The Best of
Planning
for Higher
Education

George Keller, Editor

Society for College and University Planning
Ann Arbor, Michigan

Society for College and University Planning, Ann Arbor, Michigan USA 48105-2785

© 1997 by the Society for College and University Planning
All rights reserved. Printed in the United States of America
ISBN 0-9601608-6-8

All articles originally published in
Planning for Higher Education
ISSN 076-0938

US $39.95

Contents

IV. IMPROVING THE FINANCES

PREFACE

During the past decade *Planning for Higher Education*, the quarterly journal of the Society for College and University Planning (SCUP), has emerged as the leading journal in the world for ideas and suggestions about how to plan for improvements at colleges and universities. This book is a selection of some of the best articles that have appeared in the journal in recent years. People have requested offprints of many of the articles; now we have assembled the finest of them in one volume.

The decade of the 1990s has been a whirlwind time for higher education. The emergence of a knowledge-based economy has made higher learning and advanced training more important than ever before. Changes in society—immigration, family structure, the costs of college, digital communication, new academic fields, continuing education for adults, internationalism, and more—have caused many to argue that institutions should change the way they teach, what and whom they teach, and how they conduct research. Universities have also been prodded to improve their management, overhaul their finances, and rethink the design and spaces of their campuses. Planning and renovating for the new era have become urgent necessities.

Planning for Higher Education has tried to present much of the newest and finest innovations, planning techniques, financial refinements, and architectural and equipment ideas to colleges and universities everywhere. (While the readers are mostly American college and university leaders and planners, the journal has subscribers in 30 other nations as well.) Most of the best thinkers and boldest higher education innovators in North America have contributed articles and reviews to the journal. So reading this book should give you a lively sense of several of the new directions in which higher education is moving, just as the journal has stimulated new thinking and action initiatives at many colleges and universities.

The Society, or SCUP, is devoted to the improvement of comprehensive planning. Therefore, the articles cover academic, administrative, facilities, and financial planning, not just architectural, say, or academic planning. However, the emphasis within comprehensive education planning has had some subtle shifts in the past decade. New facilities and added academic programs have diminished a bit in importance, and strategic management, financial agility and frugality, and preparations for the Internet networks have rushed to new prominence. The matter of leadership for educational change has reached a new intensity of concern. Still, planning in any one area must be sagacious about the cascading consequences for the other major segments of academic life.

We hope the contents of this book will ignite some fresh thinking and beneficial initiatives in higher education circles. *Planning for Higher Education* has worked assiduously with each of the authors to make the articles exceptionally readable, useful, and richly detailed, forsaking the triviality and obscurantism that unfortunately cripples some of the scholarship and other writings about higher education. Hence readers should find the articles lucid as well as animating.

This book is the product of many hands and minds. But three persons deserve special mention. Meredith Whiteley, the chair of SCUP's Publications Advisory Committee, set in motion the new series of publications by the Society; and Terry Calhoun and Susanne Kocsis of the Society's central office were wonderfully attentive shepherds.

George Keller

Editor, *Planning for Higher Education*
Baltimore, Maryland

V. STRATEGIES, LEADERSHIP, AND ADMINISTRATION

II. Coming Changes in Academe

What the past twenty years of research have revealed about how colleges affect students.

Designing Colleges for Greater Learning

Ernest Pascarella and Patrick Terenzini

ive years ago we decided to update Kenneth Feldman and Theodore Newcomb's landmark work, *The Impact of College on Students* (1969). Twenty years had passed, numerous studies had been conducted since 1967, new theories and statistical procedures had been developed, and activity on the assessment of undergraduate student learning had become widespread.

So we spent four years going through more than 2,600 studies trying to find out what scholars have learned, hoping to answer the questions: Does college make a difference? And if so, how? We focused on three areas. How do students change during their college years? To what extent are the changes attributable to the collegiate experience? What college practices, experiences, and structures tend to produce changes?

We summarized the outcomes of four years of college in our recent book. But we finished our research feeling a bit uneasy about the solidity of some of the findings since the *net* effect of college is difficult to determine. It is hard to separate the impact of college from other influences on students between the ages of 18 and 23. (Only a dozen or so of the 2600 studies had control groups of similar young persons not in college.) Change *during* college is not the same as change *due* to college. Nonetheless, the evidence shows that undergraduate classes, and even more, collegiate life has a significant impact.

Ernest Pascarella is professor of educational psychology at the University of Illinois, Chicago. He will be the Mary Louise Petersen Professor of Higher Education at the University of Iowa as of September, 1997. A graduate of Princeton with an M.S. in psychological measurement from the University of Pennsylvania, he received his Ph.D. in higher education from Syracuse University, where he taught before going to Chicago. He has received several national awards for his research and served as president of the Association for the Study of Higher Education in 1989-90. He and Dr. Terenzini are co-authors of *How College Affects Students* (Jossey-Bass, 1991).

Patrick Terenzini is professor of higher education and senior scientist at the Center for the Study of Higher Education, Pennsylvania State University. He holds an A.B. from Dartmouth, an M.A.T. from Harvard, and a Ph.D. from Syracuse. He worked as assistant to the president for planning and director of institutional research at SUNY at Albany, and professor of higher education at the University of Georgia before joining Penn State in 1990. He is the Editor in Chief of *New Directions for Institutional Research* and associate editor of *Higher Education: Handbook of Theory and Research*.

A surprise in the data

Most surprising was the evidence that elite or expensive colleges and universities—public or private—had scarcely any greater impact on student growth than other undergraduate institutions. (We are both graduates of Ivy League universities.) Even the

> *Most surprising was that elite colleges and universities have scarcely any greater impact than other institutions.*

return on earnings from attending a prestigious college may not be as big as people believe it is. Where students attend college appears to matter much less than what happens to them after they enroll. Clearly certain colleges and universities may be quite potent in their impact on students. But much of the difference in educational attainments between highly touted colleges and other colleges appears to be due to the family income and high ability of the students admitted.

The evidence we scrutinized suggests that two factors are crucial to lifting students to new plateaus of thinking and sensibility.

One is the quality of the student's own effort in making use of the range of learning and social opportunities on a campus. The impact of a college is not simply the result of what a college does for or to a student. Rather the impact is to a considerable extent the result of the way a student exploits the people, programs, facilities, and experiences that the college makes available. Individual student characteristics usually mediate the impact of college (Weidman 1989; Weidman 1984). Not all students benefit equally from the same experience. The greater the effort, the greater the likelihood of educational and personal returns on that investment across a spectrum of college outcomes.

The other important factor we found is the quality and actions of the other people in

a student's undergraduate life, whether other students or faculty. What stimulates is the character of the learning environments that other students and the faculty create, and the nature and strength of the interactions they provide for learning and changes of all kinds. The research makes abundantly clear the important influences that faculty members have on student change in all areas. But students also change because of other students, the academic program required of them, departmental climates, the residence hall arrangements and environment, co-curricular activities, and (to a lesser extent) institutional size and physical quality.

These two factors suggest that educational planners can actually shape the educational and interpersonal experiences and settings of their campus in ways that promote learning and achievement of the college's goals more effectively. And planners, faculty, and administrators can develop ways to induce students to exploit these experiences and settings to the fullest.

> *Impact is partly a result of the way a student exploits the people, programs, facilities, and experiences of a college.*

Nearly 25 years ago the Nobel Prize-winning psychologist, Herbert Simon (1967) charged:

> We do not, in colleges today, make use of any learning principles in a considered, professional way. We do not design the college as a learning environment. We do not give anyone a specific responsibility for bringing to the college the best available professional and scientific knowledge for designing that environment. (p. 76)

Our knowledge of how to achieve desirable outcomes in undergraduates is not yet "scientific" and certain. But we are coming closer to some answers. Educational planners and policymakers should know of the strong correlations that have been found, and employ them more deliberately.

Implications for colleges

The conventional wisdom holds that institutional quality is based on superior resources: a large endowment, huge library holdings, many attractive buildings, nearly all faculty with Ph.D.'s and noted research professors among them, lots of computers, and so on. Our findings, however, suggest the need for better measures of college effectiveness and quality. We tend to agree with Astin (1985) that "talent development" should be the proper work of undergraduate education, which means that quality should be measured by what institutions do to advance a student's learning beyond what it is when that student enters college. The quality of undergraduate education seems to be more a function of what a college does programmatically than it is of human, financial, and material resources.

Thus, any college or university can improve its educational outcomes, its "quality." Though this short article is not the place to discuss all the conditions that enhance outcomes in detail (for example, Chickering 1969, 1981; Baird 1976; Kuh, et al. 1991), it may be instructive to point to several of the areas that our study found can help produce beneficial student changes.

The importance of people

If the quality of effort by students and faculty and the quality of the interpersonal life on campus are two key determinants of a college's intellectual achievements, then the selection of, and orientation and rewards for, students and faculty are vital.

Colleges that seek to be excellent must have admissions offices, with adequate financial aid behind them, that seek a wide variety of talent. Academic credentials are, of course, important for admission, but colleges should also seek to enroll students with special talents and gifts that can enrich the intellectual and interpersonal climate on campus. Colleges should make stronger efforts to ascer-

tain the personal, attitudinal, and behavioral characteristics of their applicants, especially since these are often better predictors of minority student performance than standardized test scores (Nettles, Thoeny, and Gosman 1986). Admissions is serious business, and institutions that desire to be academically productive should gather students *with methodical energy.* Influences on the character of a college's community that are exerted by each new class of students should not be left to chance. Admissions programs should be given careful attention and investment.

Any college can improve its outcomes, its "quality."

Institutional climate is also heavily influenced by faculty members. Significant improvements in the quality of instruction and learning may require greater attention to faculty recruiting, hiring, and reward policies. If a college or university has a powerful interest in student learning outcomes, it needs to seek out faculty who care about teaching and student growth. For example, when new faculty are recruited, they might be asked to submit evidence of their teaching abilities and other student-oriented activities as well as their research bibliographies. Candidates might be required to meet with and to make presentations to students as well as to the college's current faculty members.

Significant involvement in students' out-of-class-lives and in creative instruction cannot be expected from faculty members who are recruited because of their research potential. At the reward level, decisions regarding promotion, tenure, and compensation should give considerable attention to those who have best inspired students both in and out of the classroom to stretch their minds.

There is little evidence to support the widespread belief that good undergraduate teaching and scholarly productivity are strongly linked. Indeed, the available evidence indicates that, at best, there is only a small, positive relationship between the two

3

(Feldman 1987). Institutions should recruit good teachers as assiduously as they pursue top-flight researchers and not necessarily expect the same individuals to excel in both.

Arranging the environment

The transition from high school to college involves the unlearning of past attitudes, values, and behaviors. It also means establishing a new identity and interpersonal network and learning new attitudes, values, and be-

---

The first semester is a pivotal time.

---

haviors. Thus, the first weeks, indeed the first semester, at college is a pivotal time. The initial encounters with the institution and its people can have profound effects on subsequent levels of involvement and aspirations for intellectual achievement.

Colleges should design their orientations for new students with the greatest care. Freshmen should be introduced not only to key administrators, available support services, registration procedures, extracurricular opportunities, and other freshmen but also to the institution's highest educational values and hopes and to older students and faculty who embody these. Institutional values are on display during orientation, and the program's activities send subtle but powerful messages to new students about what is valued and what is expected.

One finding we think is important for colleges is that while off-campus employment has a negative effect on both year-to-year persistence and bachelor's degree completion, part-time jobs *on campus* have a net positive impact on timely graduation and even on the probability of enrolling in graduate or professional school. Institutions should endeavor to find numerous ways for needy students to help in the work of the college.

While more research is needed to clarify the nature of the college experience among students of color and its effects on their cognitive and psychological change, it is cer-

tainly time to review and change policies that tolerate activities that are academically and socially uncongenial, if not hostile, to minority group undergraduates.

More than half of America's collegians commute to campus; and one-third of U.S. colleges and universities are commuter campuses. Nonetheless, the evidence seems overwhelming that residing at a college acts as a powerful socializing and academic agent. Residence permits natural and continuous meetings with faculty and other students. Colleges should encourage residential enrollment and provide attractive dormitories with places where students can collect to question, analyze, and encounter intellectual and aesthetic issues. The most consistent evidence linking residence with specific kinds of change points to the greater impact of those halls where there are purposeful efforts to integrate students' academic and social lives. So colleges should try to bring learning to the greatest extent possible into the living areas.

Part-time jobs on campus have a net positive impact.

Institutions should avoid huge residential towers. The size of a college or university is not that influential in helping student growth, but *psychological* size for students is very influential. That is, students need to have opportunities to become involved with smaller groups: small housing units, honors programs, clubs and cocurricular activities, fraternities and sororities, athletic teams, and the like. Campus architecture can play a significant role here by avoiding the monumental and designing smaller units for maximum student interactions. Social interaction with significant others—and encouragement from them—exerts a strong and independent influence in educational attainment.

Improving the learning scene

Unequivocally, the evidence indicates that when students are actively engaged in their classrooms, and with learning in general, mastery of content and cognitive development are highest. Too often course content is presented in ways that make students passive participants. There is too much lecturing and too little variety and flexibility.

Institutions should avoid huge residential towers.

Modern colleges, and especially universities, seem better structured to process large numbers of students efficiently than to maximize student learning. While the costs and the instructional demands on professors may be greater, colleges need to provide students with better opportunities to exercise their minds.

The possibilities are many: in-class presentations, question-and-answer exchanges, problem-solving activities, having advanced students help others having difficulty, student research, and individual tutorials for the more independent, to name some. The Association of American Colleges has recommended more frequent use of artists, writers, political leaders, business persons, and scientists in residence, more creative use of work-study programs, and temporary faculty opportunities for leaders outside the faculty ranks.

Evidence is growing that the organizational and interpersonal climate of academic departments may have a significant impact on intellectual growth. Content learning among students is highest in areas surrounding their academic major; so is cognitive and intellectual development. Departmental influence is most observable where faculty and students have common attitudes, where personal exchanges are frequent, friendly, and not rigidly hierarchical, and where department spirit is high. Institutions would do well to encourage their department heads to make more conscious and systematic efforts to create departmental environments that attract and engage students in and out of class.

It is clear from the research that faculty members have enormous influence on student change in virtually all areas. But it is also clear that the educational impact of a college is most likely if policy and programmatic efforts are broadly conceived and diverse, consistent, and integrated. Presidents, vice presidents, and deans who set policy and choose programs are therefore key players. The literature on administrator involvement in student change is only indirect, however.

Nonetheless, we believe that academic administrators exercise significant control over campus affairs and climates. Presidents, vice presidents, deans, librarians, and middle managers set a tone and standards for students, faculty, and staff. For significant changes to occur, a collective act of institutional will is needed. These changes are more likely to originate and have effect if they are initiated and guided by senior administrators.

A major shift in decision-making by administrators is needed.

In the last analysis, a major shift in decisionmaking by middle-and executive-level administrators is needed. We believe that colleges and universities should shift away from status building toward learning-centered management.

This new orientation would consistently and systematically take into account the consequences of administrative actions for student learning, for academic growth. Reward systems, the campus environment, faculty hiring and promotion, residential arrangements, the quality of the campus bookstore, extracurricular activities, and much else can and should be designed more thoughtfully and purposefully to lift students to the highest levels of intellectual development of which they are capable. ∎

REFERENCES

Astin, A. 1985. *Achieving Educational Excellence: A Critical Assessment of Priorities and Practices in Higher Education.* Jossey-Bass.

Baird, L. 1976. Structuring the Environment to Improve Outcomes. In *Improving Educational Outcomes,* ed. O. Lenning. New Directions for Higher Education, no. 16. Jossey-Bass.

Chickering, A. 1969. *Education and Identity.* Jossey-Bass.

Chickering, A., and R. Havighurst. 1981. The Life Cycle. In *The Modern American College: Responding to the New Realities of Diverse Students and a Changing Society.* Jossey-Bass.

Feldman, K. 1987. Research Productivity and Scholarly Accomplishments of College Teachers as Related to their Instructional Effectiveness: A Review and Exploration. *Research in Higher Education* 26: 227-298.

Feldman, K., and T. Newcomb. 1969. *The Impact of College on Students.* Jossey-Bass.

Kuh, G., J. Shuh, E. Whitt, et al. 1991. *Involving Colleges: Encouraging Student Learning and Personal Involvement through Out-of-Class Experiences.* Jossey-Bass.

Nettles, M., A. Thoeny, and E. Gosman. 1986. Comparative and Predictive Analyses of Black and White Students' College Achievement and Experience. *Journal of Higher Education* 57: 289-318.

Pascarella, E., and P. Terenzini. 1991. *How College Affects Students: Findings and Insights from Twenty Years of Research.* Jossey-Bass.

Simon, H. 1967. The Job of a College President. *Educational Record* 58: 68-78.

Weidman, J. 1984. Impacts of Campus Experiences and Partial Socialization on Undergraduates' Career Choices. *Research in Higher Education* 20: 445-476.

Weidman, J. 1989. The World of Higher Education: A Socialization-Theoretical Perspective. In *The Social World of Adolescents: International Perspectives,* ed. K. Hurrelmann and U. Engel. Aldine.

Six major changes may alter the directions of collegiate planning in the next decade.

The Changing Milieu for Education Planning

George Keller

The United States is going through several profound changes that have begun to affect colleges and universities and are likely to have further consequences in the coming decades. Though the changes are of numerous kinds, I will point here to just three demographic changes and three social shifts. Then I will suggest some of the ways they are influencing the practice of teaching and scholarship and the creation of knowledge.

The three demographic changes are immigration, the dissolution of the traditional family structure, and the emerging age profile of U.S. society.

Since the 1965 amendments to the Immigration and Nationality Act, the United States has been undergoing the greatest surge in immigrants in its history. For more than two decades now approximately 1 million persons have entered the country le-

George Keller is editor of *Planning for Higher Education* and an award-winning consultant and education scholar and writer in Baltimore. He did his undergraduate and graduate work at Columbia; and has taught and administered at Columbia, SUNY, the University of Maryland, and the University of Pennsylvania. He is the author of many articles and reviews, and the book *Academic Strategy* (1983). This article is based on an invited address to the annual meeting of the American Council of Learned Societies in April 1994.

gally and illegally, equaling the previous two peak years for immigration, 1907 and 1914, when 1.2 million were admitted. In the fiscal year of 1993, for example, the United States admitted 880,000 persons legally, and another 200,000 to 300,000 immigrants are estimated to have entered illegally. For three decades, the United States has been accepting more immigrants and refugees each year than all the other developed countries of the world combined.

Unlike earlier waves of immigration, approximately 45 percent have been Latinos, and roughly 40 percent have been Asians. By the year 2000—five years from now—one-fourth of all young people under 16 will be in just three states: California, Florida, and Texas.

The second change is in family formation and child rearing. The stable two-parent family with two or more children is increasingly rare. The number of one-parent families has risen from approximately 4 million in 1970 to 8.5 million in 1990; one-fourth of all U.S. children under 18 are now in one-parent families. In Britain the percentage with one parent is 17 percent, in France and Germany about 12 percent. Three in 10 births in the United States are now out of wedlock. For African Americans, two-thirds of all births are non-marital; and the illegitimacy ratio for whites has quintupled in the past 30 years. Moreover, the divorce rate has reached 38 percent of all marriages; there were 1,187,000 divorces in 1993. The U.S. Commission on Civil Rights argues that illegitimacy and divorces are "responsible for essentially all of the growth in poverty since 1970" (Lawler 1993). In 1990, 80 percent of the unmarried women who had a child before finishing high school were living in poverty, while only 8 percent of the married women who completed high school and had a baby after the age of 19 were in poverty homes.

As anyone who reads the newspapers knows, the percentage of children and teens in foster care is up; child neglect and abuse is increasing; teenage and preteen crime is widespread; and orphanage is returning.

The U.S. population is becoming more polarized.

turning. For educators, the decline of learning in American middle and high schools has been steep, and antisocial and anti-intellectual behavior is now spreading among youths. Some campuses have begun regulating manners, speech, and behavior.

The third demographic change is the aging of American society. As the number of births has declined and better health care, nutrition, exercise, and family finances contribute to keeping older people alive longer, the population is getting older. Nearly 13 percent of Americans are now 65 or older. There are 11 million more retirees than teenagers. By the year 2020, the number of Americans over 50 will soar 75 percent, to more than one-third of the population; and the U.S. Census Bureau estimates that in 2020, 9.5 to 10 percent will be over 80 years of age.

Today's elderly are the healthiest and wealthiest old people in history. Their poverty rate is lower and median household wealth is greater than that of any other American age group. The over-50s have as much discretionary income as all other U.S. age groups combined, about half the nation's total. The percentage of the U.S.

federal budget going to retirees has gone from 19 percent in 1980 to nearly 30 percent in 1993. In addition, the elderly have become a powerful political force. The American Association of Retired Persons, or AARP, now has 31 million members over age 50—one of every five voters—and is the second largest membership organization in America (after the Roman Catholic Church).

Seismic shifts in society

Of the numerous social changes, I think three may be especially consequential for U.S. higher education.

Socioeconomically, the U.S. population is becoming more polarized and less middle class. Between 1973 and 1990 the poorest fifth of the population declined in income about 12 percent, while the richest fifth increased about 25 percent. The United States now has the largest "underclass" of any developed country, with the highest crime rate, rate of drug abuse, and percentage of homeless people. On the other hand, America has the largest number of Nobel Prize winners, research scholars, artists, female executives, trained physicians, and skilled musicians and poets.

Studies suggest that three factors are especially determining: family structure, level of education, and work patterns. For instance, the growing upper middle-income group is often composed of a married couple, both college educated, and both working.

A second social change is the growing importance to Americans of the Pacific Rim countries. In 1979 U.S. trade with Asia surpassed trade with Europe, and has been growing since. Long Beach, San Francisco, and Seattle are replacing Boston, New York, and Baltimore as leading seaports. Japan has become one of the world's great industrial and commercial powers, and China, with nearly one-fifth of the world's population, is breaking out of Maoist politics and economics.

For colleges and universities this poses an academic challenge. Our intellectual roots are in Israel, Greece, Rome, and Western Europe, and the curricula of most colleges focus on that area. But our social and economic life will increasingly consist of exchanges with Asian countries, and with Latin American nations and Arab oil states.

Electronic technology offers a new kind of book.

The third change is the outburst of new communications technology: computers, cassettes, films, satellite transmission, Internet, and the like. It is as significant as the invention and spread of printed books in the 16th and 17th centuries. It has already resulted in the use of new ways to gather, store, and exchange information, novel teaching styles, new kinds of libraries, and radically different exchanges among computer-literate persons around the world. One in four telephone calls in the United States is now a facsimile transmission. Classicist Jay David Bolter wrote in his 1991 book *Writing Space* that, "Print will no longer define the organization and presentation of knowledge....Electronic technology offers us a new kind of book and new ways to write and read" (1991).

The consequences of change

The repercussions of these six changes—and others—have begun to be felt throughout academe, and will help shape the creation and dissemination of knowledge in the years ahead.

The increasing number of Latino and Asian students means different food in the campus cafeterias, different speakers and campus events, and more demands for separate residential living. It means we shall have to train many new Latino and African American scholars, both of whom are in short supply, as exemplars for the young. It has already created a movement toward "multiculturalism" and prompted substitutions in liberal education's canon, which is being denounced as a form of Western chauvinism and cultural imperialism.

The dissolution of the traditional, nuclear family has led to the introduction of new speech and behavior codes at universi-

ties, increased student services, additional counseling, and a massive increase in remedial education at most colleges. It has also resulted in alarming increases in financial aid requirements that colleges must provide—some institutions now give back one-third of their tuition revenues in grants to students—and special summer programs on campus to help prepare students for college work. Colleges have had to invent costly substitutes for parental guidance, discipline, motivation, and support.

The emerging gerontocracy has brought a new constituency into higher education: retirees. Over 45 percent of all registered students in U.S. institutions are now 25 years old or older. Universities are moving from being educational camps for the young to serving like public libraries for persons 15 to 75 years old. Communities like Ithaca, New York; Oberlin, Ohio; Santa Barbara, California; and Sarasota, Florida have become new living-learning locations for elderly persons who wish to continue learning. Florida's Eckerd College and New York

Some institutions now give back one-third of their tuition revenues.

City's Columbia University both have new academies for senior retired scholars who wish to continue teaching and research. Hundreds of colleges and universities now have academic programs in gerontology or geriatric medicine, dentistry, and psychiatry.

The socioeconomic polarization has prompted an increase in the number of honors programs, fresh demands for three-year baccalaureates, and a swelling number of graduate students. More than one-half of all masters degrees awarded by U.S. institutions have been bestowed in the past 20 years. At the other end, a rising number of those wishing admission to college are unprepared for collegiate study. Many urban community colleges have been transformed into literacy centers and remedial institutes.

The expanding connections with Asian countries have begun to stimulate more courses in Chinese and Japanese language and culture, new programs abroad in Japan, and increased exchanges with Pacific Rim countries. Religion programs are now more comparative and inclusive; and international trade has altered national economic planning models.

Because of new electronic hardware and software, nearly every classroom and campus library will need to be renovated, as some have already been.

Huge training programs for students and faculty are being established to keep undergraduates and scholars abreast of the latest electronic communication techniques and possibilities. As Richard Lanham points out in his recent book *The Electronic Word*, modern electronics may transform scholarship as we know it.

The big problem with truth

For the most learned persons in American society and their research, the changes I have briefly described seem to presage a new tension.

On the one hand, demographic, international, and social shifts are pulling scholars deeper into ethnic, gender, and social class studies, and into unique forms of knowledge. More research is devoted to analyzing distinctive voices and styles, and rhetoric is returning as a principal subject, aided by "deconstructionist" attacks. There is a growing cynicism about universal values and standards, and about the possibility of finding "truth." We live in an age of disenchantment, of relativities, as Canadian philosopher Charles Taylor has documented so well. There are, it is said, only many kinds of knowledge; and all the kinds are subjective

and context-bound and not really objective. The cold war era may have ended, but a new era of culture wars has begun.

We live in an age of disenchantment.

On the other hand, technology is pulling everyone toward certain kinds of standardization, as is contemporary mathematical and scientific research. Scholars still search for underlying similarities, unifying theories, and fundamental, abiding truths. Many persons still subscribe to the idea of timeless verities, and most universities still demand objective, unbiased teaching and scholarship.

Clearly, U.S. colleges and universities will need to rethink and restructure much of what they are currently doing. And academic planners will need to decide on what constitutes the proper content of instruction and most beneficial research in the new environment of turn-of-the century America. ∎

REFERENCES

Atlas, J. 1990. *Battle of the Books: The Curriculum Debate in America*. W.W. Norton.

Bolter, J.D. 1991. *Writing Space: The Computer, Hypertext, and the History of Writing*. Erlbaum.

Hunter, J. D. 1991. *Culture Wars: The Struggle to Define America*. Basic Books.

Lanham, R. 1993. *The Electronic Word: Democracy, Technology, and the Arts*. University of Chicago Press.

Lawler, P. 1993. The New Counterculture. *The Wall Street Journal*, (13 August).

Taylor, C. 1992. *The Ethics of Authenticity*. Harvard University Press.

———. 1989. *Sources of the Self*. Harvard University Press.

Colleges need to design the first two years with students' lives in mind.

Look Who's Coming to College

Vivian Center Seltzer

Each fall America's 3,500 colleges and universities admit about a million and a half new students aged 17 to 19 to their campuses. The young people come to learn, to sharpen their intellects, and to prepare for a career of work. But these young women and men also come to establish their identity as they leave adolescence and struggle to define themselves as independent adults. They have already spent six or seven years attempting to establish the kind of persons they are, to discover what they believe in and whom they admire and dislike, and to create a self that is separate from that of their parents without unduly violating their parents' preferences.

As most theories of adolescence proclaim (Muuss, 1988), the period from 17 to 20 years of age is when most young persons try to complete the process of defining what kind of personality they will have, what values they will adhere to, and how they will

Vivian Center Seltzer, professor of human development and behavior at the University of Pennsylvania's Graduate School of Social Work, earned her baccalaureate at the University of Minnesota and her Ph.D. from Bryn Mawr. She has held visiting professorships in Scotland and Israel and has practices as a clinical psychologist. Her latest book is *The Psychosocial Worlds of the Adolescent* (Wiley, 1989).

employ their minds in the worlds of work, service, and personal expression. This period is the last stage of adolescence, a time when young people make new lifelong friends, settle on a direction for their lives, explore the realm of sexual activity, and perhaps decide who their mates will be. Thus, U.S. higher education admits young people to begin their advanced intellectual development at the same time they are earnestly establishing identities for themselves. During the first two years of college, *two* tempestuous explorations are going on.

Many college and university leaders — and certainly most faculty — tend to concentrate on students' academic pursuit and to ignore their psychosocial pursuit. This emphasis is, of course, proper. But in the past quarter century in America, the conditions surrounding the pursuit of an identity for young persons have been transformed, and the intensity of the pursuit in late adolescence has increased. The way young people establish whom they want to be — psychosocially as well as academically — has changed considerably (Coleman and Husen, 1985). Colleges and universities must make plans dealing with the new personality dynamics of late adolescents and should, to some extent, alter college programs. The psychosocial pursuit should command attention more nearly equal to that given to the academic pursuit.

How Do Personalities Develop?

Prior to this century, most people believed that personalities were formed through genetics or, as Freud argued, in early childhood. But since the publication in 1904 of G. Stanley Hall's famous work *Adolescence*—and especially in recent decades—most scholars think that personality and character are heavily shaped by interpersonal relations during the years from puberty at ages 11, 12, or 13 to the late teens or early twenties (G. Mead, 1934; Sullivan, 1953; Coleman, 1961; M. Mead, 1961; Erikson, 1968; Keniston, 1970; Blos, 1979; Dunphy, 1980; Conger and Peterson, 1984; Bronfenbrenner, 1986). Exactly what happens in adolescence is far from being scientifically agreed upon (Adelson, 1989), but there is a tentative consensus that the teenage years are when young people, especially in radically individualist America, try on different lifestyles and construct a sense of self. As psychoanalyst-scholar Peter Blos has written, "Puberty is an act of nature and adolescence is an act of man" (1979, p. 405).

My research, and that of others, suggests that late adolescence is a final stage when most young people complete the process of selecting a self and coordinating family ties, genital activity, social behavior, value preferences, and occupational directions to make up a persona. How and where do they do all this?

The Changing Forces of Human Development

For most of today's brightest and best young persons, college is where they fashion a sense of self. College has become an immensely important place for personality development for nearly half of America's young because most of the traditional forces that helped adolescents find an identity have become weak or withered away. Puberty rites, confirmations or bar mitzvahs, apprenticeships, coming-out parties, community meetings, and town dances have lost their ability to provide self-definition. Although sons and daughters of fundamentalist Protestants, orthodox Jews, devout Muslims, and strict Roman Catholics usually are influenced by their family faith, many young persons today have weak religious ties. And religious leaders do not play the powerful role in the United States today that they do in, say, modern Iran or did in puritan England.

Conditions surrounding the pursuit of an identity for young persons have been transformed.

Parental authority has become less influential, as nearly one-fourth of American children are now born out of wedlock, as two-thirds of all mothers with children work, as divorce rates have increased, and as parents have increasingly yielded to their children's wants and needs rather than pressing their children to follow family values and behavioral patterns. As the nation's finest sociologist of education, James Coleman, says, "There has been a decline in hierarchical authority throughout society, particularly in the family. . . . Society has been invaded by an advanced individualism, in which cultivation of one's own well-being has replaced interest in others" (1987, p. 35).

Also, television and pop music present violent, hedonistic, and exotic scenarios to youth. Expert advice via magazines, newspapers, schools, TV, books, films, advertisements, and lectures competes with family guidance (Cremin, 1989). An increasingly pluralistic society makes local family, religious, and educational influences seem relative, and modern media reveal how Japanese, Nigerians, Poles, and American Indians live different lives. Rapid change causes young people to feel that values, behaviors, allegiances are ephemeral, that the important thing is to "hang loose."

The contemporary late adolescent in college is in a psychological no-man's land where the many roadsigns point in a hundred directions, the travel guides have disappeared, and few reliable others exist to tell

Adolescents are in a psychological no-man's land.

him or her what is expected. The normal confusion of adolescence, when one is separating from family care and sustenance, is compounded today by a cacophony of social and cultural voices—and academic voices too, because college educators and professors are also reluctant to inject what seems like moral guidance (although they cannot avoid the ethical implications of their views and behavior). Yet, the college youth must choose how and where to live, whom to associate with, what work to do for a living, whom to mate with or befriend, how to dress, what kind of music to enjoy, and how intellectual to become.

The Peer Groups

To fashion an identity, young people now rely mainly on others of the same age; together they establish mini-societies with their own norms and values (Coleman, 1961). They learn together how to deal with adults and the world. The peer groups have thus become the major agency through which adolescents develop themselves, particularly their personalities, although on large issues, family influence can still be quite strong. Michigan's Joseph Adelson claims, "On important questions youngsters value their parents' advice above that of their peers. . . . There is not now, nor has there ever been, a generation gap, not for most youngsters, and not on significant issues" (1989). As Table 1 shows, my research supports this view.

Alongside affiliation with chosen groups of peers, late adolescents engage in an increasingly alert search among the various peer group members and other young persons to identify those attributes they should develop in themselves or avoid. My research reveals that this informational pursuit, this

Table 1. How 12th Graders Rank the Ten Most Influential Persons in Their Lives, 1988

1. Parents
2. Schoolmates, same age
3. Special friend
4. Older brothers/sisters
5. Neighbors of same age
6. Friends, 2–5 years older
7. School teachers, counselors
8. Media
9. Clergy
10. Friends, 5+ years older

watching and comparing with others, is a primary, perhaps even the central, dynamic of the adolescent years.

Late adolescents study each other with meticulous care for cues about how they should behave, dress, speak, and regard the worlds of school and college (Seltzer, 1982, 1989). They use each other to sculpt a personal style and value system that will enable them to deal with the multiplicity of messages and uncertainty—without breaking too sharply with their parents' hopes for them or with the family's religion, politics, views on education, and moral preferences.

Watching and comparing with others is central.

It becomes clear to most American teenagers that to know who "I" am and where "I" can go in life is largely conditional on how "I" rank relative to those with whom I will go through life. This sense is especially keen among college freshmen and sophomores. Peer gatherings serve as a grist mill to observe microscopically other and competing persons, to evaluate one another, and to determine which attributes the group values most highly. (Table 2 indicates the ten most important attributes that are observed.) The late adolescent then adopts those behavioral traits that seem to fit with her or his own fuzzy proclivities or vague goals for the future.

There exists a reciprocal and unexpressed social contract in which each of the

Table 2. Peer Attitudes "Always/Usually" of Interest to Adolescents

Attribute	Rank
Loyalty to friends	1
Cleanliness	2
Clothes	3
Trustworthiness	4
General physical appearance	5
Honesty	6
Dependability	7
Maturity	8
Popularity with opposite sex	9
Complexion	10

peer group members models the others for the benefit of his or her development and the development of others. Harry Stack Sullivan believed (1953) that relationships with other people influence how we develop and what we become; we are shaped by significant others. My research seems to support this view. Comparison acts with peers appear to be the primary mechanism for the psychosocial development of most adolescents. What this means, of course, is that the shaping of a self is enormously dependent upon whom an adolescent associates with, compares herself to, and learns from.

College Freshmen

Most students entering college have already completed a good portion of the work of comparing themselves with others and becoming aware of their strengths and weaknesses. Having completed the first stage of adolescent probing, which revealed they could be college bound, they are disciplined enough to undertake sustained academic training for some important area of work. Most late adolescents who enter college, however, also see it as a period of "coming of age," of being on their own and refining themselves in an atmosphere of fun and freedom. They often nurture fantasies about "college life" (Moffat, 1989).

But the freshman year usually hurls students back into the first stage of adolescence, albeit for a temporary period. Their new peers are different from them and more high-powered, and there are many unfamiliar

others. Here are some typical responses from my hundreds of student interviews:

> When I came to college and saw the great differences in backgrounds and beliefs . . . I was at a loss.

> I was shocked by the diversity of such a large university. I really had to struggle to adjust. At first I didn't want to deal with it, so I withdrew into my studies for the first few months.

> I left behind all my security and support and had to start over in a world full of strangers.

To cope, most freshmen sharpen their observational skills and increase their watchfulness of and comparisons with others their age. They hunt for others who appear, at least on the surface, to be like themselves. The attraction of fraternities and sororities, ethnic or special purpose clubs, athletic teams, and familiar activities such as the campus newspaper, debate team, feminist circle, or political organization is huge. As a result, attention to academic studies frequently suffers. Not surprisingly, roughly one-fourth of all freshmen in U.S. colleges do not return for the sophomore year.

We are shaped by significant others.

Many students join small peer groups to assist in their search for self. For instance, they may associate with a pre-law group, a theater group, their fellows on the swimming team, a sexual partner, or a small pack interested in going to Europe the next summer. I have found many college students to be amazingly discriminating in their socially comparative searching. The psychosocial exploration can be exhilarating as students find unknown strengths and special attributes, but it can also be painful as students discover themselves deficient by comparison or unable to become an engineer or musician as they wish. Some slide into drug or alcohol abuse.

To sum up, undergraduates in the first two years are engaged in a preoccupying and to them extremely urgent psychosociological search, learning from each other. Their search is heavily visual and auditory and only partially verbal. They may be training themselves academically, but they are just as actively trying to place themselves psychosocially and to establish a satisfactory identity and lifestyle.

What About Faculty?

Professors play an important though little understood role in helping students find their way from adolescence to maturity. Some professors try to be a friend to their students, but this seldom works since the emphasis of faculty lives is too distant from student concerns. Indeed, professors are often fodder for shared laughs and speculations among younger students.

However, according to my investigations, the teaching faculty do help students in three important ways. One, they furnish students with a respite from their intensive comparisons with other students. The scholars' intellectual inquiries and lectures offer an activity so different from the psychosocial questing that classes are often perceived as a relief, or, if the instructor is good, a stimulating interlude. Two, the level of esteem that the faculty bestow on students during classes or at the end of the term via grades helps students assess the ways they should evaluate their peers and assists them in evaluating themselves.

Colleges must plan for the new psychosocial condition of their incoming students.

Three, the finest scholar-teachers, especially if they are attractive or colorful individuals, often cut through the peer-group searching and become a role model. I suspect many parents are insistent on good teaching during college because they see

great teachers as an influential factor in lifting their daughter or son out of adolescent behavior, the often hedonistic values of youth groups, and a too-narrow band of identity seeking.

What Can Be Done?

Colleges must recognize that the decline of religion, community, and family as controlling forces in young people's development and the rise of potent forces such as television, automobiles, sports, magazines, films, and pop music have contributed to placing the development of personality and character more heavily on the shoulders of young people themselves. And this process is probably at its most stressful in late adolescence, when undergraduates are in their first year or two at college. Higher education institutions, without yielding to adolescent wants, must appreciate more than they currently do that in the early college years two concurrent activities are being pursued by students: academic training for work and psychosocial formation for lifestyle, moral outlook, and social behavior.

Colleges and universities must plan for the new psychosocial condition of their incoming students. Since U.S. institutions vary enormously, planning to accommodate this intensive search for identity will vary from campus to campus. Residential colleges have responsibilities that differ from commuter schools, small colleges from large universities, and religiously affiliated colleges from secular or state institutions.

Yet some ingredients of good planning for students suggest themselves. The freshman year certainly requires more careful design and greater attention than it now receives (Upcraft and Gardner, 1989). Deans of students should place special emphasis on serving the newest students. There is much to be said for a freshman quadrangle, like the Harvard Yard or the frosh-soph quadrangle at the University of Pennsylvania, and special freshman advisers. Colleges must design more opportunities for students to be alone (via heavier study assignments, individual projects) and to be with mature adults so that undergraduates can get relief from the pressures of their peer arena.

Professors who teach freshman and sophomore courses should relate their material more closely to the psychosocial needs of their students. What do the materials taught imply for character, ambitions, ethics, relations among peoples, cultural priorities, and a philosophy of life? Biographies can be helpful at this stage. Great books courses and courses that look at values through history ("The Relation of Females and Males in Four Cultures," "Humor in Western Civilization," "The Family from the Rise of Industrialism to the Present," etc.) also present helpful comparisons to students as they work on their selfhood, their values, and their preferences for a career. Generally, American college curricula in the first two years should be designed more specifically with the students' psychosocial pursuit in mind. Intellectual inquiry can be made to support identity seeking rather than to ignore it.

A more controversial suggestion is that colleges refrain from pressing new students to experience too many different cultures, the lifestyles of all minority groups, and the diversity of world religions, governments, and philosophies. It has suddenly become modish to require a course for freshmen that promotes intergroup harmony and reduces stereotyping and prejudicial behaviors—certainly an important aim. As I earlier described, however, freshmen are already unsettled and disoriented by college life and are struggling to solidify their own identities. They need first to validate their own traits (Darley and Aronson, 1966; Radloff, 1966); when they are assured of their own worth, diversity is far less threatening.

To reduce the stress of an overload of diversity and cultural patterns, students may reject some of those who appear different from themselves. Thus, too much diversity in the early undergraduate years runs the risk of provoking the very behavior and attitudes the college is seeking to eradicate. It is better to foster reinforcing groups—sororities, a black student association, a Chinese student group, a Newman club, and the like—in the early collegiate years and then

educate for true cosmopolitan living in the upper years.

If colleges and universities understand that today's students are coming to the campus with a much heavier burden of self-definition than did yesterday's students, the institutions can—and should—design their academic programs and student activities more thoughtfully with the students' psychosocial pursuit in mind. ∎

REFERENCES

Adelson, J., ed. *Handbook of Adolescent Psychology.* New York: John Wiley, 1980.

_____. "Drugs and Youth." *Commentary*, 87 (1989): 24–38.

Blos, P. *The Adolescent Passage: Development Issues.* New York: International Universities Press, 1979.

Coleman, J. *The Adolescent Society: The Social Life of a Teenager and its Impact on Education.* Glencoe: The Free Press, 1961.

_____. "Families and Schools." *Educational Researcher*, 16 (1987): 32–38.

Coleman, J. and Husen, T. *Becoming Adult in a Changing Society.* Paris: Organization for Economic Cooperation and Development, 1985.

Coleman, J. C., "Friendship and the Peer Group in Adolescence." *Handbook of Adolescent Psychology.* Edited by J. Adelson. New York: John Wiley & Sons, Inc., 1980, 408–431.

Conger, J. and Petersen, A. *Adolescence and Youth: Psychological Development in a Changing World.* 3d ed. New York: Harper & Row, 1984.

Cremin, L. *Popular Education and its Discontents.* New York: Harper & Row, 1989.

Darley, J. and Aronson, E. "Self-evaluation vs. Direct Anxiety Reduction as Determinants of the Fear Affiliation Relationship." *Journal of Experimental Social Psychology*, Supp. (1966): 66–79.

Dunphy, D. "Peer Group Socialization." *Adolescent Behavior and Society.* Edited by R. Muuss. 3d ed. New York: Random House, 1980.

Erikson, E. *Identity: Youth and Crisis.* New York: Norton, 1968.

Fasick, R. "Parents, Peers, Youth Culture, and Autonomy in Adolescence." *Adolescence*, 19 (1984): 143–157.

Festinger, L. "A Theory of Social Comparison Processes." *Human Relations*, 5 (1954): 117–139.

Freud, A. "Adolescence." *Psychoanalytic Study of the Child*, Vol. 13: 255–278. New York: International Universities Press, 1958.

Hakmiller, K. "Need for Self-evaluation. Perceived Similarity, and Comparison Choice." *Journal of Experimental *Social Psychology*, Supp. 1 (1966): 49–55.

Hall, G. *Adolescence*. 2 vols. New York: Appleton, 1904.

Jones, S. and Regan, D. "Ability Evaluation Through Social Comparison." *Journal of Experimental Social Psychiatry*, 13 (1974): 133–146.

Keniston, K. "Youth: A New Stage in Life." *American Scholar*, 39 (1970): 631–654.

Mead, G. *Mind, Self and Society*. Chicago: University of Chicago Press, 1934.

Mead, M. "The Young Adult." *Values and Ideals of American Youth*. Edited by E. Ginzberg. New York: Columbia University Press, 1961.

_____. *Culture and Commitment*. New York: American Museum of Natural History, 1970.

Moffat, M. *Coming of Age in New Jersey*. New Brunswick: Rutgers University Press, 1989.

Muuss, R. *Theories of Adolescence*. 5th ed. New York: Random House, 1988.

Radloff, R. "Social Comparison and Ability Evaluation." *Journal of Experimental Social Psychology*, Supp. 1 (1966): 6–26.

Riesman, D.; Denny, R.; and Glazer, N. *The Lonely Crowd: A Study of the Changing American Character*. New Haven: Yale University Press, 1950.

Seltzer, V. *Adolescent Social Development*. Lexington, MA.: Lexington Books, 1982.

_____. *The Psychosocial Worlds of the Adolescent: Public and Private*. New York: John Wiley & Sons, Inc., 1989.

Sullivan, H. S. *Interpersonal Theory of Psychiatry*. New York: Norton, 1953.

Upcraft, L. and Gardner, J. *The Freshman Year Experience: Helping Students Survive and Succeed in College*. San Francisco: Jossey-Bass, 1989.

Waterman, A. "Identity Development from Adolescence to Adulthood: An Extension of Theory and a Review of Research." *Developmental Psychology*, 18 (1982): 341–358.

The public mood about and the legal basis for affirmative action policies have shifted. An expert suggests what colleges should do now.

Rethinking Affirmative Action on Campus

George R. La Noue

As education planners and policy makers know, there have been major changes in the legal standards and political views on affirmative action. There has also been a major change in the demography of the United States in the past two decades. Every U.S. college and university now must rethink their affirmative action policies which depend on racial, ethnic, or gender preferences.

In three decades as a national policy, affirmative action has meant many things, some of them diametrically opposed (Graham 1990; Belz 1991). In 1965 President Lyndon Johnson's Executive Order 11246 required that institutions take affirmative action to see that individuals were treated "without regard to their race, creed, color, or

George R. La Noue is professor of political science and director of the Policy Sciences Graduate Program at the University of Maryland, Baltimore County. A graduate of Hanover College in Indiana with an M.A. and Ph.D. in political science from Yale, he has taught politics and education at Columbia University and is co-author of *Academics in Court* (1987), among numerous other writings. He has also served as assistant to the Executive Director of the U.S. Equal Opportunity Commission and has been a trial expert in more than two dozen cases involving civil rights issues.

national origin." For the past 20 years, however, affirmative action frequently came to mean, as Justice Blackmun's dissent in the 1978 Bakke case stated, "In order to get beyond racism, we must first take account of race." Often that idea meant policies so broad and so enduring that they could be considered more as preferences aimed at reordering societal outcomes than as specific remedies for particular problems.

Now the legal validity and public support of racial, ethnic, and gender preferences is eroding and all affirmative action programs must be reconsidered. In many higher education institutions the adjustments will be wrenching, instigating a consideration of data never before gathered or released and requiring the kind of open discussions that have not previously characterized this subject. Other institutions will be better positioned and will reach a consensus easier and earlier. But all American campuses must be prepared to develop new plans for affirmative action programs. Policies should cover admission, financial aid, employment, and contracting.

The courts' new course

Recent federal court decisions provide the impetus for this planning, although other factors necessitate it as well. The new judicial rules cover all public institutions, but private institutions will also be affected by the general reassessment of policies based on racial, ethnic, and gender categories.

On May 22, 1995 the U.S. Supreme Court announced its decision not to hear an appeal by the University of Maryland, College Park to reinstate the Banneker scholarship program for highly qualified African-American undergraduates. The appeal in

---

All campuses must be prepared to develop new plans for affirmative action.

Podberesky v. Kirwan had the support of 28 other colleges and universities, most of the traditional civil rights organizations, including the ACLU, the NAACP, the National Organization for Women, the Mexican-American Legal Defense Fund, almost all major higher education associations, and the U.S. Department of Justice. The Supreme Court denied the appeal without comment, thus leaving the Fourth Circuit Court of Appeals decision that found the program unconstitutional as guidance for courts in other jurisdictions and the law in the states (Maryland, Virginia, West Virginia, North Carolina, and South Carolina) in the Circuit.

The basis for *Podberesky* and all other legal considerations of affirmative action is a 1989 Supreme Court decision, *City of Richmond v. J. A. Croson Company*. In that case, the Court determined that the legal concept of strict scrutiny, which places a heavy burden of proof on the government, should be applied to all state and local racial classifications. This scrutiny meant that race or ethnicity could not be used as a category in a government policy, unless there was a compelling reason to do so as a remedy for identified discrimination. Even then, the remedy had to be narrowly tailored, and employed only if race-neutral methods would not suffice. According to *Croson*, race-conscious policies should only be used as an "extreme measure."

The *Croson* framework for analysis of affirmative action plans was applicable only to state and local programs. On June 12, 1995, however, the Supreme Court announced its decision in *Adarand v. Pena* which involved the constitutionality of a provision in a federal highway program providing bonuses for the use of minority contractors who were presumptively considered disadvantaged businesses. Similar programs had been upheld in previous Supreme Court cases, and Adarand, the white firm challenging the preference, had lost in two lower federal courts. The Supreme Court, however, reversed those decisions and remanded the case to be decided in accord with new principles it announced.

Writing for a five-person majority in *Adarand*, Justice Sandra Day O'Connor, who also wrote the *Croson* plurality opinion, again affirmed that strict scrutiny—the most stringent judicial test—was the standard judges should apply to all programs with racial classifications. This position was based on two premises. First, that "the Fifth and Fourteenth Amendments to the Constitution protect persons not groups." Second, that the use of racial classifications is harmful to society. She noted that such classifications had been called "pernicious," "odious," and "stigmatizing" in various earlier Supreme Court Opinions. Justice O'Connor conceded that there are rare circumstances where discrimination has been so obvious and persistent that race-based remedies might be necessary, but she cautioned that judges should view their use with skepticism.

The effect of the majority decision in *Adarand* will be to require federal courts to apply the *Croson* standards to federal programs too. In a General Accounting Office survey produced in 1995 for Senator Robert Dole, some 160 federal programs were discovered that had racial classifications. Among them are at least 40 educational programs such as minority scholarships, funding earmarked for historically black institutions, and research training assistance to institutions with high proportions of minority students.

Many of these programs are now under review by Congress or the President, but *Adarand* creates additional opportunities to challenge them in federal courts. Increasing litigation against all types of racial preferences is likely because of the emergence of conservative litigating agencies. For example, the Center for Individual Rights (CIR) brought a case challenging preferences for African-Americans and Mexican-Americans in law school admissions (*Hopwood v. University of Texas Law School*). CIR is also suing Ohio State University for imposing a 100 percent set-aside for painting contracts on its campus. The Mountain States Legal Foundation brought the *Adarand* case. The Washington Legal Foundation won the *Podberesky* case. Pacific Legal Foundation is suing San Bernadino Valley College for excluding a white girl from a remedial program, a case with sufficient notoriety that it was used by Governor Pete Wilson in defending his executive order curtailing racial preferences in California.

How the *Adarand* principles will eventually be applied to all the federal race-based programs that survive congressional

The legal concept of strict scrutiny should now be applied.

and administrative review will not be known for years, but the Fourth Circuit's *Podberesky* decision is certainly consistent with the *Adarand* majority. College Park was once a *de jure* segregated campus until the 1950s and therefore was presumed to have more flexibility in using race-conscious remedies than campuses with a less clear record of discrimination. The campus argued that its scholarship program for African-American scholars was necessary because College Park's previous history has given it a poor reputation in the black community. There was also some perception of a hostile climate toward blacks on the campus, the campus leaders said, and inter-

generational effects of segregated education were still present because by some measure African-Americans were underrepresented on the campus. Nevertheless, the Circuit's three-judge panel refuted every argument the university made, particularly noting the underrepresentation had to be calculated by measuring the pool of *qualified* students for the university, not by counting the *total* population of high school graduates. The panel's decision was affirmed later on in an appeal to all the Circuits' judges by a vote of 8-3.

The Banneker scholarship program had its own particular characteristics and is not representative of all affirmative action programs in higher education. But the *Podberesky* decision cannot be prudently ignored by other campuses across the country.

The new political alignments

Beyond the new judicial rules toward affirmative action, no campus leader should overlook the general changes in public opinion on this subject. The results of opinion polls often turn on how particular questions are worded, but there seems to be broad opposition to those types of affirmative action that go beyond opening up competition toward forcing outcomes through quotas or preferences.

More significant for campuses than public attitudes is the newly crystallized opposition of the Republican party to affirmative action. The historical attitude of the Republican party on this subject has been inconsistent (Graham 1990). President Nixon was influential in creating the Philadelphia plan which set quotas for construction hiring, and he acted as a champion of black enterprise development. His administration laid the foundation for the minority business preference programs which are now honeycombed throughout the federal government. While President Reagan was philosophically opposed to affirmative action, his administration was divided and largely ineffective, except in judicial appointments, in changing its course. Even the Bush administration, initially opposed to the 1990 Civil Rights Act, which was labeled a quota bill, ended in acquiescence to that legislation in 1991.

The current Republican party, however, for reasons of philosophy and electoral strategy, now seems committed to opposing those types of affirmative action which involve preferences. All major contenders for the 1996 Republican Presidential nomination have announced their

---

No campus leaders should overlook the general changes in public opinion on this subject.

---

opposition to preferences and several have made it a major part of their platform. While there is no conformity within the Republican party on affirmative action, and some conservative Democrats are also hostile to racial preferences, the new role of the GOP has enormous significance for universities, even in states where Republicans are not a political majority.

On many, if not most, campuses there has been little debate over the particulars of affirmative action. The issues have been seen in ideological terms or as responses to external constituencies: government agencies, accrediting organizations, academic association, and foundations. Few persons not in administrative inner circles actually knew how affirmative action affected campus decisions—whether the preferences were great or small, consistently or inconsistently applied. Very little of the actual data that could lead to informed judgment about the effects of these policies has been gathered or released and it was not clear who had the right to see the data.

Current Republican activism changes these conditions. Governor Wilson's intervention into the University of California's policies may be only the opening salvo. First, it ensures a debate over affirmative action policies in most governments and gives that debate a legitimacy it has not had in the past. Issues raised by a major party

resonate on editorial pages and in trustees meetings in ways that other issues do not. This is particularly true of affirmative action, which has the support of many effective national interest groups but whose opponents have had none. Second, legislative committees will ask harder questions than before and, where Republicans control committee chairmanships, there may be investigations into the actual operation of affirmative action policies and threats of fiscal retaliation for campuses, public and private, that do not make records available or will not change their policies. Third, campus leaders will find it harder to advocate affirmative action policies involving preferences if they know there is no consensus behind them and if their advocacy could be taken for espousing a partisan position.

The new demographics of minorities

Campuses must also recognize the implications of larger demographic trends in the United States for traditional affirmative action policies. These trends affect some states more than others, but campuses that recruit in broad geographic areas or that are located in metropolitan areas are now confronted with students and employee applicants from a wider variety of ethnic groups.

The great moral engine for affirmative action was compensation for the generations of injustices towards African-Americans. But other groups have been shoe-horned into the affirmative action model constructed for blacks. Between 1980 and 1990 three times as many Asian-Americans and Hispanics were added to the nation's population as blacks. Consequently, African-Americans are now less than one-half of the population of groups that are considered minorities (La Noue 1993a). On numerous campuses Asian-Americans or Hispanics will be the dominant minority, especially since historically black institutions still enroll and employ disproportionate numbers of America's blacks.

The situation of Asian-Americans and Hispanic-Americans cannot be easily compared to that of African-Americans either in their arrival in the country, in their American experiences, or in their current status.

A substantial proportion of Asian-Americans and Hispanics are recent immigrants or first-generation Americans. There is increasing concern about whether these persons should receive the same kind of affirmative action as is intended for descendants of slaves. But few, if any, campuses have made affirmative action distinctions based on immigrant status.

Also, there are major cultural, educational, and economic differences among Cuban-Americans, Mexican-Americans, and Puerto Ricans, and even greater differences between Japanese-Americans, Asian Indians, and Pacific Islanders. To make matters more complex, extensive patterns of intermarriage are developing. For example, numerous Japanese-American women marry white men. There is a growing objection by persons of mixed parentage to being forced to choose single categories as their identity for affirmative action reasons.

Finally, some Hispanic and Asian-American subgroups have made substantial progress and now rank among the American success stories of immigrant group mobility, while other subgroups lag behind. To extend the mantle of disadvantage to all members of these groups is to divide the population along color lines that ignore reality.

Campus models to consider

In planning to review affirmative action policies, campuses can choose among three models:

- remedying past discrimination
- expanding diversity
- promoting social justice.

Each of these models start from different premises and involve different legal, political, and educational issues; but in practice, many campuses have mixed rhetoric from each to justify a melange of policies.

Remedying past discrimination. While there are some differences depending on whether the issue is admissions, financial aid, employment, or public contracting, courts have integrated the lessons from the *Croson* decision to establish some new legal parameters. The thrust of recent federal court decisions is that institutions may, af-

Other groups have been shoe-horned into the affirmative action model constructed for blacks.

ter identifying discrimination with some particularity and determining that race-neutral policies will not work, use narrowly tailored race-based remedies as a last resort. Neither diversity or social justice concerns will suffice as reasons for a public institution to employ racial classifications systematically to limit competition, or to confer or deny benefits.

For a campus to be able to use racial classifications as remedies, it will have to undertake the onerous and politically difficult task of carefully identifying the discrimination it seeks to cure. *Podberesky* suggests that even if a public campus was in a state with *de jure* segregation, history alone is not enough to confer benefits on current black students. Of course, it could not serve as a justification for preferences for non-black groups either. If the campus engaged in recent discrimination against a group, or if the present effects of past discrimination on its students or employees can be clearly identified, not just speculated about, then a narrowly-tailored remedy might be employed. Proving such discrimination according to the strict scrutiny standard will usually be a formidable task. On the other hand, campuses always have the option, and indeed the moral responsibility, to make anti-discriminatory policies and enforce them vigorously. They cannot prefer groups based on race, ethnicity, or sex, however, without a finding of discrimination.

The law about making such findings has only begun to emerge. After the *Croson* decision invalidating Richmond's 30 percent set-aside for minority businesses, some governments abandoned similar programs, some modified existing programs, and some commissioned consultant studies to assess the extent of local contracting discrimination. More than a hundred of these so-called disparity studies have been completed at a cost of at least $45 million and the outcomes have been highly controversial (La Noue 1993b).

Some studies have clearly been results-driven with predetermined conclusions. Others have floundered because of inadequate data or research methodologies. Some have found discrimination against some previously covered groups, but not against others, which has led to outcomes that were politically unacceptable. In Miami, for instance, the study found white women-owned businesses underutilized, but not firms owned by blacks or Hispanics. In Los Angeles, Hispanic-owned businesses, but not those owned by blacks, were found to be underutilized. Neither government would accept those findings. Smaller, less politically powerful groups such as Native Americans have been excluded from post-*Croson* minority business programs all over the country. Naturally, the groups that were formerly included objected to newly designed preference programs which would place them in the same non-preferred position as white males.

Only one disparity study has been the subject of full discovery and trial. In that case, a federal district court in 1995 found the study scientifically and legally inadequate, and permanently enjoined a goals program for black contractors (*Contractors Association of Eastern Pennsylvania v. City of Philadelphia,* 1995).

Expanding diversity. Some campuses have already shifted their rhetoric from affirmative action to diversity, sometimes without making any actual changes in policy. Diversity is a legitimate reason to consider racial, ethnic, and gender factors in making campus policies. But it has to be done correctly, lest courts or opponents see it as a disguise for otherwise illegitimate policies.

The source of the judicial rationale for diversity policies is the *Bakke* decision, where Justice Lewis Powell, who cast the deciding vote in the case, tried to steer a middle course between the use of quotas and the appropriate consideration of race as one of the characteristics in selecting a diverse student body. (It is an opinion worth re-reading by campus policy makers.) At its heart is a finding that any system based on racial categories which denies the right to any person to compete for any benefit is unconstitutional, but that diversity is a proper

Diversity is a legitimate reason to consider racial, ethnic, and gender factors.

goal in selecting students, and so race might be a factor in considering diversity on campus. Justice Powell went on to say that, "The diversity that furthers a compelling state interest encompasses a far broader array of qualifications and characteristics of which racial or ethnic origin is but a single though important element." (*Bakke*, 315) He then cited the Harvard College admissions policy which purportedly valued the diversity brought by Idaho farm boys as well as by minority group members.

Justice Powell's diversity concept suggests campuses will have to use categories for diversity that go beyond the affirmative action conventions. The diversity that campuses otherwise normally seek in selecting students and employees is variety in life experiences and intellectual orientations. Assumptions based on race, ethnicity, and gender are often poor surrogates for actual measures of experience and orientation. To make that assumption is to fall victim to stereotyping and to suggesting that persons with similar immutable genetic characteristics are likely to behave and believe in predetermined ways. The position that each person has many identities and unique characteristics is a more attractive posture for an academic institution, not to mention the fact that it is empirically closer to reality.

Should a campus decide to plan a new diversity policy, a number of issues need to be considered. First, what areas of academic life need to be included? Diversity may be more relevant to the selection of students and employees, but may be less of a factor in choosing firms to supply goods and services. Should diversity be a consideration in inviting speakers to campus or in selection of faculty on a department-by-department basis? Many institutions may find that the most underrepresented ideas on campus are not among those who most favor diversity policies, but those, who for religious or political reasons, are relatively conservative.

Does true diversity require campuses to replicate the marketplace spectrum of ideas? How are international students to be regarded? Is a student from Norway more diverse than an African-American from a local suburb? Is an ethnic Chinese student from Malaysia more diverse than a Chinese-American from San Francisco? Are there reasons to prefer American citizens, particularly where financial aid is involved?

Finally, what is the balance between seeking diversity and/or consensus appropriate for each campus? Some institutions seem committed to a version of multiculturalism where persons are expected and encouraged to define themselves primarily by race or ethnicity. Other institutions place more emphasis on developing a community in which separate cultures are subordinated to a common religious or secular vision.

Should diversity be a consideration in inviting speakers to campus or in selection of faculty?

Promoting social justice. Higher education has had a long tradition of seeing its mission as related to various views of social justice. That tradition offers opportunities for a kind of affirmative action that reaches out to disadvantaged persons and neighborhoods without using explicit racial classifications. If properly designed, these programs should not create legal problems. In most cases those policies will benefit minorities and other underrepresented groups relatively more than others, though the poli-

cies are not based on racial, ethnic, or gender classifications.

Institutions may bring their research resources to bear on problems of the greatest social needs. They may use admissions or financial aid decisions to assist students who have faced the greatest educational handicaps or those whose potential has been obscured by poor school preparation or chaotic families (*Bakke*, 317). They may not, however, use race or ethnicity or gender as a surrogate for disadvantages that in fact exist more broadly in society and that can be measured more objectively in economic or educational terms.

Programs could be designed to reach out to schools for assistance or to recruit students that are defined geographically, *e.g.,* inner city, or by condition, *e.g.,* schools with inadequate curriculums, high numbers of students who are eligible for school lunch assistance or who live in public housing. Students and employees who are not personally disadvantaged, but are committed to working on social problems affecting those who are disadvantaged, may receive higher priorities in admissions or hiring. Local situations and particular campus missions may suggest other alternatives. Campuses that effectively develop these opportunities may find they will be magnets for both minorities and non-minorities who are motivated by those goals.

Campus planning

The visibility of campus affirmative action policies will surely be increased in this new era and administrators will have to be prepared for more questions and requests for hard data about the actual operation of policies that exist. On most campuses this situation will require rethinking of policies and better planning about their implementation.

Because this area of law is so volatile and controversial, campuses will need careful legal advice. If current policies can be accurately described and the right questions posed, establishing the legal parameters should take place before the larger campus planning process begins. There is no point in spending long hours developing a plan that has little chance of surviving a court challenge. Legal advice may also serve to moot some of the more extreme ideological demands that otherwise might distract the planning process.

After legal principles are established, the larger planning process can begin. Many institutions will discover that opinions about

> *Administrators will have to be prepared for more questions and requests for hard data.*

affirmative action are more diverse in the various campus constituencies than was previously visible. The strong leadership commitment to affirmative action—on some campuses even deemed necessary for all employment—has suppressed some opposition; and those dissenters will now be heard from. It is particularly important to have vigorous debates about whether discrimination remediation, diversity, or a social justice strategy is the right approach for the campus.

In the planning process, it will be helpful to have a broad variety of opinions, probably supplemented by some public forums, so no one feels excluded. When new policies or options have been created, it will again be necessary to seek detailed legal advice. Some policies may be constitutional only if implemented in particular ways. For example, any policy using racial classifications now needs at least to show that race-neutral means would not suffice, that only those groups for which there is a proven history of

discrimination are included, that classifications are used only in the areas in which the discrimination took place, and that the use of race will last only as long as necessary.

It seems probable that the national debate over restructuring affirmative action will be contentious and long. There is an enormous amount of power, money, and principle at stake, and the sides are far apart. By engaging seriously in the process of review on their own campuses, academic institutions may provide models of discourse for the larger society. Resolution of these conflicts should be through creative solutions based on data rather than rhetoric, and they should be developed by people who respect one another. If the campuses fail in this dialogue, it is hard to be optimistic about the success of such efforts in the rest of society. ∎

REFERENCES

Adarand v. Pena, 1995. 63 U.S.L.W. 4523.

City of Richmond v. Croson, 1989. 488 U.S. 469.

Hopwood v. University of Texas, 1994. 861 F.Supp. 551 (W. D. Tex).

Podberesky v. Kirwan, 1995. 38 F.3d 147 (4th Cir.).

Regents of the University of California v. Bakke, 1978. 438 U.S. 265.

Belz, H., 1991. *Equality Transformed: A Quarter-Century of Affirmative Action*. Transaction Publishers.

Graham, H., 1990. *The Civil Rights Era*. Oxford University Press.

La Noue, G. 1993a. The Demographic Assumptions of Affirmative Action. *Population and Environment* 14 (5): 421-440.

La Noue, G. 1993b. Social Science and Minority Set-Asides. *The Public Interest* (110): 49-62.

Wright, L. 1994. One Drop of Blood. *The New Yorker* (25 July): 55.

Here's a guide for planners to the complex, multiplying, fast-changing activities in distance education.

Distancing Your College Courses

Deborah Allen Carey

D istance learning systems have been spreading throughout U.S. higher education, as most campus planners know. But with the availability of new technology, the rapid changes in software, and the evolving connections between colleges and schools and working adults and rural residents, it has been extremely difficult for campus administrators, planners, and facilities directors to figure out which distance learning system to install. Planning for distance learning can seem overwhelming.

It may be helpful, therefore, to understand two things about distance learning. One is that the persistent drift in distance education is away from passive lectures and information delivery (old-time distance learning) toward more interactive student learning which incorporates computer data and multi-media presentations. Increasingly, the instructors not only lecture but also promote discussion, pose problems, and guide responses with student groups in many locations simultaneously.

The other is that three models have emerged for distance education. There are also some newer ones on the horizon, but these three appear to have had some success. So education planners should know the advantages and disadvantages of each — and a little of the different costs involved with each. For simplicity's sake, I'll call these models the traditional, the transitional, and the advanced. Each can be tailored to specific college needs, local distribution resources, and budget.

Because distance education requires special equipment and different kinds of educational facilities, I have tried to be quite specific in the material requirements for each of the three models.

A traditional system

A good example of a traditional distance learning system is Manchester Community Technical College's (MCTC) Project Cable Connect, which links the college to six local high schools providing basic instruction at fairly low cost. This system has been in operation for six years. In a cooperative project with Cox Cable TV, the system allows for live, two-way, scheduled interactive audio and video among all locations. Cox Cable provides coaxial cable and

Deborah Allen Carey is the educational facilities planner at S/L/A/M Collaborative, a Connecticut architectural and engineering firm. After receiving her B.A. from Mount Holyoke College and her M.Arch. from the University of Washington in Seattle, she worked in health facility design and published a book, *Hospice Inpatient Environments*. For the past six years she has done planning and design for schools and colleges, especially in the area of educational technology.

fiber optic connections as well as channel clearance during classes.

During a typical day, five or six distance learning classes are offered over the system. The classes offered typically have low enrollment and would be difficult to justify without the combined enrollment of other sites. MCTC also offers high school students courses for college credit, such as Japanese, Criminal Justice, and Allied Health.

The operation of the system involves a video classroom at each site. In each room, students sit at tables with microphones in front of them. There is a camera in the classroom to record the students, and a TV monitor to view the teacher and teaching materials. The college classroom where the teacher is located is more technologically sophisticated with three cameras to capture the teacher and students in that room, as well as a document camera for transmission of material.

In order to maintain eye contact with students at other sites, the teacher wears a microphone, and monitors are mounted next to the "teacher" camera. A fax machine allows the students to send homework to the teacher. Cameras need appropriate lighting levels on the teacher and student. Also, moderated acoustics are important for microphone pick-up.

The technology is relatively easy to use. Robert Kagan, Manchester Community Technical College's Communications Coordinator, said, "Several of the high schools originate courses using a single-consumer, $1000 camcorder and microphone. While results may not be as polished as with a

FIGURE 1

A typical distance education set-up for delivery via cable television.

A. 4–Color Video Cameras
B. 3–Tripods with Pedistols and Dollies
C. 1–Copy stand with lightsand camera
D. 4–20" Color Receivers to monitor High Schools
E. 1–20" Color Monitor for students in TV Studio
F. 1–Wireless microphone for the teacher

G. Key Light (Mounted on Ceiling)
H. 2–PZM Microphones for the Students (Mounted on Ceiling)
I. Dry Erase Board
J. Speakers (Mounted on Ceiling
K. Back Drop
L. Teacher's Podium
M. Control Board
N. Fax Machine

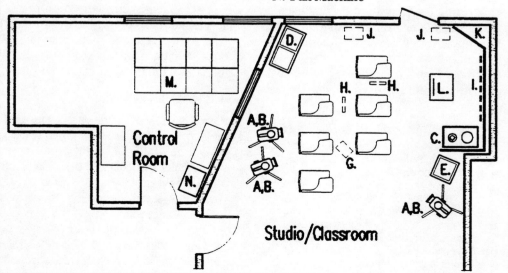

more sophisticated system, there is nothing to suggest that they are any less effective."

The MCTC system depends upon a control room and technically expert operator as well. (Figure 1 shows the layout of the control room and studio/classroom.) The control room includes video playback machines, a character generator for adding titles, a video switcher and an audio board.

In order to facilitate communication between the operator and the teacher, the control room must have a visual link with the teacher's classroom. The cost for this system is approximately $65,000 and includes the equipment shown in Figure 2.

Advantages
- The cable TV distribution system is a reliable, well understood technology.

FIGURE 2

Equipment needed for cable TV education delivery.

TV Studio/Classroom	TV Control Room
4–Color Video Cameras (include. view finder etc.)	Special Effects Generator
3–Tripods with Pedestals and Dollies	Audio Mixer
1–Copy stand with lights	4–Remote Camera Control Units
4–20" Color Receivers to monitor the High Schools	Character Generator
1–20" Color Monitor for students in the TV Studio	Talk back system
1–Wireless microphone for the teacher	6–5" monitors (1 for each camera and 2 for videocassette recorders)
2–PZM Microphones for students in the TV Studio	2–9" monitors (1 for preview and 1 for program)
White Board	13" Program monitor
	Vectorscope Waveform Monitor
	Distribution amplifier
	Wireless microphone system
	2–videocassette recorders (1 for recording and 1 for playback)
	Cassette Player
	Monitor speakers
	Power amplifier
	Modulator for signals back to cable system
	CD Player
	Waveform monitor
	TV racks to mount the equipment
	Fax machine

- The system has worked for six years with few problems.
- It has a low initial cost.
- User operating costs are low.
- The TV studio/classroom and control room were in place to teach broadcasting and studio production courses, so it was relatively easy to introduce distance learning classes.

Disadvantages

- Distribution and scheduling of air time is dependent upon cable system cooperation. Gaps of up to two minutes in the broadcast have occurred.
- The distance learning broadcast is available to all cable subscribers; thus on-the-air discretion is needed; and use of copyright materials (such as information on CD-ROM disks, videoplayers, VCRs, etc.) is severely restricted.
- Courses are available only to schools with video classrooms within the cable system area.
- The system requires a control room and a technician to monitor and control broadcast output.
- High resolution video, such as computer text, drawings, and maps, cannot be distributed on cable TV's cable system, nor is it compatible with newer standards for video transmission. Moreover, new transmission systems will be very expensive to originate locally.

The MCTC distance learning system is dependent on teacher skills and the control room operator for success. However, any college is able to provide basic instruction at relatively low cost using this system.

A transition system

Appalachian State University in North Carolina is an example of an institution that has prepared for distance learning and data resource sharing with a flexible system that takes into account the transitional nature of today's communications technology. Cable TV analog systems are being replaced by digital video and audio systems. Full-motion video signals must be digitized and most must be compressed to be sent over telephone or satellite dish systems. Cable companies and telephone companies are positioning themselves to capture computer and audio/video transmission business, and telephone companies are lining up to partner with school systems around the country. They plan to aid in the distribu-

tion of live, two-way, interactive video and audio transmission, as well as to provide computer links. This new phenomenon is changing the meaning of distance learning to *include* video (or tele) conferencing.

Although both distance learning and video conferencing are live two-way video and audio transmissions, the purpose as well as the placement of the camera(s), monitor(s), lighting and room configuration are different. In video conferencing it is important that each person have the opportunity to speak at each location, so the room is usually lighted evenly to support this purpose. Rooms are generally smaller with a conference table in the center. The rooms are linked by camera and telephone line connections. The camera angle and view in conference room A is generally controlled by someone in conference room B, and vice versa, so that people can see those with whom they wish to

The system is dependent on teacher skills and the control room operator.

talk. In video conferencing, microphones are located at the table and/or around the room, to allow equal access to conversation.

In contrast, distance learning—sometimes called "talking head" instruction—involves a "teacher" classroom and a receiver classroom with a monitor instead of the instructor. Lighting is used to highlight the instructor and chalk board or other materials used to teach class. Cameras are fixed on the instructor, on materials, and on the students in both locations. The monitor(s) displaying the other classroom(s) must be located very near the camera, as eye contact is critical to the success of the two-way link. Switching among cameras on the instructor, instruction materials, or students in the "teacher" classroom is done by an operator at the instructor site. Both the teacher classroom and the receiver rooms can be larger in this case, as the purpose is different.

Systems to provide live two-way audio/visual teleconferencing, media links, and project data stored in computers are being developed simultaneously using different technologies. For instance, James Strom, vice chancellor of advancement for Appalachian State University, notes that a good example of a transitional system is that developed at Cal Poly, in San Luis Obispo, California. The one at Appalachian State University was developed with partners such as the AT&T Corporation, Bell South, Combinet, Compression Labs, Inc., NCR, Digiboard, and Southern Bell. Although the system is using low-cost resources currently available, it provides the capacity for future change.

Using copper twisted-pair ISDN (Integrated Services Digital Network) phone lines (available in many states) links have been provided among four public schools and Appalachian State University. ISDN is the digitization of the phone line, providing the speed and the bandwidth needed to handle interactive teleconferencing and collaborative multimedia computing. Unlike the previous cable system, which is analog based, video signals distributed through ISDN phone links need conversion to a digital signal using what is called a codec. Two ISDN lines terminate at each of the elementary schools. One ISDN line is dedicated to the Vistium Unit, a portable AT&T camera/microphone/codec device at each site. The second ISDN line is connected to the school file server which operates a LAN for the computer lab and classrooms at each elementary school. Many companies make codecs; examples include V-Tel, headquartered in Texas, and PictureTel, of Danvers, Massachusetts, as well as AT&T.

Teachers develop school learning projects with each other using the E-mail available through ISDN links. Then they present the projects to their students, who use computer software to create project solutions. The culminating event is a video

The Appalachian State system can adapt without major financial impact.

conference, where students and teachers from different sites interactively share their observations and conclusions. Scott Smith, Coordinator for Impact North Carolina's project, says, "We see learners at both ends. All students have access to the World Wide Web through Appalachian State University as well." Students learn to plan, cooperate, present, and deal with controlled examples of real-world situations they will encounter outside the classroom.

A list of equipment at Parkway Elementary School, which has recently received equipment upgrades is shown in Figure 3. It is planned that the other elementary schools in the system will receive similar upgrades in the near future. Each school has a printer shared by several classrooms and a file server for the LAN. The cost to equip one classroom is $3,600 for the two computers and the network card. The portable Vistium unit is approximately $6,000, as is the school's server.

FIGURE 3

Equipment needed for receiving school classrooms in the transitional system of distance education.

Classroom	Computer Lab
1–486 Computer	25–486 Computers
1–386 Computer	1–AT&T Vistium Unit
Scanner, Digitizing Tablet and Light Pen	Rolling Cart
Network Card	Printer
ISDN link to LAN	

FIGURE 4

The State of Connecticut's advanced distance education system.

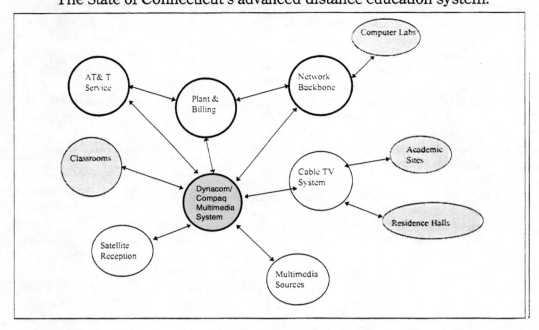

Advantages

- It has a low first cost.
- It integrates computer technology with video conferencing.
- The system is compatible with technology upgrades.
- Sites can use the Vistium unit for video conferencing by sharing its use at their school.

Disadvantages

- Use of ISDN links means an installation charge and monthly fees. Depending on the service area, the fees can be expensive.
- Multimedia information is limited on the system to some CD-ROM encyclopedias and clip art. Access to VCRs, other CD-ROMs, CD-i, laser disc player, Cable TV, is not possible on this system.
- Video conferencing is not distance learning; camera and monitors are not typically placed together in the classrooms, and control of the camera lies with the remote location.

As ISDN phone lines are replaced by fiber optic networks, the Appalachian State system can adapt without major financial impact. Other changes include the possibility of developing a multi-point video-conferencing capability so that three or more sites could have simultaneous video sessions. Currently,

North Carolina's system does not integrate multimedia sources in the system.

A technologically advanced system

At the University of Connecticut, a pioneer system is being developed in a partnering effort between the University's Communications Services group and the School of Education, Dynacom, Southern New England Telephone, Windham Public Schools, and Compaq Computers. The system will allow integration of audio/visual full-motion, two-way distance learning capability with access to multimedia and computer data on the PC desktop. The menu system is Dynalink, patented by Dynacom, which centralizes technology (video, audio, graphics, and data networking) via VCR, CD-ROM, CD-i, laser disc player, Cable TV, Digital Video Server, computer or satellite, etc. in one central location (see Figure 4).

In the classroom, the user has one PC or hand-held remote controller. Control of all resources in the system, including computer data, multimedia information, and audio video information is provided through this single remote. The system uses fiber optic, twisted-pair or coaxial cable networks to video conference or transfer data among classrooms on campus or, with T-1 ISDN lines, to the seven regional campuses. Picture Tel codes at the "head end" provide compressed video access. At the "head end" a technician monitors racks of equipment and handles search and loading of needed equipment.

The system consists of a head end room (in Babbage Library basement) which is configured as follows:

- 30' x 50' room, air conditioned, with 36 racks for equipment and control desk with monitors, a camera for remote viewing of the head end room, and area for storage.
- Equipment includes: CD-ROMs, Laserdiscs, video and audio tape players, satellite reception, CATV, local original television, conference room controllers, and computers available for scheduled use by those connected to the system.
- 10' ceiling with cable trays for fiber optics cabling systems, other cable connections to distribution system located near the university telephone switching room for easy cross connection of systems.

Currently, there are fiber optics connections to 13 classrooms on the main campus, including five, tiered-seating classrooms with monitors and cameras, eight traditional, 'flat-floor' lecture classrooms similarly equipped, and 12 small rooms equipped for teleconferencing. The University's seven regional campuses will soon each have one teleconference/classroom connected to the main system by an ATM video/audio phone line system as well.

In the classroom, there are monitors and a hand set as well as a wireless keyboard. Some classrooms have Canon Pan/tilt/zoom cameras with microphones for video conferencing as well. In operation, a teacher or student picks up a hand-held control panel, and can access two-way, interactive video, and/or any resource, such as a video tape, CD-ROM, IBM computer, satellite program, etc. with a touch of the keypad.

At UConn, a university instructor has the capacity to speak to students in several different classrooms on campus at the same time. Students are able to respond, asking and answering questions, and engaging in conversation. Back in the head end room, a technician can add a video for scheduled viewing and monitor the system. One technician and limited student support staff handle the entire system's requests, and trouble shooting and scheduling as well. Each classroom equipment system costs approximately $6,000.

Advantages

- Easy teacher and student access to the entire set of multimedia information, as well as video conferencing, with a single point of control.
- Leveraged multimedia equipment, as one source, can be scheduled for many classrooms.
- Systems can use analog or digital sources (VCR or CD-ROM) as well as fiber optic, twisted pair or coaxial network infrastructure.
- This system can use base-band, broadband and compressed video simultaneously.
- Very cost effective in large room systems of 40 or more students.
- The system has the ability to scale from a large group on a projector to one individual on (multiple) desktop PC.
- All stations have equal capabilities regardless of location.

Disadvantages

- Use of phone links means an installation charge and monthly fees. Depending on the service area, these costs can be expensive.
- The Dynacom control system is patented and, although it is compatible with other vendor systems such as Rouland, AMX or Ducane, it has a higher first cost for smaller systems and is proprietary.
- Video conferencing is not distance learning; camera and monitors are not typically placed together in the classrooms, and control of the camera lies with the remote location.

What are your options?

Fundamentally, distance learning a.k.a. video conferencing has three major elements that affect planning and operating budgets: video/audio distribution alternatives, data and multimedia control systems, and ease of technology upgrade. At MCTC the distribution system, Cox Cable, allows for cost-effective analog video transmission, but without control of the content. This is limited because copyrighted multimedia information cannot be shown over publicly available cable TV systems without the purchase of very expensive "rights." Scheduling is dependent upon cable company availability as well. Moreover, scheduling classes for simultaneous viewing can be very constraining. In addition, the technician must be present to assure both video and audio quality during the session. Moreover, cable TV systems do not currently support new technology advances in video quality or transfer.

In contrast, at Appalachian State University, transmission is over current ISDN phone networks. This means that video

The definition of distance learning is changing.

must be in a digitized and compressed format, which is arguably of poorer quality, but makes it convenient to distribute. And, once T-1 and ATM conventions are available, the existing system will be able to be adapted with a minimum of cost and inconvenience. At Appalachian State, the scheduling of video sessions is in the hands of the users. Students and teachers also control the content of the sessions, including multimedia and computer information—with a caveat, however. While the AT&T Vistium Units allow sharing of Windows data as well as audio/video, there is minimal sharing of CD-ROM sources. Only CD clip art or encyclopedias are available and metered on the local area networks; all other CD-ROM information is limited to one computer at a time (stand alone). Thus videotapes, cable TV programs and other sources are not shared in this system.

At the University of Connecticut, T-1 phone links distribute the audio-video with or without compression. Scheduling is in the hands of the users. One technician can supervise a very large system with 96 sites. Moreover, with one point of control, the teacher or student can bring up a menu to view many sources of information, from anywhere. The computer screen has become the resource for access to information, images, or real-time conversation. Rob Veitzke,

Communications Coordinator at UConn, said, "The ease of use of the hand-held controller allows the teacher and student to concentrate on the problem and the solutions, rather than the technology."

Conclusion

All these systems provide distance learning. However, the definition of distance learning is changing as technology affords us new ways to communicate; and it has changed the way we teach and learn.

Currently there is a mix of distance learning and teleconferencing networks in operation throughout the world. Distance learning ISDN networks in Western Europe, the Middle East, North and South America, Australia, New Zealand, and some Asia/Pacific countries are connected to world ISDN, but the networks are not standardized, nor all-pervasive (Latchem 1995). In the United States there are tens of thousands of instructional programs for distance learners delivered by a single teacher using a particular system. Educational institutions such as SCOLA and the National Technological University provide video

Control room for the University of Connecticut's advanced system.

broadcasts to supplement text in their courses. Many community colleges use self-produced television courses to deliver educational programming.

There are partnerships among state and local school systems and local cable or phone companies within geographically diverse institutions such as Pennsylvania State University, the University of Missouri,

Virtual universities are being created.

Murray State University in Kentucky, Appalachian State University in North Carolina, Indiana's Ball State University, and state systems in Maine, California, Connecticut, and many others. All major universities have satellite hardware, production studios, and personnel dedicated to the system. More than 1,000 post-secondary institutions sign on each year for courses broadcast by the Public Broadcasting System. A range of more than 100 college programs is provided or received by a consortium of 260 organizations NUTN, the National University Teleconference Network (Moore 1995).

Sites receiving distance learning include schools of all types, homes, and also workplaces. For example, Colorado's National Technological University consists of 94 engineering colleges sending courses directly to workplaces. Stanford is a founding member of the Collaboration for Interactive Visual Distance Learning Group, aiming to strengthen educational/industrial links with two-way video-conferencing among Boston University, Columbia University, Massachusetts Institute of Technology, Pennsylvania State University, Rensselaer Polytechnic Institute, Stanford University, and five major corporations—AT&T, IBM, PictureTel, 3M, and United Technologies Corporation.

With current expanded technology, "virtual" universities are being created where an Internet address provides instruction and email responses. Distance learning and media access are being used throughout the world to share knowledge and solve problems. As the ability to see and hear each other over long or short distance becomes a global prerogative, there has never been a better time to forge a distribution partnership with telephone or cable companies, like-minded educational institutions, and even businesses. And, with the knowledge of these three basic systems in mind, the next step is to consult a telecommunications professional who will provide the expertise needed to sift through options available within your region. ■

REFERENCES

Latchem, C. 1995. See What I Mean? In *Open and Distance Learning Today*, (ed.) Fred Lockwood, 98-105. Rutledge.

Moore, M. 1995. American Distance Learning: A Short Literature Review. In *Open and Distance Learning Today*, (ed.) Fred Lockwood, 32-41. Rutledge.

Strom, J. 1994. Distance Learning Now. *School and College* 33(12): 11-15.

Willis, B. 1994. *Distance Education: Strategies and Tools*. Educational Technology Publications.

Reengineering a faculty's pedagogy and academic programs is hard. But it can be done.

A Pioneer in High-Tech Instruction

Gary Judd and Laura Tanski

In 1987 several mathematics professors, led by William Boyce, approached Rensselaer's chief academic officer with the idea of creating a calculus course that would take some of the drudgery out of teaching calculus by using computers to illustrate and facilitate the solving of calculus problems. The provost gave them $10,000, and "workshop calculus" was born. That was the beginning of an instructional revolution at Rensselaer Polytechnic Institute, America's oldest private college of engineering and science, located in Troy, N.Y. at what was once the entrance to the Erie Canal that cut across upper New York State to the Midwest.

The teaching revolution has earned Rensselaer the first Boeing Outstanding Educator Award, TIAA-CREF's Hesburgh Award,

Gary Judd is dean of the faculty and of the graduate school at Rensselaer Polytechnic Institute in Troy, New York. He is a graduate of R.P.I., received his Ph.D. in materials engineering there, and has taught at R.P.I. since 1967. He is a fellow of ASM International.

Laura Tanski is director of academic budgets and planning at Rensselaer, from which she graduated. Since joining the Institute's staff in 1986, she has worked on numerous planning projects, and now coordinates R.P.I.'s reengineering efforts and oversees the finances of academic affairs.

and in October 1996 one of the first three Pew Leadership Awards for the Renewal of Undergraduate Education (along with $250,000 in prize money). This once-traditional five-school campus—engineering, science, management, architecture, and humanities and social sciences—has suddenly emerged as one of the pioneers in what may be the dominant pedagogy of the 21st century.

How did it happen? And what might planners at other institutions of higher education learn from our decade-long transformation through reengineering?

By the late 1980s, the personal computer, or PC, had opened the way for persons like William Boyce to experiment with radical new ways of teaching, which would allow students to stop being note takers in lecture rooms and become instead active learners with microcomputers, intensely working on practical issues of engineering, science, architecture, and management. By 1991, after support from the National Science Foundation, workshop calculus was offered to all R.P.I. freshmen, and Rensselaer's engineering school undertook a study of its core program and the way it was taught. Also, a physicist, Jack Wilson, was hired as the founding director of the Lois and Harlan Anderson Center for Innovation in Undergraduate Education, and charged with increasing the scope of Rensselaer Polytechnic Institute's pedagogical efforts.

Sparked by these grass-roots initiatives, Rensselaer's president and provost sponsored a Panel on Strategic Initiatives. This panel of 12 faculty, staff, and students worked for 18 months, then suggested three strategic emphases for R.P.I.: manufacturing materials and design (in which Rensselaer had unusual strength), environment and energy, and interactive learning. About interactive learning the report said, "Rensselaer can lead the country in innovative, effective approaches to technological education, particularly enhancement of human creativity through computational technology."

The Institute committed $6 million in institutional funds to these three initiatives over the next four years, with most of the money going to improvements in interactive learning. Lecture halls and classrooms were gutted and computer stations installed. And the Anderson Center for Innovation gradually moved toward the model of a "studio classroom," where students work actively and collaboratively on science, engineering, and management problems, somewhat the way Rensselaer architecture students had been doing already. This seemed closer to the way engineers actually work (Petroski 1996); the students became more actively engaged and less bored; and many faculty were relieved from lengthy lectures and pleased to work closely beside students.

From experiments to overhaul

In the fall of 1993 R.P.I.'s new president, civil engineer R. Byron Pipes, arrived and quickly sensed that Rensselaer was at the edge of some kind of dramatic action. Many faculty on campus also understood that enrollments in the sciences were declining nationally (with poor instruction often cited as a main reason), that the dropout rate among engineering students was high, and that college costs were escalating.

The president began a series of campus discussions, facilitated by the Pew Higher Education Roundtable, then called for a series of five retreats to discuss the possibility of major institutional restructuring. Arranged by the campus planner to include faculty, students, leading administrators and staff, and to produce actionable outcomes, the retreats met in early 1994; and the participants agreed that R.P.I. needed to make major changes in its way of operating, that the Institute should use the reengineering approach to make these changes (Hammer and Champy 1993), and that the most substantial changes should occur in the core academic programs and methods of teaching, not just in administrative procedures.

The dean of the faculty (one of the authors) was charged with leading the 10-person steering committee that was to oversee the reengineering process, which included four process teams. The four teams received

The students became more actively engaged and less bored.

two days of training in reengineering tools and techniques from an outside consultant. The teams went to work, then reported back to the campus at the end of 1994. Their recommendations were accepted in toto by the dean of the faculty and President Pipes.

The most significant recommendations came from the Design and Delivery of Education Team, who recommended that students take four courses for four credits each semester instead of five or six courses for three credits, that the curriculum requirements be simplified and electives increased, that physical education requirements be dropped, and that as many courses as possible move toward interactive learning. This meant that what R.P.I. students learned, and how they learned it, would be transformed. The faculty senate approved these and other recommendations in May 1995.

Gradually other parts of the campus community discovered an affinity for reengineering. Purchasing and residence halls maintenance processes have been altered, and the budget process, academic advising, and student services (admissions, financial aid, registration, and tuition billing) are now being scrutinized for greater efficiency and cost reductions (Seymour 1995).

More students in class now sit at tables in groups of four with their own Thinkpad™ laptop computers, and many classrooms have taken out the rows of chairs. More classroom work is collaborative, intensive, problem-oriented, and interactive. Numerous professors have reorganized their courses, and others are doing so. Rensselaer hopes to complete the transition to the new style of teaching by the end of the decade.

Naturally there are some students who don't like the new pedagogy and resist the changes. They would rather study on their own and listen to an expert scholar explain a theory, a problem, and the best way to approach major issues. Also, a minority of R.P.I. professors grumble that the institution may be overemphasizing teaching and neglecting the necessity of increased research in technology, science, business, and the humanities and social affairs. But the new studio courses require less faculty preparation, take less time, and appear to save money, as well as increase students' satisfaction with their classes. More and more faculty are becoming positive about the academic reengineering.

What we learned

Much of what Rensselaer has accomplished may be unique to its campus and the fact the R.P.I. is a heavily technological and scientific institution. But we suspect that many of the principles and practices we have employed can be applied to campuses elsewhere. Much of the way we brought about substantial changes can be found in the standard literature on leadership, university planning, and reengineering. Still, here are the ingredients we would emphasize.

Laying the groundwork. For major changes on campus to occur, the campus community, especially the faculty, must be persuaded that changes are necessary and can be beneficial. This persuasion probably has two key components. One is a common

understanding by the college's or university's administrative, academic, trustee, and alumni leadership of the institution's situation and competitive position, and a dissemination of that understanding. This

Naturally some students don't like the new pedagogy and resist the changes.

requires a knowledge of the demographic, financial, educational, facilities, and morale issues—and the trends confronting the institution. As Max DePree has said, "The first responsibility of a leader is to define reality" (1989).

Fact-gathering is essential, then serious discussions about the implications of the data. Rensselaer accomplished the discussions through a series of meetings and retreats of 50 or so persons each, at which all constituent groups were represented. Open meetings, departmental meetings, and newsletter articles can all be used. (R.P.I.'s internal surveys indicated that information given out at departmental meetings has the most creditability.)

At the informational sessions, the leaders should emphasize the depth, trends, and scope of the new environmental and internal conditions. But an inventory of major challenges or an exaggerated sense of impending crisis is insufficient; people must also understand the school's special strengths and the possibilities. In our view, the stress should be on the importance of the campus remaining in synchrony with a rapidly changing world and on the strategies for remaining ahead of, and distinctive from, competitor colleges.

A second component is obtaining agreement on the urgency of changes. It is one thing to educate everyone about the current status and possible threats to the institution. It is quite another to gain agreement that major changes are necessary. This requires a skillful chipping away at complacency, a graphic and steady presentation of the possible consequences of standing still, and a vision of what the reconstructed campus might be like or could be like.

It also requires no exemptions. Some institutions, for instance, have limited their changes to certain administrative processes and exempt the faculty from all serious renovations. At Rensselaer the decision to focus our changes on academics, on teaching and learning, on our core business was a key moment in R.P.I.'s transformation. (We were fortunate to have several champions of pedagogical change on our campus; but we suspect many other institutions also have innovative instructors in their midst.)

Selecting a change process. Choose a change process and then stick to it. At Rensselaer we selected reengineering as a process after an earlier attempt at TQM failed to catch on. You will need to select and train participants in the process, probably with the help of outside experts. The people who are expected to devise changes must be informed about the process, how it works, what is expected from them, and how they should arrive at their recommendations.

Deadlines should be firm to prevent procrastination and indecisiveness; and each group should be informed that the deliverables must be concrete, substantial, and feasible. Mere pipe dreams or simple tinkering must be discouraged. Good communication is critical. Clear and frequent messages about the developing change process and emerging ideas for restructuring should come from all levels—from persons involved in the process, through the institution's media, and from the academic and administrative hierarchy. These communications will set the stage for final, formal presentations and help win acceptance.

For change to be real, empowerment must be real. Therefore, if a campus team is charged with developing a new way of doing things, the college's leaders should be prepared to honor the team's results and resist the temptation to tweak suggestions excessively or overrule them. Administrators should exercise their oversight function by being involved with the team

throughout its deliberations and by providing gentle steering pressure while the ideas for change are still malleable.

Implementing the changes. Too often, strategy sessions or reengineering sessions end with the submission of a report. We suggest that each team be charged by the steering committee and the president to recommend how the changes should be implemented whenever practical, possibly securing approvals for the implementation from the people affected.

It is helpful to find external cheerleaders. At Rensselaer we benefited from the financial support of NSF, FIPSE, AT&T, General Electric, Hewlett-Packard, IBM, and the Pew Charitable Trusts for our efforts at transformation, and these pieces of outside recognition helped assure faculty that major changes have the interest of important agencies in society. Gathering external recognition through newspaper and

Reengineering change requires no exemptions.

magazine articles, SCUP presentations, and other means also helps add credibility to the changes. Of course, inside support is also necessary. R.P.I. devotes about two percent of its budget annually to the transformation, hosts luncheons and parties to celebrate the changes, and sends many thank-you letters.

New technology offers significant opportunities for universities to rethink their work and their processes. However, it is possible to throw a lot of money at technology and achieve no discernible improvements in student learning, client response time, or overall quality, and no reductions in costs whatsoever. It is not efficient to use laptop computers as expensive substitutes for paper notebooks. To justify investments in technology, classroom teaching and other central processes on campus must change. Therefore, we suggest that technology, both hardware and software, be viewed as enabling mechanisms for real change, not merely as add-ons.

Making change natural

In our view, nothing is so helpful and important for the transformation that colleges and universities will have to go through in the coming decade as building a culture of change on campus, where there is a desire and search for continuous improvements in all parts of the institution. Easier proclaimed than done, however.

We have found a few things to be especially conducive to shaping such a new culture. One is prompt and visible support for the internal change agents. These are the people on campus who already believe in the value of change. Supporting these persons—as was done for mathematician William Boyce and physicist Jack Wilson—spreads the message quickly and far. Often this support is as simple as providing a visible platform for the innovative person to share her or his views. Summertime grants, leadership roles, prizes, and promotions can also reward the innovators.

Plant and nurture constructive change wherever the ground is fertile. No process is too small or insignificant, no office so unimportant that dramatic improvement is not desirable. Indeed, it is frequently the "small wins" (Weick 1984) such as reducing the processing time for a piece of paperwork by 50 percent or introducing greater enthusiasm and active work in a single class that provide the examples to inspire people to undertake larger renovations.

And last, campus leaders must be fully committed to the necessity of changes and have the tenacity and courage to insist on them. With energetic and dedicated leadership almost any process will produce positive outcomes; without it, even the most tried and true methods will usually fail. No list of suggestions or formulas can replace the value of personal conviction by an institution's major administrators and trustees. The campus leaders must believe that

> *To justify investments in technology, classroom teaching must change.*

their actions and the changes will result in a stronger institution, and that the new academic culture will create a more effective and enjoyable learning, living, and working environment at their campus.

Major changes at an institution can bring out the worst in some people. But sound core values and the unswerving conviction that there will be a better future can sustain a college or university through the inevitable difficulties that structural adjustments to new conditions require. ∎

REFERENCES

DePree, M. 1989. *Leadership is an Art*. Dell.

Hammer, M. and Champy, J. 1993. *Reengineering the Corporation*. Harper Business.

Petroski, H. 1996. *Invention by Design: How Engineers Get From Thought to Thing*. Harvard University Press.

Seymour, D. 1995. *Once Upon a Campus*. ACE/Oryx Press.

Weick, K. 1984. Small Wins: Redefining the Scale of Social Problems. *American Psychology* 39(1): 40-49.

Examining one of higher education's touchiest issues.

Coming Soon: Alternatives to Tenure

Richard Chait

Tenure has become the academy's version of the abortion issue—a controversy marked by passion, polemics, and hardened convictions. The often shrill debate situates tenure as either indispensable or indefensible, as either the bulwark of academic freedom and economic security or the bane of institutional flexibility and accountability. On one side the Patrick Henrys proclaim, "Give me tenure or give me death." On the other, the champions of reform, primarily legislators and trustees, stalk tenure as Ahab hunted the white whale.

Are there any ways to bridge this gulf? I think so.

First, the discussion must be recast to focus on *objectives*. Attacks on tenure are of-

ten that and little more. "If only we could eliminate tenure, then we could...," and the strong voices of tenure's critics trail off, unable to detail the educational payoffs of a world without tenure. Rather than ask, "How do we overturn tenure?" lawmakers and regents should first identify, with substantive input from the faculty and administration, the results desired. Then they should ask administrators and faculty members to design sensible policies and practices that head the institution in the desired direction. Tenure may not, in fact, be a substantial obstacle to achieving their objectives.

Regents and lawmakers might aim, for example, to shift resources from low-priority to high-priority programs, a key concern when the University of Minnesota's Board of Regents tried to reform its tenure code last year. This might be accomplished by reallocating faculty positions among departments, encouraging early retirements, and phasing out marginal programs.

Or the goal might be to eliminate "deadwood" among the faculty. This might be done through a combination of stringent post-tenure reviews, salary reductions, and budget cuts in departments with more than an occasional substandard performer.

Often, however, academics react to any inquiries and initiatives—whether concerning productivity, flexibility, or assessment—with indignation, resistance, and fierce counterattacks. Too many faculty members

Richard Chait is professor of higher education at Harvard University's Graduate School of Education. A graduate of Rutgers University, he received his Ph.D. degree from the University of Wisconsin. He is a former associate provost at Penn State, a professor of non-profit management at Case Western Reserve, and director of the Center for Higher Education Governance and Leadership at the University of Maryland. He has published considerably on the role of trustees, and is now conducting a study of "faculty employment arrangements for the 21st century." This article originally appeared in a slightly different form in *The Chronicle of Higher Education*, February 7, 1997.

ask first, "How do we preserve tenure?" rather than "How can we achieve our educational and professional objectives?" Academics should realize that most trustees and legislators rarely attack tenure out of malice, but out of frustration with persistent educational and financial problems on campus.

When a Texas lawmaker contemplated introducing a bill last year that would have

> *The byword on tenure should be choice, not conformity.*

required the dismissal of tenured faculty members who received unsatisfactory performance reviews, the goal was to address the complaints of constituents, not to abolish tenure. Reflexively, faculty members on many campuses in the state circled the wagons. The president of the University of Houston, on the other hand, wisely advised the faculty there "to play offense, not defense," that is, to identify changes that would respond to the legitimate concerns of the legislator and the public.

Unfortunately, too many of the faculty playbooks have only one entry under the tenure tab—the American Association of University Professors' recommended policy. Having only one choice inevitably means just two sides: for and against. Small wonder, then, that we have such a polarized debate. Colleges and universities need to invent new employment arrangements, not merely to respond to criticisms of tenure by various constituents but, just as important, to create more alternatives to better serve individual faculty members and strengthen departments and institutions.

The times have changed since 1915, when the AAUP was established. Then, there were 951 institutions of higher education and no two-year colleges. By 1940, the year of AAUP's landmark statement of academic tenure, 1,708 institutions existed, including a few two-year colleges. Today, we have more than twice the 1940 total, including branch campuses, community colleges, technical institutes, and professional schools. As a result, one size no longer fits all.

In a profession that prizes autonomy, we should not bar professors and universities from creating new, and mutually beneficial, terms of employment that match individual interests and campus needs. In other words, let Bennington be Bennington. In the 21st century, the byword on tenure should be choice, not conformity.

Tenure will continue to exist as an appropriate arrangement for some faculty members on some campuses. But why not afford more professors the opportunity to voluntarily accept a term contract in return for a higher salary, as Greensboro College does, or in return for more-frequent sabbaticals, as Webster University does?

Why not offer more people the chance to serve indefinitely as full-time senior lecturers or research professors, as various schools do at Harvard and Stanford Universities, respectively? Even more creatively, the University of Virginia Medical School now has six tracks for full-time faculty members. One leads to a mandatory tenure decision, two offer the possibility of tenure, and three do not offer tenure; yet all offer the opportunity for promotion through the ranks.

Full-time, long-term, non-tenured jobs are attractive to some institutions and to some individuals, particularly in professional schools, where financial pressures mandate different employment arrangements, where faculty members with practical experience are especially valued, and where professors have the possibility of full-time jobs outside the academy. Yet, even within the arts and sciences, some faculty members elect to work on campuses with contract systems—and not out of desperation. In a recent study, "Where Tenure Does Not Reign," a colleague and I noted that the preponderance of faculty members at these colleges see their academic life as agreeable, collegial, and devoid of the caste system that tenure fosters.

Discussing other options

As the management adage cautions, solutions are the source of all problems. Therefore, we can and should argue about the relative merits of alternative career paths and employment arrangements, mindful that all such arrangements—traditional tenure included—have drawbacks. (Indeed, three separate studies published in the past year—by Eugene Rice, by William Tierney and Estela Bensimon, and by Cathy Trower—reached the same conclusion: Tenure-track faculty members are largely an unhappy lot, partially as a result of a probationary process they often view as mysterious, politicized, and stressful. However, when more options are introduced, the chance to find common ground might expand greatly.

Of course, whenever unconventional employment arrangements are mentioned, especially by "outsiders," the alternatives are immediately labeled a "threat to academic freedom," which then freezes the debate. The dogma of the academic profession posits that tenure and academic freedom are inseparable. If faculty members were more receptive to evidence that tenure and academic freedom *can* be un-

---

One half of all American faculty members do not have tenure.

---

coupled, the discussion might become more productive.

In "Academic Freedom Without Tenure," an article recently published by the New Pathways Project of the American Association for Higher Education, Peter Byrne of the Georgetown University Law Center offers a useful springboard for rational discussion. He outlines a procedure to provide academic freedom and due process to *all* faculty members—tenured or not—when disputes over academic freedom arise. The key elements include a peer-dominated review panel: a requirement that the faculty member make a *prima facie* case that a violation has occurred, whereupon the burden of proof shifts to the institution; an oral hearing held prior to the

panel's decision; and the possibility of arbitration of still-disputed claims by an external tribunal of trusted academics.

Such arrangements are not simply a matter of legal theory. Numerous four-year colleges such as Hampshire College and Evergreen State College, have comparable provisions with no adverse effects reported by their faculty (described proudly by Evergreen's president as "more cussedly outspoken than any other.").

In reality, about one-half of all American faculty members (when part-timers and adjuncts are included) do not have tenure. This fact that calls into question the unbreakable bond between academic freedom and tenure more than justifies efforts to find other ways to guarantee academic freedom for all members of the faculty. Ironically, under the current system, many junior faculty members feel that the quest for tenure and the perceived need to accommodate the preferences and prejudices of senior colleagues significantly *limit* their academic freedom.

A constructive step to unfreeze the debate about how to protect academic freedom would be to invite a group of distinguished law professors, university attorneys, judges, and other knowledgeable professionals to codify contract language that would give every faculty member a legally enforceable right to academic freedom and due process. Purists will say, "Impossible," and skeptics will charge, "Tenure by another name." However, why not try?

If we succeed, some professors who are now committed to tenure mainly as an assurance of academic freedom might voluntarily accept a 5- or 10-year appointment with academic freedom contractually guaranteed. If significant numbers of colleagues followed suit, the public might finally understand the value that the profession truly attaches to academic freedom as a fundamental principle, rather than as a rationale for near-absolute employment security.

One additional step might advance enlightened conversations about academic tenure: greater reliance on data and less dependence on anecdote. Academics normally insist on empirical evidence and factual data. Yet the debate on tenure often proceeds without either. To a remarkable degree, universities lack basic information, such as the percentage of the payroll disbursed to tenured faculty members, the projected turnover of faculty members, or the number and percentage of positions periodically shifted from one department to another. Consequently, trustees' questions about whether tenure impedes flexibility cannot be answered.

Ask a provost, president, or faculty leader, "How many tenured faculty are deadwood?" and the most common reply is, "I don't know," "Fewer than you think," or "No more than in any other profession." Such responses do not allay legislators' impressions of rampant faculty incompetence.

The importance of better data and facts

Some policy makers worry that tenure standards are too lax, while many probationary faculty members believe that the bar has been set too high or angled so as to put women and members of minority groups at a disadvantage. Vague assurances are not the proper antidote to these arguments. Why not collect and publish annually data—by race, gender, and department or school—on how many faculty members achieve tenure, much as law firms do on the rates at which associates achieve partnership? This information could confirm or correct impressions about the rigor and fairness of the tenure process, just as data about the number of faculty members prodded or compelled to resign or nudged into retirement could answer questions about the stringency and impact of post-tenure reviews.

Comparative data on personnel policies are equally scarce. In the absence of readily (and electronically) available data on the criteria and standards for tenure or the grounds for layoffs and dismissal or post-tenure-review procedures, the debate inevitably turns on anecdote, hearsay, and emotion.

Thus, a professor at the University of Minnesota unequivocally declared, at a Board of Regents meeting last summer, that the institution's ability to recruit professors would be severely jeopardized by any changes in the ironclad protection that tenured faculty members enjoyed against termination were their programs discontinued. He presented no data to support this assertion, and no comparative numbers from the scores of research universities without such

Deliberations about tenure should exemplify the best of the academy, not the worst.

a guarantee. Vehement assertions were presented as fact: a doctoral dissertation committee would have been distraught.

Opponents of tenure hardly do better. Contentions by trustees and legislators about the slothfulness and intransigence of tenured faculty members, the prevalence of deadwood, and professors' growing indifference to teaching are frequently based on a single, secondhand anecdote. While a corporate executive confronted with a comparable complaint at work might investigate such an anecdote, none would make policy based on it. Yet some trustees and legislators are too apt to do just that.

The costs are high. Jean Keffeler, a former regent at the University of Minnesota and a strong advocate of changes in the tenure code, recently remarked that much of the ultimately counterproductive debate there was marked, on both sides, by amateurish work, the absence of intellectual standards, and too little information, provided too late.

In contrast, the faculty and academic leaders of Arizona's public universities agreed last year to collect and present to the regents a yearly "tenure audit," with detailed data on all academic personnel actions—appointments, promotions, tenure decisions, and post-tenure reviews. In no small way, the faculty's agreement to provide these data reassured the regents that the quality of faculties and the effectiveness of the tenure system would be monitored.

As a consequence, support among the regents for radical solutions to the tenure "problem" atrophied.

In sum, deliberations about tenure should exemplify the best of the academy, not the worst. We regularly tell the world that the academic profession thrives on systematic inquiry, careful experiments, and robust debate. Lest we be labeled hypocrites, we must create opportunities for civilized discourse and incisive analysis about the value of tenure and alternative employment practices. And we should insist that the quality of the discussion surpass the minimum standards we set for students—no unexamined assumptions, no unsubstantiated claims, and no blind allegiance to convention.

If we fail to do this, a riskier fate may await us: public referenda, legislative incursions, and trustee initiatives that pre-empt further discussion. Even more dangerous, higher education's aversion to a robust, open-minded exploration of employment arrangements could signal to society that the bastion of academic freedom rests on a very insecure foundation. ■

As a national shortage looms, universities try more daring approaches.

Attracting Blacks into Engineering

Phyllis Denbo and Saul K. Fenster

By 1995 eight of the ten fastest-growing occupations in America will be science- or engineering-based. Between now and the year 2000, the demand for engineers, scientists, and technicians will increase by 28 percent (Commission for Professionals, 1987). By the year 2010, the United States could face a shortage of a half million technically trained professionals (Task Force on Women, Minorities, and the Handicapped, 1989). Already several other industrialized nations produce more engineers per capita than the United States does. This year Japan will graduate as many engineers as America will, despite the fact that Japan's population is half the size of this nation's. Business firms in several sections of the United States are beginning to worry, and some are starting to invest in science and engineering education.

Overwhelmingly, the scientific and engineering workforce, and even more the U.S. science and engineering professoriate, are white males. But by the year 2000, roughly 75 percent of the new entrants to the U.S. workforce will be minorities and women. Therefore, if America is to address its coming shortage of scientists and engineers, colleges and universities must plan now to educate more black, Hispanic, and women engineers and scientists.

The number of females in science and engineering has been increasing somewhat, though women received only 7 percent of the doctorates in engineering in 1988 (Sylvia, 1991). The number of Hispanics is also increasing slowly. But the paucity of African-Americans in the fields of engineering and science is alarming.

In 1988, there were 139,000 black engineers and scientists employed in the entire United States, representing only 2.6 percent of the workers in these categories. In contrast, African-Americans accounted for 10 percent of the total U.S. employment and nearly 7 percent of all professional and related workers, according to the National Science Foundation. The underrepresentation of black engineers and scientists with doctor-

Phyllis Denbo is former director of the Office of Planning and Evaluation at New Jersey Institute of Technology (NJIT) and presently directs College Leadership New Jersey, a multi-institutional public policy based leadership development program for college juniors. A graduate of Barnard College with an M.A. from the University of Pennsylvania, she formerly served as assistant director of research at the New Jersey Department of Higher Education.

Saul K. Fenster, a fellow of the American Society of Mechanical Engineers and a fellow of the American Society for Engineering Education, is president of NJIT. He graduated from CCNY, Columbia University, and earned his Ph.D. from the University of Michigan. The author of two textbooks and numerous research papers, he has worked as a research engineer in industry and is a member of the National Action Council for Minorities in Engineering.

ates is even more dramatic—less than 2 percent of the engineers and 1 percent of the physical and life scientists, mathematicians, and computer scientists.

Until 1987, the situation with respect to African-Americans in engineering and science was worsening; between 1977 and 1987 the number of blacks receiving bachelor's degrees in science and engineering dropped from 22,600 to 21,300 (National Science Foundation, 1990). At the master's degree level, black scientists and engineers declined from 2,900 in 1977 to 2,400 in 1987; at the Ph.D. level, black recipients decreased from 288 in 1979 to 231 in 1988 (National Science Foundation, 1990). This decline occurred despite a powerful demand for African-American engineers and scientists. Between 1978 and 1988, the employment of blacks in engineering and science increased twice as fast as that of whites, and the black labor force participation rate in these fields was 97 percent, compared with an 87 percent rate for all black college graduates.

Recently, though, hundreds of new efforts and dozens of new programs have been put in place, and since 1987 there are signs that U.S. colleges and universities have been enrolling more black and other minority engineers and scientists. According to a 1990 study by the National Action Council for Minorities in Engineering, freshmen enrollments by blacks, Hispanics, and American Indians have grown from 9.7 percent of all new U.S. engineering students in 1986 to more than 12 percent in 1990. And the number of black Ph.D.s in engineering, though not in biological science and psychology, rose slightly in the past three years.

What is responsible for this apparent turnaround? How can more colleges and universities plan to encourage higher African-American participation in engineering and science and thus address the growing national shortage?

We offer some suggestions, and we will explain what our institution, New Jersey Institute of Technology (NJIT), has learned in the past two decades. At NJIT, black and Hispanic students currently account for 23 percent of the full-time undergraduate enrollment, and the Institute has consistently been among the top twenty institutions in the country in the number of minority engineers graduated annually.

Four precepts

Our experience and that of others suggest that planning for improvements in this area should keep in mind four principles.

1. *The preparation of engineers and scientists begins early, perhaps as early as the third grade.* Any college or university hoping to increase African-American enrollments in these fields must work with primary and secondary schools, and university education schools must do more to train school teachers in handling mathematics and science more expertly.

The training of engineers and scientists begins early.

2. *A comprehensive, multifaceted approach is imperative.* Constant encouragement, inspiration, internships, research assistantships, and role models of black adults from teaching and industry are essential. Alumni can be particularly effective. A campus environment rich in encouragement despite setbacks and difficulties is imperative. One or two lines of attack seem inadequate. Colleges need to install numerous practices—mathematics study groups, field trips to industrial workplaces and research labs, parental and family ties, special organizations to allow black camaraderie and mutual support, rewards of many kinds—to bolster black confidence and proficiency in engineering and science.

3. *Lots of money is needed.* Science and engineering education is more expensive than programs in, say, the humanities. But science and engineering education for young African-Americans, many of whom are poor and educationally disadvantaged and in need

of extra support, is all the more expensive. At NJIT, we have had a continuing struggle to find enough funds from corporations, foundations, and the state and federal governments to keep our ambitious programs for minority engineering going. There have been some encouraging increases in interest in educating more black engineers and scientists, but a much greater investment by society is urgent.

> # A much greater investment by society is urgent.

4. *Universities need to be ready to experiment and to keep learning.* They need to be willing to break out of standard patterns, academic calendars, and academic procedures. The situation is serious and requires extraordinary and inventive initiatives. Leaders in this effort must watch carefully to see what works, and they must keep learning and fine tuning. There are no templates. The situation is one of *terra incognita*. A great deal of trial and error and applied research is needed.

The importance of starting early

Numerous factors contribute to the low rate of minority participation in science and engineering in college and graduate school. The highest correlates are the lack of adequate academic preparation before college and study habits. Family background characteristics such as parental education level, family support for learning, and income are also very important, as are mentors, role models, financial aid, and caring, skillful teachers. Minority science students report that childhood exposure to science and to scientists and engineers is determinative, along with seeing members of their own ethnic and racial groups working as scientists and engineers (Garrison, 1987).

The simplest reason is that few young African-Americans pursue the necessary course of studies required for scientific careers. When is it too late to start a student along a scientific career path? Some say as young as seven years of age. Somewhere between the third and sixth grades the interest in science appears to diminish. Studies indicate that the education of successful engineers and scientists begins in elementary school where motivation is instilled and mathematical and scientific skills are developed (Nettles, 1987). This finding does not mean that students cannot be ignited in high school, but the task becomes harder with each adolescent year.

The results of primary grade experiences are evidenced in the test scores of the National Assessment of Educational Progress (NAEP), which surveys proficiencies in several content areas among nine and thirteen-year-old students. Among the nine-year-olds, for example, 99 percent of the white students and 93 percent of black students scored above the lowest level (simple arithmetic facts); but at a more advanced level (basic operations and problem solving), 25 percent of the whites and only 5 percent of the blacks were proficient. Similar results were obtained on the assessment of science facts and operations.

In high school, black students are less likely to enroll in the academic track, more often enrolling in the general or the vocational track, where there is less mathematics and science. While black students often choose the less rigorous courses, teachers also counsel young blacks inappropriately or with lowered expectations (Pearson and Bechtel, 1989). Blacks take less advanced algebra, geometry, and calculus and much less chemistry and physics than do whites in U.S. high schools. As a result, there is a 100-point differential between white and black scores on the college-entrance mathematics SAT. While 10 percent of whites taking the math SAT in 1988 scored above 650 (out of 800), only 1 percent of all black students scored above 650. Science test scores reveal similar differences (Anderson, 1989).

The principal remedy is obvious. Colleges and universities wishing to increase the nation's supply of African-American engineers, applied scientists, and mathematicians need to work more closely with primary and secondary schools and host campus programs for young blacks during the summer, on Saturdays, and after school.

Is helpful action increasing?

Though we believe a major and widespread national effort of intervention and assistance is needed to prepare and attract young black and other minority students to engineering and science, several new national and institution-based programs have sprung up in the past decade.

Since the early 1970s, the National Institutes of Health have sponsored two programs for students at historically black colleges and universities (HBCUs). The Minority Access to Research Careers (MARC) and Minority Biomedical Research Support (MBRS) programs have been influential in stimulating scientific careers among African-American students at HBCUs, and recently both programs have been extended to a few campuses with large minority populations. Project SOAR at Xavier University in New Orleans, the only predominantly black Roman Catholic institution in the United States, is a pre-freshman program for students planning to enter the health sciences, featuring actual laboratory experiments and motivation and study skill sessions. Two offshoots now serve tenth- and eleventh-grade black students too. (Over half of Xavier's students major in the sciences or mathematics.) (Clewell, 1989)

The National Science Foundation supports the Mathematics Engineering Achievement (MESA) project in partnerships with schools, universities, parents, and corporations. MESA centers identify talented high school students, offer them guidance and counseling, and provide them with tutors. The college-going rate is 90 percent, with 66 percent majoring in engineering and science.

One promising program that is being tried at several universities was started by mathematics professor Philip Uri Treisman

at the University of California at Berkeley. He wondered why blacks and Hispanics of-

Universities must plan now to train more black engineers and scientists.

ten failed his calculus course while other students, especially Asians, often did well. His research found that a major difference lay in study groups, which Asian students usually utilized while blacks tried to solve math problems by themselves. Now he runs group-study math workshops which contain 80 percent blacks and Hispanics, and the minority students have been succeeding at higher levels (Fullilove and Treisman, 1990).

About eighty-nine colleges and universities use the Minority Engineering Program, a six-week summer orientation program before the students begin their freshman year. They learn to study in groups, correct their shortcomings, and are introduced to engineering science.

Numerous individual colleges and universities have also established their own programs of nurture for women, Hispanics, and African-Americans. One such institution is the New Jersey Institute of Technology, where we work.

To produce more black engineers

NJIT is the state's technological university, enrolling about 7500 students, 30 percent of whom are graduate students. It is located in the city of Newark, which has a large and mostly poor African-American population.

For many years, NJIT sought to increase the number of blacks in engineering; in 1968, NJIT began one of America's earliest programs to provide special assistance to black students to help them make it in engineering. What has evolved is one of the most comprehensive and integrated collegiate efforts in the nation, beginning at the elementary school level and continuing through graduate school. We try to keep learning and experimenting. We are quite self-critical and believe we are boldly innovative. We also have come to believe that multiple approaches are necessary.

Multiple approaches are necessary.

NJIT's program has three principal components: the Center for Pre-College Programs, the Educational Opportunity Program (EOP), and Project CAP, a career-advancement plan program for minorities and women.

The Pre-College Programs are an effort to interest middle school and high school minority students in engineering and science. NJIT began twenty years ago with one program and twenty students. Today we educate nearly 3000 younger students and their teachers each year through twenty-six programs that range from one-day workshops and six-week summer programs to instruction in the schools during the school day and after school.

Academically, the focus is mainly on urban engineering, with help on mathematics, chemistry, and computer science. There is even a summertime program in marine biology at the New Jersey seashore. Since 1984, the center has pioneered with instructional programs at the elementary school level (as early as the fourth grade), making NJIT one of the first universities to do so. While the emphasis is on sharpening academic skills, communication skills, and problem solving, the young boys and girls take field trips, visit university facilities, participate in parent programs, and learn how engineers live and work. A special feature is the use of NJIT minority graduate students as instructors alongside school teachers in the classrooms. Studies reveal that approximately 80 percent of those youngsters touched by NJIT's Pre-College Programs go on to college, with more than 70 percent pursuing careers in engineering and science.

The second component, EOP, serves the college-age students at NJIT. EOP tries to provide a total package of assistance to poorer, underprepared blacks and other minorities at NJIT so that they can graduate as engineers and scientists. There is a mandatory six-week, residential program in the summer before entering for all EOP students. There are financial aid, tutoring, mentoring, and extensive counseling. There is an articulation program for minority students transferring from two-year colleges, and an undergraduate research experience (URE) offering minority students the opportunity to work with faculty is being developed. There are also social activities, to create bonds, and a staff of credentialled minority counselors to encourage, remind, advise, prod, and cheer. Of the NJIT freshman class of 600 last year, about 125 were admitted as part of the Educational Opportunity Program.

The third component of the minority initiative is Project CAP, a cooperative program for blacks, Hispanics, and women undergraduates who do not qualify for the EOP programs. The centerpiece here is job preparation and counseling and placements in industry so that students can do real work in engineering or science positions. The students also have corporate mentors. About 230 undergraduates participated last year, working in nearly 200 companies.

These three components have helped NJIT turn out a considerable number of black engineers and applied scientists. Last year 16 percent of the graduating class were minority students. But we keep learning and refining. A new dean of freshman studies was appointed this year to intensify freshman counseling, establish an early warning and intervention system, and perhaps initiate freshman mathematics workshops modeled after those at Berkeley.

NJIT still needs to do more to increase the number of black graduate students, who are less than 6 percent of the total, and black engineering faculty, who are less than 3 percent. While these numbers are consistent with those of similar universities, they are, to us, unacceptably low. The university does participate in the Minority Academic (MAC)

Program, a state-subsidized loan program to increase minority success in Ph.D. programs, but adequate funding remains an obstacle. However, NJIT has just begun fund raising for a special endowment for its minority student initiatives.

The United States clearly needs more engineers and scientists, and it will be very difficult to fill that need without more young African-Americans and other minorities entering these fields. Affirmative action alone will not suffice. A broad array of fresh initiatives and enticements seems imperative. Each institution with technical and scientific programs should plan now for how it can help. ∎

REFERENCES

Anderson, B. "Black Participation in High School Science." *Blacks, Science, and American Education.* Edited by W. Pearson, Jr., and H.K. Bechtel. New Brunswick, NJ: Rutgers University Press, 1989.

Carter, D. and Wilson, R. *Eighth Annual Status Report: Minorities in Higher Education.* Washington, D.C.:American Council on Education, 1989.

Clewell, B. "Intervention Programs: Case Studies." *Blacks, Science, and American Education,* 1989, 105-122.

Commission for Professionals in Science and Technology. *Competition for Human Resources in Science and Engineering in the 1990s.* Washington, D.C., 1987.

Davis, J. "The Mathematics Education of Black High School Students." *Blacks, Science, and American Education,* 1989, 23-42.

Ellis, R.A. "Engineering and Engineering Technology Degrees, 1990." *Engineering Education,* 81(1), 1991, 34-44.

Fullilove, R. and Treisman, P.U. "Mathematics Achievement Among African-American Undergraduates at the University of California, Berkeley: An Evaluation of the Mathematics Workshop Program." *The Journal of Negro Education,* 59(3), 1990, 463-478.

Garrison, Howard H. "Undergraduate Science and Engineering Education for Blacks and Native Americans." *Minorities: Their Underrepresentation and Career Differentials in Science and Engineering.* Washington, D.C: National Technical Information Service, 1987, 39-65.

National Science Foundation. "Reclaiming Our Past." *Journal of Negro Education.* 59(3), 1990, 246-259.

Malcom, S. *Women and Minorities in Science Engineering.* Washington, D.C., National Science Foundation, 1990.

Nettles, M. "Precollegiate Development of Minority Scientists and Engineers." In *Minorities: Their Underrepresentation and Career Differentials in Science and Engineering.* Washington, D.C.: National Technical Information Service, 1987, 33-38.

Pearson, W. and Bechtel, H.K., eds. *Blacks, Science, and American Education.* New Brunswick, NJ: Rutgers University Press, 1989.

Sylvia, B. "Promoting Equality for Women in Academe." *Planning for Higher Education,* 19(3), 1991, 38-47.

Task Force on Women, Minorities, and the Handicapped. *Changing America: The New Face of Science and Technology.* Washington, D.C., 1989.

Vetter, B. *American Minorities in Science and Engineering.* Washington, D.C.: Commission on Professionals in Science and Technology, September, 1989.

Equality requires some new kinds of action.

Promoting Equality for Women in Academe

Barbara Sylvia

What are the prospects for achieving parity for women in the faculties of America's colleges and universities? And what steps should education leaders take now to arrive at parity by, say, the year 2010?

The current status of women in academe is a subject of considerable debate (Hyer, 1984; Weis, 1985). Some claim that the climate on campus is still not receptive to women (Sandler, 1986) or that the status of women in academia has not improved (Simeone, 1987), or that the prospects for parity are bleak because colleges will not enlarge their faculties soon (Heath and Tuckman, 1989). Others acknowledge gains. A few researchers have looked at the status of women in specific disciplines (National Academy of Sciences, 1983; Weis, 1987), with recommendations even suggesting the need to feminize the sciences and its pedagogy (Harris, Silverstein, & Andrews, 1989).

A graduate of the University of Pennsylvania, *Barbara Sylvia*, Ph.D. is Associate Professor of Management and Education at Salve Regina University in Rhode Island, where she previously served as Vice President and Dean of Academic Services. A holder of two master's degrees, she is currently pursuing an M.S.W. at Rhode Island College.

But, what scholars have failed to offer department chairs, deans, and presidents is an assessment of specific applicant pools for new faculty. Only after examining the number of females in the pools of potential faculty can colleges and universities plan a realistic affirmative action policy for women's equality. A discrete analysis of the number of women training to be scholars in each of the academic fields also suggests exactly in which fields the strongest affirmative action efforts need to be made.

What is the situation now?

Women have undeniably made substantial educational progress toward equality in academe during the past two decades. Women are earning doctoral degrees in far greater numbers than ever before, thereby meeting the credentialing requirement for entry into the academy's more prestigious institutions. Although in 1973 only 18% of all doctoral degrees awarded were earned by women, by 1986 that percentage rose to over 35%, where it has remained relatively constant (National Research Council [NRC], 1989, p. 11). The realized gain was that over 5,700 more women were earning doctoral degrees in 1986 than in 1973, while the number of male doctoral recipients actually decreased by more than 6,000 during the same period (see Table E of NRC, 1989 for complete data).

The increase in doctoral degrees earned by women has not been evenly distributed across fields of study, however. Women earned 55% of all doctoral degrees granted in the field of education, for instance. This constitutes almost 30% of all female doctoral recipients. But women are relatively under-represented in other fields of study. As Table 1 shows, the social sciences and humanities are the only other fields in which women received at least 40% of the degrees granted (NRC, 1989, p. 62–63).

The statistics show parity in male and female degree attainment has been nearly achieved in three of the five degree classifications. In 1985–86, women earned 56% of all associate degrees, 51% of all baccalaureate degrees, and 50% of all masters degrees. But, females earned only 33% of all first professional degrees and 35% of all doctorates. (*1989–90 Fact Book on Higher Education*, p. 205). The most notable increase, has been in the proportion of female attainment of first-professional degrees, which advanced from a low of approximately 4% in 1966–67 to over 32% by 1988. The actual number of women earning first-professional degrees is more than *fifteen times* the number of two decades ago, whereas male degree attainment in this area did not even double over the same period (*1989–90 Fact Book on Higher Education*, p. 202).

Only after examining the pools of potential female faculty can colleges plan a realistic policy for equality.

The progress in reaching parity among professors may seem slow in comparison to progress made by women in other arenas. Yet, projections indicate that women could receive 46% of all doctorates to be awarded over the next eight years (*1989–90 Fact Book on Higher Education*, p. 205). The National Research Council (1989) suggests that gains in the rate of degree attainment at the doctoral level usually lag behind progress at the baccalaureate level by 10–12 years. For 1988 doctoral recipients the median lapse of total time from baccalaureate to doctorate was 10.5 years for all fields of study. But the "production period" for doctorates varies significantly across disciplines, and longer periods of time elapsed for those in fields of study more heavily populated by women. The median time period was 10.5 years for social sciences, 12.2 years for humanities and 16.9 years for those in education (NRC, 1989, p. 24). The total time elapsing between attaining the baccalaureate and doctorate is far more pronounced for females; they average 2.5 years longer than their male counterparts in earning their doctoral degrees. Differences between genders are less significant within each discipline (NRC, 1989, p. 23).

Since women doctoral students attend graduate school an average of 6–7 months longer than do men, it is clear that they tend to take more time to earn a degree even after finally enrolling (NRC, 1989, p. 24). This is probably due to higher proportions attending on a part-time basis, which is at least partly a function of finances. The National Research Council (1989) discovered a correlation between fields of study in which women were primarily self-supported and those in which the total elapsed time prior to

Table 1. Percentage of Female Doctoral Recipients in Various Fields of Study

Field of Study	1973 % women	1988 % women
Engineering	1	7
Physical Sciences	7	17
Professional fields	13	32
Life Sciences	18	37
Humanities	29	44
Social Sciences	21	45
Education	25	55
TOTAL	18%	35%

Source: NRC, *Summary Report: 1988 Doctorate Recipients from United States Universities*, (1989).

doctoral completion was longest. Field of study, rather than gender, appears to be the determining factor however, since disparities between male and female completion rates varies within two months of one another when field of study is held constant.

Colleges, doctorates, and women

The national data useful for examining some questions are five years old. Therefore, we are uncertain as to how some proportions may have changed over the past few years. We do know that 65.1% of all faculty in four-year institutions in the United States held a doctorate in 1984. The percentage of all faculty who were women in 1985–86 was only 28%, up slightly from 22.3% in 1972–73. While these percentages vary across institutional types, with independent two-year institutions having almost 50% of their faculty female, and certainly vary across institutions within each type, the overall percentage of female faculty remains rather low and, therefore, warrants further examination (*1989–90 Fact Book on Higher Education*, p. 171).

A closer analysis of the composition of faculty at four-year institutions in 1984 reveals that 70.2% of the males and only 50.1% of the females held doctoral degrees (*1989–90 Fact Book on Higher Education*, p. 172). This indicates that women have gained academic appointments even when their academic credentials, on the average, have not been comparable to those of their male colleagues. However, an academic appointment should not be equated with a tenure-track position. Here again, numbers are inadequate in relaying the full story since women are most underrepresented in tenure-track positions (National Center for Educational Statistics, unpublished, as reported in *Professional Women and Minorities*, 1987).

If the median of each interval presented in the tables of data drawn from the 1985 Carnegie Survey of Faculty can be assumed to represent the age of those in the interval, then the average age of the male faculty member was approximately 47, while the average age of female faculty was about 42 (*1989–90 Fact Book on Higher Education*, p.

172). If we assume that females will remain in academia as many years as their male colleagues, female faculty may increase in proportion if only by default, given differences in age. However, more research will be needed to examine the differences in retirement patterns after 1994.

This will not be sufficient in and of itself to create equity soon since women are currently less than 40% of the full-time assistant and associate professors at four-year institutions (*1989–90 Fact Book on Higher Education*, p. 171). Therefore, without a dramatic increase in female representation in these lower ranks, equity between male and female representation in academia can not be achieved in our generation.

The distribution of 1988 doctoral recipients in Table 2 shows the percentage who are women, the percentage with postgraduation employment commitments to working in academe, and the percentage with an interest in teaching as their primary post-doctoral

Some academic disciplines lack a sufficient number of females.

activity. The aspirations of the 1988 doctoral recipients tells us something about how the actual supply of doctoral recipients is shaped to become an applicant pool for a faculty appointment in academe. The disaggregation by field of study allows us to look more closely at the prospective applicant pool for a given position in academia, since it addresses the question of the percentage of doctoral recipients in each field who are primarily interested in a teaching position versus other employment opportunities. (Note the low percentages of doctoral students in some fields like engineering, physical sciences, social sciences, and even education who intend to use their doctorates at colleges and universities.)

When the composition of the doctoral recipients in each field are further examined by gender, another dimension of the problem

Table 2. Comparative Percentages: 1988 Doctoral Recipients v. 1984 Faculty @ 4-yr Institutions

Field of Study	1988 Doctoral Recipients			1984 Faculty
	Primary Activity to be Teaching	Commitment to Academe*	% Female	% Female
Business & Management	57.7%	90.0%	23.8%	1.7%
Computer Science@	27.2	56.6	10.9	-na-
Education	35.5	43.8	55.2	15.1
Engineering@	20.6	28.5	6.8	.6
Humanities	70.2	79.3	44.3	26.0
Life Sciences	28.7	51.9	36.8	4.3
Mathematics	50.1	75.9	16.2	-na-
Physical Sciences@	24.7	36.2	16.6	4.5
Social Sciences	29.7	45.1	45.0	14.4
Other Prof. Fields	46.6	73.8	40.4	33.4**
All Fields	36.3%	49.8%	35.2%	100%
n =			33,456	-na-

NOTES: 1988 data are from the National Research Council (1989) *Summary Report, 1988*, p. 42–63. 1984 faculty data are from the Carnegie Survey of Faculty as reported in the *1989–90 Fact Book on Higher Education* (p. 173, 4-Year Institutions), Macmillan Co.

* Academe includes two- and four-year colleges and universities, medical schools, and foreign universities. Elementary and secondary schools are not included.

** Over one-third of this group majored in a Health Science.

@ Over 50% of the 1988 graduates from these fields were committed to postgraduate employment which was primarily research and development oriented. Some of those R & D positions were in academe, of course.

of parity emerges. Women may well be competing against other women for positions in the humanities, social sciences and especially education if, in fact, the distribution of percentages interested in teaching is similar for female and male doctoral recipients. If there is a significant difference between the gender mix of those interested in teaching versus other opportunities, that information would be critical for discipline-specific policy development based on an anticipated demand curve.

Furthermore, in comparing this data to participation rates of female faculty in four-year institutions across fields of study in 1984 (last column), some patterns are revealed about the composition of prospective applicants versus those presently in academia. While some fields of study have a sufficient supply of female doctoral recipients to make a substantial change in the proportion of female faculty (business and management, education, life sciences, and social sciences), *other disciplines (especially engineering and the physical sciences) lack sufficient numbers of females to generate a sizable applicant pool of prospective female faculty.* This is important to examine since those fields of study with lowest participation rates may well be the ones in which affirmative action policies should be most stringent. However, equity policies may be unrealistic if the supply of female doctoral recipients is not considered in determining goals.

Women's academic preferences

The data on 1988 doctoral recipients is encouraging in that women are strongly represented in both the humanities and social sciences, fields in which the greatest faculty demand is predicted to exist over the next two decades (Bowen & Sosa, 1989). More clearly revealed in Table 2 are the areas in which there are low female participation rates, coupled with low levels of interest in teaching, creating an applicant pool which is seriously underrepresentative of the total female population.

Colleges will need to stimulate interest in both the study of specific disciplines and the teaching of those disciplines among women to make a significant impact on participation rates in academe. For example, if only 1 in 5 engineering graduates are interested in teaching as their primary post-doctoral activity, and if women comprise only 6.8% of that population, very few female applicants can be expected to be in the applicant pool for a faculty position in engineering. Contrast this with the humanities, where 7 out of every 10 graduates will seek a teaching appointment and 44% are women. The data are more complex for the field of education where numerous doctoral recipients interested in teaching seem to be contending for elementary or secondary teaching positions, not positions in higher education.

The National Science Foundation has projected academic retirement patterns and the demand for doctoral graduates in the fields of science and engineering. The findings suggest that:

> up to 12%, or 5500, of the current full-time S/E faculty in the departments surveyed may retire (by 1991) . . . Among these departments, the largest number of retirements would be expected in civil and electrical engineering, physics, mathematics and economics (National Science Foundation, 1986, p. 2).

Of course, these job opportunities will affect far fewer women than men since women are highly underrepresented in these fields of doctoral study. This factor should be taken into consideration even though a study of the changing status of female faculty at doctorate-granting institutions (1971–1980) found that "an increase in availability of female doctorates . . . did not translate into automatic increments in female representation on all campuses" (Hyer, 1984, p. 1).

The comparison of 1988 doctoral recipients with 1984 female faculty further emphasizes the high correlation which exists between traditional fields of interest among women and current fields of study. That is, one might conclude from this data that women remain highly represented in fields of study similar to those of two decades ago.

Female college students have evidenced major shifts in attitudes.

However, female college students have evidenced major shifts in attitudes over the past 20 years. The American Council on Education (1987), based on surveys directed by UCLA's Alexander Astin, reported that women are less likely to enter fields such as teaching, which had attracted substantial percentages of women in 1966. Business, medicine, and law are reported as being in greater demand by women. The effects of these changes in attitude have not as yet found their way to the doctoral degree level. But, the changes may become more evident later in the final decade of the 20th century.

Supply and demand

That women remain, at this time, most substantially represented in fields such as education, humanities and the social sciences, where over 46% of all U.S. doctoral degrees were earned in 1988, means that female applicants are even more significantly underrepresented in applicant pools for positions in other disciplines (NRC, 1989, p. 62–63). That is, while females earned 35.2% of all doctoral degrees in 1988, the true pool of prospective applicants is a function of both the percentage of those with degrees in that field who have an interest in teaching and the percentage of that subpopulation who are female.

When the number of doctoral recipients are compared to actual faculty appointments for specific years, the relationship between total supply and demand is made more apparent. Data reported by Bowen and Schuster (1986, p. 176), across five-year intervals since 1970, suggest that the marginal excess of annual supply of doctoral recipients (1970–79) became much larger by 1984. Given the projected student enrollment decreases over the next several years and the uncertainty of retirement patterns after the uncapping of retirement, the supply of doctoral graduates may continue to exceed the demand in academia. Even if the estimates of faculty demand advanced by Bowen and Sosa are accurate—approximately 160,000 faculty appointments over the next 25 years in four-year institutions alone—the next eight years remain a period of proportionally lower demand (1989, p. 213).

The fields of study in which women earn their doctorates will be an ever more important issue, therefore, in determining their possible appointment to a faculty position. Perhaps the lack of congruence between the fields of study traditionally pursued by women and the relative demand for persons in those disciplines, is a primary cause of female underrepresentation in academia. This lack of fit between the supply and demand functions relative to female doctorates may be the reason that "given the overall surge in enrollment and degrees granted to females, women have not done nearly as well in obtaining professional positions as they have in obtaining degrees" (Weis, 1987, p. 47).

A specific institutional plan must therefore consider not only percentages of doctoral recipients across various disciplines with an interest in teaching and percentages of those interested in teaching who are female, but also the type of institution offering the position as well as the average attainment of equity that has been realized thus far by comparable institutions.

In examining the supply of female doctoral recipients (Table 3) across selected fields of study, one need only compare current data with that of approximately a decade ago to see the progress which has been made by females in male-dominated fields. For purposes of comparison, I selected doctoral fields of study on the basis of their being "high participation" fields or "low participation" fields for that year. The field was tagged as being a high participation field if the percentage of female doctoral recipients, in that field of study, exceeded the overall participation rate of females earning doctoral degrees in that year by at least five percentage points. Likewise, low participation fields were those whose percentage of female graduates fell at least five percentage points below the overall participation rate of women earning doctorates in that year. While the margin of five percentage points in either direction was determined arbitrarily, this allowed a range within which various fields of study might fluctuate in enrollment pattern without their participation rate being overemphasized. The following results emerged:

With the exception of some subfields within the biological sciences, disciplines in which female participation had strong representation over a decade ago had stronger representation in 1988. The participation rate in the biological sciences shifted somewhat with subdivisions of that field of study jumping across the margin bordering against average participation rate levels. (This is probably due far more to the arbitrary interval determinants, derived by using the margin of five percentage points, than to any significant variation.) The gain has been far more than minimal in areas traditionally dominated by males, albeit the gain still does not approach parity with male representation.

With the percentage of doctoral degrees earned by women in computer science and engineering having finally crept up to 7.2% in 1988, the pool of applicants for a position requiring these credentials would be expected to reveal a dearth of women (NRC, 1989, p. 62). This would be the case whether the position was in academia or in industry. Therefore, it seems ludicrous to expect equal representation of women in these disciplines.

A study conducted by the National Academy of Sciences-National Research Council (1983) found that among science and engineering faculty, "recent women Ph.D.'s (were) found in junior faculty positions in proportions exceeding their availability in the doctoral pool" (p. 16). Bowen and Sosa (1989) project the demand in mathematics

Table 3. Female Doctoral Recipients

High Participation Fields of Study	1975 >=26%	1988 >=40%	Low Participation Fields of Study	1975 <=16%	1988 <=30%
Humanities			Humanities—		
English	41%	58%	Philosophy	15%	24%
French	65	71			
German	44	54	Social Sciences—		
Spanish	47	61	Economics	8	20
			Political Science	16	24
Education	31	55			
			Biological Sciences—		
Social Sciences			Botany	13	@
Anthropology	35	52			
Psychology	31	55	Physical Sciences—		
Sociology	30	53	Chemistry	11	21
			Mathematics	11	16
Biological Sciences—			Physics	5	10
Bacteriology/Micro.	26	@			
Biology, General	28	@			

@Note: Not a high participation field in 1985–86.

@Note: Not a low participation field in 1988.

NOTES: 1975 data are from *1989–90 Fact Book on Higher Education*, p. 94. 1988 data are from the *National Research Council*, 1989, p. 56–63.

and physical sciences to exceed the supply by 1997. Therefore, that degree of relative overrepresentation of women among junior faculty in these fields may soon become history.

Where does inequity begin?

The above analysis leads us to question where the differences in male and female degree attainment begins to take shape. If women are falling, or jumping, off track in securing credentials necessary for entry into academe, the points at which this is observable must be identified if we are to move beyond the charges related to hiring practices. As Bernice Sandler writes, "Clearly, the challenge of truly integrating women into academic life has not been surmounted by the passage of laws and the ending of many overtly discriminatory practices" (1986, p. 2).

Increasing the quantity of females in the pool of applicants is the only long-run solution to the problem of parity. This is of criti-

cal importance whether the position is sought in academia or business and industry.

This is an important distinction to make because employment opportunities in business and industry are a realistic alternative to higher education for doctoral recipients. If women reach parity in academe by securing 51% of all faculty positions, while failing to increase their level proportionately of doctoral attainment, simple mathematical deduction suggests a serious underrepresentation of women in leadership positions in business and industry.

The issue is one of progress and empowerment through education, rather than through position attainment alone. Given that premise, it is logical for universities to focus on the educational variation in the composition of the applicant pool and to examine means by which that pool of applicants can be more representative of the female population in the future.

There is much we do know about the shape of female and male educational enrollment patterns, although many extraneous variables impact upon the development of the actual patterns. For instance, we know that the percentage of female high school graduates under 24 years of age who were enrolled in college, and/or completed one or more years in college, has grown from 46.5% in 1970 to 55.3% in 1986 (*1989–90 Fact Book on Higher Education*, p. 29). Also, college enrollment among women is now comparable to that among men. Therefore, women are beginning the post-secondary educational experience in numbers comparable to men.

We also should bear in mind that while over 82% of all 18–24-year-olds were high school graduates in 1985, only 34% of all 18–24-year-old high school graduates were enrolled in college (*1989–90 Fact Book on Higher Education*, p. 30). This fact suggests another possible source of increased female enrollment in the future: the lower college enrollment rates among females in earlier years (26.3% versus 41.8% for men in 1970) may be supplemented by the complement of this group enrolling in college during a later period of their lives (*1989–90 Fact Book on Higher Education*, p. 29). Therefore, there is still ample opportunity to regain some women who have stepped out of the formal educational system.

The solution to the problem of maximizing female participation in academia is one of comprehensive programming throughout the educational experience, rather than merely at any one plateau. Women who evidence strong mathematical and scientific skill need to be recognized in their youth, and given stronger incentives for continued achievement. It is disheartening to learn that a 1987 study by the Stevens Institute of Technology found that "counselors and friends were most often identified as people who discouraged girls from going into engineering . . ." (Association of American Colleges [AAC], 1987, p. 6). Feldman (1974), acknowledging the importance of individual differences, warns against the tendency of counseling women either into or away from male-dominated fields simply because they are women.

The National Science Foundation has established a variety of programs aimed at increasing female participation in scientific research including Standard Research Awards, Research Initiation Awards, Research Planning Grants, Career Advancement Awards and Visiting Professorships for Women (AAC, 1987, p. 5). The Stevens Institute of Technology, for example, has a Women in Engineering Summer Program which claims a "strong, positive, long-term impact on students, increasing the number of women enrolling in engineering throughout the country" (AAC, 1987, p. 6).

Parity for women will not be achieved by invective or quotas.

The efforts of the University of California in promoting female participation in academe are worthy of mention too since they relate directly to the specific underrepresentation of women in the applicant pool for positions as faculty. The President's Fellowship Program provides significant financial support to women interested in eventually becoming a faculty member after pursuing studies in fields such as engineering, mathematics, business, computer science, or life and physical sciences. The University of Michigan's School of Dentistry developed a "Women in Science Videotape Series" to promote female participation in science and mathematics careers. Guidance counselors might do more by way of utilizing such resources to promote interest and affirm acceptance of females with demonstrated potential in these disciplines (AAC, 1986, p. 4–5). As noted by Chamberlain (1988), women now comprise approximately 25% of the most highly trained professionals in science and other professional areas, with this figure having increased from only 5% just two decades ago.

Bowen and Schuster's proposal for a national program to foster and promote exceptionally talented persons interested in faculty appointments would benefit both males and females. The four-part proposal includes more graduate fellowships, research support for young scholars, support for mid-career faculty development, and faculty appointments for young scholars (Bowen and Schuster, 1985, p. 15). A national program might be fashioned in such a way as to include some of the recommendations of others suggesting mentor programs for young scholars and faculty. The idea of sponsorship has been advanced by Clark & Corcoran (1986) and defined as "advancement of a favored protege, mentoring and/or coaching a novice through the informal norms of the workplace and/or discipline" (p. 26). The research support for young scholars, recommended by Bowen and Schuster (1985), may be enhanced through the introduction of sponsorship programs within universities. Likewise, graduate fellowships developed in conjunction with an outreach effort by faculty and students in the physical sciences and engineering departments (Weis, 1985) may serve as an effective coupling of stimulants.

Discipline-specific action

Clearly, the collective ingenuity of many will be needed to ensure that women continue the pattern of substantial educational progress. However, the true challenge for administrators and faculties of higher education extends far beyond the development of even the more creative of these programs. The ethical and professional imperative of our times commands us to apply our most discerning analytic skills to an examination of the factors which influence female participation in each of the varied disciplines of our institutions, developing *an affirmative action plan for each field of study*. Once the plans are developed, they must be acted upon at each level of the hiring and advancement procedures.

The status of women in U.S. higher education is far more encouraging than many would have us believe. But we must guard against the tendency of setting unrealistic timetables and goals to achieve our desired ends. Blakely (1989) provides a careful examination of the realities of equity achievement in Canadian institutions of higher education, delineating the detailed implications

for faculty hiring and promotion practices necessary to reach specific goals. Such an outline provides clear evidence of the fallacy of unrealistic goal setting and raises serious questions as to whether such a practice does not, in and of itself, foster widespread institutional underachievement of objectives.

Our goals should be only so lofty as our strategic planning methods can support. Some institutions, including the University of Pennsylvania, have conducted studies of current faculty and doctoral recipients by race, gender, and discipline. These studies can form the basis for *discipline-specific* affirmative action planning.

Planning for parity should begin early.

Parity for women in academe is a proper goal. But it will not be achieved by invective or quotas. It can be achieved by colleges and universities planning now to encourage and support female scholars in a more targeted way in such underrepresented fields as agriculture, business, chemistry, economics, engineering, mathematics, philosophy, political science, and physics. And planning for higher education parity should begin early, with counselors and teachers in the schools. ■

REFERENCES

Association of American Colleges. (1986). *On Campus with Women* (v15 n4). Washington, DC: Project on the Status and Education of Women. (ERIC Document Reproduction Service No. ED 273 180).

Association of American Colleges. (1986). *On Campus with Women*. (v16+17 n1). Washington, DC: Project on the Status and Education of Women. (ERIC Document Reproduction Service No. ED 286 408).

Association of American Colleges. (1987-88). *On Campus with Women* (v17 n2-3). Washington, DC: Project on the Status and Education of Women. (ERIC Document Reproduction Service No. ED 293 423).

Blakely, J. H. (1989). What should the goals be? Employment equity for female faculty in Canada. *Canadian Journal of Higher Education, 19*(1), 29-48.

Bowen, H. L. & Schuster, J. H. (1985). Outlook for the academic profession. *Academe, 71*(5), 9–15.

Bowen, H. L. & Schuster, J. H. (1986). *American professors: A national resource imperiled.* New York: Oxford University Press.

Bowen, W. G. & Sosa, J. A. (1989). *Prospects for faculty in the arts & sciences.* New Jersey: Princeton University Press.

Chamberlain, M. K. (Ed) (1988). *Women in academe: Progress and prospects.* New York: Russell Sage Foundation.

Clark, S. M. & Corcoran, M. (1986). Perspectives on the professional socialization of women faculty: A case of cumulative disadvantage? *Journal of Higher Education, 57,* 20–43.

Feldman, S. D. (1974). *Escape from the doll's house: Women in graduate and professional school education.* New York: McGraw-Hill.

Harris, J., Silverstein, J. & Andrews, D. (1989). Educating women in science. In C. S. Pearson, D. L. Shavlik, & J. G. Touchton (Eds.), *Educating the minority: Women challenge tradition in higher education,* 294–310. New York: Macmillan.

Heath, J. A., & Tuckman, H. P. (1989). The impact on labor markets of the relative growth of new female doctorates. *Journal of Higher Education, 60,* 704–715.

Hyer, P. (1984, April). A ten-year progress report on women faculty at doctorate-granting universities. Paper presented at the Annual Meeting of the American Educational Research Association (68th), New Orleans, LA. (ERIC Document Reproduction Service No. ED 247 838).

National Academy of Sciences. (1983). Climbing the ladder: An update on the status of doctoral women scientists and engineers. Washington, DC: National Research Council, Office of Scientific and Engineering Personnel. (ERIC Document Reproduction Service No. ED 239 861).

National Center for Educational Statistics [NCES]. Unpublished. In B. M. Vetter, & E. L. Babco, (1987), Professional women and minorities, Washington: Commission on Professionals in Science and Technology.

National Center for Educational Statistics [NCES]. (1988). *Projections of educational statistics to 1997–98.* Washington, DC: U.S. Government Printing Office.

National Research Council [NRC]. (1989). *Summary report 1988: Doctoral recipients from United States universities.* Washington, DC: National Academy Press.

National Science Foundation, Division of Science Resources Studies. (1986). Recent doctorate faculty increases in engineering and some science fields. *Science Resources Studies Highlights.* Washington, DC: National Science Foundation. (ERIC Document Reproduction Service No. ED 288 427).

1989–90 Fact Book on Higher Education. (1989). American Council on Education/Macmillan Series on Higher Education. New York: Macmillan.

Sandler, B. (1986). *The campus climate revisited: Chilly for women faculty, administrators, and graduate students* [Final Report]. Washington, DC: Association of American Colleges. (ERIC Document Reproduction Service No. ED 298 837).

Simeone, A. (1987). *Academic women: Working towards equality.* South Hadley, MA: Bergin and Garvey.

Weis, L. (1985). Progress but no parity: Women in higher education. *Academe, 71*(6), 29–33.

Weis, L. (1987). Academic women in science, 1977–1984. *Academe, 73*(1), 43–47.

Teaching at our colleges and universities has gone through an irreversible shift. What should institutions do?

Education's New Academic Work Force

David Leslie and Judith Gappa

To maintain high-quality instruction and academic programs, a college or university must identify and hire the best faculty persons who will teach devotedly and work together collegially. But where do institutions find such people? Where are the faculty who bring commitment, energy, exposure to the problems of the time, and a deep interest in teaching young people?

The surprising answer is that many of the best teachers on campuses today are part-time faculty. This is what we found in our recent study, *The Invisible Faculty*. We also found that most institutions do not see the value of this veritable gold mine of experienced and skilled instructors, those faculty who are already teaching considerable portions of the undergraduate and graduate curriculums and on whom institutions rely to a greater extent than they like to admit.

Colleges and universities are using more part-timers than ever. Yet they remain a largely invisible resource—a resource that has invigorated academic programs with fresh enthusiasm, new perspective, and novel kinds of expertise.

Part-time faculty now constitute more than 35 percent of the teaching faculty in the United States (by head count). At two-year community colleges they can be more than 50 percent or 60 percent of the faculty. In the public universities in Florida, 60 percent of the lower division undergraduate courses are taught by non-tenure track faculty, an undetermined but large number being part-timers. Roughly the same situation is true at many other state colleges and universities, including many of the most fa-

David Leslie is professor of education at the College of William and Mary. He received his B.A. in psychology from Drew University in New Jersey and his Ed.D. in higher education from Pennsylvania State University. He has taught at Universities of Virginia and Illinois, and Illinois State and Florida State Universities. He is former president of the Association for the Study of Higher Education.

Judith Gappa is vice president for human relations and professor of education at Indiana's Purdue University. After earning her B.A. and M.A. degrees in musicology at George Washington University, she earned an Ed.D. from Utah State in educational administration. She previously taught at Utah State and San Francisco State, where she was also associate vice president for faculty affairs, and has worked at NCHEMS in Colorado. She and Dr. Leslie recently co-authored *The Invisible Faculty* (1993).

mous ones, and many private universities. Altogether, the National Center for Educational Statistics estimates the number of part-time faculty serving U.S. colleges and universities at 270,000.

Many assume that part-time faculty are largely drawn from those who aspire to a full-time academic career. But part-timers are actually a highly diverse work force. On average they are younger than full-time faculty; but 42 percent are over 45 years old. Part-timers express a high degree of satisfaction (87 percent) with their work, but they are vocally dissatisfied with their conditions of employment: pay, benefits, support services, office space, parking, and membership in the teaching community. Part-timers usually have a remarkably high motivation to teach. Some teach for purely economic reasons, but substantial numbers do not. They bring highly diverse backgrounds, experience, and skills to America's classrooms. We found that they seem to divide into four distinct groups.

Four kinds of faculty

The largest category is composed of *specialists, professionals, and experts*. More than half of all part-time faculty are fully employed elsewhere. They typically do not teach for economic reasons but because they want to, or because they are asked to by deans and department chairs. They teach in highly specialized fields such as applied mathematics, public administration, law, medicine and allied health, business, foreign languages, music, economics, education, and social work. Some also teach, often enthusiastically, in general education courses.

About 60 percent of the part-timers in higher education with full-time jobs elsewhere have taught at the same institution for more than four years (National Center for Education Statistics 1990). This means they are a far more stable group than is often assumed. Given their continuity, it is apparent that colleges and universities rely on this pool to teach important parts of the curriculum.

A second group are the *career enders*. These are persons who have reached or are

approaching retirement age, and they see college or university teaching as a way to remain intellectually active. Career enders often bring rich backgrounds in professional practice or decades of teaching experience to their classrooms. They may be retired insurance executives or college presidents, or just-retired professors of

Colleges are using more part-timers than ever.

Latin, sociology, or European history, or no longer active engineers, military officers, or lawyers. Typically they are motivated by the intrinsic enjoyment of teaching and a desire to pass on knowledge and training acquired over their lifetimes.

Third are the *free lancers*. They have usually made a choice to teach in higher education part-time as a way of realizing career or life goals that require flexible commitments. Musicians, writers, consultants, artists and designers, dancers, and small business entrepreneurs often have several simultaneous interests and find they cannot accept the confining role of a full-time faculty member. Nor do they wish to be isolated from cutting-edge scholarship and art or work in academe. Some teach for the pay until their own careers take off. These free-lancers tend to be quite independent, highly resourceful, and multi-talented people.

Fourth are the *aspiring academics*, who are typically younger women and men, often new Ph.D.'s or other doctoral recipients looking for tenure-track positions, or ABD's (all but dissertation) who are teaching part-time to finance the writing of their doctoral thesis. Aspiring academics are the most ambivalent about their status. They often report that they have to calculate how much time and energy to commit to their marginal faculty role. Women in their childbearing years or in a dual-career families appear in this group disproportionately.

Part-timers in all four categories tend to be energetic and committed to teaching, and most are surprisingly loyal to their institutions. The data reveal that one-third of all part-timers have taught at their current institutions for seven or more years.

The use of part-timers

We found great pressures to continue the use of part-time faculty at most colleges and universities, and even to expand their use. Among the reasons: fiscal reductions, changing student characteristics, the desire for more "practical" expertise, and shortages in the supply of faculty in some fields (Bowen and Schuster 1986; Bowen and Sosa 1989).

The use of part-time faculty is already more varied than is commonly known. Although they are frequently described as "temporary" and "substitute" appointments, part-time faculty have been heavily and continuously used to cover substantial amounts of instruction at a wide range of institutions. They are far more central to the academic and fiscal viability of U.S. colleges and universities than would be true if they were casual or temporary employees.

When institutional leaders and professors gave us their reasons for hiring part-time faculty, the reasons seemed to fall into two clear categories: institutional and educational.

Universities gave institutional reasons most often when the were constrained financially or they enjoyed a nearby pool of talented people who wanted to teach part-time. One frequent reason was the institutional bind of steady state or slightly enlarging enrollment combined with financial cutbacks because of their state's fiscal problems or a national recession. For institutions in this bind, part-time faculty represented a way to absorb continuing demand without increasing—or even reducing—costs.

Also, some institutions had faculty who preferred to conduct research and wanted to teach only the advanced or graduate courses. So institutions assigned lower-division courses to part-timers. Others have freshman writing requirements that required numerous small classes in English, and part-time instructors seemed especially appropriate. Metropolitan institutions often strengthen their programs in the arts, law, computer science, accounting, public policy and politics, and engineering—among others—by adding outside experts to teach in their specialties.

Educational reasons for hiring part-time instructors are important too. Part-time faculty can be hired to keep sections small, when economics would seem to dictate large, unwieldy classes. Part-timers allow colleges to offer courses for which they could not justify a full-time faculty member: courses in Italian or Chinese language, international finance, labor law, wildlife management, manufacturing, or instruction for the oboe or jazz piano. Universities can use part-timers to develop and test new academic programs without having to make a large investment for the long term.

Further, part-timers can be introduced to improve the teaching at a college, since many part-timers seem to bring unusual skills, expertise, and devotion to their classes. As one part-time teacher told us, "I love the challenge of dealing with students who are not interested in my subject, but who are required to be in my class. I feel I can bring real world examples to motivate and interest them." Part-timers often present students

Half of all part-time faculty are fully employed elsewhere.

with fresh ideas, introduce them to important networks of outside influentials, and give them access to the most modern equipment.

In sum, part-time faculty actually strengthen institutions rather than weaken them as numerous full-time professors—and the AAUP—allege. They enhance both the efficiency and the educational effectiveness of colleges and universities. They contribute to the quality of education at many institutions.

But part-timers, we found, are usually treated as second-class citizens. They are denied access to office space, paid on a separate low salary scale, and excluded from the core activities of campus life.

The worst offenders were colleges and universities that practiced an *unplanned* use of part-time faculty. These institutions made last-minute, off-the-street hires. They failed to orient the part-timers to the institution, its students, and good teaching standards. They neglected to provide mailboxes, office space, or support services. And they offered exploitative pay and no fringe benefits.

Part-timers often present students with fresh ideas.

However, we found a small but growing number of institutions and academic departments that are beginning to recognize that part-timers are now a permanent part of the academic force. These institutions recognize the threats to quality and their own responsibility for changing the professorial system in significant ways. They are planning to accommodate the new teaching force in academe. These institutions recognize:

- Part-time faculty are a permanent part of their academic work force. They are not "temporaries" but an integral portion of their instructional team.
- Part-timers now teach substantial parts of the undergraduate and graduate curriculum. They are a vital element, not marginal people.
- Faculties are now bifurcated into high and low "castes," with full-time, tenure track persons on top and part-time instructors or adjunct professors at the bottom. They think that this bifurcation damages quality and sense of academic community.
- Part-time faculty are victims of an expanding situation that exploits them and treats them shabbily.

What to do?

What should colleges and universities do now that one-fourth to two-thirds of their instructors are part-timers? We suggest several things.

First, become proactive about incorporating part-time faculty into your academic community. Many institutions temporize and avoid making strategic decisions about this development. Don't dodge the facts. Create a strategy that includes the part-time teachers.

We discovered that many universities which felt they were controlling costs were actually engaging in false economies, especially economies that damaged quality. Hidden costs accrue when a college tries to save money without attending to educational impact.

For example, thinning the ranks of full-time faculty leaves fewer persons to handle advising, curriculum development, and program coordination. Department chairs must assume the added burdens of recruiting, supervising, and managing the part-timers. Individually part-timers may be highly productive, but the aggregate cost of instruction may show inefficiencies.

The proactive institutions usually help part-timers understand why they have been hired and how the university expects them to do their jobs. They also provide office space, telephone numbers, and support staff. These institutions tend to have a plan about how to use part-time faculty as a

Many institutions had large gaps in their data.

regular part of their department or school responsibility.

A good example is one large mathematics department we visited. It has a program to hire 12 graduate students a year, who teach highly structured remedial courses under the supervision of an internship advisor. A second tier of part-time faculty holds master's degrees and has college or high school teaching experience. They teach the required lower-division courses. A third tier with Ph.D.'s help teach the upper-division courses. These are long-term part-timers or experts with full-time positions in industry.

Second, collect data about your institution's part-time faculty. Too many institutions we visited had large gaps in their data on part-timers, and some had no information at all. Since good planning depends on a solid understanding of current conditions, we suggest that academic planners and institutional researchers become more specifi-

It is time to bring the two "castes" together.

cally aware of the characteristics of their part-time faculty, their work assignments, and the pressures that compel the use of part-timers. You should gather and analyze data on a routine and continuing basis: what their backgrounds and qualifications are, their employment histories, how much they teach, what they teach, to whom they teach it, how much they are compensated, how they are evaluated, and their attitudes toward the institution and its students.

Third, your institution should have clear policies about the use of part-timers. At present deans and department chairs have so much freedom that part-timers may be treated capriciously and unevenly. Without central administration policies about part-timers, the various divisions struggle to create their own policies, which may vary considerably. They need guidance from the institution, and a clear set of good practices, incentives, pay scales, and support.

Fourth, whatever plans you devise for part-time faculty, they should include the views of the part-timers themselves. They need to be asked about their status, working conditions, terms of employment, and ways they could make a better contribution to departmental, school, or institutional goals. Part-timers have different and valuable perspectives on the courses they teach and on the curriculum of which their course is a part.

In effect, many students are being taught by two different faculties who do not talk with each other. It is time to bring the two "castes" together. The planning process is a great place to begin.

Fifth, you should treat part-time faculty fairly. Part-timers should receive decent and

consistent treatment. They should have the same tools to do their work as full-timers: some office space, telephones, access to a computer, secretarial help, a mailbox. Also, they should have a voice in expressing their needs, interests, and suggestions for improved education, perhaps through the faculty senate.

Policies need not be the same for full-time and part-time faculty; but they should speak to the same issues. For example, if employment security is important to full-time faculty, it should be addressed in the case of part-timers too. We can imagine some part-timers being given three or five-year contracts, and some of the best being granted tenure. Likewise, if full-time faculty receive merit pay increases for superior teaching or scholarship, then merit pay should be awarded to the more outstanding part-time faculty.

Sixth, try hard to change the attitudes of full-time professors toward part-timers, who are too often treated less as a valuable new resource and more as a "throw-away" commodity. Instead of turning part-timers over frequently, we think colleges should concentrate on developing them as skilled, experienced, and dedicated teachers. They should be involved in major campus decisions; their achievements should be recognized in the campus newspaper and at special events; they should be included in significant social events; and they should be helped to develop their intellectual, artistic, and pedagogical skills. Department chairs are the key. They should be give clear directions and the responsibilities for the hiring, supervision, and development of part-timers.

Recognizing the new

What is essential is that academic planners and leading faculty recognize that a truly significant shift has changed higher education unalterably. Many American students now complete at least the first two years of college taught largely by instructors and graduate students who are not on the tenure tack. The granite fact is that the undergraduate experience is now substantially shaped by one class of faculty while another class is increasingly concentrating on research, graduate study, or upper division courses.

In our view, tenure-track, full-time faculty must squarely face the corollary of their decision to delegate so much responsibility to non-tenure track, part-time faculty without a commitment to their working conditions, professional development, fair salaries, and full acceptance as members of the faculty. They can, of course abdicate. But they will have to convince the taxpayers and tuition-

A truly significant shift has changed higher education unalterably.

paying public that their non-teaching activities are worth supporting at the resource level the tenure system demands.

We found a disturbing inertia in the culture of academic life. The existing professorial culture seems driven by the tenure-track faculty's efforts to hold on to their own special privileges, perquisites, and power. Frankly, there is snobbery (even though many part-timers have educational credentials, publications, experience, and expertise comparable to most full-timers). There is a baffling reluctance by full-time faculty to recognize what is really happening to instruction on their own campuses, and there is a dangerously short-sighted view. Higher education is under powerful pressure to change; the marketplace and many public policy makers want higher quality education for college students at a reasonable cost. Part-time faculty are part of the solution, not a major piece of the problem.

We think it makes sense for the traditional faculty members to make common cause with the growing number of "new" and often invisible faculty in their midst—to conceptualize and design a new kind of high-quality undergraduate experience. A united faculty of full-timers and part-timers working together has a far better chance of improving higher education than does a divided, competitive, and two-caste faculty.

It is time to concede that the structure of America's faculty and the teaching in academe has gone through a radical and irreversible shift. The task now is to take advantage of this new condition, not ignore it or disdain it. Only by properly harnessing the skills and energetic devotion of higher education's many, new part-time faculty will the United States and its young people in colleges be adequately served. ∎

REFERENCES

Bowen, H. and J. Schuster. 1986. *American Professors: A National Resource Imperiled.* Oxford University Press.

Bowen, W. and J. Sosa, 1989. *Prospects for Faculty in the Arts and Sciences.* Princeton University Press.

National Center for Educational Statistics. 1990. *Faculty in Higher Education Institutions, 1988.* National Center for Education Statistics.

Gappa, J. and D. Leslie. 1993. *The Invisible Faculty: Improving the Status of Part-Timers in Higher Education.* Jossey-Bass.

Colleges may need to refocus their retention programs.

Reconstructing the First Year of College

Vincent Tinto

nterest in student retention has not waned. If anything, it has grown in the past few years. Retention programs have grown to include such initiatives as improved advising, expanded orientation sessions, tutoring and developmental education efforts, peer mentoring, new residence hall arrangements, and the increasingly popular freshman seminars (Upcraft, Gardner and Associates 1989).

While these retention programs have helped some students complete their college education, their long-term impact on retention has been surprisingly limited, or at least more limited than they need be. The reasons for this are many. But perhaps the most important one is that most retention programs have done little to change the quality of the *academic* experience for students, especially during the critical first year of college.

How can colleges and universities improve their first-year academic encounters?

Vincent Tinto is professor of education and sociology at Syracuse University. A graduate of the University of Chicago with a Ph.D. in education and sociology, he is an authority on why students fail to complete their collegiate studies and author of *Leaving College: Rethinking the Causes and Cures of Student Attrition*, 2nd edition (1993).

How can they enhance the impact of their programs upon student retention? To begin to answer these questions let's first review what we have learned in the past decade about the scope and causes of student leaving.

We know that more than 40 percent of all students in America who start at a four-year college still fail to earn a degree; and nearly 57 percent of all dropouts from four-year institutions leave before the start of their second year. We also know that student departures during college take a variety of forms and arise from a diversity of sources, individual and institutional. There is no one form of behavior, no single prevailing reason for leaving. There are many types of leaving. Of these, researchers have been able to identify seven major causes of student withdrawal.

Academic difficulty. Some students leave because they are unable or unwilling to meet the minimum academic standards of the institution. They are asked to leave, or soon expect to be. Most of these leavings arise because of insufficient academic skills or poor study habits.

But while the incidence of academic dismissals seems to be increasing, and on some campuses now makes up a majority of all student leavers, it remains the case that departures for academic reasons still represent only 30 to 35 percent of all leaving nationally. The majority of departures continue to arise voluntarily, and they usually do so despite sufficient levels of grade performance. These types of departures typically arise from the following causes.

Adjustment difficulties. Even the most academically gifted and socially mature students experience some difficulties making the transition from secondary school to the demands of college. For most, these difficulties are transitory. But for some the adjustment to the more rigorous academic work and to the different, more competitive social life is quite difficult, and can lead to early withdrawal from college, often in the first six weeks of the first semester.

Some individuals feel awkward among strangers, or find it hard to deal with other new students. Others are unprepared for the greater diversity of associates, or come from backgrounds that differ markedly from most of their classmates. For them, college is a sometimes "foreign" experience, the transition to it, difficult.

Goals: uncertain, narrow, or new. Entering students vary in their clarity and intensity of purpose. Many students begin college with only a vague notion of why they have done so. But while some uncertainty of career goals is typical of most undergraduates, difficulties arise when goals go unresolved for too long because such uncertainty can undermine the willingness of students to perform the work needed to remain in college.

Other new students enter college with narrow or limited goals such as preparing for a career in theater or in professional sports, or using one college as a stepping stone for transfer to another university, so they may leave before earning a degree. And, of course, some students will alter their goals after a year or two on campus. They decide they don't want to be scientists, physicians, or school teachers after all, so they drop out even when their grades are satisfactory. Or they discover a deep interest in jazz piano, designing new computer software, or making films, and they leave.

Commitments: weak and external. Earning a baccalaureate degree over four years requires a high level of commitment. Not all students possess that degree of commit-

ment. Some are unwilling to spend the effort to complete their college degree requirements. They have the ability to do college work, but not the commitment.

Others, however, though wanting to stay, are pulled away from college because of external commitments. They leave to handle a divorce, death, or drinking problem at home, to explore a relationship with a loved one in another state, or to help with

> # Researchers have identified seven major causes of student withdrawal.

the family farm or business. A majority of these departing students are likely to be stop-outs rather than dropouts. Given the opportunity or a change of external circumstances, they frequently will return to college at a later date.

Financial inadequacies. In exit interviews, departing students most often give lack of money as the reason for leaving, often combined with unspecified "personal reasons." But follow-up interviews reveal that the decision to leave is not so much cost per se but the perceived quality and value of what they are receiving for the cost. "Inadequate finances" often turns out to be a smoke screen too for more complicated or personal reasons for leaving.

Nevertheless, numerous students, especially those from working class, broken-family, or disadvantaged backgrounds, do leave because they are unable to pay for tuition plus living costs away from home, even with a part-time job, loans, and some college aid. Many of these persons will likely continue to work on their degree part-time, or return at a later date when they have earned money to pay for their college costs.

Incongruence. Some students leave because they feel they do not "fit" or do not "belong" socially or academically. They feel the college is "not right" for them. In the jargon or researchers, there is a lack of congruence between the individual and the institution.

Frequently, the student has chosen unwisely. But just as frequently it is the institution that fails with its unfriendly atmosphere, lack of concern for student needs and growth, or a poorly designed academic program. Some students, for instance, leave a college because they are bored or unchallenged intellectually. In this case the students leave not because they have failed but because they want to take a positive step toward receiving a better education elsewhere. Transfer rather than permanent withdrawal is typically the result.

Isolation. Finally, some students drop out because they feel lonely, isolated, unable to establish connections with their classmates or upper class students, or with the college's professors and administrators. Leavers of this type, which is especially common in the first year, express a sense of not having made any significant contacts and not feeling membership in the institution. They feel marginal, unconnected, isolated.

The rise and shortcoming of retention programs

In response to these types of student departures, many colleges and universities have put in place a variety of retention programs.

In response to the need for academic assistance, for instance, institutions have introduced a range of remedial (or developmental) courses, tutorials, and supplemental instruction activities to enhance the skills of these students. As a way of easing the transition to college, institutions have increasingly turned to extended orientation sessions and required freshman courses, such as "University 101," which stress coping skills as well as the provision of information about the ways of negotiating the demands of college life. Some colleges have also emphasized better advising and career counseling as ways of helping students make more informed academic and career choices. Other institutions have stressed freshmen social activities and faculty and student mentor programs as mechanisms for the development of much needed affiliation among new students and between students and faculty.

But while several institutions report sizable increases in student persistence as a result of their new retention efforts, most colleges report only modest gains. In analyzing why this is so, I have increasingly come to think that the main reason for the

Most retention programs are non-academic in nature.

modest gains is that most retention programs are largely non-academic in nature.

Most retention programs are managed by, indeed staffed by, student affairs personnel. Though faculty involvement has usually been sought, most professors have been reluctant to participate in these new efforts. As one scholar said to me, "If it weren't for the admissions office admitting students who don't belong here, we wouldn't have a retention problem. And if we have a retention problem, it's the responsibility of the student affairs people to deal with it."

Of course, some faculty members do get involved in first-year programs. But most do not. And some retention programs emphasize academic issues, but most do not. When they do, they are largely peripheral or supplemental to the academic experience, not an integral part of it. As a result, existing retention programs have done little to improve the daily *academic* experiences of students in the classrooms and laboratories.

This should change. Faculty should become more actively involved in retention efforts; and retention programs should include initiatives that change the everyday academic experience of students, especially during the critical first year. (This is especially urgent for commuter students since classrooms and laboratories are often the only places where commuters actively engage with faculty and other students.)

After more than a decade of research in this field, I am persuaded that the roots of successful student retention lie in better education during the first year. Sure, finer orientations to college, closer freshman advising, more financial aid, stronger development courses, more freshman mixers, and improved residence hall arrangements are all a help to new students. But unless students become keenly involved in higher learning from the first month, a considerable number of them will be reluctant to stay.

Rather than merely tinkering at the margins of academic life academic planners need to direct their attention to a major reconstruction of the learning settings that mark undergraduate life, especially during the foundational first year of college. The question they must ask is not what programs are needed to retain students, but how the learning settings of the first year should be constructed so as to promote student education in that year and beyond.

Fortunately, a small but growing number of colleges and universities have begun to turn their attention to the task of educational reform in the first year. They have sought to alter the settings, classrooms, and laboratory experiences in which education occurs. Among these reforms, one of the most promising, in my view, is the creation of "learning communities" for new college students.

Learning communities in the first year

In their most basic form learning communities are a kind of co-registration or block scheduling that enables students to take courses together. The same students register for two or more courses, forming a sort of study team. In a few cases this may mean sharing the entire first-semester curriculum together (Gabelnick et al. 1990) so that all new students in that learning community are studying the same material. Sometimes it will link all freshmen by tying two courses together for all, most typically a course in writing with a course in selected literature, or biographies, or current social problems. In the larger universities such as the University of Oregon and the University of Washington, students in a learning community may attend lectures with 200-300 other students but stay together for a smaller discussion section (Freshman Interest Group) led by a graduate student or upperclassman. In Seattle Central Community College, however, students in the Coordinated Studies Program take all their courses together in one block of time so that the community meets two or three times a week for four to six hours at a time.

Typically, learning communities are organized around a central theme which links

> *Despite new retention efforts, most colleges report only modest gains.*

the courses—say, "Body and Mind"—in which required courses in human biology, psychology, and sociology are linked in pursuit of a singular piece of knowledge: how and why humans behave as they do. At New York's LaGuardia Community College, learning communities are designed for students studying for a career in business (the Enterprise Center) as well as for students requiring some developmental academic assistance (the New Student House). In these cases, the character of the learning experience is very much a reflection of the quality of faculty collaboration and the degree to which the experience of the linked courses form an educationally coherent whole.

Clearly there is no one type of learning community. There are many. Experimentation is rife as colleges seek to create the best kind of learning communities at that campus. But nearly all the experiments have two things in common. One is *shared learning*. Learning communities enroll the same students in several classes so they get to know each other quickly and fairly intimately and in a way that is part and parcel of their academic experience. The other is *connected learning*. By organizing the shared courses around a theme or single large subject, learning communities seek to construct a coherent first-year educational experience that is not just an unconnected array of courses in, say, composition, calculus, modern history, Spanish, and geology.

A feature of learning communities that has made them easy to install is that some types of communities require relatively little from the faculty. It is possible for faculty to continue to teach much as they always have. What may be different for professors is the content of the freshmen courses and some of the assignments. Students may be given group or team projects instead of being asked to do individual study. But the restructuring is largely in the way students are registered together and the way the first-year courses are packaged around a common topic, theme, or study project. The change in faculty behavior required is minimal, except for possible ventures in team teaching.

This is not to say that some learning communities have not involved faculty in important ways and have not required faculty to make significant changes in their behavior. Some have. Those at Seattle Central Community College, for instance, require a good deal of faculty collaboration in the construction of course content and a healthy dose of collaborative teaching—a form of teaching that is not often found in the repertoire of teaching skills that faculty bring to the classroom. My point is that altered faculty behavior, though desirable, is not required to reap some of the benefits of first-year learning communities.

By registering students for the same courses or having all new students study the same topic, the entering students form their own self-supporting associations to give each other academic and social support. They spend more time together out of class than do students in traditional, unrelated, stand-alone classes. The common study of a subject and co-registration brings them together fast as small communities of learners.

Academic planners need to direct their attention to a major reconstruction of learning settings.

Not surprisingly the students in these new learning communities tend to report themselves more satisfied with their first year experiences in college. And they are more likely to persist beyond the first year.

For example, at Seattle Central Community College, learning community students have continued at a rate approximately 25 percentage points higher than those students in the traditional curriculum. Indeed, even in institutions where retention rates are high, such as at the University of Washington, students in that institution's Freshmen Interest Groups persist more frequently than those taking stand-alone courses. And it is all be-

All the experiments have two things in common.

cause of the simple strategic change of allowing students to share much of a more connected first-year curriculum together.

As one student told us in our recent study (Tinto, Goodsell, and Russo 1994):

In the cluster we knew each other; we were friends. We discussed everything from all our classes.... If we needed help, or if we had questions, we could help each other.

Actually, many of the new learning communities, as I noted above, do more than co-register students around a topic. They often change the manner in which students are educated. Some faculty members employ collaborative pedagogies, asking students to take an active role in the construction of knowledge rather than merely listening to lectures. Other teachers require the students to work interdependently by assigning work that cannot be completed without the responsible participation of each group member. In a few cases, faculty members assign carefully constructed group projects, inducing students to integrate the intellectual matter of several of their classes. Occasionally the results have been startling.

The fruits of innovation

These freshly designed learning communities for new undergraduates appear to be yielding important benefits. First, students become more actively involved in classroom learning. And as students spend more time learning, they learn more (Astin 1984). Second, the new students spend more time *learning together*. This enhances the quality of their learning; and by learning together, everyone's understanding and knowledge is enriched. Third, these stu-

They provide lessons that no lectures or homilies can provide.

dents form social groups outside their classrooms, bonding in ways that increase their persistence in college. Fourth, students often develop a deeper appreciation of the value of cooperation and of including many voices in the construction of knowledge. Fifth, learning communities enable students to bridge the large divide between academic classes and student social conduct that frequently characterizes student life (Moffatt 1989), especially in the first two years on campus. They tend to learn and to make close friends at the same time.

Learning communities also encourage the student services staff to work more closely with the faculty by jointly constructing a first-semester curriculum specifically tailored for new students. At New York City's LaGuardia Community College, the First Year Seminars are in fact staffed by both faculty and student affairs people. At Leeward Community College in Hawaii, advisors, counselors, and peer-student mentors meet weekly with new students to discuss both their classwork and the requirements for making it through college. With such approaches the two separate fiefdoms of faculty and student services staff can be brought closer together.

One last outcome, one that is especially important in our time of what Robert Bellah calls rampant "expressive individualism" and of growing racial, gender, sexual, and ideological divisions on campus, is that of increased collaboration among students. Cleverly arranged learning communities stimulate a great deal of cooperative learning. They provide lessons that no lectures or homilies can provide. They teach students that their learning and that of their peers are inexorably intertwined, and that, regardless of race, class, gender, or background, their academic interests are at bottom the same. Thus, the introduction of learning communities for first-year students can not only increase retention but also develop educational citizenship, a quality that is in danger of eroding throughout the nation. ∎

REFERENCES

Astin, A. 1984. Student Involvement: A Developmental Theory for Higher Education. *Journal of College Student Personnel* 25:297-308.

Gabelnick, F. et al. 1990. *Learning Communities: Creating Connections Among Students, Faculty, and Disciplines*. New Directions for Student Learning, No. 41. Jossey-Bass.

Moffat, M. 1989. *Coming of Age in New Jersey: College and American Culture*. Rutgers University Press.

Tinto, V. 1993. *Leaving College: Rethinking the Causes and Cures of Student Attrition*. 2nd edition. University of Chicago Press.

Tinto, V., Goodsell-Love, A., and Russo, P. 1994. *Building Learning Communities for New College Students*. National Center on Postsecondary Teaching, Learning, and Assessment, Pennsylvania State University.

Upcraft, M., Gardner, J. and Associates. 1989. *The Freshman Year Experience*. Jossey-Bass.

Community colleges are moving toward becoming something more than a college.

The Approaching Metamorphosis of Community Colleges

Jon Travis

The two-year community college, an American invention, has demonstrated a remarkable capacity for change and accretion of duties during the past century of its existence. Begun in the Midwest under the influence of such persons as University of Chicago president William Rainey Harper as "junior colleges," they provided the general courses of the first two years of higher education. Also created as extensions of high schools, and governed by the public school districts, these two-year colleges soon incorporated vocational and technical programs. In the 1970s, they added two more roles to job training and transfer preparation: adult continuing education of many kinds—both credit and non- credit—and

Jon Travis is assistant professor of higher education and director of the Center for Community College Education at Texas A & M University—Commerce. A graduate of the University of Iowa and West Virginia University, he received an Ed.D. from Arizona State University. He has taught at Yavapai College and the Maricopa Community College Distract, both in Arizona, and served as district coordinator for faculty and staff development for the Maricopa District. He is the author of several articles on two-year colleges.

community services. "Comprehensive" has been the adjective of choice to describe the modern community college.

Now another metamorphosis is upon us. Because of the deteriorating social conditions in many urban areas, new ethnic tensions, homelessness, drug abuse, dissolution of the traditional family, immigration, and youth unemployment, community colleges have been placing community needs more and more at the top of their priorities. The very fabric of our society appears to be threatened (Commission on the Future of Community Colleges 1988), and a growing underclass faces a widening gap from the rest of society (Harlacher and Gollattscheck 1992). The only institutions that seem able to halt the deterioration are the nation's 1,200 community colleges.

But this means that community colleges will need to accept a new primary mission—that of helping to rebuild their local communities. In the next decade, two-year colleges may become community education and service centers, entities that no longer resemble a college. The name "college" may even be dropped to make them more user-friendly and to describe their activities more accurately.

Several analysts have already called for a whole new outlook for the community college (Boone 1992; Griffith and Connor 1994; Hankin 1992; Harlacher and Gollattscheck 1992; Perkins et al. 1984). Meanwhile, other college-watchers, noting a perceived decline in the number of transfers to four-year institutions and the increasing remedial and social rehabilitation work, have demonstrated their concern that community colleges are becoming places that no longer resemble a college of higher education (Cohen and Brawer 1987, 1996; Eaton 1992, 1994; Richardson and Bender 1987). Although no single mission will be adequate for all two-year colleges, the new needs of American society will force a reconsideration of mission for the majority of community colleges. Indeed, many colleges in urban locations have already expanded their focus.

This metamorphosis will require community college leaders, planners, and faculty members to redesign the nature of their institutions. Planning for anticipated community college roles, structures, faculty needs, and new alliances may be one of the most challenging educational planning tasks of the next decade. Actually this planning process is taking place even now.

The new situation

Each year, more than 10 million people take at least one credit or non-credit course at the 1,200 public two-year colleges, which are located in most sections and nearly every city in the 50 states. Nearly half of the nation's undergraduates and half of the first-time college students attend a community college. A cohort with an average age of 32, the community college student body includes almost half of all minority students in higher education.

Yet, during the past 20 years the kind of educational services that most community colleges provide has changed appreciably. While most institutions continue to offer course work in the traditional, lower-division transfer programs, they have expanded their programs in vocational/occupational training, workforce retraining, developmental education and basic literacy, English for immigrants, parenting courses,

drug counseling and rehabilitation, and community services. Fewer students currently complete a two-year degree. Most two-year college students work part-time, and perhaps half are working full-time, fitting college courses into their lives rather

The name "college" may even be dropped.

than putting their work and family life on hold as they pursue their education full-time (Griffith and Connor 1994).

A radically new kind of community service center is emerging within today's comprehensive community college, compelled by the poignant needs of the bottom third of the U.S. population. Students entering two-year colleges are demonstrating increasing educational inadequacies. The traditional support systems that have fortified young people—families, neighborhoods, churches, community centers, small businesses—have either lost influence or eroded. Neither volunteerism nor government welfare programs seems to halt the deterioration.

To prevent the rise of a permanently uneducated underclass, some group or institution needs to devote itself to replacing the support systems and training efforts that have nearly disappeared and to provide a nurturing environment and mature, encouraging human interaction. The logical choice seems to be the community college (Boone 1992; Commission on the Future 1988; Hankin 1992; Harlacher and Gollattscheck 1992; Sanchez 1994). The United States simply cannot afford to have a growing semi-literate, unskilled, increasingly criminal, unemployed segment in its midst. Some institution needs to step in to offer hope and educational skills, helping to reduce the despair and violence. Fortunately, the work of rebuilding communities has begun.

Innovations and initiatives

A multitude of initiatives have been launched by community colleges. To present a sampling of these efforts, let me categorize them into three areas:

- community-based education
- new collaborations
- new community services

Community-based education. One of the oldest innovations of community colleges is the delivery of instruction at sites remote from the college campus. More recently, these outreach efforts have been located in communities targeted for their special needs. For example, Frontier College in Toronto has sought to provide literary skills and self-esteem to people living on the streets through its Beat the Street program. The college even employed volunteer instructors who once had lived on the streets themselves (Pearpoint and Forest 1990). Oklahoma City Community College offers introductory courses in the city's branch libraries to provide more comfortable neighborhood settings (Roueche *et al.* 1995).

Urban community colleges, in particular, are committed to community-based programs. In New York, Bronx Community College supports off-campus learning in local apartment buildings. Colleges in Chicago, Kansas City, and Chattanooga have delivered courses in housing projects; and Jacksonville's downtown campus has offered programs at the Blodgett Housing Project and the Liberty Street Center, stressing vocational and personal skills. Jacksonville also developed a Return to Learn—Then Earn program for disadvantaged adults over 54. In Miami several outreach centers have been established: the Interamerican Center in "Little Havana," one each in Hialeah, Liberty City, Coconut Grove, and Homestead, and another opened in Overton after riots struck the area (Griffith and Connor 1994). Courses in Denver have been taught in the local prisons, two housing projects, and in juvenile centers. City College of Los Angeles has provided basic educational skills and job training to mothers on welfare.

Several colleges have offered instruction in individual homes. The Adult Armchair Education Project in Philadelphia includes basic skills, community problem-solving, and consumer education, while the Appalachian Adult Education Demonstration Project in Kentucky and the Homebound Project in Butte, Montana stress literacy and basic skills (Irish 1980). The list of innovative, community-based, proactive efforts to teach the least educated in their local settings is a long one. Since the poor are often intimidated by the world outside their immediate environments, such opportunities are particularly significant for meeting their needs and developing a sense of community.

New Collaborations. To reach into their communities more effectively, numerous community colleges have been developing collaborations or alliances with other community institutions; such as public libraries, high schools, churches, and businesses. Examples of collaborative efforts developed by community colleges are abundant. Recent reports indicate the growth and widespread use of this contemporary innovation (Doucette 1993; Mawby 1992; Mittelstet 1994; Pincus 1994; Roueche, et al. 1995; Taber 1995).

Among the collaborative programs developed by community colleges with public libraries are those organized by Chattanooga State Technical Community College, North Lake College in Dallas, and Metropolitan Community College in Omaha (Roueche, *et al.* 1995). Alliances to reach educational goals may ap-

Nearly half of the nation's undergraduates attend a community college.

pear to be the most natural arrangements. Arizona's Maricopa Community College District, for instance, participates in the Phoenix Think Tank, a partnership between the district and other local educational institutions to promote numerous learning initiatives.

Perhaps the majority of community colleges across the nation are collaborating with their local secondary schools, from Greenville, South Carolina and St. Petersburg, Florida to Cedar Rapids, Iowa and Denver, Colorado (Roueche, et al. 1995). These collaborations could be the initial step in creating novel community education centers that deliver courses ranging from literacy training and introductory English for immigrants to adult education courses in computer science/information management and Japanese culture (Commission on the Future 1988; Harlacher and Gollattscheck 1992; Perkins, et al. 1984). And, of course, community colleges have long worked contractually with industry to upgrade employees' skills, develop their overall knowledge base, and improve teamwork and human resource management capabilities.

New Community Services. The comprehensive community college has traditionally served community needs with non-credit courses, cultural events, and similar educational activities. With the expanding problems of U.S. society, a number of two-year colleges have introduced additional programs to help individuals and their communities recover. From courses in parenting and personal behavior training to services like child care and drug counseling, community colleges are striving to meet basic human necessities in an attempt to improve society.

Frequently colleges have teamed up with government agencies to offer multiple services; such as mental health counseling, employment services, and job retraining at one convenient location on campus. For example, Oregon's Chemetka Community College designed a program to provide mental health services, job placement, and similar community services (Hendley 1994). After Hurricane Andrew struck Florida in 1992, Miami-Dade Community College provided food, supplies, shelters, and transportation to people in need. The Saint Vincent Quadrangle Project was launched through the leadership of Cuyahoga Community College to elevate living conditions for the citizens of Cleveland's inner city. As segments of American society exhibit an abundance of distress, institutions must address a range of personal problems prior to or in conjunction with the education process.

Planning different centers

Essentially what is happening is the metamorphosis of the traditional community college into something different philosophically, structurally, and educationally. The resulting entity is a *community education center* that incorporates a range of educational services as well as social and community services for both the public and the private sectors.

Recently, the San Diego Community College District developed such a center with its Educational-Cultural Complex

A new kind of educational institution is evolving in America.

(Parnell 1990). In addition to classrooms, the design included a community theater, a public library, and food services. Using a plan resembling that of a shopping-center, the Collin County Community College District in Plano, Texas, built its Spring Creek campus under one roof, including classrooms, common areas, and a conference center for use by the local community.

A new kind of educational institution is evolving in America, something foreseen by a few visionaries such as Edmund Gleazer, president emeritus of the American Association of Community Colleges (Gleazer 1980). Combining education and training with a wide range of community services, depending on local needs, the community education center (CEC) can accommodate child care, a senior center, a movie theater, family and mental health counseling, testing, job placement, nutrition counseling and consumer education, conferences and forums about local issues, a public library, TESOL language training, fitness rooms, and more. Community colleges will truly live up to their innovative heritage.

The conditions for such a change are ripe. Many four-year colleges have considered or adopted open-door admissions; more state colleges and urban state universities are available for students who are prepared for college-level courses; and workforce training and career development are emphasized in four-year colleges as never before. Furthermore, the transfer function of the two-year college is no longer its strongest program, and relatively few starters earn a degree. Instead, a different set of problems has arisen in many communities. As analyst Lawrence Mead (1992) has written:

> The main challenge is no longer to battle the evils associated with the economy. Instead, it is to overcome social weaknesses that stem from the "post-marital" family and the inability of many youths to learn enough in school to be employable.

Decidedly, community college planners have some major work to do. If the new education center is to concentrate on community renewal, the community and its needs must be well-known. The CEC will need to be more *research-oriented*, scanning its changing local environment regularly and conducting both applied research and action research (Harkavy and Puckett 1992) to understand its community's needs and problems and to determine available resources for solutions. (Action research means involving local groups in planning and conducting programs.) The CEC also will need to take a

---

The CEC should probably abandon most traditional educational procedures and techniques.

---

more active role as a *convener*, bringing local government agencies, schools, libraries, churches, and businesses into conferences and collaborations, while providing joint educational and training programs.

In terms of instructional offerings, the CEC should probably abandon most traditional educational procedures and techniques that demonstrate inflexibility in scheduling, fee payment, facilities, and instruction. Educators will need to balance traditional institutional practices with novel student needs. For example, most forms and other paperwork should be used only if they enhance the learning process. More classes must be short-term or open-entry/open-exit.

Additionally, the CEC should serve as an aggressive advocate of the vital importance of learning and self-discipline in reac-

tion to lingering anti-intellectual and materialistic values in our society. In response to the fear of crime, family reconfigurations, economic exigencies, and a host of other familiar social maladies, the CEC is needed as a catalyst for community cooperation and interdependence. Understandably, a new funding paradigm will be imperative for these CEC's.

Unlike the older, more traditional universities, community colleges historically have acted as "paradigm busters." These two-year colleges were born as innovations. While many institutions are already experimenting with innovative programs and approaches, the imperative to design the community college of the future is directly at hand. The task is to plan intelligently for these new CEC's so that their mission and their structures, faculty, and programs are in synchrony.

Not every community college should abandon its more traditional collegiate programs, particularly those that remain vibrant. Some institutions may decide to divide into two separate entities—a collegiate provider and a community service center—as dozens have already done. As community colleges shift to comprehensive community education centers, they must continue to meet the needs of the community.

Clearly, for the majority of America's community colleges, careful planning for the metamorphosis seems a necessity. ∎

REFERENCES

Boone, E. 1992. Community-Based Programming. *Community College Review* 20(3): 8-20.

Cohen, A. and F. Brawer. 1987. *The Collegiate Function of Community Colleges.* Jossey-Bass.

Cohen, A. and F. Brawer. 1996. *The American Community College* (3rd ed.). Jossey-Bass.

Commission on the Future of Community Colleges. 1988. *Building Communities: A Vision for a New Century.* American Association of Community Colleges.

Doucette, D. 1993. What Presidents Need to Know About the Impact of Networking. *Leadership Abstracts* 6, 10. (ERIC Document Reproduction Service No. ED 367 433).

Eaton, J. 1992. The Coming Transformation of Community Colleges. *Planning for Higher Education* 21(1): 1-7.

Eaton, J. 1994. *Strengthening Collegiate Education in Community Colleges*. Jossey-Bass.

Gleazer, E. 1980. *The Community College: Values, Visions, and Vitality*. American Association of Community Colleges.

Griffith, M. and A. Connor. 1994. *Democracy's Open Door: The Community College in America's Future*. (Portsmouth, NH) Boynton/Cook.

Hankin, J. 1992. Moving Your Institution into the 21st Century. *Community, Technical, and Junior College Journal* 62(4): 36-40.

Harkavy, I. and J. Puckett. 1992. Universities and the Inner City. *Planning for Higher Education* 20(4): 27-33.

Harlacher, E. and J. Gollattscheck. 1992. Building Learning Communities. *Community College Review* 20(3): 29-36.

Hendley, V. 1994. Building Communities: As the AACC/Kellogg Beacon Project Draws to an End, Participants Look to the Future. *Community College Times* 6(14): 1, 6.

Irish, G. 1980. Reaching the Least Educated Adult. In G. Darkenwald and G. Larson (eds.), *Reaching Hard-to-Reach Adults*. New Directions for Continuing Education No. 8: 39-53. Jossey-Bass.

Mawby, R. 1992. The Role of the Community College in the Decade of the Community. *Community College Review* 20(3): 21-25.

Mead, L. 1992. *The New Politics of Poverty: The Nonworking Poor in America*. Basic Books.

Mittelstet, S. 1994. A Synthesis of the Literature on Understanding the New Vision for Community College Culture. In G. Baker (ed.), *A Handbook on the Community College in America*. Greenwood Press.

Parnell, D. 1990. *Dateline 2000: The New Higher Education Agenda*. American Association of Community and Junior Colleges.

Pearpoint, J. and M. Forest. 1990. Beat the Street: An Urban Literacy Program. *Convergence: An International Journal of Adult Education* 23: 71-84.

Perkins, C., P. Powell, D. Seyler, S. Trachtenberg, and L. Tyree. 1984. What America Will Need From its Community Colleges by the Year 2000. *Community and Junior College Journal* 55(1): 36-40.

Pincus, F. 1994. How Critics View the Community College's Role in the 21st Century. In G. Baker (ed.), *A Handbook on the Community College in America*. Greenwood Press.

Richardson, R. and L. Bender. 1987. *Minority Access and Achievement in Higher Education*. Jossey-Bass.

Roueche, J., L. Taber, S. Roueche, and Associates. 1995. *The Company We Keep: Collaboration in the Community College*. Community College Press.

Sanchez, A. 1994. Trends as Opportunities: Community Colleges Will Need to Re-engineer Their Organizations. *Community College Times* 6(14): 2.

Taber, L. 1995. ERIC Review: Collaboration as a Vehicle for Community College Facilities Development. *Community College Review* 23(3): 73-86.

III. Facilities for Tomorrow

*Universities must become better
guardians of their academic villages, and
maintain three essential elements.*

Restoring the Values of Campus Architecture

Werner Sensbach

I t has been said that campus architecture is too important to be left to architects. Whether pointing an accusatory finger at design professionals or calling for a more passionate involvement by campus leaders in shaping their learning environment, the observation hints that all is not well with campus architecture.

It is no secret that numerous college buildings constructed in the past 40 years in the United States have torn the delicate fabric of traditional campus design and, despite the passage of time, have remained unloved

---

Werner Sensbach was director of facilities planning and administration at the University of Virginia from 1965 to 1991. Educated at the University of Heidelberg and the architecture school at the University of Karlsruhe, he also has an M.S. in urban planning from the University of North Carolina, Chapel Hill. He practiced in school and college architecture in upstate New York and did urban planning for Columbia, South Carolina and Roanoke, Virginia before going to the University of Virginia, where he has also taught courses in campus design and urban planning. He is a member of this journal's editorial advisory board. All illustrations are by Mr. Sensbach.

intruders. To many trained observers a large number of the modern, technically advanced buildings erected at American colleges and universities in recent decades have caused a loss of aesthetic and academic architectural values that once accounted for a sometimes exquisite ambiance in the U.S. academic environment.

How has this happened? How can universities restore the special values of campus architecture?

Nearly two thousand years ago, the Roman architect Vitruvius wrote that architecture should provide firmness, commodity, and delight. It is the definition of "delight" that still troubles us today. This is especially so on college campuses. Many who try to give voice to what it is that brings delight in a building or an arrangement of buildings may mention the design, the placement on the site, the choice of building materials, the ornamentation, or the landscaping. But mostly it's just a feeling, or a sense that things are arranged just right, or a sensation of pleasure that comes over us. So academics, like nearly everyone else, often are unsure when planning for new campus construction about what is likely to be delightful.

Although much of the American public has long held dear to its heart college campuses and regarded them as small, ideal communities with handsome stone buildings enclosing lovely green spaces, neither college administrators and professors nor architects and art historians have paid much scholarly attention to the peculiar aesthetic needs of university environments. When Paul Venable Turner wrote his book *Campus: An American Planning Tradition* in 1984, he was surprised at how little had been written about the design and architecture of colleges and universities, even though the United States has 3,400 colleges while most other advanced nations have only a few dozen. We simply have not developed in the United States a sensibility, a vocabulary, a body of principles, an aesthetic for campus architecture.

Neither scholars nor architects have paid much attention to the peculiar aesthetic needs of university environments.

In addition, in the past half century we have come to put great faith in the professional classes. We obey the advice of lawyers, physicians, scientists, and engineers—and architects—almost without question. This appears to be changing, but we are still reluctant to challenge "experts." The professionals increasingly speak in their own language, which can be intimidating. Very often, the design committee of a university is subjected to a professional architectural rhetoric that leaves them feeling lost and scratching their heads as they listen to metaphoric manipulation that speaks of bilateral symmetry, paradoxical pastiches, canonical diagonals, ironic references, deep structure, and design messages to the future. As Alexander Pope observed, "He gains all points who pleasingly confounds, surprises, varied and conceils the bounds." Knee-deep in ar-

chitectural jargon and hyperbole, not many university building committees dare to admit they have understood little of the linguistic pyrotechnics surrounding the addition of a new building on campus.

Good campus architecture requires knowledgeable, caring patrons, administrators, deans, and leading faculty and alumni who can guide the professional architects. Without enlightened patronage, many outside professionals can too easily go astray.

Even a superficial glance at the interior of most campuses reveals a break between the small scale of the pre-1950 buildings and the massive scale of the newer structures. The self-referential, fortress-like, nearly windowless, and often faceless structures of the past few decades that have muscled their way into the university architectural context are visually disconcerting. Some modern architects, by abandoning ornament, have felt a need to turn their whole building into an ornament, giving rise to some egregious and faddish forms. The importance of academic and social interaction on a college campus seems to have gotten lost. Many of the newer structures ignore the prior presence of their architectural neighbors and resist integration into the campus fabric; and they appear interchangeable with modern buildings anywhere else in the country.

Restoring control

In my view, America's colleges and universities—and especially their physical planners—need three things to become better architectural patrons. One is a renewed sense of the special purpose of campus architecture. A second is an unswerving devotion to human scale. The third is a sense of the uncommon and particular aesthetic—the delight—that a college or university campus demands.

A surprisingly large sector of the American public has conceded a special purpose to higher education. Usually situated in sylvan settings, away from the heart of commerce and manufacturing, college campuses have provided a special place for those engaged in the earnest pursuit of basic or useful knowledge, for young people devoted to self-improvement, and for making the country smarter, wiser, more artful, and more able to deal with competitor nations.

Therefore, college and university campuses have a distinct and separate purpose, as distinct as the town hall and as separate as a dairy farm. For most students the four to seven years spent in academic pursuits on a university campus are not only an important period of maturing from adolescence to adulthood but also years of heightened sensory and creative ability, years when the powers of reasoning, feeling, ethical delineations, and aesthetic appreciation reach a degree of sharpness as never before. During college years, young minds absorb impressions that often last for a lifetime: unforgettable lectures, noisy athletic contests, quiet hours in a laboratory or library, jovial dormitory banter, black-robed commencements, encounters with persons of radically different views, the rustle of leaves, transfigured nights. The American college campus serves superbly as an example of Aristotle's idea of the good urban community as a place "where people live a common life for a noble end."

No architect should be permitted to build for academe unless he or she fully appreciates that his or her building is an educational tool of sorts. New buildings should add to the academic ambiance and enrich the intellectual exchanges and solitary inquiries. They should never be a mere personal statement by the architect or a clever display of technical ingenuity or artistic fashion.

Good campus architecture is necessarily subordinate and integral. New structures should be thoughtful, artful and handsome but fitting and modest. No planner or president should ever hire a world-famous or "hot" architect just to have one of "his" buildings decorate the campus, though even great institutions like Harvard (with Corbusier) and Cornell (see illustration 1) have fallen into this status-seeking desire.

Scale: the critical element

In a letter to L.W. Tazewell in 1805 Thomas Jefferson wrote:

> The greatest hazard for new colleges will be their overbuilding themselves. Large buildings are always ugly, inconvenient, exposed to accident of fire. . .A small building for the school and lodging for each professor is best. . .connected by covered ways out of which the rooms of students should open. . .In fact an university should not be a building but a village.

That each campus should be an "academical village" was one of Jefferson's finest architectural insights. Higher learning is an intensely personal enterprise, with young scholars working closely with other scholars, and students sharing and arguing about ideas, religious beliefs, unusual facts, and feelings. A human scale is imperative, a scale

Illustration 1. "Signature" buildings create an uneasy alliance with the older structures on campus, as this addition at Cornell University shows.

Illustration 2. Harvard's "Yard," built in colonial times, is typical of the semi-enclosed pedestrian spaces that have become the hallmark of American campus architecture.

that enhances collegiality, friendships, collaborations on research.

To a remarkable extent, American colleges and universities have followed Jefferson's advice, not just in the semi-enclosed intimacy of Harvard Yard (see illustration 2) and famous "lawn" design of Jefferson's University of Virginia but also in 19th and 20th century campuses, even in urban areas. With Rockefeller largess, the University of Chicago built quadrangles in south Chicago. In 1884 Temple University erected an enclave in a working class neighborhood in northeastern Philadelphia to provide a "street car college" alternative to the artistocratic University of Pennsylvania that Benjamin Franklin helped start. McKim, Mead, and White, fresh from work at the University of Virginia, constructed a whole new campus

in upper Manhattan for Columbia University that had Italianate baronial style and density but maintained a human scale with largely enclosed green spaces. Elsewhere in New York City, the citizens built free-tuition CCNY and Brooklyn College for future intellectual leaders; and to this day Brooklyn College is a charming oasis in a crowded neighborhood. And in California, the post-war University of California at Santa Cruz tried to create a human-scale, village-like atmosphere at a campus designed for 15,000 or so students.

One of the continuing debates in campus architectural circles is about the appropriate style for a campus: Gothic, Greco-Roman, Georgian, 19th-century stone, or modern. Is there a proper building style for colleges?

Well, Jefferson designed Virginia's build-

Illustration 3. Style is often a reflection of values. Thomas Jefferson's University of Virginia emulated the architecture of democratic Greece and republican Rome, whose values he revered.

ings in a neo-classical style to reflect the values of democratic Greece and republican Rome. (See illustration 3.) But Yale, in the late 19th century, tore down its colonial brick dormitories to replace them, under the influence of John Ruskin's theories, with the "only proper, Gothic style;" and numerous other universities also decided that the medieval cloister was a more appropriate style for semi-reclusive scholars. In 1922 the University of Colorado adopted an Italian hill-town style using rose-colored sandstone from the nearby Rocky Mountains and red tile roofs to reflect its location in the foothills of the Rockies.

Scale, not style, is the essential element in good campus design.

A favorite of architectural explorers is Rice University in Texas. The architectural firm of Cram, Goodhue, and Ferguson, having successfully employed a soaring Gothic style at Princeton and West Point, invented a wholly new style during a Mediterranean cruise by Cram. Ralph Adams Cram reports in his autobiography, "I reassembled all the elements from southern France and Italy, Dalmatia, the Peloponnesus, Byzantium, Anatolia, Syria, Sicily, and Spain and set myself the task of creating a measurable new style." To his credit, Cram succeeded in combining these far-flung influences into a creditable and visually pleasing college style. The Rice campus, in the words of biologist Julian Huxley, who taught at Rice from 1912 to 1916, "is an extraordinary spectacle, as of places in a fairy story."

I believe the style of the campus buildings is important; but style is not so important as the village-like atmosphere of all the buildings and their contained spaces. University leaders must insist that architects they hire design on a warm, human scale. Scale, not style, is the essential element in good campus design. Of course, if an inviting, charming campus enclosure can be combined with excellent, stylish buildings so much the better.

Possibly the most instructive and inspir-

Illustration 4. Eero Sarrinen's design for the Cranbrook Schools and Academy of Art in Michigan is a brilliant example of an urban, modern version of the traditional academic village.

ing example of 20th-century college architecture was created by the Finnish-born architect and city planner Eliel Saarinen in the 1930s at the Cranbrook Academy of Art in Bloomfield Hills, Michigan, where Saarinen was director. Saarinen combined Bauhaus modernity, traditional building materials, superb urban design, landscaping, sculpture, and the uniquely American idea of a college campus to compose a contemporary academic village. (See illustration 4.) In the words of the architectural critic Wolf von Eckart,

> Saarinen achieved unity by linking buildings in a web of walkways, passages, courts, terraces, stairs, and walks. He invites us to stroll in this compact, intricate, almost medieval townscape. At the end of each vista, a sculpture or other

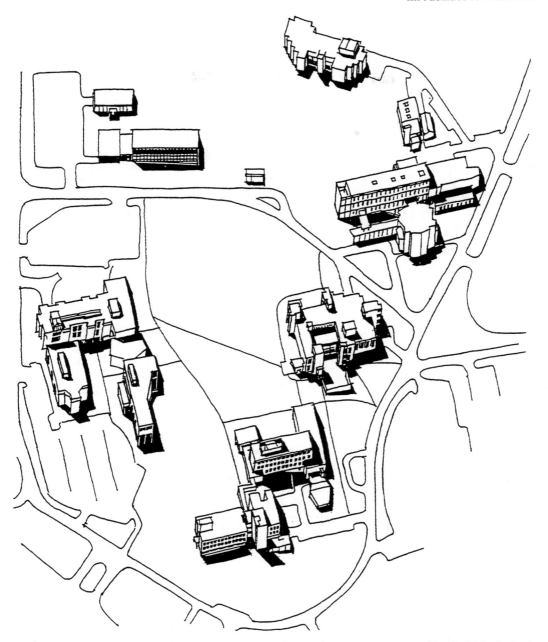

Illustration 5. Even with fairly good individual buildings, as at the University of Hartford, the lack of respect for traditional campus forms and spaces inhibits the sense of an academic environment.

point of interest draws us from one place to the next. Cranbrook's crescendo is the classic grand peristyle. . .with fountains in front and back, splashing Swedish sculptor Carl Milles' sensuous bronzes.

A campus that has handsome individual buildings but does not have a tidy web of buildings, relatively enclosed spaces, and a village-like human scale seems uninviting, cold, haphazard. (See illustration 5.) But even a campus that has a melange of building styles, as at Princeton, but is reasonably well assembled, can be alluring and conducive to important, cooperative academic work. Miami of Ohio doesn't have a single outstanding piece of architecture but is one of the country's most beautiful campuses, with a memorable ambiance. And UCLA, in the populated area just west of Beverly Hills,

The village-like university campus is a unique American architectural invention.

with eight parking garages at the campus edges, has a delightful, semi-tropical pedestrian quality despite its high-rise buildings and lack of distinguished individual buildings.

The enigma of delight

As I said earlier, the third imperative for campus planners, the special aesthetic of campus architecture, or the element of delight, is the hardest to define. It is the residue that is left after you have walked through a college campus, a sense that you have been in a special place and some of its enchantment has rubbed off on you. It is what visitors feel as they enjoy the treasures along the Washington Mall, or others feel after leaving Carnegie Hall, Longwood Gardens in southeastern Pennsylvania, Chartres Cathedral, the Piazza San Marco in Venice, or the Grand Canyon.

On a college campus the delight is generated by private garden spaces to converse, by chapel bells at noon or on each hour, by gleaming white columns and grand stairways, by hushed library interiors, by shiny gymnasiums and emerald playing fields, by poster-filled dormitory suites, by a harmony of windows and roofs, and by flowering trees and diagonal paths across a huge lawn. The poet Schiller once said that a really good poem is like the soft click of a well-made box when it is being closed. A great campus infuses with that kind of satisfaction.

Campus facilities planners need to be sure that the architects they choose are able

to incorporate surprise, touches of whimsy, elegance, rapture, and wonder into their constructions. This special campus aesthetic is definitely not a frill. It is what graduates remember decades after they have left the college, and what often prompts them to contribute money to perpetuate the delight. It is what captures high school juniors and their parents in their summer pilgrimages by automobile to numerous college campuses to select those two or three institutions to which they will apply.

The importance of guidelines

I think the best way to preserve the peculiar values of the American college campus is through a three-pronged effort.

The first is to recognize that the village-like university campus is a unique American architectural creation. No other nation has adopted the "academical village" as an architectural and landscaping form, though the ancient Oxbridge colleges came close.

Academic leaders should become more knowledgeable about the distinctiveness of their garden communities and more proud of and assertive about maintaining the values of this inventive form.*

Second, universities should have a broadly representative and expert blue-ribbon committee to watch over all new construction, not leave it to the vice president for administration, a facilities planner, or a trustee committee. The campus environment should be guarded and enhanced as carefully as the quality of the faculty.

Third, each college and university should draw up a set of design guidelines to help it become a patron who can list what is essential in its campus architecture. These guidelines will differ from campus to campus, but nearly all institutions should include concern for the three fundamentals: academic

---

* "The American campus possesses qualities and functions different from those of any other type of architecture or built environment. . . .It is like a city. . .But it is not exactly a city; it requires a special kind of physical coherence and continuity." Turner, *Campus: An American Planning Tradition,* p. 304.

Illustration 6. At Yale, Eero Saarinen's Morse-Stiles colleges created an intimate, medieval-like enclosure at the edge of a campus facing a commercial street.

purpose, human scale, and a special campus aesthetic. Architects can design more effectively and sympathetically if they understand the expectations of the college.

To be more specific, let me list what I think are the kind of design guidelines that universities should have in place.

> # *The campus environment should be guarded and enhanced as carefully as the quality of the faculty.*

1. New campus buildings should be subordinate to the campus spaces in which they participate, be they quadrangles, malls, or streets.

2. There should be a hierarchy of spaces, from large to successively smaller units. Likewise, buildings should have a hierarchy of size; no tall buildings should be placed directly among smaller ones.

3. Campus spaces should be thought of as outdoor rooms, in which buildings are the walls, lawns and walkways the floor, and trees and sky the ceiling. Each space should be considered a place of destination as well as a space to pass through. (See illustration 6.)

4. To maintain a human scale, the ability of the human eye to recognize objects and activities should be respected. Since the eye can recognize facial expressions up to a distance of 40 feet and faces at 80 feet, but cannot identify most objects beyond 450 feet, intimate campus spaces should not be wider than 80 feet across, and civic spaces should not be larger than 450 feet across. Monumental spaces require 3,500 feet or more across.*

5. A pedestrian precinct must be preserved, with only smaller buildings in the precinct. Larger building volumes should be set back from the pedestrian precinct to avoid overwhelming scale, giant shadows, and blinding reflections from large building facades.

6. "Signature" buildings are discouraged. All new construction should be in some ways harmonious with the rest of the campus architecture through the use of scale, fenestration, materials, design, roof, or other uniting elements.

7. The landscape should be treated with as much respect as the buildings. The choice of trees, shrubs, flowers, and ground covers should be employed expertly to enhance coherence, create vistas, and provide delight. "Prettifying" landscape scenes in a manner more appropriate to a private home should be avoided.

---

* A useful guide, with delightful drawings, is Paul Spreiregen, *Urban Design: The Architecture of Towns and Cities* (McGraw-Hill, 1965).

8. Avoid "dead" walls. Light and shadow should be introduced in the design of the exteriors of the building.

9. Symbolic architecture is welcome. Columns, arched entrance ways, covered walks, fountains, ramps, and stairs should enrich the architectural environment of the university.

10. The visual sensations of scholar-pedestrians should be the ultimate measurement of design satisfaction.

The visual sensations of scholar-pedestrians should be the ultimate measurement of design satisfaction.

This list of desiderata could be doubled. And it might be modified to reflect the climatic setting, urban proximity, and institutional mission of your own college or university. But each institution should have in place a set of architectural guidelines so that architects unfamiliar with the unique requirements of campus architecture do not violate the values of this distinctive American creation.

American campus architecture is too important to be left to architects. ∎

Students need a place to hang out.

Making College a Great Place to Talk

Ray Oldenburg

Two problems especially seem to be plaguing the nation's colleges and universities. One is the so-called "crisis in community," manifesting itself in rising campus crime rates, sexual harassment, ethnic and racial hostilities, dormitory and other property damage, substance abuse, apathy, and a decline in civility (Carnegie Foundation 1990).

The other problem is that higher education's teaching process is said to be yielding a faulty product. Curriculum changes, increased tutoring, new science labs, and bigger libraries seem to have accomplished little. Colleges therefore need to revitalize their learning community, bringing persons of all kinds together more often, and they need to find a way to increase learning around and outside the classrooms so that the campus ambiance is a more intellectual one.

Ray Oldenburg is professor of sociology at the University of West Florida in Pensacola. A graduate of Mankato State University with a Ph.D. from the University of Minnesota, he taught at Minnesota and the University of Nevada before joining the West Florida faculty. He is the author of articles on urban and informal public life and *The Great Good Place: Cafes, Coffee Shops, Community Centers, Beauty Parlors, General Stores, Bars, and Hangouts* (1989).

As a sociologist of community life, I suggest a giant step toward improving both problems can be taken if higher education's leaders and faculty would pay more attention to promoting better talk among students, and if architects and planners would provide better places for students to "hang out." Great conversation, abundant, joyous, earnest talk, is indispensable in academe. Without it, we create diligent students but not intellectuals. As one scholar put it:

> Intellectuals are created only where people feel a commitment to public life and a duty to speak to that public. Dedicated newspapermen may chase down stories and dog down a hot lead; that does not make them intellectuals...Professors, theologians, jurists may follow the exacting standards of their profession, may be honored and revered. But if they feel no moral duty to speak out about public concerns, broad questions which touch a broad public, they are not intellectuals. Only a place with a great public life can create intellectuals. That kind of place makes the ordinary into the extraordinary, the extraordinary into genius (Kahn 1987, 116).

Learning, talk, and hangouts

At the risk of simplifying the learning process, I suggest that learning takes place in three contexts. There is the classroom, where experts impart knowledge to novices and instruct them. There is private reflection: reading and reflection, writing and reflection, imagining and reflection. Call it contemplation, pondering, or thought, it takes place in quiet rooms, quiet libraries, quiet outdoor places, and during quiet walks and travels. And there is conversation with others, especially with one's peers, but also with people who are different: younger, older, richer, poorer, wilder, funnier, more political, less educated. It is often talk that is boisterous, noisy, and heated.

Of the three, the classroom gets inordinate attention for obvious reasons. After all it is the professors' realm. But I submit that conversation, great talk, may be nearly as important as the preoccupation with class-

---

Conversation contributes as much to community and personal growth as it does to learning.

---

room instruction. Most colleges neglect to plan adequately for informal discussions, for hangouts, for gathering places on campus. European exchange students I encounter often register disappointment with American university students because they appear to be so poor at intellectual discussions and debates and lack an appetite for them. I'm reminded of Ralph Waldo Emerson's famous essay on conversation, in which he laments Americans' failure to avail themselves of the "power of their companions" (1932). Participating in a superb conversation is like reading a fine novel or essay, so good hangouts are as vital to colleges as a good library.

I recall one class I taught in research methods, which met in a room across the hall from a student lounge. It also met right after the lunch hour. Students would gather on their own an hour early, bringing sandwiches with them, to discuss their assignments and my course's subject matter. At mid-term time, one young man informed me, to my chagrin, that he was learning more in the lounge than in my class. At the end of the term, the grades in this class were higher than those I usually give; this student group really comprehended the material better then most. Too many campuses do not tap into the power of one's companions. The auxiliary power of peer discussion, of informal conversation is too important to ignore. .

Articulating what one is learning has real benefits. Talking about the information and ideas strengthens one's grasp of it while putting the grasp to a test. Can a student clearly state the case? Can she defend it against critics, and answer questions relating to it? And listeners not only test; they supplement, offering illustrations, personal experiences, other sources, embellishments, as well as an occasional *bon mot* or witticism. They encourage the learner by their very willingness to talk about the subject in detail.

Woodrow Wilson, when he was president of Princeton wrote:

> The real intellectual life of a body of undergraduates, if there be any, manifests itself, not in the classroom but in what they do and talk of and set before themselves as their favorite objects between classes and lectures. You will see the true life of a college...where youths get together and let themselves go upon their favorite themes—in the effect their studies have upon them when no compulsion of any kind is upon them, and (when) they are not thinking to be called to a reckoning of what they know (Wilson 1909).

I speak, therefore I am

Conversation contributes as much to community and personal growth as it does to learning. Community life is shaped all over the world in hangouts: the French *cafe*, the Arabian coffeehouse, the Italian *taberna*, the German bierstube, the country store of earlier America, the ghetto bar, the well-designed college student union, and the college's fraternities and sororities.

Righteous reformers and dictators have never liked seeing people hanging around on street corners, in ice cream parlors, beer cellars, barber shops, children's playgrounds, and other public places. Our culture seems to disdain the use of time for hanging out, for released conversation and banter. But great hangouts break down social barriers and prejudices, develop one's personality and character, and enrich our understanding of life in all its variety. While formal associations—of law students, of African-American students, of young Republicans, Baptists, or socialists, of chemical engineering professors—tend to narrow and restrict human exchanges, excellent hangouts serve to expand one's association with people of many backgrounds, interests, and viewpoints. The emphasis is on the quality of talk, not on social status, religion, or age. At better hangouts, the charm and flavor of one's personality, irrespective of his or her station in life is what counts. Stories, twinkling eyes, back-slapping, and an ability to laugh and express compassion for troubles are essential, not university degrees or majors. Every topic of discussion is a trapeze for the exercise and display of wit, of style. By emphasizing style over vocabulary, hangout conversation increases the egalitarian values.

Great hangouts also allow college students to try out new personalities and they teach manners of a democratic kind. In the classroom, at campus meetings, or at home, students need to assume an expected role. But hangouts provide freedom from social roles and expected demeanors. In meeting places, those of us who are not singers, comedians, orators, psychologists, political activists, hustlers, or planners may become them. It's a wonderful stage because the audience appreciates amateur actors no matter how bad the act.

Hangouts enforce a democratic etiquette too. One cannot be a bore, an insulter of others (except in jest), an egotist or braggart, or a monopolizer of talk. Whatever interrupts conversation's lively flow is ruinous, be it a horde of barbaric fellow students, angry outbursts, or music turned up too loud (even Bach or Mozart), making talk inaudible. Fellowship has its rules.

In Santa Barbara, California, there is a tavern called "The English Department,"

which is operated by a man who did not get tenure. He has listened to talk in seminars, classrooms, offices, and university meetings, but to him the talk in his tavern is better. "Listen to these people," he said of the students, staff, faculty, and townspeople who were his customers, "they are all interested in what they are saying. There's genuine inquiry here." (The English Department 1982)

Requirements for hanging out

Meeting places off campus are often as important for learning and community as those on campus. While a graduate student at the University of Chicago, Elijah Anderson gradually gained admission to the circle of regulars at a nearby bar and liquor store called Jelly's. The predominantly black bar was not held in high regard, yet to be accepted there one had to be employed, treat other people "right," have a strong character, be of some "count"

College students in the University of Pennsylvania's Houston Hall, one of the oldest student centers in America.

(rather than be "no count" like a pusher), and be interesting to have around. Jelly's gave young Anderson "a chance to be." He wrote, "Other settings, especially those identified with the wider society, with its strange, impersonal standards and evaluations, are not really so important for gaining a sense of personal self-worth as are the settings attended by friends and other neighborhood people." (Anderson 1976, 1)

Hangouts have certain requirements. They should be easy to get to. You shouldn't need an automobile to get there. They are likely to be older structures on campus or near the campus. Students will

---

Great hangouts allow students to try out new personalities.

---

often battle fiercely to get into the older residence halls, to keep a long-time sports saloon from being razed, and to prefer ancient feeding holes ("the tables down at Morey's"). At a recent meeting of university architects, one campus planner told me his sad story of building a modern, well-lit, multi-million dollar student center that the students were boycotting. They detested its "Howard Johnson" ambiance and resented even more the loss of their old, dimly lit haunt. The planner said the old place reminded him of "the catacombs of Domitilla," complete with bad air. But the university students felt the place had character, history, and was uniquely theirs.

Great hangouts are often connected with what Emerson called "our institutions of daily necessity," namely eating and drinking. Growing undergraduates love to munch, graze, and nibble; and college and university students do more drinking than any other category of people of comparable size in the United States. Universities need to pay careful attention to dining halls, snack places, and rathskellers.

Too few campus planners and decision-makers are sufficiently mindful of the rituals

of table talk. Dining halls should have round tables and long tables for group eating and conversation, and have an inviting interior design that encourages students to linger, rather than eat and run. The recent invasion of fast-food franchises and vending machines in academe is destructive of good talk.

The specialness of college places

Civilizations throughout history have built gathering places from public baths, market squares, and river docks to inns, pool halls, and gymnasiums. But since World War II Americans have been building new, sterile, suburban "edge cities" (Fishman 1990; Norris, et.al. 1990; Garreau 1991) and abandoning or tearing down many of the great urban and country hangouts. Men's clubs, lodges, famous saloons, beauty parlors, granges, public playgrounds and sand lots, ice cream parlors and the like are disappearing. Some new suburban developments don't even have sidewalks. We are impoverishing our community life (Scitovsky 1966; Oldenburg 1989), with fewer and fewer places for people to gather.

Colleges and universities, however, are like towns or small cities. They can remain a geographical community. Students eat, sleep, work, drink, study, play, walk, and socialize—all on the same acreage. Unlike the larger society, the American college and university retains the stuff of active community life, of places with lively argument, conversation, and boisterous talk. Campuses can be a little Paris, Vienna, Greenwich Village, or Shanghai, striking all who visit them as a great place to talk, to meet people of many kinds, to experiment with new personas.

But this requires that campus planners, deans, and faculty understand the critical importance of hangouts, great good places to meet, talk, and linger. Colleges should pay greater attention to places for talk: residence hall suites with a common room, student lounges, dining halls and snack bars, bookstores, local taverns and pizza parlors, outdoor cafes, conversation nooks, and gardens outdoors on the campus grounds and indoors too, student centers, generous lobbies in all classroom buildings, the faculty club, conversation

---

Campus planners and architects must understand the critical importance of hangouts.

---

pits in the library, benches in the classroom halls and along outdoor walkways, fraternity and sorority houses, television rooms, and games rooms for Ping-Pong, billiards, and card-playing.

Some years ago I helped plan a student center, and managed to get a room included for playing cards. To my dismay the dean of students installed video games there. So instead of conviviality and repartee the room added to the already excessive individualism and isolation, and became a source of "revenue." Educators would do well to notice how returning alumni love to visit the old hangouts of their student years. Graduates recall the good times and the education they received there.

We assess colleges and universities by many criteria. Higher education probably should add the quality of its student hang-

outs and the strength and exuberance of its community to the criteria. Real intellectuals will ask, "How good is the conversation?" ∎

REFERENCES

Anderson, E. 1976. *A Place on the Corner.* University of Chicago Press.

Carnegie Foundation for the Advancement of Teaching. 1990. *Campus Life: In Search of Community.* Princeton University Press.

Emerson, R. 1932. Table talk. In *Uncollected Lectures of Ralph Waldo Emerson.* William Edwin Rudge.

The English Department 1982. *Playground Daily News.*, 25 November.

Fishman, R. 1990. Megalopolis Unbound. *Wilson Quarterly* 14: 25-45.

Garreau, J. 1991. *Edge City: Life on the New Frontier.* Doubleday.

Kahn, B. 1987. *Cosmopolitan Culture: The Gilt-edged Dream of a Tolerant City.* Atheneum.

Norris, D., E. Delaney, and K. Billingsley. 1990. America's New Cities and the Universities. *Planning for Higher Education* 19 (no. 1): 1-8.

Oldenburg, R. 1989. *The Great Good Place: Cafes, Coffee Shops, Community Centers, Beauty Parlors, General Stores, Bars and Hangouts.* Paragon House.

Scitovsky, T. 1976. *The Joyless Economy.* Oxford University Press.

Wilson, W. 1909. The Spirit of Learning. In *Selected Literary and Political Papers and Addresses of Woodrow Wilson.* vol 1. Grossett and Dunlap, 1925.

*Why colleges must renovate their classrooms,
and how it should be done.*

Classrooms for the 21st Century

Michael Owu

During the past 20 years or so the mix of large lecture rooms, small seminar rooms, and medium-sized classrooms has changed. Professors and students now want to be closer to each other during instruction. Dependence on a chalkboard is being replaced by new audio-visual techniques using film, computer projection, and slide projectors. We now know more about acoustics and lighting. New furniture designs have changed the way we sit. Yet many classrooms in America's colleges and universities were built 35 or 70 years ago and have changed relatively little. Colleges seldom budget for classroom renovations on a regular basis.

The typical undergraduate spends as many as 400 hours a year in classrooms. Of course learning also occurs in faculty offices, but the rooms where students meet with their teachers are central to effective instruction and higher learning. College classrooms deserve more than a half-century-old chalkboard and two dozen old wooden chairs on a bare floor. The time has come to convert antiquated classrooms into warm, attractive arenas that maximize student growth. Modernizing America's college classrooms may be one of the top priorities of the next decade.

Classrooms should be carefully designed to support the teaching style of the better instructors and to reduce distractions to a minimum. Good chalkboards are important, but so are the size and shape of the room, the lighting, the color of the finishes, the sight lines to the board and projection screen, the floor covering, and several other elements. The state of knowledge about classroom design has recently reached a point where campus planners can now assist professors substantially in their teaching efforts.

How can educational planners help institutions modernize their classrooms? After preparing for such renovations at my institution (MIT) and researching the subject for years, I believe there is a seven-step strategy that planners should follow.

1. Conduct a survey and inventory of all teaching spaces.

2. Carry out a utilization study to evaluate how classrooms are currently used, and how they match current teaching requirements.

3. Assess faculty and student requirements and their preferences through interviews and questionnaires.

Michael Owu is a senior planning officer at the Massachusetts Institute of Technology. A graduate of MIT, he has been responsible for administering MIT's classroom renovation program. The author thanks his colleague, Julia Vindasius, who assisted in developing MIT's assessment and procedure.

4. Develop the design criteria for seminars, classrooms, and lecture halls.

5. Calculate estimates for the costs of renovating each of the rooms.

6. Devise a program of renovation, with a financially realistic sequence of improvements.

7. Review regularly the teaching styles, specific program and course enrollments, and college teaching policies to monitor changes in classroom needs on campus.

The classroom inventory

The first step is to conduct a physical survey which counts, measures, and evaluates the physical elements of each teaching space. The survey should include room dimensions, finishes, furniture, room arrangements, conventional equipment, utilities, lighting, window treatment, ventilation, noise level, safety features, and audio-visual equipment.

In addition to these objective measurements, it is useful to assign a rating to each space as a guide to measuring the overall quality of the classroom. In a survey conducted at MIT (Vindasius 1987), a rating

scale of 1 to 5 was used, with the worst rooms for teaching rate 1, the best 5. MIT's survey revealed that 66 percent of the 154 general-purpose teaching spaces were rated 3 or

---

The typical undergraduate spends as many as 400 hours a year in classrooms.

---

below (Figure 1). Most of the worst classrooms were located in buildings built between 1913 and 1937. Most commonly, these classrooms were characterized by a stark, half-century-old environment, with poor lighting, old chalkboards, unsightly finishes, and HVAC systems that were worn, broken, and/or shabby in appearance. But even classrooms built more recently lacked the attention to detail required for effective teaching.

How are the rooms used?

The next step is to conduct a utilization study. Such a study measures the degree to which classrooms are actually used compared to

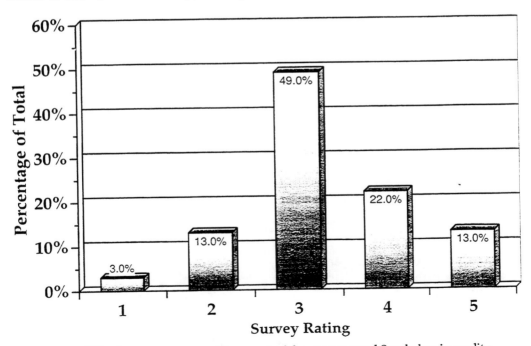

Figure 1. In MIT's classroom survey, 66 percent of the rooms rated 3 or below in quality.

their total possible use. (WICHE has issued a useful manual for calculating classroom utilization rates.) Three indicators should be measured:

- *Scheduling,* which describes the hours in use as a percentage of a 40-hour week;
- *Net utilization,* which describes the initially-assigned occupancy as a percentage of the total capacity of each room;
- *Fullness,* which portrays how "full" a room is when is it occupied by students.

You need to be careful in interpreting the results of the utilization study. You will probably find utilization to be surprisingly low, as we did at MIT. This has several causes. One is the presence of limited-use classrooms such as science laboratories, engineering classrooms, architecture studios, and machine-filled rooms for technology courses.

> *Classroom design has reached a point where planners can now assist professors.*

Another cause is that most faculty prefer teaching in the middle of the day, between 10 a.m. and 3 p.m. and universities often cater to faculty preferences. Also, colleges with an abundance of elective courses are likely to have a low rate of room utilization. And, classrooms located in remote areas and those in very poor condition are likely to be underutilized. Faculty will be reluctant to teach there, and students will not want to attend classes there.

What we found at MIT was that we had too many large classrooms and too few smaller seminar rooms for the mix of courses taught at MIT today. Specifically, half the course-hours taught were in seminar-sized classes with enrollments of fewer than 20 people. Yet only 16 percent of the Institute's classrooms were seminar rooms for 20 or so students. At the other end, nearly one-third of the Institute's classrooms seated 40 to 60 students whereas only 7 percent of our course hours had enrollments of 40 to 60 students.

Generally, there has been a trend to smaller classes in U.S. higher education in the past few decades. However, this trend could be reversed in the 1990s and beyond as very tight finances force colleges to reverse the tendency toward course proliferation and highly specialized, boutique courses with tiny enrollments.

> *We found we had too many large classrooms and too few smaller seminar rooms.*

Interviewing for preferences

The third step is to interview faculty members and students as well as asking them to respond to questions about classroom preferences through conventional survey instruments. Interviews at MIT revealed that both faculty and students had a strong interest in creating warmer, more intimate, and more attractive classroom spaces that promote faculty-student exchanges.

Interviews at other colleges and universities may reveal a desire for terraced lecture halls, better audio-visual equipment, elimination of the pale green walls that seem to be prevalent at some campuses, better chairs, more evening classes, improved display boards, and carpeted, attractive seminar rooms that encourage lively discussions.

Designing tomorrow's classrooms

Fourth, your college will need to develop criteria for the design and renovation of classrooms and lecture halls. This is a very important step that will most likely determine the learning environment for your institution for the next half century.

You will need to display a balance in the design criteria. On the one hand a number of standards can be used as a starting point, such as those employed at the University of California, Santa Cruz (Brase 1988), or Pennsylvania State University (Allen 1991). And architectural experts on office, restaurant, and school design might be consulted. On the other hand, each college or university needs to create its own standards that reflect the needs and preferences of its own faculty, students, and administrators and the institution's traditions and financial ability to make changes.

I believe that classroom design should be grouped into four categories: physical considerations, environmental factors, furniture, and audio-visual equipment.

Each of the four categories of design criteria should satisfy the following four design requirements.

Function. The classroom must be able to function effectively for the type of instruction to be carried out within its walls. A classroom used to teach physics needs to accommodate live demonstrations whereas a classroom used for music performance must have a completely different set of criteria. A general purpose classroom has to be able to satisfy a range of teaching styles.

Focus. The room should focus the student's attention on the instructor, screen, and presentation area. A focused room makes it easier for teachers to convey information, communicate energy and enthusiasm, and elicit questions and challenges. Focus is achieved through an arrangement of architectural elements, proper acoustics and lighting, and the absence of visual distractions.

Flexibility. Because many classrooms have multiple uses, they must be flexible enough to seat 50 students while making a 20-student class seem comfortable in the same room. And most classrooms need to permit lectures as well as slide presentations with note taking. Flexibility is also necessary to accommodate changes in the technology of teaching over the next 20–30 years.

Aesthetics. Attention to aesthetics allows students to enjoy their classroom encounters, and feel like learning. Attractive classrooms lend dignity to the learning process, and announce silently that the cultivation of the mind is a beautiful and dramatic activity. Mean and dingy classrooms—especially if the athletic facilities and art center are handsome—suggest that classroom teaching is a lesser enterprise. Attention to form, line, color,

texture, and variety can be achieved at relatively little additional cost and a tremendous return on the investment.

With these design requirements in mind, planners can work on the four categories of classroom design.

First, physical considerations. Faculty members need to engage students; so raised platforms for the teachers should be avoided, even in the largest lecture halls. Instructional space should be level, or below that of the students.

To improve sight lines and sound transmission, floors should be tiered in all the larger lecture halls. Light-frame construction can be used to build over existing flat floors usually. Ceilings should be not less than ten feet high, and should be angled at the front of the room to better project sound to the rear (Figure 2).

Mean and dingy classrooms suggest that teaching is a lesser enterprise.

Entrance doors should always be located at the rear of the room, not at the front where latecomers can disturb the class in progress. Vision or see-through panels should be installed in all doors to allow students to check whether they have the right class or whether the classroom is in use. The vision panels should be narrow to reduce the spillage of light from the hallway lights during video shows in class. If the doorway cannot be relocated, it may be necessary to reorient the room 90 or 180 degrees during renovations.

Second, environmental factors. Acoustics and lighting have an enormous influence on the classroom experience, but are often neglected in the design of classrooms. Good acoustic design must control the sounds and voices in the room so that they are heard easily and accurately, and it must prevent unwanted background or outside noise from intruding.

In small classrooms modest acoustic treatment may be required. But in medium-sized and larger classrooms good acoustics probably require the introduction of tapered side walls and an angled front wall (Figure 3). There should be acoustically reflective surfaces at the front of the room and acoustically absorbent surfaces at the rear.

The importance of lighting in classrooms cannot be overemphasized.

In rooms of any size, I strongly recommend carpeting to absorb unwanted sounds such as the sound of chairs being moved or feet being shuffled. Anti-static carpeting should be used in rooms that use equipment with magnetic tape and memory. Other sources of unwanted noise—squeaky chair arms, rattling windows—should be identified and fixed or replaced.

As for lighting, its importance for classrooms cannot be overemphasized. Most classrooms at U.S. colleges and universities are lighted horribly, with a few blue-white fluo-rescent panels stuck up on the ceiling. With the desire by faculty and students for a warmer atmosphere and the increased use of overhead, slide, video, and computer projection during classes, classroom lighting design needs far greater attention.

Most important, each student's ability to take notes needs to be maintained at all times. (A light-level of two foot-candles is sufficient for college students.) The best way to achieve this is by using incandescent downlights which can be dimmed over the entire seating area, and a series of additional fixtures for general purpose lighting, chalkboard lighting up front, podium lighting, and special instructional space lighting as needed. A set of incandescent lights over the instructor's area should illumine the chalkboard or science presentation tables. If fluorescent fixtures are used, soft-white bulbs should be used. Recessed fixtures are preferable, and fixtures should be placed at the periphery of rooms as well as at the ceiling center.

Almost as important as the lighting are the lighting controls.

Controls should be simple to use, very clearly labeled, and conveniently located. Usu-

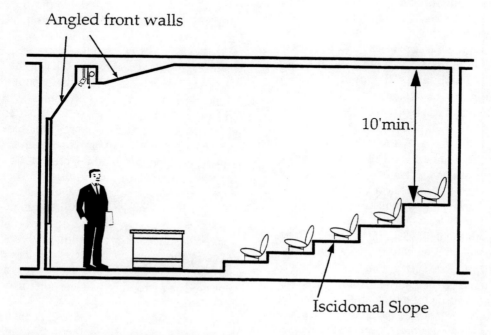

Angled front walls

10'min.

Iscidomal Slope

Figure 2. Research is revealing the ideal classroom design.

ally, controls should be located at room entrance (at the rear), in the projection booth if there is one, and at the instructional space in the front of the room so that the teacher can adjust the lighting. Also, light from outside the room needs to be controlled. Sunlight spilling into the room can wash out projected images, so blackout shades or blinds are imperative.

Then there is the need to control heating and cooling to make students comfortable. Thermostats in the classrooms should keep temperatures at 65–68°F in winter and at 72–74°F in summer. Humidity levels should, if possible, be maintained at close to 50 percent. If there are windows, they should be capable of being opened in spring and fall.

Third, the furniture. I think a college is wise to invest in durable, high-quality furnishings rather than cheaper, plastic chairs and metal tables. Initial costs will be higher, but the payoff in wear, comfort, and aesthetics makes better furniture a smarter choice for the long run.

For larger lecture halls (and even smaller ones) and for seminar rooms, continuous writing surfaces for the students should be used. Tables provide students with more room to spread out their materials and are

> *Chairs should be upholstered and writing arms should be at least 130-square-inches.*

more suitable for open-book examinations. In seminar rooms, oval tables are the most effective. In lecture halls, the tables should be arranged in long concentric arcs facing the instructor, and fixed, upholstered tilt-swivel chairs should be used behind the curved tables. In smaller classrooms or seminar rooms, however, fixed seating is a deterrent to group activity and flexible use. In medium classrooms tablet-arm chairs are almost obligatory, but the chairs should be upholstered and tablets should be large (at least 130-square-inches in size). A minimum seat of 21 inches should be specified. And several

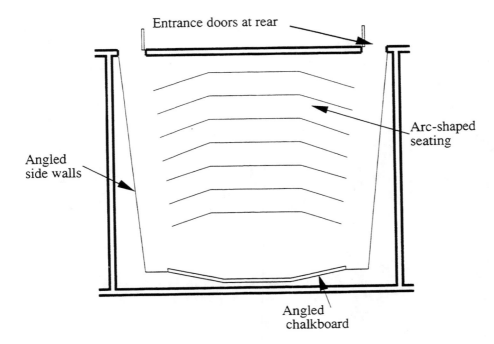

Figure 3. Entry, acoustics, and lighting are very important.

tablet-arm chairs for left-handed students should be in each classroom with movable chairs. The wheeled chairs should have book storage under the seats.

Chalkboards should be black for contrast; brown and green chalkboards should be shunned. Preferably the board should be ample, covering most of the forward wall with panels four feet high. In large lecture halls motorized chalkboards, with manual overrides, should be installed. Where audio-visual equipment or computers are used extensively it is better to install white marker boards with water-based markers.

Classrooms also should have a bulletin board near the entrances-exits, and have coat racks where students can hang their coats during class. Unobtrusive, lockable, built-in storage units, with cabinets and drawers, should be present in most classrooms so that overhead projectors, television sets with VCRs, or science equipment can be secured after class.

Fourth, there is the matter of audio-visual equipment, which is increasing rapidly in classrooms presentations. Designers might begin by reading a good book to become familiar with the latest technology, such as that by Jerome Menell (1982) or Robert Simpson (1987). For large lecture halls it is prudent to consult an audio-visual specialist early in your renovations.

There are four types of projectors that are being used currently in classrooms: overhead projectors, slide projectors (35 mm and lantern), movie projectors (16 mm, 35 mm, and 70 mm), and large-screen display systems capable of receiving signals from television, videotapes, laserdiscs, and computers. There are also two projection methods: front-screen, where audience and projector are on the same side of an opaque screen; and rear-screen, where audience and projector are on opposite sides of a rigid, translucent screen. With this complexity, you can understand why an audio-visual specialist is required.

The relationships between screen height, distance to the first row and last row of seats, and optimal viewing angles are all well established for traditional projection methods. But these are based on assumptions about the minimum size of the pictorial image and text. For text displayed from a computer source, however, those same assumptions cannot be

MIT's Boynton Hall, 1968.

accepted because computer text is small and difficult to read.

Computer technology is changing so fast the equipment installed today may well be obsolete in 3–5 years. Planning for that day is challenging; no one can be certain in what direction the industry is moving. But it is wise to accommodate the technological innovations and maintain flexibility by building wiring conduits that can handle future connectivity to cable, computer networks, or an ISDN telephone system.

How much will the changes cost?

The fifth step of the classroom modernization strategy is to develop cost estimates. These estimates are extremely difficult without specific architectural plans and actual rough estimates before they approve substantial classroom renovations. So you need to generate some general costs per square foot for categories of space rather than for individual classroom space. For example, you can use one cost per square foot for all classrooms from 200 to 400 square feet in area, and another for rooms in the 400 to 600 square feet range, rounding the costs out to the nearest $10,000.

Classroom renovation, especially of older classrooms, is seldom inexpensive. For example, at MIT we renovated a 150-seat, 1500-square-foot lecture room that had not received attention since 1933, and that had been described by one faculty member as a "travesty," into a beautiful, paneled, ultra-modern, 21st-century award-winning lecture hall at a cost of nearly $1,000,000. Once used begrudgingly, the room is now full nearly 60 hours a week. But most classrooms can be renovated handsomely for one-tenth that sum.

Next, if the president and trustees agree that the teaching spaces should be made into contemporary and attractive rooms for the crucial work of teaching, you need to begin the renovations. The sequence of the renovations is important. In general, the rooms with the poorest ratings should be modernized first; and renovations should be distributed with one eye on the various constituencies so that no one sector of the university feels neglected. Depending on the money and the space available for moving classes, you will need to schedule about two to five renova-

MIT's Boynton Hall after it was renovated, 1989.

tions a year over 5–10 years. At MIT last year we had an ambitious, six-classroom, $1.9 million renovation program in place.

Are more professors demanding large-screen displays for computer and laserdisc projections?

The last of the seven steps, once the renovation schedule is underway, is to monitor the direction of your college and seek to predict the coming alterations in classroom space that may be required.

Are the institution's enrollments increasing or decreasing? Which departments are losing students and which are gaining majors? Is the financial situation mandating fewer classes under ten students? Is the university inviting more outside speakers and holding more conferences, which necessitate elegant lecture halls? Is there a new program of freshmen seminars being planned so that more college seminar rooms will be needed? Are more professors demanding large screen displays for computer, VCR, and laserdisc projections? You will need to stay on top of these changes and forecast the different classroom implications of these shifts. Close relations with department chairpersons and the best teaching faculty are a great help in this monitoring.

If teaching in the classrooms is the heart of higher education's enterprise, then investment in these classrooms to make them attractive, modern, and highly conducive to learning should be central to any college or university's physical planning. ∎

REFERENCES

Allen, R. 1991. *Design of General Purpose Classrooms and Lecture Halls*. Penn State University-wide Classroom Improvement Committee.

Brase, W. 1988-89. Design Criteria for Effective Classrooms. *Planning for Higher Education* 17 (Fall): 81-91.

Menell, J. 1982. Audiovisual Communications. In *Handbook of Specialty Elements in Architecture*. McGraw-Hill.

Murgio, M. 1986. A Room with a View. *Progressive Architecture*, Sept., 148-153.

Western Interstate Commission on Higher Education. Planning and Management Systems Division. In cooperation with the American Association of Collegiate Registrar's and Admissions Officers. 1971. Section 4. The Development and Education of Institutional Utilization Criteria for Classrooms and Class Laboratories. In *Higher Education Facilities Planning and Management Manuals, Manual Two: Classroom and Class Laboratory Facilities*. WICHE.

Reznikoff, S. 1986. *Interior Graphic and Design Standards*. Whitney Library of Design. Watson-Guptill.

Simpson, R. 1987. *Effective Audio-Visual: A User's Handbook*. Focal Press.

Sommer, R., and H. Olsen. 1980. The Soft Classroom. *Environment and Behavior* 12 (no. 1): 3-6.

Vaughan, T. 1991. Good Teaching Rooms: A Campus Resource. *Academe*, July/Aug., 10-15.

Vindasius, J. 1987. *A Meeting of Minds: An Assessment of Classroom Facilities Needs at MIT*. MIT Planning Office.

Suddenly the design of college residence halls has become a new priority.

New-Wave Student Housing

Earl Flansburgh

Americans have become more deeply concerned about higher quality in higher education. And several studies have shown that residential living can increase the quality of learning. But there are other factors too that suggest that attention to student housing may be one of the most significant matters of the 1990s. Colleges and universities should be planning now for the new demands for improved residential living.

For one, off-campus housing in many areas is getting scarcer and more expensive. On a national scale, U.S. housing starts and apartment construction did not keep pace with family formation in the 1980s. In 1989, for example, there were 2.4 million marriages, according to the National Center for Health Statistics, but only 1.38 million housing starts. With more families competing for housing units, the inevitable inflation has

Earl R. Flansburgh, FAIA, is president of a Boston-based architectural, master planning, and interior design firm. A graduate of Cornell and MIT, he has taught architectural history at Wellesley and design at MIT. His firm has designed more than 300 educational facilities, including a new law library and master plan for Boston College Law School and a residence hall-dining hall at Worcester Polytechnic Institute that recently won the Walter Taylor Award as the best U.S. educational building of the year.

taken place. And families have been competing with students for these units. Landlords, given a choice, will frequently take couples, who are perceived as more stable and quiet, over students, perceived as more disruptive and noisy. The growing problem of off-campus housing is often particularly acute—and time-consuming for students—where the college or university is located in a small town or residential suburb. In cities, the problems of public transportation, safety, and parking, have made off-campus housing less attractive.

Another phenomenon begun in the 1980s is that an increasing number of students want to live on campus. Unlike the 1960s and 1970s, when students often wanted to get away from authority and community, today's students seem to have rediscovered camaraderie and the pleasure of getting to know new and different colleagues.

An additional factor is the intensifying competition for good students. As the applicant pool for traditional undergraduates—and graduate students—has declined, and will continue to decline until the mid-1990s, colleges doing market research have learned that the lack of attractive quarters in which to live is often cited as an important element in college choice. Institutions are being forced to provide better residential spaces to attract and keep the students their faculties want.

Attractive quarters in which to live is often cited as an important element in college choice.

Also, as universities become more diverse in their student population, with more minority students, sons and daughters of Asian and Hispanic immigrants, and foreign students, campuses are rethinking what this requires in student living arrangements, food in the dining halls, and support facilities. Should there be Third World houses, foreign language houses, an international house, and gender-specific housing?

But perhaps the biggest factor compelling a new look at student housing in the 1990s is the revolution in what students do in a dormitory room today as opposed to a decade ago. More about this major change a little later.

Renovate or build?

For all these reasons, and others, colleges and universities should be giving renewed attention to campus residences. But should colleges renovate existing dormitories or build new ones?

The renovation of old residence halls may be desirable if the buildings are well-built, reasonably spacious, and not too old. Renovation may be almost obligatory if the buildings form an integral part of the college's traditions. Sensitive and ingenious renovations can maintain the aesthetics and charm while introducing 21st-century features.

However, it is important to realize that

Figure 1. Founders Hall at Worcester Polytechnic Institute. This award-winning design comprises several residences around a dining hall (at the left). The buildings are broken into separate structures to fit in with the residential nature of the surrounding neighborhood.

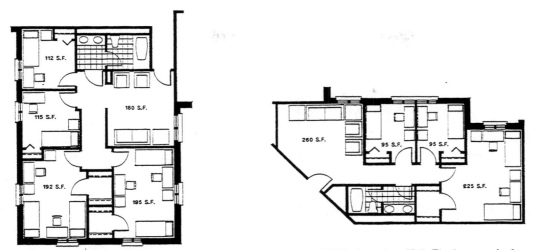

Figure 2. A six-person-suite (left) and a four-person suite at WPI's Founders Hall. The larger suite has two doubles and two singles; the smaller suite has one double bedroom and two single bedrooms.

renovating an old residence hall can approach the cost of new construction, or actually exceed it. Many existing dormitories must be extensively remodeled to be brought up to the same building code as new buildings. Existing residences often do not have adequate access for the handicapped, or fire stair enclosures. Back-up emergency lighting and generators are often antiquated. Also, some older dormitories are constructed of wood which is not adequately fireproofed. If the work also includes the removal of asbestos, renovation costs can be startling.

If a university decides to build, it may believe that hiring an experienced residential building developer will allow them to provide residences for students more economically. Sometimes construction by private developers has been fairly successful. But speculative developers will usually build to standards of quality different from those an educational institution deems appropriate. The college will usually have little control over the design. And the institution's tax-exempt status may be called into question by a private development project. A for-profit developer building on non-profit land may find the project taxed, particularly if the developer owns the building for a period of time. The legal aspects of private building for collegiate use can become exceedingly complicated in some communities.

So it is usually advantageous for a college or university to study seriously the creation of its own new residence halls. Financially it is appealing because such buildings produce revenue that will amortize the mortgage. Residence halls are frequently an attractive gift for affluent and loyal old graduates. Many states also have low-interest bonds that help colleges finance student housing.

It is important to bear in mind, however, that residential housing projects on campus seldom break even for the first three or four years. After the first three or four years, with modest inflation, revenue from student housing will slowly begin to exceed running costs slightly.

I think that a college or university planning for increased excellence in the coming decades should in nearly all cases where renovation is not necessary for strong historic or aesthetic reasons build its own housing for students. Student residential space should reflect the special nature and culture of the institution, and should be used to enhance the quality of total learning on campus.

What kind of residences?

In planning student residences, one of the fundamental questions is how large a group of students should be combined in one facility. There are several opinions on this matter, some based on sociological studies, some based on economics, and others based on long experience. Sometimes the institution's tradition in student housing will argue for a certain size. For instance, Smith College, the noted women's college in western Massachusetts, has a tradition of small houses, so the Friedman House residences our firm built there are tiny townhouses for four students each. Urban universities often have high-rise dormitories.

How large a group of students should be combined in one facility?

My view is that, if land permits, housing students in groups of approximately 200 works best—in terms of student friendships, economics, and human scale. If at all possible residence halls should be limited to four floors of rooms. Higher than that requires elevators, which should be avoided as the primary means of circulation. Circulation of students going to classes is a major problem, especially in the mornings, or at evening meal; elevators cause delays and vandalism because they cannot handle crowds at one time. If you are building for many students, it is best to build multiple structures of 180–200 each.

What about the number of students per room? Most college administrators think that either individual rooms or rooms with two students are preferable. I agree. Rooms with more than two students should be avoided because three or four students in a room makes studying extremely difficult.

A second question for basic unit planning is whether the residence hall will have rooms along a corridor (hotel-style) or suites (several single or double rooms built around a central, shared living space).

Single or double rooms on either side of a corridor is an economical form. But it does little to enhance collegiality, and done properly for students is not quite as frugal as

many believe. What happens with undergraduates, especially males, is that the corridors get used as a common room, or even a playing field, for "corridor hockey" and other games that energetic young students devise. The hallways thus receive lots of abuse. The carpet on the corridor floors needs to be replaced every three or four years; the corridor walls should be brick to handle hard pounding; and light fixtures should be sturdy. I think corridors should have some windows to the outside too.

A suite is really an apartment without a kitchen, built to accommodate two, four, or six students. They should not be designed for three, five, or seven students because many years of experience and some research have shown that an odd number of students usually isolates individual students while pairs enhance friendship. The bathroom in a suite should be divided into two or three spaces, with shower and wash basins separated, to handle peak-hour usage.

Some universities are building residence halls with suites containing small kitchens and dining areas so that the residences can be converted if need be to conventional rental apartments, open to tenants who are not part of the university, should student interest in on-campus housing decline sharply. I think that in most cases this is not a good idea. Kitchens are expensive. They attract insects. Keeping them clean in a suite leads to arguments. And kitchens in dorms prevents students from dining together with others and learning from them.

The problem of room size

The size of the student room is always an issue. Students and residence halls administrators want the largest rooms possible; the college's business manager wants the most compact and economical space. As a compromise, most single study-bedrooms should have a net (inside the walls) area of 105 to 115 square feet, or roughly a 9 × 12 layout. Two-person rooms should have a net area of 190 to 210 feet. These sizes are compact, but have space enough for some flexibility of layout. Some colleges or very budget-con-

Figure 3. The Friedman House at Smith College—townhouses for four students each—were tucked into spaces among existing buildings in the residential neighborhood.

scious state universities build smaller rooms, but this often results in inflexibility of layout, student complaints, and a damaging of the walls; and it actually provides only limited dollar savings.

If anything, student rooms for the future should be larger. Nothing has altered the way our society operates—and the way stu-

dents work—as much as the personal computer. Computers have transformed the uses of dormitory rooms. This requires colleges to rethink the space and facilities students need.

Compact computers have had an impact on dormitory rooms in two major ways. They demand additional space for the com-

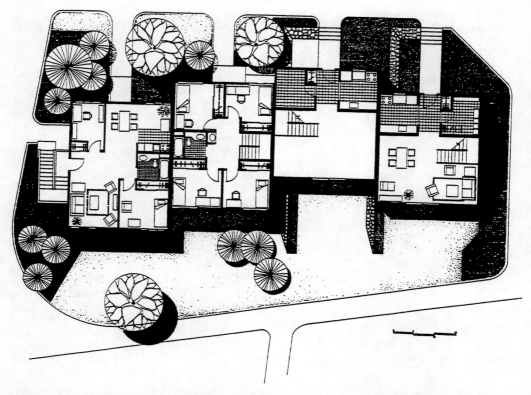

Figure 4. Floor plan of Smith College's Friedman House. Note the ample common room space.

puter and printer and they contribute to a significant increase in the needs for electrical power and outlets. The screen, computer terminal, and printer occupy an area of approximately two feet by four feet, not including space for the seated student. Student rooms for the future need to be designed with a computer and printer in mind.

The presence of the computer, and other new electrical items, also mandate that new residence halls be designed for a significant increase in electrical power. Students today arrive on campus with stereo systems, small television sets, VCR's, hair dryers, electric shavers, radio/alarm clocks, portable irons, coffee makers, lamps, and even toaster ovens or microwave units, as well as computers and printers. Yet the current electrical code requirements for a bedroom indicate only one duplex outlet for each wall. This is barely sufficient for single-occupant rooms. For two-student rooms, the code minimum number of outlets should be dou-

bled so that there are four duplex outlets for each student. In addition, telephones should be installed in each room, and cable TV hookups are now almost obligatory for new residence halls.

The widespread use of computers by students also means that the residence halls need to be designed to handle power interruptions. It is not uncommon to have power halted by an event in one of the rooms. To contain the power disturbance so that it affects only one suite and not the entire dormitory, a small circuit breaker box should be installed directly adjacent to the entrance of each suite. This will ensure that a short circuit in one room or suite does not "dump" all the computers on the floor.

Handling noise

The popularity of rock-and-roll music, often played at high volume, requires that colleges pay greater attention in the new residence halls to sound muffling. In planning dormitories and residence halls, it is important to provide as much acoustical isolation as possible. That is not easy.

The physics of acoustics is relentless. A wall between two spaces with a one-inch-square opening or the equivalent of a one-inch-square opening, where air can filter from one space to another, has 50% of the effectiveness as a solid, airtight wall. Therefore, a good starting point in acoustic isolation is to make sure that there are no openings between one space and the adjacent space. That means no openings under doors, no pipe openings in a wall, and no duct openings between two spaces.

When two spaces are adjacent and there is no possibility of air transmission, there is still a problem with the vibration of the common partition or floor. In other words, a student who turns a high-fidelity system up to 60 or 80 decibels will vibrate the walls, floor, and ceiling of the space, which in turn will vibrate the spaces next door, above, and below. This vibration of surfaces causes sound transmission. One way to mitigate that sound transmission is to increase the mass of the floor, walls, and ceiling. Higher mass allows less substantial vibration, and therefore less transmission of sound.

In addition to mass isolations, vibration of the walls of adjoining spaces can be diminished by ensuring that there is limited or no structural connection between the wall in the space with the student and the wall in the adjoining residence unit. This means that the studs that hold up the finish side of the partition in the rooms with the music do not touch the studs in the finish wall treatment of the wall in the adjoining room. This system, called "staggered studs," reduces the problem of sound transmission by isolating one space from another.

The third method of limiting sound transmission is through planning. This means that you do not place the room that is likely to have the greatest amount of noise, such as a living room, next to a room where quiet is desired, i.e., a bedroom, but rather next to another space that is likely to be noisy, i.e., a living room. So in planning dormitories and residence halls, living rooms are placed adjacent to each other and bedrooms are placed adjacent to each other wherever possible. This type of preventive design reduces the amount of disturbance from one space to the next.

In fact, acoustic isolation is best achieved by embracing all three of these processes of wall, floor and ceiling mass, of isolation, and of planning.

Non-living spaces

For any college desirous of encouraging exchanges among its students, the design of common spaces, or lounges, is a major matter. Residence halls usually have two kinds

---

Computers have transformed the use of dormitory rooms.

---

of lounges for informal social interaction. One is the "destination" lounge, the large space adjacent to the front door of the building or a closed space on each floor of the hall where students may gather. The other is the "circulation" lounge, an attractive space to intercept students along the corridor or next to the stairway or elevator. Circulation lounges on each floor are particularly important in buildings with rooms along a corridor instead of suites with a common living room attached to the room groupings.

Too often lounges are cold and utilitarian and the furniture tacky. To be sure, lounges need to be durable because of hard use. But they should also be home-like. The large entry lounge to a residence hall especially should be handsome and inviting, with plants, rugs, and excellent furniture. For students it is a major place to meet and talk.

Another common room in most contemporary residence halls is the laundry room, which on some campuses has become a new social center. Students today prefer to do their own laundry. Given the semi-social nature of the use of this facility, colleges should try to locate the laundry room adjacent to the "pub" or the vending machine area, and seating should be provided. An important design element of the laundry, pub, or vending machine areas is the acoustic isolation of the noisy activities from student work and sleeping rooms.

The design of dining halls is of immense importance.

A third common room that is gaining popularity fast, and will probably be a fixture of the 1990s, is the weight room. Physical fitness, weight control, and aerobic exercise are no longer only for athletes. I think each 200-student residence should provide for a weight room with appropriate exercise equipment. Here again sound isolation is important in the construction of these spaces.

A fourth kind of common room is the television lounge. Television has become a ubiquitous part of our daily life. But the television rooms of the 1970s residence halls need to be replaced with large TV screens in the lounge spaces, without separate TV rooms. Today most students have small TV sets for their rooms, and casual viewers stay in their own rooms. But large groups of students still gather for elections, extraordinary news happenings, major athletic events, and other special moments, and this requires a TV screen in a lounge area for dozens of students.

The storage issue

Since dormitory rooms, for economic reasons, are relatively small, residence halls of the future need to provide more storage space in the building than in the past. Not only do students now need a place to store out-of-season clothing, but they also need storage space for bicycles, skis, roller skates, knapsacks, climbing equipment, and similar items. Residence halls are home to students nine months of the year, and their homes contain more possessions than in the past. Failure to provide adequate central storage space means that students construct their own makeshift forms of storage in their rooms or in the outside hallways.

Bicycles have become especially popular. Residence halls of tomorrow will need bicycle racks near the entrance of each dormitory so that students can have easy deposit and access. Providing shelter from rain or snow for the bicycles next to resident halls' entrance is a considerable design problem.

Where to eat?

The dining hall, of course, is a very important space in student life. Many of us remember impassioned discussions over a meal in college as we debated the way we would settle world issues, interpret an author's writings, or determine what is reality. Ideas get shaped and lifelong friendships are made in college dining halls and pubs. Their design is of immense importance as colleges seek to enhance out-of-class learning and unite resident and commuter student populations.

Should a college have one huge dining hall? It depends on the size of the college. Small colleges under 1000 students probably should. Larger colleges and universities cannot. Huge, cavernous dining halls should be avoided; smaller ones that seat 200 or so students are preferable because they encourage intimate exchanges. (Each 200-seat dining room serves roughly 400 students.) Smaller dining rooms are now possible because of the increasing use of a central preparation kitchen on campus, with warming kitchens in each dining hall.

Everything affordable should be done to make the dining halls not only a warm, attractive place to eat but also a pleasant place to have vigorous discussions, meet fellow students, and contemplate significant issues. Window treatment to provide lovely views needs attention. The aesthetics of the interior, the acoustics, and especially the lighting in the hall are design elements that require artful and sensitive handling. The table groupings should have variety, from small tables for two to one or two long tables for a team, sorority, or chemistry class; but many tables should seat six to eight students to encourage new acquaintances and group discussions.

Today's students frequently "graze," or eat small meals at odd hours from early morning to midnight. This has led some universities to install fast-food franchises in their campuses. While this may be financially helpful, conviviality and good nutrition are often sacrificed. The "pub," as it was called before the national drinking age was raised from 18 to 21, is preferable as a gathering spot for after-hours eating, drinking, and talk. Again, durable, comfortable furniture and a lighting level that encourages intimacy and conversation should be provided for this important, informal gathering place.

Those other spaces

What about apartments for resident advisors, or RA's? Or a large suite for a faculty family? Or classrooms or seminar rooms on the ground floor of the residence hall?

I think that planning a residence hall must include suites for the resident advisors. The sheer animal vitality and emotional turmoil of young students need to be proctored by older, stable students. Since the resident advisors have an ombudsman's role, their suites require a small room for private and often intense conversations.

Faculty suites in student residence halls have not worked well. Faculty are reluctant to accept such living accommodations, and the institution usually needs to provide additional money for the faculty family's "real" home elsewhere. (Faculty apartments adjacent to residence halls work better than those in the dormitory.) Classrooms in the dormitories have a similar record. Residence halls are usually located at the perimeter of the campus and professors—and students—tend to prefer classes near the professors' offices, which are normally in the heart of the campus.

One of the most perplexing problems of modern universities is providing parking for students. Students will often not use their cars for a week or two at a time, but they want them nearby when they do need to use them. There is no easy way to solve this vexing problem. Solutions vary from campus to campus. At some institutions multi-storied parking garages have been built, but these are not economically feasible for low-cost student parking.

Planning for residence halls should take into account the need for outdoor recreational spaces that allow students to spill out from the building onto a terrace, a pleasant balcony, or a small grassy playing field. These too help build community and increase retention.

The way students live and work today is different from that of the past.

Should tomorrow's residence halls be air-conditioned? Air-conditioning is almost mandatory for college dormitories in the southern half of the United States, but it is an arguable installation in the northern climates. Each college needs to ask itself how it will use the residence halls in the summer. If they will be used heavily for the whole summer, air-conditioning may be economically feasible.

Seeing residential life whole

Too often college and university residences have been treated as unfortunately necessary and utilitarian structures. Amenities, student needs, and the many opportunities for creating a more studious, more friendly body of students have been overlooked.

But campus residence halls are home for students for four years, or two or three years for graduate students. They are not normal homes with families, but with a special peer group home of energetic, bright, adventurous, and sometimes frustrated students. So durability, control of acoustics, and arrangements for group encounters are essential. The rules of standard residential construction and design need to be altered so that colleges can, in an economical way, provide the optimum conditions for higher learning—and for bonding affectionate alumni who will help support the college in future decades.

The way students live and the way they work intellectually today is different from that of the past. Colleges need to build new kinds of dormitories for the electronic age, and for achieving the higher retention and quality of learning the public now expects. Residential renewal and new construction should be a major part of planning capital facilities improvements in American higher education.

Winston Churchill once said (of his House of Parliament): "We shape our buildings. Then our buildings shape us." For college residence halls this seems a basic truth. ∎

How colleges can design buildings to foster collegiality and productivity.

Campus Architecture That Shapes Behavior

James Burlage and Wendell Brase

As available land at colleges and universities becomes scarcer, institutions have been forced to build taller buildings—four to eight stories instead of two or three. This has led to the separation of people on campus by floors because visits, conversations, and socializing tend to take place more easily in horizontal spaces. Floors are more confining than walls. Persons will often walk 160 feet down the hall to visit someone, but balk at going up or down one flight of stairs to confer with someone closer.

This architectural situation exacerbates the already fragmenting academic life that exists at all but the smallest colleges; and it contributes to the increasing loss of community, friendship, and scholarly collaborations on campus. So the question arises: how can architects design for improved social interactions and better academic productivity in the new mid-rise college buildings?

First, an assumption. We believe that built environments should serve people's needs, especially their social needs. To us this is the essence of good architecture. Buildings should be more than masonry sculptures or imaginative flights of architectural artistry. We can shape social behavior to a certain degree by the spaces we create.

Social and intellectual exchanges are critical for colleges and universities. This seems to be particularly so for the laboratory-based sciences and engineering, where teamwork rather than the efforts of isolated individuals is vital to research productivity. But the need for interaction is not limited to the sciences and engineering. Academic and facilities planners should demand that building renovations or new architecture pay attention to the enhancement of exchanges and visits among all faculty, students, and staff. How can this be accomplished?

James Burlage, FAIA, is a principal of Burlage & Associates Architects of Sausalito, California, and an award winning architect who has designed 17 college and university libraries as well as campus office buildings and scientific research laboratories, and has conducted master planning at institutions such as Stanford. He is a graduate of the University of Notre Dame who received his M.Arch. from Columbia.

Wendell C. Brase is Vice Chancellor – Administrative and Business Services at the University of California, Irvine. With nineteen years of experience in the UC system (thirteen years at UC Santa Cruz, six years at UCI), Mr. Brase is responsible for UC Irvine's administrative, financial, and business services including a comprehensive program of process improvement and administrative streamlining (recently awarded first-place in NACUBO's Higher Education Awards Program).

Distance as an enemy

The most important factor in determining the amount of interaction in a workplace is the distance that two people have to travel to converse. Several studies indicate that strong interaction is most likely within a 30-foot radius. One professor of engineering management, Thomas Allen of MIT, has shown that the probability of exchanges drops close to an asymptotic level when the distance within a building between two individuals exceeds 50 meters or so, or 165 feet (Allen 1977, 1980).

Planners should demand that architecture pay attention to the enhancement of exchanges and visits.

So the first thing to keep in mind is the desirability of keeping university people close together as much as possible. With mid-rise buildings this may actually be easier to do than with low, sprawling structures.

For example, in the design of the Sinsheimer Laboratories at the University of California, Santa Cruz, the building's designers, ED-2 International of San Francisco, made use of this finding. Peter W. T. Wong, ED-2's principal-in-charge, and key science faculty visited Dr. Allen at MIT and toured Boston area projects to study features that promote collaborative work and research productivity. As a result, the architects clustered all the faculty and staff offices at Santa Cruz in a central mid-rise building, segregated from the laboratories, which are contained in two flanking wings. In the 50-meter envelope (including the vertical transition distance), they carefully placed numerous "magnets" to pull people together: drinking fountains, restrooms, mailboxes, bulletin boards, photocopiers, vending machines, and conference rooms. The "magnets" are important to draw faculty out of their offices or laboratories to the interactive node of the building. And separating the offices from the labs requires walking, and encourages chance meetings and communication.

Thomas Allen has said, "The Sinsheimer Laboratories building goes further than any other university project I know in making use of the behavioral research that links internal architecture to academic productivity." Wong and ED-2 International have recently extended the interaction-producing design concepts to laboratories at the University of Minnesota and IBM.

Faculty who work in Sinsheimer Labs seem to like the building too. Charles Daniel, a biology professor, reports, "One of my recent grant proposals would never have come about without the discussions I had with John Tamkun and Cliff Poodry [faculty in other specialties]." Others use words like "obvious" to attest to the design's benefits from tighter interaction patterns. And Howard Wang, chair of the biology department, says, "The more frequent interactions translate into new ideas for research and different approaches for experiments. You can actually feel the way the building acts as an intellectual catalyst."

The four promoters of talk

We think there are four spatial arrangements that are most conducive to greater faculty, faculty-staff, and faculty-student meeting and exchanges:

1. public spaces
2. functional rooms
3. support spaces
4. circulation

Public spaces. Nearly everyone knows about the town squares of European cities or the village greens of East Coast towns in America. These are the places where the public gathers. They unite a city, town, or village (Whyte 1980), allowing people to eat, talk, trade, stroll, or rest together. Some campuses also have quadrangles, inner courtyards, or central lawns bordered by patios where people gather.

Universities can provide such public spaces for their mid-rise buildings, through the design of one of three kinds of public space. One means is through the location of a new building adjacent to a campus space that allows for the creation of an outdoor area where faculty, students, and staff can gather, whether in a small park-like setting or a small, landscaped plaza with special paving. This is obviously more appropriate for colleges in warmer climates.

Stairway at the Sinsheimer Laboratories at the University of California, Santa Cruz. In mid-rise campus buildings vertical circulation becomes especially vital.

The other two kinds of public spaces are a courtyard and an atrium. The building can be a hollow square or U-shaped structure with an inner courtyard containing a fountain, sculpture, trees, shrubbery, benches, or flowers. The courtyard is a more private realm than the "town" square beside a college building, but it draws people together effectively too, as medieval cloisters and Spanish inner spaces do.

An atrium was an open courtyard in large Roman houses; but today the term is usually used to describe a covered courtyard or glazed winter garden inside a building. Modern atrium design incorporates special wall enclosures, sunshading, ventilation devices, and subtle means of controlling temperature and humidity. The Ford Foundation's headquarters in New York City has a striking atrium, and Graham Gund placed one at the heart of Davidson College's Visual Arts Center. (Gund and Dorsten 1994, p. 23). Atriums have become popular recently for linking floor levels within a large interior space because they increase visual awareness between floors—people can see both horizontally and vertically to the other floors—and help break the sense of enclosure. The building's users share views, light, noise, and smells and can gather easily in the central space.

Functional rooms. These are rooms that allow faculty or other campus persons to carry out some task. Daily routines are filled with such tasks. These include formal rooms such as lecture halls, laboratories, conference rooms, and libraries, and infor-

Magnets are important to draw faculty out of their offices.

mal rooms such as cafeterias, lounges, exercise rooms or gymnasiums, locker rooms, and administrative offices. The location of these functional rooms can enhance meetings, as can the rooms' shape, enclosures, scale, furniture, light, and views.

For instance, the Sinsheimer Laboratories have two-story conference rooms designed to function with either closed or open doors, inviting unscheduled, spontaneous use. Faculty have found these conference rooms most useful when their use is

Atriums have become popular for linking floor levels.

least structured, and meet there frequently for impromptu discussions. One problem is that students also find the conference rooms attractive places in which to study or discuss academic assignments.

Support spaces. A majority of traffic in a building results from the movement to and from certain necessities during the day: restrooms, supply rooms, vending areas, information display spaces, drinking fountains, coffee stations. What is common to these support spaces is their opportunity to attract people. So their location and the design of these spaces must be such that they induce conversations.

At Stanford University's Terman Building the snack bar and lounge spaces were located in a highly trafficked area and created a wonderful activity space. To get to the restrooms in the basement, persons had to penetrate this activity zone, further enhancing the use of these support spaces. Also at Stanford, in the Keck Building, the drinking fountains, copy machines, coffee machines, bulletin boards, and writing boards were all situated along the atrium corridor, pulling people into meetings and conversations informally all day long. A unique device for drawing people together was the seismograph machine in Stanford's Mitchell Building. During periods of ground tremors in California or elsewhere people on campus rushed to the machine. (It is probably the only crowd attraction in the Mitchell Building.)

Moving people on campus

Circulation. The circulation spaces may have the greatest effect on how people perceive a campus building. Also, one's orientation to a building is highly dependent on her or his understanding of the circulation configuration. The paths connecting the various functions can promote or deter interaction. Circulation networks include both horizontal and vertical movement. Especially important, the intersections and terminations of circulation paths are among the most active social spaces in a building.

Horizontal spaces are made more welcoming to interaction if the corridors can be single loaded, with office doors on only one side of the corridor. Atriums or courtyards facilitate this kind of corridor. Double loaded corridors, with doors on both sides like hotel corridors, have a strong institutional feel and retard social exchanges. But corridors have four faces, and the walls, floors, and ceiling can be manipulated to establish greater variety and interest. Walls, for instance, can be punctuated with lounges and other open spaces. As for the larger horizontal spaces such as the entrance lobby or a courtyard, these can be partitioned by columns or low walls to define movement and by furniture and indoor landscaping to create tidy interaction spaces.

Vertical circulation connecting the floors of a building has become more important as university buildings have increased in height.

But stairs can be designed to be inviting and attractive, with large landings where passersby can stop and converse. An especially nice touch is if the landings have a view into active areas, perhaps through location open to an atrium space, to encourage persons to pause and observe the building's users.

Elevators are of course necessary for multi-story buildings and for the disabled. But elevator speed can encourage movement up and down. And the lobbies in front of each elevator entrance can contain bulletin boards, a few chairs for impromptu discussions, and

Campus architecture should be grounded in the research on behavior.

acoustics that permit informal comments and introductions. As campus buildings shift from low-rise to mid-rise, the importance of fresh, imaginative design of vertical circulation cannot be overemphasized.

Robert Geddes, dean of Princeton's architectural school in the 1960s, once wrote:

There are limits of size for every group beyond which friendships do not form...The frequency of involuntary, personal face-to-face

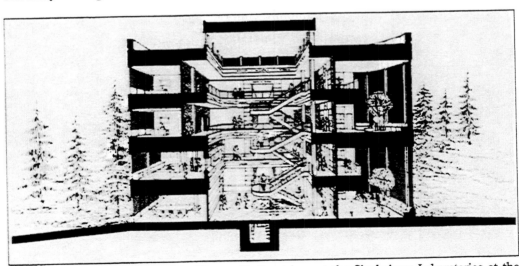

Cross-section of the office core building, with its atrium, at the Sinsheimer Laboratories at the University of California, Santa Cruz. The aim is to provide maximum exchanges among the faculty and between faculty and students.

contacts is one of the most important factors in the formation of groups and informal friendships. The layout has a direct bearing on the formation and maintenance of informal social groups. Circulation, as well as various programmatic and support spaces, must be designed to facilitate interaction.

With the advent of more and more mid-rise buildings at colleges and universities, the necessity of designing spaces that encourage and increase chance meetings, informal discussions, intellectual exchanges, and views of other persons at work has increased. Campus architecture should be grounded in the research on behavior, especially intellectual work behavior; and must make good social interaction and high productivity a goal for its design. ∎

REFERENCES

Allen, T. 1977. *Managing the Flow of Technology.* MIT Press.

Allen, T., Lee, an M. Tushman. 1980. R & D Performance as a Function of Internal Communication, Project Management, and the Nature of Work. *IEEE Transactions on Engineering Management.*

Ching, F. D. K. 1979. *Architecture: Form, Space, and Order.* Van Nostrand Reinhold.

Consentini Associates and Architects Collaborative. 1985. *Atriums: Four Case Studies.* AIA Foundation.

Gund, G. and J. Dorsten. 1994. Art Buildings and Ideology. *Planning for Higher Education* 23(1): 15-23.

Whyte, W. 1980. *The Social Life of Small Urban Spaces.* The Conservation Foundation.

Restoring fine old buildings is now easier and less expensive, with the right planning.

Dos and Don'ts of Historic Preservation on Campus

Stanton Eckstut and Ezra Ehrenkrantz

Only a generation ago, numerous colleges and universities destroyed some of their oldest and historic buildings in the name of progress. But today more and more academic institutions preserve, and even honor, their historic architecture. However, some universities continue to neglect their fine, old buildings or they carry out insensitive renovations. It is essential that historic preservation be done properly, with considerable planning done in advance.

What constitutes a historic building on campus? Well, some college buildings are historic by any measure, such as the red-brick Massachusetts Hall of 1718 facing Harvard Yard, or Thomas Jefferson's circular Rotunda at the University of Virginia.

But only a small number of America's 3,500 institutions, mostly those on the first-settled East Coast, can boast of such distinguished national landmarks.

These older colleges and universities do not, however, have a monopoly on historic buildings. Newer constructions, such as the turn-of-the-century Chapel at Duke University or the Campanile at Berkeley, and newer campuses, such as the Gothic-style University of Chicago or Tuscany-inspired University of Colorado at Boulder, are also historic, particularly in the context of their geographic location.

Generally, historic campus buildings fall into two categories. There are *buildings of merit* which have one or more intrinsic values. The architecture may be outstanding or significant. The building may have been de-

Stanton Eckstut is principal of Ehrenkrantz & Eckstut Architects of New York City and an award-winning architect. A graduate of Penn State with an M.Arch. from the University of Pennsylvania, he has served as director of the Urban Design Program at Columbia's Graduate School of Architecture. He lectures frequently and writes occasionally on the importance of historical and site considerations in design.

Ezra Ehrenkrantz is a principal of the firm and a national authority on the technology of construction. He received a B.Arch. from MIT and an M.Arch. from the University of Liverpool in England. Among his numerous awards is the 1993 AIA/New York Chapter's Medal of Honor for a distinguished history of architectural achievements. He is completing research on the impact of new technology on the design of educational facilities.

signed by a famous architect. An important national or regional event may have occurred there, or a famous person is associated with the building. Or the building has an appeal for generations of former students.

Second, there are *buildings of place*. These may or may not be architecturally distinguished structures but they are a vitally important component of some historic precinct. They enhance the historic character of that section of the campus. As part of a lovely architectural ensemble, these buildings assume a value beyond their own presence, and become historically noteworthy.

What good is historic preservation?

In the past several decades historic preservation has captured the interest of many Americans. So the first reason for making historic preservation a guiding principle for campus planning and development is that many people now favor such preservation.

Some 19th-century buildings or dormitories which were once scorned as too old and rundown are now loved because they are old. Others which were ridiculed for their flamboyant Victorian style or imitation

Many people favor such preservation.

Spanish architecture are now regarded as camp or charming.

Second, historic preservation implements the idea of sustainable development, a set of values now favored by many environmentalists, younger architects, and faculty. Why, the reasoning goes, construct a new building if an old structure can be renovated for another half century of use?

Third, historic buildings give a college or university much of its venerability and

The main floor of the U.S. Customs House in lower Manhattan, one of the grandest public spaces in New York City, was rated a 1 for historic preservation.

character. These landmark structures not only help create an appropriate setting for the transmission of knowledge and values from earlier generations but they also assist students to look beyond themselves and their moment in time.

Historic buildings give a college venerability and character.

Fourth, historic buildings can offer inspiration for the design of new spaces and structures on campus. The new buildings need not copy the old ones, but they can reflect the old ones in scale, materials, and massing, and thereby complement the landmark buildings and strengthen the institution's overall design and setting.

Fifth, historic buildings are assets for alumni allegiance and admissions recruiting. For older graduates, the students, faculty, administrators, and most academic programs and residential rules have changed, so it is reassuring to see the buildings they remember fairly much as they were decades ago when the alumni were callow undergraduates. And those same historic buildings help the college enlist potential students, and their parents. For decades, Princeton has operated its admissions office in the handsome, old (1836) West College building overlooking even older and more historic Nassau Hall. All-female Smith College recently moved its admissions office from busy Elm Street to an attractive 19th-century house at the campus center, overlooking the college's Paradise Pond. Mills College in Oakland, California just completed a five-year restoration of Mills Hall, the 1854 administration building at the heart of the campus.

The new direction of preservation

A generation ago nearly all colleges and universities restored and renovated on an "as needed" basis. That probably worked for most institutions because preservation and renovations were simpler then—no high technology, fewer government mandates, and fewer historical buffs looking over your shoulder. But today historic preservation has become more complicated, more scholarly, and more expensive, the technology has become elaborate, the ADA regulations are comprehensive, and universities have less money for capital construction.

What should colleges and universities do? As a firm that has to some extent specialized in planning and historic preservation, from the old City & County Building in Salt Lake City to the famous and luxurious Dakota Residence apartment house in Manhattan, we have developed some new guidelines. Our work at large institutions such as Columbia, Harvard, Tufts, and Georgetown as well as at smaller colleges like Swarthmore, Stevens Institute of Technology, and the U.S. Merchant Marine Academy has given us, we think, a higher

It is surprising how few planners know their buildings well.

education perspective as well. One thing seems imperative: colleges and universities should look beyond historic preservation as usual, and adopt a more thoughtful, strategic approach based on careful planning.

We suggest a three-part planning strategy which should be an integral part of the long-term facilities plan. If this is done, most historic buildings can be renovated for the same cost as new construction or less.

Preservation Strategy: Part One. In this first part, we suggest four fundamental steps. The first step is obvious: gather basic information about each building on campus: its size, materials, date of construction, additions and renovations, architectural quality, and historic significance. Though obvious, it is surprising how few facilities planners in academe know their buildings well.

Second, the facilities planner and campus architect, perhaps with the aid of an architectural historian from the faculty or an outside expert, must grade each zone of the historic buildings. That is, each portion or detail of the building should be rated for preservation purposes. Our firm uses a 1 to 5 grading system, with 1 representing a magnificent facade, interior space, or detail that must be kept intact or fully restored and a 5 signifying an architectural space or element of little or no historical importance which can be modernized.

In our just completed work at the historic U.S. Custom House in Manhattan, for example, our firm employed this grading approach to determine which parts of the 550,000-square-foot, seven-story building should be fully restored and which portions could be adapted to other uses. The main floor of the U.S. Custom House contains some of the grandest old public spaces in New York City, including a two-story, columned Main Hall whose floor and walls are finished in different polished marbles, and a dramatic series of murals painted on the vaulting of the 48-foot-high dome by Reginald Marsh in 1937, depicting early shipping in the New York harbor. These spaces we rated a 1. Much of the rest of the building, however, is less important architecturally and could be adapted to contemporary uses. These spaces we rated 3, 4, or 5.

The grading of building zones is particularly useful in the restoration and renovation of historic college and university buildings. At the time of their construction they were usually meant to serve as spaces for classrooms, dormitories, or offices, not to be major architectural statements. The facade and entrance may be handsome, but the interiors are seldom distinguished except for some lovely details, a stairway, or a special room or

Square footage is not so valuable as cubic footage.

three. For instance, at Swarthmore College outside Philadelphia, Trotter Hall is one of the school's historic and best-loved buildings, with original portions dating to the 1850s. Yet Trotter Hall is also one of the school's least practical and most outdated buildings. It was slated for demolition.

Our firm, in joint venture with Margaret Helfand Architects, instead prepared a multi-phase plan to renovate Trotter Hall and construct a new 40,000-square-feet building nearby. We began by zoning the building's facade and interior for architectural and historical importance. The gray stone of the facade is a vital component of the entire Swarthmore campus and thus needed careful restoration. But much of the lower-graded interior had minimum importance or quality, so we had considerable

Swarthmore College's Trotter Hall, one of the best loved and most outdated buildings, was slated for demolition—but was rescued for preservation.

freedom in planning the reconfiguration of the internal spaces for contemporary educational purposes in a cost-effective manner.

Third, college planners should assess each campus building's technological proficiency. A technology feasibility study will help determine whether a building can be technologically upgraded at a reasonable cost. This is what our firm did for Columbia

How modern should a college make a historic building?

University as part of their five-year plan for facilities renewal. Columbia is one of America's best designed city campuses, a superb product of McKim, Mead & White in the 1890s. But we found that some historic buildings had thick, load-bearing walls, awkward floor plans, and significant architectural features (like elaborate plaster ceilings) which made high-tech upgrades all but impossible or too expensive. Because an old building cannot accommodate high-tech uses does not mean it can't be renovated for other uses.

A technology feasibility audit can result in some nice surprises. Consider the recent conversion of the historic 1902 Carnegie Laboratory at Stevens Institute of Technology in Hoboken, New Jersey. In 1990 officials at Stevens Institute of Technology asked our firm to renovate the antiquated lab so that it could be used for an ultra-modern Design & Manufacturing Institute. We discovered that the interior partition walls were not load-bearing and could be cleared out. Essentially the building had an open space plan with cast-iron columns 17 feet apart on the high-ceilinged first and second floors and a single open-truss space on the third floor. We also found that the cast-iron columns are hollow.

So the lighting and HVAC ducts were installed along the sides of the rooms. The hollow columns now carry communications and services between the floors inexpensively. The old building has become a

highly flexible, highest-tech, research powerhouse—for $2 million. True, Stevens Institute of Technology could have constructed a new 18,500 square-foot lab for the same cost. But the building would have lacked the architectural beauty and historical associations of the renovated Carnegie Laboratory. Moreover, the new building would not have afforded the same *cubic* footage. Too many buildings are evaluated solely for their *square* footage, which is not nearly so valuable as cubic footage.

Fourth, as the final part of the first strategy—the analysis—colleges should anticipate which buildings might become historic or architecturally distinctive in the next several decades. There may be neo-Georgian structures of the 1920s, modern buildings erected in the 1950s, or even faculty homes at campus edge that will be campus landmarks for the next generation. These buildings need careful maintenance and should be protected from demolition.

Administrators certainly do not have to keep all their old buildings. But facilities planners should help the institution's leaders decide which facilities are the best representatives of the period.

How's your master plan?

It is too seldom recognized that a facilities master plan can save a college or university enormous amounts of money by helping institutions to act, not react, to building requirements. Such a master plan serves as the framework that unites maintenance, preservation, renovation, and new construction into a cost-effective whole. What should a good facilities master plan include?

Preservation Strategy: Part Two. Each university should create a *phased* plan, spelling out what needs to be done each year for the next decade or so. Your part one analysis of every building on campus will tell you what needs to be fixed, and when it should be done. Leaky roofs, for instance, can cause serious damage to historic buildings and should be fixed as soon as possible.

Plan to add new space before you empty out an old building for renovations. Set aside money, or collect money, for major preservation projects in the near future. Your facilities plan should have a clear sequence of work, with rough cost estimates, as Harvey Kaiser has recommended (1993). Anticipate preservation projects. Don't wait until the historic edifices begin to crumble.

Second, build in flexibility so that each campus building can serve new uses over time. Technology is changing fast, and wireless communication may become a reality before long. No longer should most buildings be built for single use as they often were in the 19th century. Now building uses and technologies change with startling speed. Air conditioning changes window design. Elevators are necessary supplements now to stairways because of new ADA requirements (McGuinness 1993). The large computer center built only 20 years ago may soon become a high-tech lecture room.

Preservation Strategy: Part Three. Having inventoried the campus buildings and updated the facilities master plan, a college

or university should next identify the means and methods for the restoration of its best historic buildings. Look at each building's potential. What are the possibilities for adaptive reuse of each structure? Weigh the specifics. To what extent can the old building's materials be duplicated with today's materials? How modern should a college make a historic building? What era do you select for restoration? (Numerous buildings have been modernized or altered over the years. Should you take the building back to its appearance in 1925 when it was modernized, or take it back to its original 1880 design?)

Restoration need not be costly

Historic preservation need not be more expensive than new construction if facilities planners use our three-part strategy. Yes, the painstaking top-to-bottom restoration of an entire building which has important and intricate architectural details will be more

The historic, many stanchioned Carnegie Laboratory at Stevens Institute of Technology in New Jersey was renovated inside for the ultra-modern Design and Manufacturing Research Institute.

expensive than the construction of a new building of the same size. However, very few university buildings deserve that kind of total restoration.

For most renovations of a historic building, the costs will be one half to three quarters of the cost of new construction. Under a typical scenario, only 20 percent or so of the building will receive careful restoration because of its artistic or sentimental importance. Another 50 percent will require considerable renovation, with the remaining 30 percent needing little more than cosmetic upgrading.

Some administrators worry, where will the college find the skilled craftspeople to carry out the restoration of historic buildings? Believe it or not, such persons still exist. Our firm, which tries to keep a file on the best of them, has had to fly them in for special assignments. But the need for splendid stone carvers or skilled plaster restorers is usually not a major concern for college architecture.

One last piece of advice. Great historical preservation requires an architect who can subdue his or her ego, someone who sees that preserving the life of an important and historic building can be as exciting as designing a new building. The best of every age should be preserved. Choose architects and builders who love history as much as they love creating something new and different.

Preserving can be as exciting as designing a new building.

But above all, plan for preservation. Colleges and universities exude the learning of the ages, of all cultures. Their architecture should similarly respect history and culture. ■

REFERENCES

Kaiser, H. 1993. *The Facilities Audit: A Process for Improving Facilities Conditions.* Association of Higher Education Facilities Officers.

McGuinness, K. 1993. Redesigning Your Campus for Disabled Students. *Planning for Higher Education* 22 (1): 23-27.

An expert describes the vital role of acoustical planning for the sound of music.

Frontier Acoustics for Music Buildings

Russell Cooper

Music buildings are different. They require sophisticated advance planning to control and direct sound and noise. They are more expensive. The architecture and construction engineering need to be shaped to accommodate acoustical needs. And the interior design requires special handling to enhance or to muffle sound. Any college or university that is building a new music hall or renovating an existing one must recognize that there are exceptionally difficult design problems that necessitate early and expert acoustical planning.

Music buildings must provide appropriate music environments for teaching, practice, performance, rehearsal, and recording, and they must satisfy the tastes of numerous professors, some of whom are outstanding

Russell Cooper is senior consultant at Jaffe Holden Scarborough Acoustics in Norwalk, Connecticut, and an expert on architectural acoustics and noise control. He is a graduate of the University of Hartford where he received a B.S. in acoustical engineering and minored in music. He has worked as a manufacturer of acoustical equipment and a consultant to an architectural firm that builds music and theater facilities and studios. He continues to play timpani in two regional symphony orchestras, and has helped design a dozen music and performing arts centers.

instrumentalists or composers themselves. These music environments raise design issues such as the acoustics of individual rooms, sound and vibration isolation from external and internal noises, and mechanical system noise control. Acoustical requirements raise the cost of these buildings way beyond the cost of classroom buildings.

Most campus music schools are also used for performances for and by community groups, and for touring dance, music, and theater groups, as well as individual artists. Of course, each locality has different requirements. For example, a music school in a major city like New York or San Francisco which has several concert and recital spaces does not need to build a hall for professional concerts. However, when Cleveland State University planned its new building it had to include a 1000-seat recital hall because Cleveland did not have a satisfactory mid-size concert hall. (See Figure 1.) Likewise, when the University of Indianapolis planned a fine arts extension, the president asked for a 500-seat recital hall so that the college could attract touring performers and groups to raise revenue.

At Interlochen Music Academy in Traverse City, Michigan, the curriculum included musical theater, dance, and drama as well as music; and the city lacked a main performance venue. So the stage at Corson Hall was designed in a proscenium format,

Figure 1. Cleveland State University had to build a mid-size recital hall.

incorporating a limited capacity for flying scenery, so that dance and drama could be presented as well as acoustically sharp music performances. (See Figure 2.)

Thus, the first planning consideration for college leaders is how the music building will be used, and by whom. Then you will be ready for specific acoustical planning.

Those handsome recital halls

The crown jewel of every music education facility is its recital hall. This is what campus visitors come to admire and musicians want to be perfect.

Recital halls are very difficult to design, and college recital halls are especially tough. University and conservatory halls need to accommodate everyone from a single piano, violin, or harp soloist to a full symphony orchestra with a chorus of 200 or 250 voices. So the design of a conservatory recital hall should have a larger volume-to-seat ratio then would the 2,500 seat symphony hall downtown. Whereas the symphony hall might have 350 cubic feet

per seat, the college hall should have 450 to 600 cubic feet per seat. This translates into spaces that can be 45 feet high.

Also, university music hall platforms should be large enough to handle an orchestra and a large choir, so approximately 2000-2500 square feet is the minimum required. Yet, when smaller groups perform on stage, they must not feel alone and tiny on a sea of stage. So portable sound-reflective and diffusive shell panels should be used to surround the smaller groups. The difference in sound power between large symphony orchestras and small chamber groups requires architectural elements such as variable draperies and panels, portable absorptive units, tunable reflectors, and demountable shell panels to enable the hall to function properly. Because of all these acoustical requirements, it is common for the cost of a college recital hall to be a high $150-$175 per square foot.

The most sought-after acoustics for a recital hall is a noise-free environment where listeners feel enveloped in a sonic environment that is considered "warm."

Figure 2. Corson Hall at Interlochen Music Academy in Michigan had to include a proscenium stage to allow dance and dramas as well as music.

Noise-free simply means being very, very quiet. Being enveloped means having the sound be heard by the listener from all around, particularly from the sides. Warmth is associated with an abundance of low-frequency sound. How does a college achieve these qualities?

The crown jewel is the recital hall.

Even the lowest energy instruments, such as a solo violin, deserve a chance to be heard distinctly. Hence it's imperative that the hall be exceedingly quiet, as noise-free as possible. Air conditioning or heating fans should not be heard. Nor should environmental noise from overhead airplanes, nearby subways and trains, or automobile roars, screeches, and horns.

This means that air conditioning equipment for recital halls should be located in a basement far away from the hall or in a sepa-

rate building, never on the roof. The air ducts should be larger than usual for low-speed, quiet air delivery. Air is usually "dumped" or allowed to trickle down from holes in the ceiling, and is returned via numerous openings near the hall's floor. In urban sites where environmental noise is a problem, it is necessary to have four to six-inch-thick concrete roofs, 12 to 24-inch-thick exterior concrete walls, acoustical doors and windows, and "floating" structural systems.

As I said earlier, the proper volume for the hall will insure that the sound energy is contained and reinforced to provide loudness. But architectural details can influence the quality of sound. These details include wall and ceiling geometry, the selection of proper materials for surfaces, and specialty acoustical elements. This leads us to the second requisite: envelopment.

Envelopment, or being immersed in the sound, can be achieved by reflecting or diffusing the sound from the musicians off the side walls and ceiling to arrive at the listeners from all angles. Actually this reflected sound should reach the listeners slightly later than the direct sound from the stage. This time delay creates a perception not unlike that of hearing in stereo. When we listen to music outdoors it can sound flat and one-dimensional because there are no reflections. So it is important that the side walls and ceiling be carefully angled and shaped to reflect and diffuse sounds. In some instances suspended ceiling reflectors need to be installed.

The third sought-after quality is warmth. Warmth is associated with low-frequency sound, so music hall architects must make sure that materials selected for the hall do not absorb low-frequency energy. This requires that most boundary surfaces be solid and rigid since vibrating panels absorb low-frequency energy. This means concrete, plaster, and gypsum board surfaces. Contrary to common belief, wood often hampers good acoustics, although wood applied directly to a massive back-up material such as concrete so it won't vibrate can avoid low-frequency absorption.

The greatest absorber of sound is the audience and its clothing.

The greatest absorber of sound in a recital hall is the audience and their woolen, cotton, or synthetic clothing. But sometimes there are empty seats, so the seats must simulate acoustically the effect of being occupied. This can be accomplished by installing chairs with upholstered seats and backs with a tightly wrapped fabric over a $1\frac{1}{2}$-inch cushion. Since the seats cover much of the floor area, recital halls do not need carpeting except in the aisles.

Just as the audience needs good acoustics, so too do the musicians. Therefore, the performance platform must incorporate wall and ceiling shapes that reflect and diffuse sound not only out to the audience but to the other musicians on stage. In this way the orchestra members can hear themselves and adjust the balance and tone of

their sound. Lower, suspended reflectors over the performance platform are often necessary to help reflect sound within the

Architecture details can influence the quality of sound.

orchestra. These panels should be integrated into the architecture of the hall, and should be more "open" spaced than "closed" to allow for low-frequency sound energy to communicate with the volume above the reflectors to preserve the "warmth."

A reminder. A recital hall is essentially a single-purpose music space. College leaders should not try to make it function as a theater also. I have seen terrible acoustical disappointments where a music hall is expected to satisfy several different uses.

Rehearsal, teaching, and practice rooms

These rooms are more dedicated spaces. They vary in size and cubic volume, depending on the sound power levels of the instrumentalists or ensembles using the space. Rehearsal rooms for an orchestra or chorus should not be less than 25 feet in height. Choral rooms require 20 square feet per person, instrumental rooms 30 square feet per person. Rooms smaller than this tend to be loud and oppressive. Some try to put absorptive panels in the room to reduce the loudness, but this results in a "boomy" or "muddy" sounding room.

These practice and rehearsal rooms should not be as reverberant as the recital hall, but neither should they be "dead." The goal is to provide a pleasing musical environment in which the professor and ensemble can hear themselves and identify articulation and pitch problems. I recommend movable acoustical elements for these rooms so that the acoustical environment can be tailored to the different user group preferences. Among the simplest devices are velour draperies that track

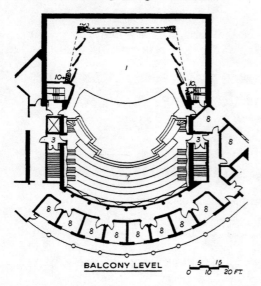

Bennett Hall

1. Performance Platform
3. Sound Lock
7. Balcony Seating
8. Practice Rooms
9. Control Room
10. Acoustic Drapes

BALCONY LEVEL

Figure 3. Bennett Hall in Highland Park, Illinois, has moveable acoustical elements for different user groups.

along the walls and can be hidden in pockets when not in use. (See Figures 3.)

Sound and vibrations

One of the most important tasks in a campus music building is the isolation of sound from space to space, especially since the rooms are usually in close proximity. Spaces used for high-sound power instruments such as percussion, organ, brass, and large chorus should be larger and of double height, and should be located on grade. Wherever possible, corridors and storage rooms should be used as acoustic buffers between these noise-sensitive rooms. These two steps can reduce costs by eliminating costly floating floors and double masonry wall constructions.

Studio and practice rooms are usually located next to each other, so sound isolation between adjacent rooms is imperative. This can be done by the following construction:

- Combination masonry and gypsum board walls
- Floating wood floors over concrete slabs
- Resiliently mounted gypsum board ceilings. (Figure 4.)

For practice rooms, universities should consider modular, pre-fabricated construc-tion, which offers a low-cost, guaranteed acoustical alternative to general construction.

Doors to music practice rooms should always be acoustical steel doors with a rating of Sound Transmission Class (STC)-47. (Regular doors have a STC rating of 20 or so.) A door of this type costs about $1,500 but is worth it because the cost of all the other isolated construction will be wasted if the doors are acoustically ineffective. Architects also need to avoid sound-flanking paths from one room to another. Conduits, piping, and ducts that penetrate the walls and ceilings should be isolated from the portions by the use of resilient gaskets and caulking materials.

To control noise

Heating, ventilating, and air conditioning (HVAC) systems create noise, and noise in music buildings must be reduced as much as possible. Colleges can employ several strategies. They can place mechanical equipment in a remote location. They can use low air velocities, and reduce fan noise with in-line silencers and sound-absorbing duct lining. And they can provide silent supply and return grilles.

131

In studios and practice rooms, however, a low level of noise is actually desirable to mask the outside sound that inevitably seeps through wall, floor, and ceiling constructions. This low-level "acoustical perfume" can be done by installing a

Practice rooms need "acoustical perfume."

quiet air conditioning outlet or vent that generates and diffuses a moderate amount of continuous noise. This must be done very carefully so that the level of introduced noise is not objectionable.

The design of the air conditioning system is crucial. A common misconception is that putting a silencer in the duct, or by lining the duct, noise problems caused by air conditioning will be solved. A silencer, by restricting air flow, regenerates noise itself. When a portion of duct length traverses a

critical acoustical space, architects must encase the duct in serveral layers of gypsum board to prevent noise from breaking out of the thin sheetmetal duct enclosure.

To control noise there are several important design practices. One, never locate air conditioning equipment on the music building's roof. Instead, use a basement or a remote location. Two, support all mechanical equipment—chillers, pumps, fans, etc.—on vibration isolation devices; and for ducts, pipes, and conduits that serve the mechanical equipment attach them with flexible connections and suspend them on vibration isolators for a distance of at least 20 feet from each machine.

Three, place the supply and return ducts for teaching suites and practice rooms in the corridors outside the rooms. Branch ducts containing sound traps can then be tapped from the main duct into each practice room. This requires either wider corridors or taller plenum spaces over the corridors in which to stack the duct work. (See Figure 5.)

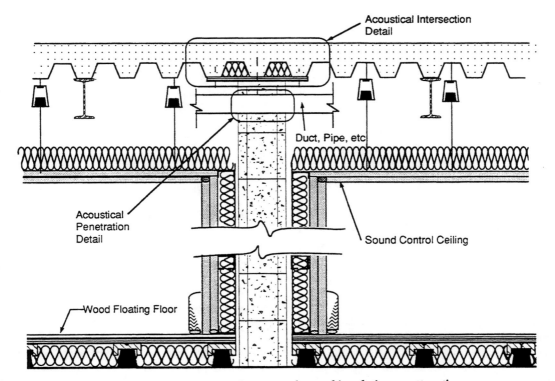

Figure 4. Studio and practice rooms require unusual sound insulation construction.

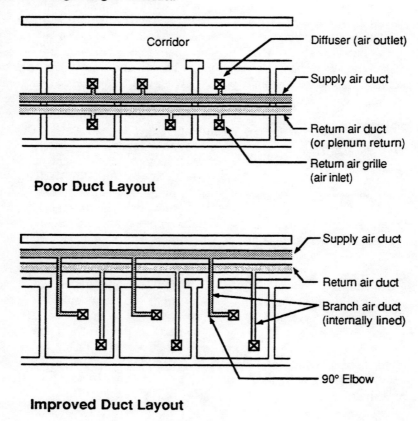

Poor Duct Layout

Improved Duct Layout

Figure 5. Air ducts for music practice rooms should be placed outside the rooms.

The matter of costs

What every college or university should remember is that music building costs are greater then most other buildings. Construction costs for music buildings in 1992 range from $125 to $135 per gross square foot, twice the construction costs of standard classroom buildings. Any architects and builders who come in with lower budgets should be questioned meticulously because they are probably making acoustical compromises and reducing the quality of sound and noise control.

Special attention should be given to the ratio of net to gross square foot. Music schools, with their complex and thick floor/wall/ceilings and large ducts and remote mechanical spaces, have larger grossing factors than standard construction. Whereas the standard construction grossing factor is 1.2, the figure for music buildings is 1.4 or 1.5. Colleges that accept low-bid estimates from builders who do not understand the special and expensive acoustical needs of music buildings will either receive poor-quality buildings acoustically or be forced to add money to the estimate to make late additions and changes.

> *Acoustical requirements raise costs way beyond those of other buildings.*

I suggest that campus facilities planners submit a detailed, written description of the music building's sound isolation concept to the cost estimators at the beginning of the project. It should include details about construction materials (double-layer gypsum stud wall, fiberglass batt, etc.) yet be generic enough to permit tuning of the partitions as the design develops. Such guidelines make it easier for estimators to judge costs correctly, and avoid surprises down the road. I believe it is wise to employ an acoustical expert for this early planning stage to help develop the sound isolation concept.

As I said at the beginning, music buildings are different. Universities must realize that structures in which to practice and perform the musical art require a high degree of advanced acoustical planning, specialized building design and construction, and above-average expenditures. ■

A different kind of educational bookstore is being created within colleges and universities.

The New College Bookstore

John Finefrock

What is difficult for most people, not only booksellers, is to acknowledge responsibility for creating a better future. In the distraction of daily details, caught in the web of existing practices, and seduced by old habits and the latest fads, we fail to undertake strategic changes that can remake our lives, our professions, and our institutions so that

John Finefrock is manager of the bookstore at Kenyon College in Gambier, Ohio, where he also teaches Chinese. He earned a B.A. from the University of California, Santa Barbara and a M.Div. from the Graduate Theological Union in Berkeley. Before coming to Kenyon in 1982, he managed the Chautauqua Bookstore in upstate New York and was head of publications there. The Kenyon College Book Shop has been called "best U.S. college bookstore" in Lisa Birnbach's *College Book* and in *Rolling Stone* magazine, and has been cited by *Publisher's Weekly* as having "the highest sales per student in the USA."

Featured in *The Wall Street Journal* in 1992, Mr. Finefrock won the 1995 Kenyon Faculty Cup for Distinguished Teaching, was a John S. Knight Fellow in 1995-96, and is also the author of *The Future of the Campus Store*, 1993.

they contribute to a fresh and finer future, especially for the young.

But some bookstore managers at American colleges and universities have begun to transform the campus bookstore into a every different kind of place, a new kind of college center. They think this strategic change will contribute significantly to the intensity of intellectual life on campus.

The traditional college bookstore mostly provides items directly necessary for college work: notebooks, pens, textbooks, basic art supplies, and college memorabilia (pennants, mugs, T-shirts, and the like). It is usually cramped, strictly functional, uninviting, and open only during normal business hours. Some of these store managers don't even like books but see them as "merchandise." And most colleges treat their bookstore managers as clerks; campus bookstore managers are among the lowest paid professionals at academic institutions.

The managers of the "new" college bookstore, however, (and I include myself among them) are trying to create a radically new kind of gathering place on campus. Frankly, we are dreamers who are using our practical skills to build a dream in the heart of academe. This may sound grand, but some of us believe that the search for and accumulation of good books by students can be like the quest for one's soul or the meaning of life. We are trying to build a physical facility appropriate for young people's hungry search for culture, self-identity, and intellectual acumen.

Most colleges treat their bookstore managers like clerks.

The college store business

According to the National Association of College Stores, there are 4,500 member stores in the U.S. and Canada. They grossed about $8 billion in 1992. Books and texts account for 60 percent of sales, but in the past decade non-book items have been increasing—food, clothing, candy, backpacks, posters, hair dryers, computers—because the profits are higher in such merchandise. As a result, many college stores now resemble crowded convenience stores, and in some of

The search for good books by students can be like the quest for one's soul.

them books have become a minor part of their activity, relegated to a back section because the number of items in the store has increased but the space of the store has not.

Not so at the Seminary Students Coop in Hyde Park, Illinois, which has a splendid stock of books. Or at the Hungry Mind, the attractive bookstore for Macalester College in St. Paul, Minnesota, with its great spaces and lofty ceiling. Or at the bookstores of Dartmouth College, Kentucky's Centre College, the University of Toronto, or the University of Washington in Seattle. Or at the magnificent University of Iceland bookstore in Reykjavik. These, and others like them, are college stores where books are central, the spaces handsome, and where students and fac-

The trade book section of the University of Toronto Book Store in the great reading room of the former Metro Toronto Central Library. The Bookstore is the third largest bookseller in Canada with more than 50,000 book titles in stock and more than 300 magazine titles.

ulty hang out as if the bookstore were an intellectual community center.

These new bookstores are places where university presidents and planners have insisted on a facility that looks and feels good, that invites with visible cues all the campus constituencies to the great party of life in which learning together is the most fun of all. A visit to buy the *Washington Post*, the *American Scholar*, or a new book on 20th-century music leads a student past a display of the best new academic books, into a meeting with his or her philosophy professor, near an admissions officer with parents and prospective student in tow, and past members of the soccer team reading magazines while they wait to get picked up by a bus for their next game. These new bookstores have poetry readings, autograph signings, jazz concerts, and comfortable chairs in which to read. They are gossip-central, the major meeting place for students and faculty to meet informally. Alumni, local citizens, tourists, and students from other colleges come long distances to spend a day at these stores.

The new college bookstore is usually the result of a daring president, a demanding faculty, and a creative, bookish store manager coming together. That is how our

The Kenyon Book Shop is open 365 days a year.

bookstore at Kenyon College began. The Kenyon professors were unhappy about their college store, which was the only place to buy books in Gambier, Ohio (pop. 2,100), and a faculty committee drew up an idealistic wish list for an enlarged exemplary bookstore. The president endorsed their report. To the amazement of the faculty, I took their report seriously and a decade ago begun to build their ideal store. We expanded into a former pizza restaurant next to the college, renovated the basement for sales space, and built an addition to the building so that Kenyon now has a 15,000-square-feet store.

A most unusual place

The Kenyon College Book Shop is open from 7:30 a.m. to 11:00 p.m., 365 days a year. The floor is carpeted and the 14-foot high walls are covered from floor to ceiling with oak shelves of books. In the rear of the store we have a living-room-like reading area with sofas and upholstered chairs, and large windows that look out into a green, wooded area. There is piped-in classical music, and kites hanging from the ceiling. (Above the cash register, a local artist quilted a replica of Michelangelo's Sistine Chapel ceiling to hang from our ceiling.) We used to have flowers and plants all around, but that became too expensive.

You can get coffee, bagels, ice cream, and rootbeer.

The Kenyon College store stocks about 80,000 book titles a year. With certain publishing houses like Oxford University Press or Harvard University Press we buy a copy of every book they publish, and we have them on our shelves months before the reviews come out. (Our librarians thus can inspect new books before they buy them.) You can find an extraordinary range of just-published books in our store, from medieval medicine to the latest poetry of Maya Angelou. We keep new books for one year or two, then return most of them to the publishers if they don't sell, so we seldom compete with our college library.

We also stock about 500 magazines and scholarly journals, from Rolling Stone to Vogue, covering computers, tennis, foreign affairs, religion, and African arts and culture (*Callaloo*). These are very popular with students and faculty, who often read an article, walk to one of our photocopy machines to make a copy, then replace the magazine. (As with books, most magazine publishers accept returns, so we feel we can stock as many as we have space for.) The texts for courses are in a separate section.

There is an area where you can get coffee, bagels, Ben and Jerry's ice cream, and

10 varieties of root beer. You can have break-fast and lunch in the store and spend all day till nearly midnight browsing and reading in an armchair without buying a thing. No one is pressured to buy; but curiously the more we let people explore and read, the more they buy. The Kenyon store sales have qua-drupled in the past 10 years. Our staff con-sists of 22 full-time and four part-time trained professionals. We use no student clerks.

There is a conference room, and we hold classes in the store. There is a huge brag board with newspaper clippings about our students, Kenyon's teams, and faculty book reviews and articles. We have poetry readings, small concerts, and displays of the best student art.

The Kenyon College Book Shop also tries to provide for all the daily needs of stu-dents, faculty and staff. So we sell music tapes and CD's, basic hardware and furni-ture, cards, art supplies, stationary, aspirin, printer ribbons—really a bazaar of student and faculty needs. We also try to provide sur-prises so that people keep coming in. The

---

We are inventing an on-campus intellectual community center.

---

store once sold live baby rabbits and fuzzy, yellow baby chicks for Easter; but the crea-tures chewed on electrical wires, created safety and health problems, and the adminis-tration and maintenance staff told us, "Never again." When we opened a camping section, we brought in six-foot stuffed bears to sleep in our pup tents, complete with jars of honey, canoe paddles, and magazines that bears might read. Little did we imagine that faculty children would crawl into the tents and use the large bears as couches while they read their children's books. Our store gets clut-tered from time to time, but our view is that where there is occasional mess there is life. The students love it.

The Kenyon store does a considerable mail-order business. We order all the books

for the college library. We even order books for the University of Tokyo! (They heard of us, and our book prices are cheaper than those in Tokyo). We also help faculty with out-of-print book searches, and have a service desk to answer any student questions about books or journals. Surpris-ingly, the Kenyon bookshop has no secu-rity guards, and has almost no pilferage, or "shrinkage" as store managers call it. Stud-ies have found that one in eight store visi-tors steal, especially in urban areas; but we have so far not had a problem.

The Kenyon Book Shop has elements of a library, newsstand, student center, Viennese cafe, and convenience store but has mixed the elements. We believe Kenyon—and other institutions like us—are inventing a novel kind of place, an on-campus intellectual community center. Students write their class papers in our chairs and play chess. A few faculty and stu-dents have written novels in our bookstore.

Does it make money? Properly run, these new college bookstores can and should earn a small profit, as the Kenyon store does. In fiscal year 1995-96 we had revenues of $2.4 million (excluding com-puter sales)—in a tiny Ohio town of 2,100 people. One hundred percent of our net profit—about four percent of total gross sales—goes to the college's student schol-arship fund, which we think is proper but which also helps sales because students know they get back some of the money they spend.

But the real "profit" comes in other forms. The Kenyon College Book Shop is used by the admissions office to attract the best students; and at least a few recruited faculty have chosen Kenyon because they have the same access to new books, jour-nals, and magazines in Gambier, Ohio as they would in Cambridge, New York, or San Francisco. A store like Kenyon's says to visitors, "This is a college where learning is taken seriously." Our bookstore makes a statement about Kenyon College. It differ-entiates us.

Perhaps the largest profit is the sheer pleasure of large open spaces, warm in winter and cool in summer, where one can read, explore, talk, eat, relax, and listen to the world's best music and informal little concerts, where sophomores can literally bump into their professors, discover new journals and ideas, savor the latest clothing fashions, poetry, and tips on bicycles, and buy delicious new chocolates from Switzerland.

What are the ingredients?

This new kind of college bookstore has several features I think are imperative.

Space. Space is the key element. Most university stores are only one third or one

---

Space is the key element.

---

half the size they should be. You need more room for tables, chairs, and sofas, and aisles that are wide enough. The ceilings should have height too. The most stunning, inspiring bookstore I have ever seen is in Helsinki, Finland. It was designed by the noted architect Alvar Aalto and has a very high curved ceiling, giving the shop a cathedral-like grandeur.

The walls should be lined with books; that creates a lovely ambiance, as it did in J.P. Morgan's magnificent library. You'll need to provide chairs and tables for 100 to 200 students, racks for 500-600 magazine and journals, as well as a dining area where students, faculty, and staff can have coffee, a soft drink, and a gourmet snack.

Long hours. One reason many people don't visit bookstores is because they are usually closed. Colleges need to find a way to have their community center-bookstores open earlier each day and later each night, seven days a week. Bookstores should have hours like a cafe, not like a bank.

Quickness. Colleges can get Sunday book reviews from leading newspapers on Friday. There's no reason to wait for the reviews before buying new books. Ideas should be handled like hot news, not like yesterday's beer. Students and faculty appreciate a college store that helps them stay at

The Kenyon College Bookshop has classical music, bagels, and 500 magazines and journals, and stays open 365 days a year.

the forefront, especially in non-popular fields. Professors get a jolt by discovering new stuff they didn't know was published yet.

Provision for daily needs. The best new stores on campus are really attuned to supplying student and faculty needs: a well-

The best new campus stores bristle with life and activity.

brewed cup of coffee, the best cheap pens, computer discs, comfortable jogging shoes. Know your students and professors and what they require in their daily intellectual work and their best leisure.

Intimacy with the college. It is surprising how little most campus book shops relate to the special activities of their institutions. Often the local taverns feature photographs of the sports stars from the college teams, and local restaurants list the coming lectures, concerts, and dramatic shows on campus more than the campus bookstore does. Faculty books, articles, and photographs, and student accomplishments and productions should be prominently displayed, and bulletin boards should pin up references to the college, to alumni, to trustees, and community leaders.

Life. The best new campus stores bristle with life and activity. Students especially are a boisterous, irreverent, athletic group. They are different from other adult commercial shoppers. The campus bookstores of the future will reflect that energy, as well as young people's quieter quests for learning and love, friendships, and a philosophy or religion to live by. ■

POSTSCRIPT

John Finefrock has updated the information contained in this 1993 article to reflect more recent data. In addition, he offers the following postscript.

A trend toward leasing?

There appears to be a growing trend toward leasing out bookstore space and associated operations. In 1990, according to the National Association of College Stores, 655 college bookstores were managed by lease companies. By 1996, the number of leased stores grew to 1,065, or about twenty-five percent of U.S. college bookstores. Institutional stores represent half of all college stores, while private stores represent fifteen to twenty percent of the total, and cooperatives make up roughly five percent.

Among the recently leased bookstores are those at Harvard, Yale, and the University of Chicago. The University of California at Berkeley is taking this option under consideration. Meanwhile, Columbia University has retained its lease operator for textbooks and supplies, while simultaneously providing space in a new building for a privately-owned academic bookstore. Columbia promotes the private bookstore on its web site.

There are a number of reasons for this apparent trend. College stores, which have existed in some cases for a hundred or more years, are facing increased competition from the burgeoning ranks of the superstores. In many instances the profitability of college stores, usually marginal to begin with, has dwindled significantly.

Even when financial officers are not demanding high rent or high return from an institution's investment, they are less and less willing to support a bookstore's annual losses. Leasing is seen as a way to bail out a faltering operation while increasing income to an institution. It is also a way to continue offering bookstore services to the campus community, often in space that has been newly renovated and decorated at the lessor's expense.

Will bookstores cease to exist?

Does the apparent trend toward leasing bookstore space and operations presage the future on college campuses? The shift toward leasing may also ultimately affect libraries and computer centers, particularly if lease operators can offer students more services at a lower price than traditional institutional libraries and information services.

Why, some might argue, is a physical location or building even required for a bookstore? Such may be the case as colleges engage in distance learning and explore alternatives for delivering commodities currently provided by bookstores. Yet, bookstores are potentially very different from each other, grounded in distinct institutional identities and providing privileged commodities such as books along with generally available items such as sweatshirts, pens, and mugs. If these campus-run bookstores are homogenized into a superstore or another centrally commercialized entity, much would be lost.

A change in undergraduate interests has created a new kind of campus building.

The Outburst of Student Recreation Centers

David Body

During the past 15 years a new kind of building has begun to appear on campuses. It is becoming a feature at large and small universities and has started to appear at some private colleges and community colleges. The buildings are called student recreation centers, wellness centers, or centers for student physical activities.

The student recreation center is neither like the gymnasiums that have been part of campus life for a century, nor like the student centers built in the post-war years to be hubs of undergraduate social and extracurricular life. Yet they incorporate parts of both. These earlier buildings were designed to serve a different set of students. Athletics was less prominent, and women's sports programs were minimal and frequently

David Body is the principal-in-charge at Cannon-Parkin for master planning, programming, and design of sports facilities, for which the firm is noted. A graduate in architecture from England's University of Sheffield, he is a former Canadian Tennis Open and California State Squash champion and has played lacrosse and paleta argentina at the international level. He has visited and consulted on sports facilities on four continents and worked for more than 40 colleges and universities nationwide, has lectured at Harvard and the University of Arizona, and has been a leader in the design of the modern student recreation center.

housed separately. The lines between intercollegiate competitive sports and recreation and intramurals were not as clearly drawn. Intercollegiate sports were not the subject of present-day media scrutiny, and the expectations of players, coaches, and spectators were lower with regard to the quality of playing surfaces, lighting, safety zones, seating, sight lines, and restrooms.

The student recreation building of today is a far cry from its predecessors. And it is increasingly regarded not as a non-academic luxury but as an essential structure for the education of a young person's body, mind, emotional qualities, and self-discipline. It is also seen as a preventative health resource—a wellness center.

A good number of the early gyms were architecturally delightful, as evidenced by the conversion of some into art or computer centers or into libraries. But most athletic facilities have become dinosaurs, with unsafe pool depths, labyrinthine circulation patterns that make them impossible to secure, with code and ADA deficiencies, and with inadequate spectator space. Yet what principally caused the explosion of the new recreation centers were several major shifts in students' values, mores, and interests.

Propellants for the emergence

In my judgment, four big changes gave impetus to the development of student recreation centers as we know them today.

1. *The increased quantity and quality of intercollegiate sports competition.* More of the sports now require year-round practice and training and place impossible demands on facilities shared with recreational users.

2. *The large increase in participation by women* in athletics, exercise, aerobics, recreational games, and after the passage of Title IX in 1972, in intercollegiate competitive sports (Emmons and Wendt 1996).

3. *The extraordinary growth of student interest in fitness and regular exercise.* Beginning in the 1960s with President John F. Kennedy's advocacy of fitness programs, and medical research on the causes of heart disease and obesity, undergraduates have now made better health, nutrition, and physical fitness an integral part of their weekly lives. Many faculty and staff have done so also.

4. *An expansion of the number of students who demand facilities for individual or small pickup-team recreation at nearly all hours.* From early morning swims or runs to lunchtime or midnight basketball, volleyball, squash, or ice hockey, today's undergraduates want to engage in exercise or athletics between long sessions at the computer, in the classrooms, and in the library. Significantly, they are even willing to put money up for the new facilities, often in the form of a student fee to support a bond issue.

These four changes and the resulting space requirements at first led to design responses to meet the new program requirements. Often the responses took the form of a multi-purpose facility where the emerging recreational component was located around and under the seats of a spectator facility. Examples of such design projects include the 1973 Recreation Hall at the University of California, Davis, and the facility at the University of Southern Illinois. The University of Washington in Seattle also built a single-purpose recreation and intramural structure during this period.

Then in the late 1970s and early 1980s some serendipitous liaisons occurred which led to the birth of the contemporary recreation and health center. Students grew more insistent. Recruited athletes became more demanding. Faculty and staff too began fitness regimens. Some campus administrators grasped the new national interest in exercise, fitness, wellness, and around-the-clock recreation and impromptu games. And some

Undergraduates have made better health and fitness a part of their lives.

architects realized that something new —not just a larger gym or field house, or a student center with fitness rooms added—was required. One early prototype was UCLA's John Wooden Center, which opened in 1983. Here a visionary recreation director, the health-conscious California environment and their assertive student leaders, and a pro-health and recreation chancellor collaborated closely with the campus architect and a specialized consulting architect to create a new kind of campus facility.

When the Wooden Center design began in 1979, there was a good deal of searching for the forms that would embody the new intensity of physical activity on campus. But gradually the program for the building and the design came together. The exterior materials may reflect the university's budget constraints, but the organization of the interior spaces and general ambiance represent a breakthrough. The controlled single point of entry to the building, the greater clarity of circulation, the visual links between activity spaces, the introduction of natural light into the interior, carpeted floors and contemporary colors, glass-walled courts, ample lounge spaces, and original artwork are now all accepted as design standards for recreation centers. Other early examples of the new genre may be found at Texas Tech University, the University of California, Berkeley, and St. Mary's University in Halifax, Nova Scotia.

Recent Student Recreation Centers

Project	Year Opened	New Area GSF	Other Recreation Facilities	Spectators	Pools	ICA Component
ARIZONA STATE UNIVERSITY Student Recreation Complex	1989	150,000	Yes	No	Outdoor Recreation	No
LOMA LINDA UNIVERSITY Drayson Center	1995	98,000	No	No	Outdoor Recreation	No
MISSISSIPPI STATE UNIVERSITY Sanderson Recreation Center	1997	160,000	No	No	Indoor Comp./Rec.	No
OAKLAND UNIVERSITY Student Recreation and Athletic Center	1998	260,000	No	3,000 Main Gym	Indoor Comp./Rec.	Yes Div. II
POMONA COLLEGE Rains Center	1989	86,000	No	1,800 Main Gym	Outdoor Comp./Rec.	Yes Div. III
RANDOLPH MACON COLLEGE Sports and Recreation Center	1997	70,000	Yes	No	Indoor Comp./Rec.	Yes Div. III
UNIVERSITY OF ARIZONA Student Recreation Center	1990	120,000	Yes	No	Outdoor Recreation	No
UNIVERSITY OF CALIFORNIA, LOS ANGELES Wooden Center	1984	100,000	Yes	1,800 Main Gym	No	Some Div. I
UNIVERSITY OF CALIFORNIA, RIVERSIDE Student Recreation Center	1994	89,000	Yes	3,000 Main Gym	No	Some Div. II
UNIVERSITY OF CALIFORNIA, RIVERSIDE Student Recreation Center	1994	89,000	Yes	3,000 Main Gym	No	Some Div. II
UNIVERSITY OF CALIFORNIA, SAN DIEGO Recreation Intramural Athletic Center	1995	188,000	Yes	4,000 Main Gym	No	Yes Div. III
UNIVERSITY OF GEORGIA The Ramsey Center for Student Physical Activies	1996	384,000	No	2,500 Volley Ball 3,000 Swimming	Indoor Comp./Rec.	Yes Div. I
UNIVERSITY OF MIAMI George A. Smathers Student Wellness Center	1996	114,000	Yes	No	Indoor Recreation	No
UNIVERSITY OF SOUTHERN CALIFORNIA Lyon Center	1989	80,000	Yes	1,800 Main Gym	Adjacent 1984 Olympic Pool	Some Div. I
VANDERBILT UNIVERSITY Student Recreation Center	1990	130,000	No	No	Indoor Recreation	No

The basic elements

Since the mid-1980s the design of student recreation centers has evolved. The type, quantity, and size of spaces vary widely. The programs have been influenced by factors such as an institution's enrollment, commuter or residential campus, other existing athletic facilities on campus, geographical location and climate, the regional recreational sports, the number and type of intercollegiate sports, size of the surrounding community, and the funding available. But many elements have remained constant.

- A single, controlled access entrance/lobby equipped with computer-monitors with the numerous required exits alarmed and enunciated to the control desk.
- High-bay court space for basketball, volleyball, badminton, indoor soccer, etc.
- Weight training and exercise rooms with free weights and cardio-vascular equipment.
- Racquet courts for squash, racquetball, and volleyball.

- Multi-purpose rooms of varying sizes for aerobics, combatives, yoga, Tai-chi, etc.
- Indoor elevated jogging track.
- Administration offices and conference spaces for sports and recreation staff and for student clubs.
- Locker/shower rooms, with separate facilities for men, women, faculty, and staff.
- Equipment checkout and storage, and sometimes laundry facilities.
- Lounge spaces, because the center has increasingly become the campus social center.
- An aquatic facility. The large universities with an intercollegiate swimming program have a competitive facility, with a 50-meter constant-depth pool, diving well, and practice tank, allowing the separate recreation pool to be sized for instructional swim classes and recreational uses such as lap swimming, inner-tube polo, and water basketball. The recreation pool may also have a zero-level (beach) entry, shallow water for instruction and water aerobics, deeper water for scuba diving

Photo Credit: Christopher Barone

Exterior of the Drayson Center for student physical activities and recreation at Loma Linda University, near San Bernadino, California.

and life saving classes, and more convenient access for disabled persons.

At smaller universities and most colleges both the pool and the gymnasium are often shared by intercollegiate competitive teams and recreation-seeking students. The design challenge of meeting the conflicting needs of competitive sports and "fun" recreation is diffi-

> *The design challenge of meeting the conflicting needs of competitive sports and recreation is difficult.*

cult, but it is being resolved in creative ways nationwide. Not only must the design of the pool itself accommodate both swimming and diving competition and student recreational uses, but the issue of spectator facilities and access must be addressed. For gymnasiums too, most colleges must combine the uses of intercollegiate competition, intramural, and recreational activity—and, at other times, events such as concerts, dances, and ceremonies.

Fortunately, the greatly improved technology of retractable seating, and motor-

ized curtains and backdrops, have facilitated such shared use. For example, the University of California, San Diego, has recently completed a facility accommodating 4,000 spectators for an athletic event, all on retractable seats. When the seats are fully retracted, the floor area released holds five recreational basketball courts. At UCSD an auxiliary gym actually makes basketball hoops available to recreational users even during an intercollegiate game.

The financial impact of accommodating spectators in a student recreational facility that is required to be open at all hours should never be underestimated. Provisions must be made for a lobby with ticket booths, multiple easy exits, concessions, numerous restrooms, press and TV space, team rooms, coaching offices, significant storage space, and additional circulation without impacting the facility's recreational use unduly.

As student interest in new forms of health maintenance, recreation, and intramural competition continues, campus and outside architects must also consider secondary spaces, the inclusion of which usually engenders debate during the programming phase. Such spaces include a wellness center, climbing walls, saunas, a cardio theater, rooms for

Photo Credit: Christopher Barone

The fitness area at the Student Recreation Center at the University of California, Riverside.

gymnastics or dance, MAC's (multi-use athletic courts with dasher boards similar to those in hockey rinks), a first aid room, and—yes—computer study rooms.

Location, location

Where should the student recreation center be located? After all, the building has an architectural mass that is difficult to insert graciously into the human-scaled heart of the campus. Parking needs, the spectator flows, and other considerations would seem to suggest a peripheral location. Also, if the recreation center is open to the local community in early mornings and other offpeak hours to generate some revenue, that too suggests a perimeter location.

However, this new genre of building has become more and more the social center as well as activity center of the campus; and students, faculty, and staff like to enjoy a more central facility that permits a fairly quick return to academic work and chores. So institutions such as the University of Miami, UCLA, and the University of Southern California have located their recreational centers on the central campus. But other universities from the University of Georgia to the University of Arizona have preferred an outer site.

Another frequent planning debate is whether to construct a single, large facility which allows the entire campus community to meet in one location or to build several satellite buildings around the campus, related to playing fields, parking fields, or student residential houses. The University of Virginia, for example, has chosen to develop satellite facilities. This scattered approach has significant management implications, and at Virginia at least it has resulted in a degree of "ownership" of the facilities by discreet community segments. Also, some colleges and universities choose to have separate facilities for individual competitive and recreational sports: a Tennis and Racquets Center, a fieldhouse, or a Natatorium for all water activities.

This leads to the question: What is the appropriate size for these new campus recreation centers? This is a difficult question to answer. As I noted earlier, it depends on the size of the university, whether spectators and community persons are introduced, whether one or two swimming pools are included, and more. It may also depend on the formulas of the state officials or some generous alumnus. Indeed, size is most frequently driven by the available funds.

Frequently a college or university will base its decision in part on comparisons with peer institutions, but unfortunately

Where should the student recreation center be located?

there is considerable misinformation about the square-foot cost of student recreation centers, even centers which have been built. The discrepancies stem not only from the bid date, zone of country, whether the site is complex, self-contained, or served by a central plant, and exclusive or inclusive of site development costs, but also from the confusion between construction cost and

Entrance to the 384,000-square-foot physical activities center at the University of Georgia, which more than 5,000 students use each day.

total project cost, and between assignable area and gross area, which can result in bizarre square foot numbers. Campus architects and administrators need to take great care to avoid inaccurate budgeting at the start of the project.

How much should a college or university plan to budget for a new state-of-the-art recreation center? In my experience, it is difficult to construct a building that provides for the full range of today's preferred activities for less than $8 million. The majority of projects I know of have fallen within a cost range of $8 million to $30 million, with projects for a large university that include a separate competitive pool and considerable spectator facilities at the high end.

Are these new student recreation centers worth the expense? One way to get an answer is to visit these centers and observe the traffic. The University of Georgia's Ramsey Center has averaged 5,500 visits a day since it opened; that of smaller Loma Linda University's Drayson Center has averaged 1,500. The center at Arizona State

University is usually filled until midnight. Obviously the recreation centers respond to a new desire by many young people and adults to keep themselves fit, agile, healthy,

Are these new student recreation centers worth the expense?

and strong. The recreation centers teach healthy lifestyle habits, preventative medicine, safe and fair competition. The facility is a valuable tool for recruitment and for retention. It is a place where students, faculty, and staff—and perhaps alumni and others from the surrounding community—can meet, workout, and play together. Also, for architects the centers are a new challenge and great fun to design.

Looking ahead, campus leaders and planners need to consider too: What of the future? Will financial difficulties force institutions to lease parts of the buildings to franchisers, or to various sports company sponsorships? Is intercollegiate athletics about to experience some cost-cutting restructuring? Should colleges continue to make wellness, the inculcation of healthy lifestyle habits, and the development of physical energy to carry out important intellectual and artistic work an integral part of their educational program?

Whatever the future holds, the student recreation center has become a new kind of building for new kinds of activities on campus in the past 15 years. Campus planners who have not already done so will need to take note of this latest addition to American university architecture. ∎

Photo Credit: Robert Barclay

Recreational pool at the Student Activities Center at Central Michigan University, looking through a hallway window.

REFERENCE

Emmons, P. and Wendt, D. 1996. What is Equitable in Athletic Facilities? *Planning for Higher Education* 24 (3): 27-31.

How traditional and virtual environments can be integrated to alter campus life and learning.

Stimulating Change Through Recombinant Facilities

Rodney Rose

C olleges and universities depend heavily on their campus facilities. The quality of instruction and research, the meetings of scholars and of students and faculty, the quality and variety of student life, and even the institutional culture, and all tied inexorably to physical resources. College campuses—land, academic and research buildings, studios, student unions, housing, athletic fields and recreation areas—give form to the learning communities and are inseparable from the programs, research, learning, and living that goes on within them. Higher education is shaped by the place in which it is conducted.

But the cost of maintaining, renovating, replacing, or building new facilities has increased dramatically. The older facilities have become more difficult and expensive to renovate. (The cost of deferred maintenance alone is estimated to be more than $60 billion for the nation's colleges and universities.) Then there is the cost of adding more buildings and new campuses to accommodate the still increasing demand for spaces. And now, rapid development of advanced computing and telecommunications technology raises fundamental questions about the traditional campus as a place—a thoughtful arrangement of buildings, fields, and spaces—in which to study. The development of new models such as the proposed Western Governors' University (WGU), backed by a commitment of 11 governors, and California's version of the WGU, the Virtual On-Line University, are considered by some to be an alternative to the continued construction of traditional campuses.

However, a pioneering approach to new buildings and major renovations has emerged and promises to revolutionize both campus facilities and the way scholars teach and students learn. These innovative learning environments integrate the advantages of a "virtual" learning environment with traditional campus-based approaches to enhance the quality of learning relationships between faculty and students. I call them *recombinant facilities*.

Rodney Rose is vice president of The JCM Group, a Los Angeles firm specializing in facilities planning and project management. A graduate of the University of California at Berkeley, he served as director of capital planning at UCLA from 1974 to 1991 and continues to help colleges and universities conduct strategic planning and create innovative capital development strategies. He was president of SCUP in 1991-92.

Take Harrison Hall at Portland State University in Oregon. Completed in 1996 at a cost of about $2.5 million, Harrison Hall could be perceived as merely a large new classroom building with built-in high-tech computing and telecommunications equipment. It's much more than that. It is 9,000 square feet of space dominated by a flat-floor, flexible seating auditorium, seating approximately 400. Because of its flexible design, however, the space can easily be converted from traditional classrooms to a ballroom, banquet facilities, a video conference center, a multi-media laboratory, or interactive television facilities in a single, cost-effective space.

All of its $500,000 of advanced telecommunications and multimedia technology are built into one wall of the room, dominated by

A pioneering approach to new buildings and renovations has emerged.

three 9 by 12-foot high-resolution video screens. A moveable podium has built-in controls that enable the speakers or technicians to operate all the functions, including electronically operated window shades. Staff support for the entire facility can be provided by only one technician, working in concert with one or a group of speakers.

Traditional classes, seminars, and lectures are held in Harrison Hall. But it is also possible to gain access to the facility and the programs and classes generated there without ever stepping inside. Course materials provided in its classes and lectures are recorded automatically, to allow accessibility to students at any time and from any location. Because the building is capable of taking full advantage of the Internet, EDNET, and video conferencing, students and other learners can take advantage of programs conducted in Harrison Hall from anywhere, on or off campus.

Or take Glendale Community College's Innovation Center in Phoenix, where a small group of faculty, students, and staff have de-

veloped a CD-ROM-based learning module which teaches basic anatomy students how to dissect a fetal pig. In addition to its use locally, the module is marketed internationally through corporate partnerships established by the college. Other multimedia projects developed at the Innovation Center include modules on Surgical Asepsis and Transcultural Assessment for the Department of Nursing, and a tutorial CD on Past-Tense Verbs, using both animation and sound, to provide undergraduates in English courses with a technique for improving their grammar skills. The purpose of the Innovation Center is to provide assistance to faculty in the integration of technology into curriculum development and preparation of classroom materials.

The Innovation Center occupies only part of an integrated learning facility called the High Tech Complex (HTC). The HTC actually consists of two facilities: the first, a 31,000 square-foot facility opened in 1987. The second, slightly smaller at 26,400 square feet, opened in 1991. These are multi-discipline facilities, designed to provide instructional support for open-entry/open-exit classes as well as traditional courses, computing support for administrative functions, technology and support. Also incorporated into the two facilities are language laboratories, seminar rooms, video conference and video production facilities, and faculty offices.

Both facilities have a large area called the "pit," with more than 400 microcomputer workstations. Students have access to these workstations as well as other HTC services more than 100 hours a week. They may check out software, work by themselves, or obtain immediate assistance from Instructional Associates who are available at the facility during all operating hours. The Instructional Associates assist students with both the hardware and software technologies, and with their particular assignments or course material.

Other facilities within the HTC include an Electronic Classroom, where students learn through various experimental instructional delivery methods, and an Authoring Lab, for creation of materials, manuals, and documentation for faculty and staff, which serves as a focal point for computer-related curriculum design and development. There is a small reference library and a number of traditional classrooms and seminar rooms as well.

A new category of buildings

Harrison Hall and the High Tech Complex are examples of recombinant facilities. As most persons know, recombinant DNA technology creates new organisms by splicing and recombining segments of DNA, or genes. Similarly, recombinant facilities create new kinds of facilities through the process of realignment or rearrangement of existing facilities and traditional functions, with the addition of novel functions, forming new combinations that change the interaction of people with their physical environment.

What is becoming clear is that campus facilities can no longer be only about architecture, landscape design, and master planning as a *response* to specific campus needs. Buildings and facilities need to be thought about and planned as part of an institution's higher learning strategy. Solving the facili-

ties problem for colleges and universities now requires strategic programming of functions, management, technology, and ready resources to affect new institutional outcomes: increased quality of learning, additional revenues, reduced costs, and more efficient delivery of programs and services.

Not many new buildings have accomplished this. We usually don't think of buildings as the mechanism for making change happen, certainly not in the same way we think of the steam engine, the printing press, automobile, or the telephone as having changed our lives. But, networked or linked together in new and creative ar-

> *Buildings can change the way we live, work, and play.*

rangements, buildings can change the way we live, work, and play in dramatic ways.

Let me cite four examples of recombinant facilities that have significantly changed life in the United States. The fully *planned communities* that began with entire

The "pit" at the High Tech Complex at Glendale Community College in Phoenix, Arizona. The 400 workstations are open 100 hours a week, with Instructional Associates.

new towns such as Reston, Virginia and Mission Viejo, California built in the 1960s have changed zoning, work and living relationships, and redefined urban life. The large *shopping malls*—enclosed and controlled environments—have not only replaced the traditional boulevard and store front commercial streets but have also become a new kind of village green, community center, and "downtown" for millions of people by recombining stores with theaters, restaurants, and landscaped atrium spaces, free parking, extended hours, and a clean, safer ambiance.

Theme parks resulted from the innovation of splicing new services into traditional entertainment attractions (rides, boardwalk exhibits, games, food concessions, etc.) to create a major new industry, dominated by Fortune 100 companies such as Disney, Six Flags, and Universal-MCA. The resulting environments now include modern hotels, restaurants, educational and sports facilities, and museums to become centers for family activities, extended vacations, or entertainment.

The newest recombinant facilities are *integrated health centers*. These combine the traditional hospital, clinics, pharmacies, physicians' offices, and laboratories with new wellness-focused complexes that include fitness and exercise centers, acupuncture and chiropractic services, massage therapy, health food stores, cardiac rehabilitation, and family counseling services. The result is a completely new strategy for health care delivery, designed to produce a healthier population for the 21st century. Michigan's Saint Lawrence Medical Center and the St. Joseph Medical Center in Kansas are only two already in operation.

Can universities recombine?

Transforming colleges and universities is a gargantuan challenge, and traditional campus facilities planning is often a considerable barrier to the transformation. Facilities are frequently underutilized, inflexible, and expensive to adapt to new uses or new technologies. It is still common for colleges to plan buildings to provide for specific functions or academic program needs: a life science building, a recreation center, a library. Buildings

tend to be "owned" by departments or divisions, and representatives of those departments usually play a dominant role in planning the building for their own needs.

Campus facilities planning can no longer be only a response to specific needs.

Recombinant facility design, however, requires college and university administrators to think very differently about facility planning and the role of their facilities: how they are used, who uses them, and how they can be more productively utilized. Campus planners, including faculty and administrators, need to view their facilities as a way of enhancing the learning process for both students and faculty, employing the best technologies available to improve outcomes, rather than as a means of satisfying the wishes of special units.

Recombinant facilities are not the same as older facilities that have been modernized. They are not libraries with new on-line services and reader stations, or stadiums with new private sky boxes and television instant replay. Recombinant facilities represent a rethinking of how students learn, alumni gather, and professors teach in their physical surroundings. Campus facilities, properly recombined, should alter the way faculty, students, and staff behave, study, and live, just as a shopping mall changes our buying patterns and an integrated health center changes how we take care of our bodies and our health.

An example of a major, new recombinant facility is the University of Michigan's $45 million Media Union. Opened in the fall of 1996, it is one of the most spectacular models of a recombinant facility on any American campus. The 250,000 square-foot facility houses an electronic library, more than 500 workstations in open areas, interactive multimedia classrooms, a virtual reality laboratory, theater and performance space, design and innovation studios, and more than two dozen "collaboration rooms" to encourage interdisciplinary team projects.

By the fall term of 1997, the services and facilities of the Media Union will be accessible 24 hours a day, 7 days a week, available to the entire campus community as well as to the community at large. Designed by Albert Kahn and Associates, the structure has impressive cathedral ceilings and uses glass extensively on exterior and interior walls. A first impression may suggest an ultra-modern library, but that would be a mistake. The Media Union does not "belong" to the library or to any single department or school. It is a radically new facility in which scholars and students in art, engineering, architecture, the sciences, music, medicine, philosophy, and the humanities can come together to design new courses, study multidisciplinary topics, and invent new forms of pedagogy—at any time of day or night.

President James Duderstadt maintains that the Media Union is a hothouse for developing the new learning-teaching environment of the 21st century. The mission statement never mentions academic disciplines or special reserved spaces. Promotional materials describe the facility as "an

---

Recombinant facility design requires administrators to think very differently.

---

interactive playground for imaginative scholars, a place for creativity, using knowledge to serve our society." Its occupants will "explore new avenues for creative collaboration, extend human cognition and sensory powers, invent new paradigms for learning and teaching, discover new art forms, design new buildings for new forms of community, and create new devices for industry and home." The university's leaders hope to break down department walls and reduce the isolation of such schools and departments, and to allow new forms of behavior, cooperation, research, and scholarship to emerge.

What makes this a significant model of recombinant facilities is not just the realignment of relatively traditional functions and spaces to create a new learning environment. It is the organizational structure, the investment of collaborative resources, the integration of a wide variety of management, staffing, and technical expertise that make this unique among university facilities. The management team of the facility, for example, is headed by an executive committee of twelve, consisting of deans and directors representing the Schools of Architecture and Urban Planning; Engineering; Information and Library Studies; Literature, Science and the Arts; and Music; as well as the Academic Outreach Program, the Information and Technology Division, and the University Library. Each school or program has invested resources, including a commitment of faculty and staff, to try to make this collaborative effort work.

Lobby and elevator tower at the University of Michigan's $45 million new Media Union, a radically new kind of teaching-learning facility.

A facilities revolution?

The Media Union, the High Tech Complex, and Harrison Hall are each examples of recombinant facilities, models for breaking down traditional barriers and creating a new physical and technological environment for interactive, collaborative learning.

What makes them important as models is that they begin to redefine the campus as a *place*—focused on the needs of learners, with unrestricted access to a diverse learner population and learning styles, and an integration of technology to provide access to the global network of learning resources, creating additional value for its community. These characteristics may also make the college or university more attractive to potential partners, investors, or donors, and less vulnerable to the fiscal exigencies of tight-fisted legislatures.

The three facilities are not alike, but their "gene-slicing" design, global reach, interdisciplinary collaboration, and flexible, multiple uses are similar. All focus primarily on students and their learning in an entirely new way, much as enclosed shopping malls and integrated health centers have rearranged the way people think about shopping and taking care of their health.

Traditional Campus Facilities	New Campus Facilities
• Single discipline	• Interdisciplinary
• Limited access	• Unlimited access
• Restricted funding	• Diverse, collaborative funding
• "Owned" by users	• Institutional ownership

However, the recombinant facilities on campus need not be limited to the types of learning spaces illustrated here. Others might include an integrated instructional laboratory facility, focused on a wide range of physical, natural, and/or social sciences disciplines; or a multi-purpose telecommunication center, devoted to the production, distribution, and marketing of educational materials; or a telecommuting center, providing short-term office, research, or support services for part-time students and faculty.

In fact, the recombinant facilities approach may not require building a new facility at all. For example, existing facilities such as classrooms, laboratories, and media sup-

Campus architecture may be at the edge of a major shift.

port facilities, which are frequently autonomous, separately managed units, could be networked through the use of shared technical and staff resources, shared computer and telecommunications technology, centralized scheduling and management, and collaborative funding. Some renovation, realignment of programs, and installation of new equipment would be necessary; but construction of a new facility, or major structural renovations, might be avoided.

For example, linking existing campuses and buildings by networking technology and faculty resources is integral to the development strategy of the Maricopa (Phoenix, Arizona) and Dallas community college districts. By creating organizational, financial, and facilities networks that cross traditional district boundaries, students in Phoenix and Dallas have achieved greater access to instructional programs. In addition, there have been significant savings in capital costs, increased revenue streams generated by marketing of learning modules and telecourses, and a greater response to community and business needs.

As the University of Michigan has learned, recombinant facilities require university planners to reevaluate how buildings are conceived in the first place. That means that all facilities must become college or university buildings, not owned by some discipline or department. It means rethinking who gets appointed to planning and programming committees, and how capital budget priorities are created and how fundraising is conducted. Above all, it means taking creative risks to invent these new recombinant facilities, and it means keeping the needs of students and their learning paramount.

Recombinant DNA technology can be used to create healthier, better new organisms. Recombinant facilities, splicing new "genes" into traditional, old college patterns of behavior, can be used to help reshape colleges and universities as a different kind of place for higher learning. Campus architecture may be at the edge of a major shift in both design and purpose, and this new kind of facilities design may be a powerful lever for prying colleges and universities into the structural changes that many persons are now demanding. ∎

IV. Improving the Finances

A primer for planners about higher education's "cost disease" and its future effects.

How To Think About Rising College Costs

William J. Baumol and Sue Anne Batey Blackman

College planners and administrators are painfully aware that the costs of higher education have for decades grown faster than the inflation rate, and have risen dramatically since 1980. This "cost disease" of higher education has led critics to demand that colleges reduce duplications, administrative "bloat," and the proliferation of courses, introduce stricter financial controls, and trim their sprawling academic programs. Numerous states have reduced their appropriations for public higher education, occasionally to force tighter financial management.

Just a cursory review illustrates the magnitude and persistence of the growth rates of the real price of higher education (that is, the price increase above the rate of general inflation). As Figure 1 shows, for the 42-year period 1949 to 1991 the Consumer Price Index, or CPI, and education costs have both increased throughout the postwar period. But the curve for education prices lies above the CPI curve every year since 1949 and has drawn far ahead of the CPI since the late 1970s. Virtually without respite since 1949, higher education rose in price more rapidly than prices were rising on average in the economy. While the CPI's rate of increase was 4.2 percent, higher education prices rose 7.6 percent a year. Because of compounding, this apparently small difference means that, in dollars of constant purchasing power, the cost of American higher education has *quadrupled* over the 42-year period!

The rapidly growing costs of higher education are not peculiar to the United States. Despite other industrialized countries' greater central control over their university budgets, there are very few other

William J. Baumol is Joseph Douglas Green Professor of Economics emeritus at Princeton and director of the C.V. Starr Center for Applied Economics at New York University. A graduate of CCNY in New York, with a Ph.D. from the London School of Economics, he has taught at Princeton since 1949. He is author or co-author of 27 books and nearly 500 articles, a past president of the American Economic Association, recipient of the Frank Seidman Award in Political Economy, and a member of the National Academy of Sciences.

Sue Anne Batey Blackman is senior research assistant to Dr. Baumol and co-author with him of *Productivity and American Leadership: The Long View* (1989). She is a graduate of the University of Colorado at Boulder and is co-author of two books and author of several articles on economics, national policy, and environmental issues.

advanced nations in which similar complaints about the rates of cost increase for higher education are not heard. Figure 2 shows that for the period 1965-1991 the rates of growth in real costs for higher education in five other countries also have grown rapidly. Indeed, the U.S. record is far from the worst. So the higher education systems of other major countries provide no models for a quick fix for the problem of rapidly rising college costs in the United States.

Why the cost disease?

To be sure, U.S. colleges and universities can benefit from stronger financial management, and their means to slow down their escalating costs have not been exhausted. But the reasons for rising college costs are complex (Getz and Siegfried 1991); the increase has no single explanation. Moreover, the extraordinary rise in higher education costs is not unique. Much the same "cost disease" infects such other service fields as health care, legal services, library services, insurance, auto repairs, live artistic performances, police protection, fine restaurant meals, and a number of others.

For many of these services, the federal government keeps tabs on their price increases and productivity performance; and these data confirm that their prices also have grown persistently faster than the rate

The cost of American higher education has quadrupled over the 42-year period.

of inflation and their productivity growth has been usually small. The price of a doctor's services has doubled in constant purchasing power over the past four decades, and the price of hospital rooms has risen 700 percent.

Why is it that the prices of higher education, and of health care, dramatic and orchestral performances, legal services, excellent restaurants, auto repairs, and similar services are rising faster than the prices of food, clothing, computers, and manufactured goods?

FIGURE 1

Index of U.S. Education Expenditure per Student vs. Consumer Price Index
1949–1991 (1949=100)

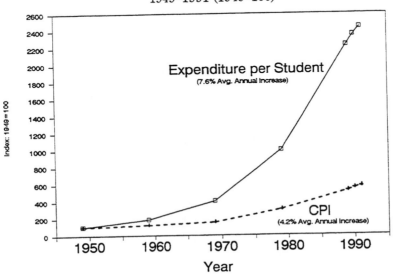

Sources: U.S. Dept. of Education and U.S. Dept. of Labor, Bur. of Labor Stats.

There is one influence that goes far in accounting for the price increases in higher education and other important services. *They are each characterized by a persistently slow growth in productivity relative to other economic activities.* That is, in these particular services the output per work-hour rises more slowly than the output per work-hour in other economic activities.

This explanation is supported by the available data on crude labor productivity growth in higher education, or labor productivity figures unadjusted for changes in the quality of the product. According to the *Digest of Education Statistics, 1994* (p. 175), in 1869-70 there were 563 institutions of higher learning in the United States, with 52,286 degree students enrolled and 5,553 faculty members, or 9.4 students per faculty member. In 1991-92 there were 3,601 institutions of higher learning with 14,358,953 students and 826,252 faculty members, or 17.4 students per faculty member. This means that crudely measured labor productivity (the number of students taught per teacher) grew over the course of the past 120 years at an annual rate of one half of

one percent. This is only one quarter of the average rate of growth of labor productivity in the U.S. economy as a whole, some two percent a year.

In higher education the nature of the products make their production a handicraft activity.

The fact is that in higher education and similar personal services the nature of their products tends to make their production a handicraft activity. The services are labor-intensive, and consumers and the products demand personal attention. Most of these services resist standardization. No two sick patients are exactly alike. No two wrecked automobiles are alike. It takes individual, highly skilled, human attention to diagnose their problems and repair the damage.

Second, these services have labor requirements that are difficult to reduce through technology. College teaching can

FIGURE 2

Real Education Price Growth Rates
Six Countries, 1965–1988

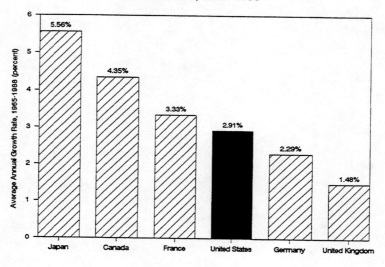

Sources: UNESCO and U.S. Dept. of Education
Filename:HIGHED2.drw

be complemented by computer-assisted instruction, video cassettes, interactive television, and E-mail, but live professors are still considered essential. Moreover, their labor-time cannot be reduced much without cutting quality. Labor content in higher education or medicine or the performing arts cannot be reduced year after year as it can in, say, computer or auto manufacturing and in the production of corn. Personal services are condemned to productivity growth slower than the economy's average.

This slower productivity growth leads directly to the persistent rise in their real costs. An example may make this point clearer. If the wages of workers in a computer plant rise 4 percent but their productivity—the number of computers produced per worker—rises 6 percent, then the costs per computer will fall. Wages rise, but output per worker rises even faster. In contrast, if the salaries of professors rise 4 percent a year, but productivity in higher education goes up only 1 percent, then the labor costs of higher education will rise roughly by the amount of difference. Instructors' salaries rise, but output per instructor does not rise as fast.

Thus, it is the difference between productivity improvements in personal services like higher education and productivity improvements in many other segments of the economy that is a primary driving force in the relative price increases in relatively stagnant personal services like higher education. There are very few villains here. Wasteful expenditures, greed, and poor management exist in higher education as they do elsewhere, but do not play the critical role. Rather, it is the relatively stagnant technology of education, health care, the performing arts, gourmet restaurants, police, and similar services, each of which requires lots of personal, highly skilled attention, that accounts for the compounding rise in their costs—a rise that threatens to strain the budgets of families, municipalities, states, and central governments of the entire industrialized world.

Can we afford higher education?

This situation seems to imply that higher education's cost increases, along with rising costs in health care, the arts, and other personal services, may inevitably price the services beyond the reach of an ever-grow-

FIGURE 3

Hypothetical Changes in Total Output Over 50 Years,
Assuming Historic Productivity Growth

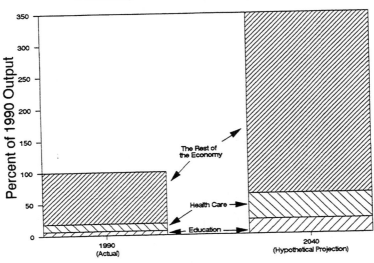

Filename:HIGHED5.drw

160

ing share of the population. But that is not true. Contrary to appearances, the United States can afford ever more expensive college education, medical care, police protection, and musical performances.

To see why, we must recognize that the problem of slow productivity growth in the handicraft services is balanced by the rapid productivity growth in the rest of the economy. Productivity is growing almost everywhere in the economy, even if it is growing more slowly in some parts. And in an economy in which productivity is growing everywhere, an hour of labor can buy more of every product, including higher education. This conclusion may strike educators and education planners as utterly Pollyannaish. But the conclusion is inescapable, if only our future productivity continues to grow as it has in the past century. There are two fundamental reasons why this is so.

First, there is a small, but nevertheless positive, growth rate in productivity in those stagnant personal services such as higher education. To take an example from the performing arts, it still takes as much labor-time to perform a half-hour Mozart quartet as it did when the music was composed 200 years ago.

So there seems to have been no productivity improvement. However, today Viennese musicians can travel to Frankfurt to perform in a few hours. In Mozart's time, the trip from Vienna to Frankfurt took six days. Developments in science and technology have reduced the real cost—the number of hours of labor required to deliver the service. The musicians are able to be more productive.

Personal services are condemned to slower productivity growth.

In university education, productivity has surely been assisted by films, computers, telephones, microphones, airplanes, and larger class sizes, as well as by other technological developments. Many colleges now offer evening courses, weekend programs, and summer schedules, using their facilities more efficiently. Even though college and university productivity grows at only a snail's pace, it is growing. This rise in labor productivity means that less labor-time is required to produce this

FIGURE 4

Hypothetical Changes in Total Spending Over 50 Years,
Assuming Historic Productivity Growth

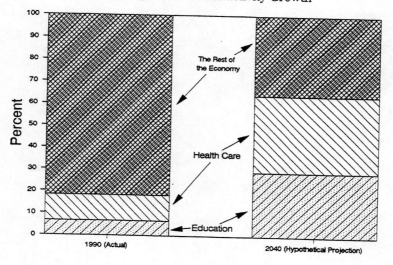

service, and thus that much less labor-time in other economic activities is needed to acquire the wherewithal to purchase a higher education. In a sense, higher education has become a bit more affordable even as it appears to draw steadily beyond our financial means.

By 2040 education and health care alone could well absorb over half of the entire GNP.

Second, productivity growth in the rest of the economy gives us the means to afford more of everything. This is because in an economy in which productivity is growing in almost every sector, consumers can have more of every good and service. But there needs to be a transfer of funds from the savings created by high-productivity industries to the costs of low-productivity services. To prevent the demise of important handicraft services, societies and families must change the proportions of income that they devote to different products.

Reallocating national resources

Just how much of our national output will Americans have to devote to our stagnant personal services?

We can suggest the magnitudes by using some current U.S. data on price trends and on expenditures for health care and education. What would happen if the real prices of health care and education continue to grow at their current rates for the next 50 years, and if overall U.S. productivity rises in that period at its historic rate of approximately 2 percent while real health care and education outputs maintain an unchanged share of the gross national product (GNP)? That is, what if the economy were to produce more of health care, education, and everything else, yet keep their relative output proportions unchanged? (We do not intend this as a forecast, only as a suggestive extrapolation.)

In Figures 3 and 4, the left-hand bar shows the actual shares of the 1990 U.S. GNP by three categories: education, health care, and a catch-all "rest of the economy." In 1990 education and health care constituted less than 20 percent of the total activity in the economy. The right-hand bar in Figure 3 shows what might happen to outputs 50 years down the road, if the number of hours of labor performed remains constant but productivity in the economy grows at its historic average rate and each industry's output level is adjusted to retain the same share of total output. Each of the three segments in the right-hand bar (the year 2040) in Figure 3 is more than 3.5 times as tall as in the left-hand bar.

Figure 4, however, is the crucial one for our argument. It shows how the apportionment of real expenditures has to be modified by Americans in order to achieve the output result in Figure 3. Health care expenditures, instead of constituting 11 percent of the total as they did in 1990, must rise to roughly 35 percent of the total by 2040. And the share of expenditure devoted to education will have to rise from 9 percent in 1990 to more than 20 percent in 2040.

In other words, if current relative price trends and output proportions continue as they are now, by the year 2040 education and health care alone will absorb well over half of the entire GNP! Consumers will have tripled their consumption of every good and service, including manufactured necessities and luxuries; but they will be devoting a much larger share of their total spending for education and health care.

Devoting half the country's national income to education and health care sounds frightening and troublesome. In some ways, it is alarming. But in other ways, it is not so. It is as though the real price of computers and printers in the future will be cut drastically but the cost of computer software programs will rise to 50 percent of the total cost of operating the computers effectively.

The huge job of persuasion

Our hopeful take on this economic phenomenon, however, is beset with daunting difficulties. Most immediate perhaps is the enormously arduous task of getting the general public to recognize the difference between reality and illusion in the behavior of costs. It will not be easy to convince the intelligent nonspecialist that, even though the prices of personal services like a college education appear to be rising at a rate that is out of control, in fact the costs of these services (in terms of labor-time equivalent) are really declining gradually because of increases in people's labor productivity. The drop in the relative price of many goods will allow them to have more money for services like education or auto repairs.

Yet the task of explaining this changing economic situation should not be beyond the abilities of skilled journalists,

Higher education is an example of the need for reconceived practices.

educators, medical experts, economists, political leaders and others who specialize in effective communication.

Another difficulty that bedevils the effective treatment of the cost disease of higher education and other services is that of acquiring the tax revenues necessary to help maintain these services. A large portion of the budget of every state government consists of the expenditures for education, health care, police, libraries, and other services likely to exhibit rising price behavior. This means Americans can expect the real outlays for these services to treble or more by 2040, if these service outputs are not to fall behind the outputs of the economy's remaining activities. The political task will require unusual courage and persuasiveness. And we admit that even if the necessary tax increases are achieved, it is disturbing that such an enormous share of the GNP will have to flow through government channels rather than the private sector of the economy.

Surely it is urgent to think now about the implications of the escalating costs of higher education, health care, and other important public services, and about the

practical means for grappling with the increase. Better financial planning and management within higher education and other services, and structural changes in the delivery of these services can help; but new tax and other revenues will also be needed.

Higher education is an example of the need for reconceived practices. Many state colleges and universities are already feeling the destructive effects of budget cuts, and a few colleges are beginning to show signs of erosion in the quality and breadth of their services. Yet higher education, professional training, and research are engines of economic growth. The irony is that, to the extent that education, training, and university research fuel productivity growth in the economy as a whole, the threatened undermining of colleges and universities can handicap the very process of economic growth that provides the nation's educational resources. ■

REFERENCES

Baumol, W. and W. Bowen. 1966. *Performing Arts: The Economic Dilemma.* Twentieth Century Fund.

Baumol, W., S. A. B. Blackman, and E. Wolff. 1989. *Productivity and American Leadership.* MIT Press.

Eckhaus, R. 1990. The U.S. Economy and Higher Education. In K. Hanson and J. Meyerson (eds.), *Higher Education in a Changing Economy.* ACE/Macmillan.

Getz, M. and J. Siegfried. 1991. Costs and Productivity in American Colleges and Universities. In C. Clotfelder *et al, Economic Challenges in Higher Education.* University of Chicago Press.

Organization for Economic Cooperation and Development (OECD). 1990. *Health Care Systems in Transition: The Search for Efficiency.* Paris.

Ryan, P. 1992. Unbalanced Growth and Fiscal Restriction: Public Spending on Higher Education in Advanced Economies Since 1970. *Structural Change and Economic Dynamics* 3(2): 261-288.

United Nations Educational, Scientific, and Cultural Organization (UNESCO). *Statistical Yearbook. Paris.* Various issues.

U.S. Department of Education. 1990 and 1994. *Digest of Education Statistics.* National Center for Education Statistics.

U.S. Department of Labor. *CPI Detailed Report.* Bureau of Labor Statistics. Various Issues.

*A transformation is taking place in the
nature of wealth, and higher education is
at the core.*

Education and Family Wealth

John Langbein

T he ancient field of trust-and-estate
law has entered a period of serious decline. Within law firms,
even some seasoned practitioners
have begun to diversify away from
the field, despite the fact that
nearly one-eighth of the U.S. population is
now over 65 years of age and the number
and percentage of elderly is growing.

While some of the decline is owed to the
1981 revision of federal transfer taxes, the
decline in probate is rooted in several little-
noticed but profound changes in the nature of
wealth in our time. These changes in the
nature of U.S. wealth, along with major demographic changes, have radically altered
traditional patterns of the transmission of
wealth between parents and their sons and
daughters. We are living through a quiet but
powerful inheritance revolution.

Education, and especially higher educa-

tion, is at the center of this fundamental
shift. Since most colleges and universities
are dependent on family contributions and on
wills for their financial health, it is obligatory
that university leaders, planners, and the
fund-raising staff understand what is taking
place. The financial future of America's colleges, especially the private institutions,
could be affected.

Family wealth in the past

Often we can best broach the new by identifying important characteristics of the old. In
the days when Abraham Lincoln lived on the
prairie and his contemporaries were building
cities on the Atlantic seaboard, around the
Great Lakes, and in the Ohio and Mississippi
River valleys, the prototypical unit of production was the family. Nineteenth-century
America was overwhelmingly a nation of
small farms, and in the towns and cities an
economy of small shops and small-scale fac-
tories. For many farmers, artisans, and the
shopkeepers the entire family worked in the
enterprise.

In those circumstances, Americans had
little occasion to distinguish between what
we think of as earned income (income from
one's labor) and investment income (the return on property); the two incomes merged.
I do not mean to slight the importance of

John Langbein is Chancellor Kent Professor of
Law and Legal History at Yale University. A grad-
uate of Columbia University and Harvard Law
School, he also has an L.L.B. and Ph.D. from
Cambridge University in England. Prior to coming
to Yale, he was Max Pam Professor of American
and Foreign Law at the University of Chicago Law
School. This article is based on his essay in the
February 1988 issue of the *Michigan Law Review*.

We are living through a quiet but powerful inheritance revolution.

property. Ownership of a farm, a store, or a small business rescued you from a life of stoop labor in someone else's field, mill, or household. Accordingly, people of means aspired to nothing so much as to leave their children the family farm, firm, or store, to make for their children in the quaint phrase of the time "a provision for life."

There was relatively little formal education. In this low-tech age, the transmission of skills, like so much else, occurred within the family. You learned your trade alongside your parents and relatives. The family was not only the primary unit of production, it was also the primary source of education.

Transfer of ownership rights in these multigenerational enterprises occurred upon the death of the parents, typically of the father. Various arrangements were made for the widow, but the tendency was to limit the widow to a life interest so that the bulk of the property could pass to the next generation, assuring continuity of the enterprise.

Life expectancy 100 years ago was about 45 years, so parents often died in middle age. The successors were typically young adults, as compared with middle-aged or near-elderly adults who usually inherit today when parents die. To complete this snapshot of 19th-century wealth transmission patterns, I need to remind you that daughters received much less than sons. Family firms associated the son or sons with the firm's name; for example, the pianomaking firm is called Steinway & Sons, not Steinway & Daughters. Wealth transmission favored the male line.

In sum, wealth in the last century was tangible—land, the family business or store, and possessions like furniture, tools, and personal valuables—and it was transferred on the death of relatively young parents to their children, especially the sons.

New forms of wealth

In the first half of the 20th century, the family gradually ceased to be an important unit of production. To be sure, you can still find remnants of cottage industry in America; there is a fair amount of mom-and-pop retailing; and numerous small firms are still owned by families. In the main, however, the complexity of modern modes of production, marketing, and distribution impose enormous capital requirements. Village blacksmiths cannot manufacture automobiles, airplanes, and oil rigs. The characteristic unit of production in our age is corporate, not domestic.

This development extends to farming as well. Family farms still exist in America, but many of them are hobby farms or secondary enterprises run by people whose main livelihood derives from employment away from the farm. Farms have become fewer and larger, and American agriculture is ever more technology driven and capital intensive. Whereas 44 percent of Americans lived on farms in 1880, only 4 percent did in 1990.

The family has undergone a specialization of function. In economic terms, the family remains a unit of consumption but is very seldom a unit of production anymore. Production and distribution commonly take place in large entities: assembly plants, oil refineries, retail store chains, and large commercial firms. These modern modes of production are capital intensive and require specialized institutions to finance their huge capital needs: banks, insurance companies, securities firms, and other financial intermediaries.

These large financial enterprises now absorb the savings that families used to devote to family enterprise. Family savings are now invested externally—in stocks, bank deposits, insurance policies, and the like. Financial assets have become the characteristic form of transmissable wealth. Property has increasingly become paper property. (I'm concerned here only with private-sector wealth, not the benefits of government largess—"new property" as Charles Reich called it[1]—such as Social Security, Medicare, food stamps, federal retirement payments and other entitlement programs.)

The productive world of education

The same technological and economic forces that caused the dissolution of the family-based enterprises have also stripped the family of much of its role as an educational institution. These forces have created a second new form of modern wealth: human capital.[2]

Economists now see educational expenditure as an investment, akin to conventional investment in plant, equipment, and inventory. Education produces skills, and skills are as much an input in the productive process as machines. Whether we speak of new fields like aeronautics or ancient ones like health care, the story is the same. While plant and equipment become increasingly sophisticated—robotics, CAT scanners, and all that—the skills of the workforce become still more decisive. Human capital more and more substitutes for nonhuman capital. New knowledge not only displaces old knowledge, it also displaces plant and equipment.

Human capital more and more substitutes for nonhuman capital.

Human capital has steadily increased over the 20th century as a fraction of total capital and a fraction of the gross national product. The percentage of GNP spent on education and job training grew by 80 percent from 1929 to 1969, in which year it stood at 15.4 percent of GNP.[3]

More and more, Americans expect personal wealth to take the form of earned income, that is, a return on human capital. A major source of wealth today is a person's breadth and depth of knowledge, one's skills and expertise. Creating this human capital has become a gigantic industry in the United States—a vast array of pre-schools, schools, summer camps, training centers, colleges

and universities, and advanced learning institutes and conferences.

In 1870 only 2 percent of the population graduated from high school; by 1970 the figure was 75.6 percent. In 1870 all higher education awarded only 9,371 bachelor's degrees and one doctorate. By 1970 the number of degrees conferred had increased one hundredfold over 1870, with 30,000 Ph.D. or equivalent degrees alone. As recently as 1940, only 4.6 percent of Americans had completed four or more years of university study; by 1987 19.9 percent had done so.

The creation of superior human capital—a principal form of modern wealth—has become a central activity of this nation. In today's economic order it is education more than tangible property that gives a young person advantages.

Paying for human capital

The development of human capital through education has required huge investments from many sources. In 1900 the total expenditures for formal education stood at $289.6 million. In 1989–90 the total expenditures on formal education were $330.5 billion, about 7 percent of the GNP. Two-fifths of it went for higher education.

There is no mystery about who has been paying for this vast expenditure of education. Even allowing for scholarships, loans, and student labor, the main burden falls on parents. Of course, even childless people pay taxes to support public education. But for this essay, I want to focus on families who are raising children.

The astonishing growth of education in our time has resulted in a revolution in the transfer of wealth within families. The business of educating children and adolescents has become the main occasion for intergenerational wealth transfer. At the beginning of this century, parents were concerned to transmit the partrimony—the farm, the firm, the belongings—so that their offspring would have a better life. Today, parents are more likely to be concerned to provide the best possible education for their children so their offspring can enjoy a richer life.

The process of delivering educational advantage to children begins early. According to U.S. Department of Education statistics, there has been a huge increase in formal preschool education in the past 25 years. During the years of their children's primary and secondary school education, propertied parents either seek housing in suitable school districts or send their children to private schools. Parents who can do so tend to move into the better school districts when they have school-age children, then move out when they no longer need the schools.

And then there is college. *The Digest of Educational Statistics, 1989* reports that the average annual charge for tuition, room, and board for undergraduates in 1987–88 was $3,960 in public colleges and $10,390 in private colleges. For parents who send their son or daughter to one of the prestigious private colleges or universities, the total cost in 1991–92 will be between $21,000 and $23,000 a year. In the best graduate and professional schools the price tag is higher still. Yale Law School will cost about $25,000 in 1991–92. Thus, college and three years of graduate study at leading private institutions can cost a family more than $150,000.

Very few families can afford to pay such education bills on what accountants would call a current basis. That is especially true when the family has more than one child in the educational mill at the same time. For most families these education expenses represent capital transfers in a quite literal sense. That is, the money for college comes from savings or a refinanced mortgage, or from debt (money borrowed from the family's future capital).

A recent *Newsweek* article[4] recounts the saga of a parent named C.Y. Lu who had the financial misfortune to have one son attending Princeton while the other was enrolled at Harvard Law School. Mr. Lu was reported to have sold off investments, taken out educational loans, and refinanced his home mortgage by $60,000 in order to raise a total of $140,000. Mr. Lu is quoted as saying, "I've told my sons, your education is going to be your inheritance."

Mr. Lu's words encapsulate my thesis.

Today's offspring expect that parental wealth will be transferred during their parents' lifetime.

Education payments are replacing property as an inheritance, and lifetime transfers are displacing succession on death. Eighty years ago Mr. Lu would have husbanded his wealth and left it to his two sons at his death. Today, in mid-life he cashes out and goes into debt in order to fork over his savings to Princeton and Harvard in the expectation that those universities will furnish his sons with the human capital that they can employ to gain wealth.

Parents understand full well what economists have been demonstrating with their studies of human capital. Degrees from high-quality colleges and graduate schools are superior investments when compared to any class of financial assets. The degrees help produce a far larger income stream. In 1985 the median annual income of full-time male workers aged 25 years and over who had not graduated high school was under $20,000. For those who had completed four years of college, however, the figure was above $30,000. And for those with more than four years of higher education, the figure approached $40,000. The comparable earnings figures for female workers were lower, but differences in educational attainment among women produced similar disparities in favor of the well-educated. Moreover, the returns on higher education appear to be increasing, widening the gap between the well-off and the poor.[5]

So, whereas children once expected the transfer of the farm or firm, today's children expect help with educational expenses. And whereas sons and daughters once expected to wait until the death of their parents for their inheritance, today's offspring expect that parental wealth will be transferred during their parents' lifetime. No wonder trust-and-estate lawyers have less to do.

The pension explosion

There is one other major contributor to the inheritance revolution: the massive growth of pensions for the elderly and the longer life expectancy that brought about the amazing expansion of retirement income.

No one in Abraham Lincoln's day had ever heard of a pension fund. If you lived beyond your period of productive labor, you were usually cared for within the family. Even as late as World War II, the private pension system was miniscule.[6] But today, the assets of nonfederal pension plans (private plans plus the pension funds of state and local government employees) exceed $2 trillion. By the mid-1980s, pension funds owned nearly one-fourth of all equity securities and one-half of all corporate debt in the United States. For many middle-class and especially upper-middle-class families, pension wealth is their largest asset.

The growth of pensions is the product of a remarkable demographic change. While life expectancy a century ago was about 45 years, today it is about 75 years, and still climbing. Modern sanitation, better nutrition, and modern medicine have combined to help people live longer than ever before. The very causes of death have changed. A century ago you were likely to die of infectious disease. Today, antibiotics and other advances have largely eliminated infectious disease as a cause of death, and people live long enough to die from the diseases of old age such as cardiovascular disease and cancer. The growth of pensions has also been spurred by the federal government creating irresistable tax incentives to encourage people to conduct much of their saving for retirement in a special mode, the tax-qualified pension plan.

From the standpoint of family wealth transfers, what is important about the pension system is that it has been deliberately designed to promote the exhaustion of accumulated capital during one's lifetime. Only a negligible fraction of pension wealth finds its way into intergenerational transfer.

The mechanism by which pension wealth is consumed is annuitization. Annuitization allows people to consume their capital safely, that is, without fear of running out of money while they are alive. But accounts that have been annuitized disappear on the death of the annuitants, as do Social Security benefits. This leaves not one penny of pension wealth for the heirs. Annuitization is the enemy of inheritance.

Truth and consequences

Transfer of wealth at death, the pattern of former times, is therefore ceasing to characterize the wealth transmission practices of the broad middle classes. Parents today tend to transfer wealth to their young in mid-life by means of investing in human capital, especially through education. And parents tend to consume their remaining wealth—real estate, savings, pension wealth, and Social Security payments—during their old age, and especially their very old age. Both developments lead away from traditional wealth transfer to their sons and daughters on death. The days of routine, lawyer-guided wealth-transfer-on-death have largely passed.

The changes in wealth transfer I have been describing are much less important for the very rich. Dynastic wealth cannot be stuffed into a pension account. And even after large transfers of family money for prep schools, colleges, and professional schools, the very well-to-do have considerable wealth to pass on to the young, and the trust-and-estate bar survives among the carriage trade.

For college and university presidents, and for their fund-raisers, the inheritance revolution will require new strategies to gather support. But support for colleges and universities should continue strong since higher education is a major contributor to the formation of human capital. ∎

NOTES

[1]Reich, C., "The New Property," *Yale Law Journal*, 73 (1964) 733–787.

[2]Becker, G., *Human Capital* (National Bureau of Economic Research, 1964); T. Schultz, *Investing in People* (University of California Press, 1981).

[3]Johnson, G. "Investment In and Returns from Education," in P. Hendershott (ed.), *The Level and Composition of Household Saving* (Ballinger, 1985).

[4]"Fuming Over College Costs," *Newsweek*, May 17, 1987.

[5]Levy, F. *Dollars and Dreams: The Changing American Income Distribution* (Russell Sage Foundation, 1987); Murphy, K. and F. Welch, "Wage Premiums for College Graduates," *Educational Researcher*, 18 (1989), 17–26.

[6]Greenough, W. and F. King, *Pension Plans and Public Policy*, (Columbia University Press, 1976).

Is it time for higher education to abandon fund accounting?

The Necessary Revolution in Financial Accounting

Gordon Winston

The financial accounts of a college or university do not report economic information for the institution as a whole. Instead, the institution is divided into separate activities and a separate set of financial accounts—income statement and balance sheet—is reported for each of those activities. In effect, each activity at a college is treated as if it were a separate firm (Garner 1991). Often-complex loans and transfers between these "firms" are recorded in each set of accounts. Typically eight or nine separate fund accounts and their interwoven transfers make up the annual financial statement for even a small college. This peculiar system is called fund accounting.

Fund accounting has been a source of complaints among college and university trustees for decades, and among others

Gordon Winston is professor of economics at Williams College. He received his Ph.D. from Stanford University, and has written two books and numerous articles on economic theory and development, and the economics of higher education. He has been a member of the Institute for Advanced Study in Princeton and a visiting scholar at the Institute for Economic Studies in Stockholm, and he served as provost at Williams from 1988-90.

who seek to determine the true financial condition of a college or university. Like the old saw about the weather, everyone complains but no one does anything about it.[1] I think a better way should and can be developed, especially since much of higher education is experiencing increasing difficulty in financing its operations. This article is an attempt to point the way.

My alternative to fund accounting is the result of a six-year effort to organize the vital economic information about a college's performance in a different and more useful way. I call the alternative *global* accounting because it presents an encompassing—all inclusive and integrated—view of a college's economic activities and its financial status. It is the kind of information that is essential to the management and governance of a college, the kind needed by the Board of Trustees, a faculty oversight committee, and top administrators. It describes the economic effects of each year's activities, and specifically the effects on the college's real wealth.[2]

The structure of global accounting is the antithesis of fund accounting. Instead of dividing the institution into a set of self-contained and balkanized accounting entities, global accounting brings economic information together about the whole college. The aim is to provide an annual picture of the financial condition of a college that is accurate, clear, and accessible.

The trouble with fund accounts

Fund accounting has an honorable history of service to government and nonprofit institutions; and there are still important questions that only fund accounts, or something like them, can answer. What is at issue is the inadequacy of fund accounts to provide the *sole* or *primary* way to frame economic information for colleges and universities. Here are some of the inadequacies:

1. Fund accounts obscure an overall, global understanding of an institution's economic performance.

2. Fund accounts are very hard to read and understand. That is, they are inaccessible without a significant investment of time to grasp their mass of detailed information repeated for each fund and their often complex transfers and interactions among funds.

3. They cause people to focus attention on understandable information that may be partial, misleading, or just marginally relevant. For example, people tend to focus on such items as the size of the operating budget, the budget surplus or deficit, or the market value of the endowment. But the operating budget leaves out a third or more of all current economic activity; budget surpluses or deficits are easily manipulated; and the endowment is only a fraction of the total wealth in even the best endowed universities (Winston 1988).

4. There is an inherent temptation to present misleading information. Separate funds are potential shells that invite shell games. For instance, Williams College, in moving $5 million of current spending off the operating budget in the 1980's, markedly reduced the apparent (but not the actual) growth of its operating expenditures. Swarthmore boasted of 40 years of exactly balanced operating budgets (Swarthmore 1987, 17), a feat which was apparently achieved by transferring to the operating budget fund from other funds (after the fact) whatever dollars were needed to cover operating expenses. Harvard and MIT followed the same convention in the 1970s (Bierman and Hofstedt 1973).

5. Fund accounting reduces higher education's ability to make economic comparisons among colleges and even to understand economic performance over time at a single school.

Fund accounting has been a source of complaints for decades.

The rationale for fund accounts in colleges has been that the separate accounts make it easier to monitor performance in specific areas supported by outside agents, donors, and government agencies who give funds to the college for restricted purposes and need to know if those purposes are well served and managed (Harried, et al 1985, 722). That stewardship role remains. But it doesn't justify the use of fund accounts as the primary way of organizing economic information.

Some have tried to make fund accounting serve purposes of both stewardship and governance, for instance, by using ratio analysis (Chabotar 1989). But these efforts have been only partially successful since they retain the shortcomings of fund accounting. On the other hand, global accounts that define the context and inform the governance and management of a college will always need to be complemented by sub-accounts fitted within the global reporting so that restrictions on the use of funds and other detailed information can be handled.

What is global accounting?

The basic structure of global accounting is simple. For each year's economic activity, three elemental facts are reported:

1. How much the college took in from all sources;

2. With it did with that money; and

3. The effect of these on the institution's real wealth.

That is the essential framework. (It is also the framework, often honored in the breach, of the familiar Income Statement and Balance Sheet.) What is centrally important is that the global accounts encompass the institution's complete activities. No flow or claim between the college and some outside agent—of income or expenditure or saving or liabilities—should be left out. And no financial flows or claims between funds should be included.

When we began constructing our system of global accounts, we intended only to reorganize the economic information already reported in the fund accounts. Our global accounts were derived from the audited, published information, largely by combining fund activities and eliminating double counting among them (Winston 1988). And that worked, at first.

Indeed, a major question was whether the approach that generated global accounts from Williams College's fund accounts would work too for other colleges. We answered that question when Duncan Mann and I were able to create global accounts for Wellesley, Carleton, Swarthmore, and, for contrast, the 65-institution system of the State University of New York (Winston and Mann). The result was an accounting of the year's total income, total current spending, and total real financial saving or change in the institution's financial wealth.

But not all wealth. It has become increasingly clear that global accounts that merely reorganize existing information create a useful set of global *financial* records which monitor real financial wealth, but they share the shortcoming of fund accounts in being inadequate to the incorporation of *physical capital wealth*. Neither system could account for all of an institution's wealth. At Williams College, for example, they ignore more than half of the college's $645 million of net worth.

So the set of genuinely global accounts presented here, while still heavily dependent on a reorganization of published information, augments those data with a more realistic treatment of land, plant, and equipment, a treatment very much in the spirit of the current literature on capital planning in colleges (Dunn 1989; Probasco 1991). For some potential users, these full global accounts may go too far; not everyone is ready to monitor all of his or her institution's wealth.

The structure of global accounting is the antithesis of fund accounting.

These users can retreat to the halfway house of global financial accounts, a system that is no worse than conventional accounting in its neglect of capital wealth and is a whole lot better in dealing with the other problems of fund accounting I have noted. So considerable improvement lies in using the global financial accounts, even if they are importantly incomplete. (Table 1 is repeated in the appendix as Table 1-A to show the same college in the abbreviated form of global *financial* accounts. But the rest of the text will deal with the fully global accounts that include all institutional wealth.)

In a significant and encouraging recent development, Harvard's new annual *Financial Report*, published in March of 1992, treats the physical capital stock much as described below, even though the increased realism raised Harvard's reported operating expenses by $77 million and gave the university a $42 million budget deficit (Harvard 1992). Harvard's decision not only reduces the risk to other schools of adopting these innovations in reporting economic information, but it indicates another way for an institution to move toward fully global accounts without embracing them all at once.

A caveat, before I describe the global accounts in detail. Their application is more immediately appropriate to private than to public institutions. The reason, of course, is the often-Byzantine arrangements of responsibility, ownership, and governance that have grown up between public colleges and state and local agencies, arrangements that can affect, *inter alia*, ownership of the school's capital stock, responsibility for tuition levels, and for salaries and fringe benefits, and even control over the use of any endowment wealth. So at public campuses the scope of responsibility and control may sometimes be different from that implied by these accounts. It remains, however, that global accounts, or something like them, are essential to public institutions if anyone is to know the real costs of public education and the effects of a state's policies on each institution's educational wealth.

The operating budget leaves out a third of all current economic activity.

How elements of global accounts work to form a coherent system of information will be clearer if they are embedded in a concrete example. Two years' data are presented in Table 1.[3] Consider the components in turn.

College income. The income elements in Table 1 are fairly straightforward at a small school, but a few comments are useful nonetheless. The set of income sources is exhaustive: *all* income flowing into the college in the year is included, whether it comes from students,[4] donors, government, borrowers of the college's wealth, or purchasers of services from the college. Gift and Grant Income in Table 1 is separated according to the donor's wishes to recognize the fact that part of the gift income is intended to expand the college's wealth and that that part is potentially different from gifts that donors intend should be used at the discretion of the college. Asset earnings include interest, dividends, and capital gains or losses (whether realized or not). Auxiliary income, in a small liberal arts college, consists largely of student charges for room and board. For a university, that line would be both larger and more complicated as would be "Sales, services and other," the catchall income line here.

Current Expenditures. Current expenditures in the global accounts is both a more and a less inclusive category than "spending from the current fund" in fund accounting. It includes all current expenditures and it excludes maintenance spending. Current expenditures are included whether they appear within the operating budget, elsewhere in the current fund, the capital budget, the endowment fund, or somewhere else in the fund accounts. So in global accounting, there is no opportunity to reduce the apparent level or growth of current expenditures by shifting some of them from a closely monitored area like the operating budget to a less scrutinized part of the accounts, like off-budget current fund or

TABLE 1

Global Accounts

	1989-1990 $	1990-1991 $
1. COLLEGE INCOME		
Tuition and Fees	29,262,691	32,543,540
Gifts and Grants:		
To Endowment	7,066,669	8,744,806
To Plant	1,016,397	713,124
All Other	12,664,824	13,951,045
Asset Income:		
Interest and Dividends	17,039,521	15,859,257
Appreciation	18,582,670	6,873,486
Sales, Services and Other	1,950,970	2,724,059
Auxiliary Income	11,599,559	11,862,813
Total College Income	99,183,301	93,272,130
2. CURRENT EXPENDITURES		
Operating Budget Expenditures	62,425,303	66,924,329
Other Current Expenditures	6,304,914	5,634,728
less Current Acct Maintenance	703,276	642,167
Total Current Expenditures	68,026,941	71,916,890
3. ADDITIONS TO CAPITAL STOCK		
Investment in New Plant	9,334,326	2,310,285
less Deferred Maintenance		
Real Depreciation	7,500,000	8,097,195
less Maintenance Spending:		
In Current Account	703,276	642,167
In Plant Fund	3,477,560	4,639,692
Total Deferred Maintenance	3,319,164	2,815,336
Total Additions to Capital	6,015,162	(505,051)
4. OPERATING COSTS		
Current Expenditures	68,026,941	71,916,890
Real Depreciation	7,500,000	8,097,195
Total Operating Costs	75,526,941	80,014,085
5. WEALTH (EOY)		
Financial Wealth		
Assets	346,203,972	358,726,081
less Liabilities	50,596,648	49,355,661
Net Financial Wealth	295,607,324	309,370,420
[Endowment Value]	[333,553,551]	[341,572,081]
Physical Capital Wealth:		
Replacement Value	323,887,799	341,438,861
less Accumulated		
Deferred Maintenance	3,319,164	6,290,686
Net Physical Wealth	320,568,635	335,148,175
Net Worth	616,175,959	644,518,595

endowment fund spending. Spending on maintenance of the plant and equipment is excluded because it is *not* a current expenditure; it is spending that buys a durable good, the restoration—"renovation and adaption"[5]—of the physical plant.[6]

Additions to the Capital Stock. Predictably, the greatest departure from conventional reporting comes in the global accounts' treatment of the physical capital stock since that aspect of college management and college wealth is so effectively neglected in fund accounting. The purpose of global accounting of the capital stock is to report its real value and record the effects of the year's activities on that value. It serves, too, to inform a more accurate measure of the college's operating costs that recognizes both current spending and real depreciation of the college's physical wealth.

Additions to the capital stock are simply the year's gross investment in new plant less any value lost through deterioration of the capital stock—the year's "deferred maintenance." Investment in new plant is uncomplicated. It includes all additions, acquisitions of new land, plant, and equipment that will augment the capital stock. Deferred maintenance describes how much of the year's real depreciation of the capital stock was not repaired or renovated, how much the physical plant was allowed to deteriorate over the year.[7] Given depreciation, repairs and renovation reduce deferred maintenance. Deferred maintenance is not a money expenditure, *per se*, of course, but it is an expenditure of part of the capital stock—consequent on time and its use in production—and therefore a very real *cost* of the year's operations. Recognition of deferred maintenance is essential if the full effect of the year's activities on the value of the college's wealth are to be reported.

Real depreciation is an estimate of the potential amount of capital stock worn out or used up in the course of the year's operations, the amount it would have depreciated had there been no repairs, renovation, or adaption. The emphasis on "real" depreciation is intended to distinguish this estimate of *actual* decline in the value of a capital

stock over the course of the year, due to time and its uses, from the more familiar but quite different matter of income tax liability in a for-profit firm. (For many, that's what "depreciation" has come to mean, both in accounting and the public mind.) In the global accounts it is pure economic depreciation.

Recognition of deferred maintenance is essential.

Finally, maintenance spending, as noted above, is much the same as investment in new plant; it increases the value of durable capital through renovation and adaption. So it is treated the same in the global accounts. To the small amount of such spending found in the current account is added that portion of a conventional "investment in plant" entry that in fact pays for renovation and adaption.

In Table 1, real depreciation is estimated as 2.5% of the $324 million capital stock with which 1990-91 started, or $8.1 million.[8] But since that was offset in 1990-91 by an estimated $4.6 million of maintenance spending from the capital budget and another $0.64 million from the operating budget, deferred maintenance for the year is estimated, with rounding, at $2.8 million[9] If current spending on maintenance had been $8.1 million for the year, deferred maintenance, of course, would have been zero.

Additions to the capital stock are the net result of all this: investment in new plant is augmented by maintenance spending and reduced by depreciation. Additions to the capital stock will be *positive* when new plant and maintenance, together, are larger than real depreciation, and *negative* when they are overwhelmed by the year's depreciation.

Operating Costs. In the global accounts, the year's total real operating costs are reported directly. To total current expenditures is added the year's depreciation of physical plant. So both forms of current spending are recognized as operating costs: current expenditures of the usual sort (less maintenance spending) and current spending of the capital stock through depreciation. Together, these describe the costs of the year's operations.[10]

Wealth: Assets and Liabilities. Assets and liabilities together describe the state of a college's wealth at the end of each fiscal year. They are the college's *stock* variables. Two aspects of the reporting of assets in global accounts should be noted. One is de-emphasis of the college's *endowment*. It shows up in Table 1 as a parenthetical notation sandwiched into the list of assets and liabilities that make up the college's wealth. The reason for this dismissive treatment is, simply, that the endowment has come erroneously to be seen as synonymous with "total financial wealth." While that was nearly true when colleges had very few non-endowment financial assets and, importantly, very little debt aside from some stray accounts payable, it is not true for many colleges now.

There is an inherent temptation to present misleading information.

Again, Williams' numbers are instructive. In 1989, its endowment had a market value of some $307 million. But the college had another $22 million in non-endowment assets[11] for total financial assets of $329 million (Williams 1991). But those assets were encumbered by some $51 million in debt. So the global accounts report net financial wealth of $278 million—total financial assets less total liabilities—as the appropriate measure of the college's financial wealth. In 1990, the endowment was up to $334 million, but net financial wealth only to $296 million.

The other important differences in global accounts' wealth reporting are that physical capital assets—land, plant and equipment—are (a) accounted for in current replacement values rather than "book values" that the college originally paid for them, and (b) adjusted for accumulated de-

ferred maintenance. At Williams, which is an old college, one major instructional building with seven large classrooms and 13,000 square feet has a book value of less than $50,000, and one faculty residence, not large but pleasant, is valued at only $850 (Williams 1991). Most other campuses would offer similar examples of the distortions inherent in using book values. So while the estimates of replacement values inevitably involve some guesswork, they are clearly a whole lot closer to the truth than are historical values. Accumulated deferred maintenance is treated as an offset against the replacement value of the physical assets, leaving net physical wealth as the measure of value of the capital stock. Table 1 assumes that there was no deferred maintenance before 1989-90, so there is little immediate difference between capital assets and net physical wealth. But Table 4 shows that over a long period, deferred maintenance will significantly reduce the college's net physical wealth. An example is Yale's current pressing problem (*New York Times*, February 3, 1992), with more than $1 billion of deferred maintenance.

Because financial and physical assets and liabilities are measured in the same current value terms, they can be added together to report the college's total wealth, its total net worth. We are adding apples and apples. For many purposes, it is essential to distinguish between these two forms of wealth (and saving); but for others it is useful to recognize total wealth, regardless of its form. In Table 1, reporting a total 1991 wealth of $645 million tells a very different and more complete story than either reporting an endowment of $342 million or financial wealth of $309 million.

Saving and Wealth: Flow-stock Relationships. The usual tautological accounting relationship between economic flows and stocks apply to global accounts. Saving is the difference between income and spending over the period. Any change in wealth between two dates equals and must be due to saving over that period; net worth (wealth) at the beginning of a period plus income minus spending has to equal net worth at the end of the period. Of course, real depreciation must be added to current expenditures to account fully for the year's total spending. This done, the stock-flow identity holds for total saving and wealth (net worth) as well as for financial and physical saving and wealth, separately. It is just as relevant to global accounts as it is to one's checking account.[12]

Operating and Capital Budgets. Operating and capital budgets are embedded in the global accounts, serving their managerial and planning functions, but firmly in the context of the college's overall activities. So total operating expenditures—the bottom line in an operating budget like that of Table 2—appears in the global accounts as a component of current spending (the largest). The effect, then, of operating budget performance on the college's wealth is incorporated immediately and directly. Though it is not made explicit here, the same is true for a capital budget which is mapped directly into the global accounts in the form of either new investment or as current spending on renovation and adaption.

Note that while operating *expenditures* are reported in a line in the global accounts, operating *revenues* do not appear. The reason is that a college's decision on how much of its total income to allocate to an operating budget as "revenue" is an internal and essentially arbitrary one. That decision may be influenced by some accumulated tradition: tuition and fees, for instance, may all go to the operating budget while only some gifts and a formulaic portion of asset income do. But a college can, by assignment and transfer of its income to and from the budget, make a budget deficit or surplus virtually anything it wants it to be, including, as Swarthmore and others have shown, always exactly zero.[13] Clarity is served, then, by focusing the global accounts on *spending* in the operating budget—or more broadly, on all current spending—as it encompasses an important set of activities in the college's educational enterprise. Attention to the arbitrary assignment of operating budget revenues—

the result of shifting money between pockets—and the consequent budget "deficits" or "surpluses" can be replaced by attention to real current spending and to actual performance relative to an approved spending plan.[14]

Using global accounts

The global accounts structure was first used to organize an historical review of Williams' economic behavior in order to provide a descriptive context for evaluating present and future performance (Winston 1988). It was done at the height of public criticism of cost growth in higher education when it was deemed wise to know how present performance compared with the past. We were able to generate long data series[15] on income levels and changes in its composition; on spending, its composition and real rates of growth; and on real saving and its distribution between financial and physical capital wealth. The result provided a foundation for economic policies.

But the broader significance of global accounts appears to lie in their ability to describe, monitor, and evaluate a college's current economic performance and in the structure they give to economic planning. First, let's look to how they can help monitor and evaluate economic performance.

The global accounts don't force any specific criteria of performance evaluation on a college except implicitly in describing the totality of the school's economic

TABLE 2

Global Accounts:
Current Expenditure Component

	1989-90 $	1990-91 $
OPERATING BUDGET		
Salary Pools:		
Faculty	10,194,014	11,415,331
Administrative/Prof	6,029,465	6,315,789
Weekly	11,568,273	12,101,430
Total Salary Pools	27,791,752	29,832,550
Fringe Benefits	7,258,226	7,816,225
Financial Aid	6,517,892	7,719,186
Other Restricted Spending	2,720,321	3,505,429
Manager's Budgets	18,137,112	18,050,939
Total Operating Budget Expenses	62,425,303	66,924,329
Other Current Expenditures	6,304,914	5,634,728
less Maint. Spending in Current Account	703,276	642,167
Total Current Expenditures	68,026,941	71,916,890

TABLE 3

Global Accounts: Summary

	1989-90 $	1990-91 $
1. SAVING – GAIN (LOSS) OF		
TOTAL REAL WEALTH:	10,171,785	(651,974)
Gain (Loss) of Real *Financial* Wealth	4,156,623	(146,923)
Gain (Loss) of Real *Physical* Wealth	6,015,162	(505,051)
Gifts to Increase Real Wealth	8,083,066	9,457,930
Savings to Increase Real Wealth	2,088,719	(10,109,904)
2. INCOME	99,183,301	93,272,130
Real Growth Rate	-3.26%	-10.19%
3. SPENDING		
Operating Costs	75,526,941	80,014,085
Deferred Maintenance	3,319,164	2,815,336
Investment in New Plant	9,334,326	2,310,285
Real Growth Rates		
Operating Costs	4.51%	1.18%
Deferred Maintenance	36.27%	-18.99%
Investment in New Plant	4.35%	-76.36%
4. SAVING: GAIN (LOSS) OF		
TOTAL REAL WEALTH USING		
SMOOTHED ASSET INCOME	7,276,151	8,600,747

activity. But they do make it especially easy to monitor the effects on its real wealth of the college's behavior and the economic circumstances it operates in: the difference between income and current spending is saving (or dissaving) and that, dollar for dollar, increases (or decreases) wealth. And global accounts make it easy to break that down to monitor, separately, the effects of college behavior on financial wealth and on physical capital wealth. There are many good reasons why a governing board might consider a dollar saved in a liquid financial asset to be very different from a dollar saved in constructing or renovating a building. Both are saving, but their different forms carry quite different implications for future flexibility, costs, returns, and performance. Even at the level of total saving, a board may think it wise to maintain real wealth or to increase it or to spend some of it down.[16] Or it may prefer only to monitor real wealth or income or spending or their components, rather than to define explicit policies in those respects. These are all decisions on which the structure of the global accounts is agnostic.

Using the data from Table 1, Table 3 illustrates one sort of evaluative summary that global accounts can produce to describe, in the broadest terms, a college's performance for a year.[17] Other summary data could be generated, but these I have listed

are especially useful in informing broad questions of strategy and governance.

The first line of Table 3—saving, or the gain or loss of real wealth—is, in a sense, "the bottom line" of the global accounts. It describes the change in total real wealth that results from the college's activities for the year, recognizing all its sources of income, all its expenditures on current account and new capital and maintenance, all the depreciation of its physical capital stock, and the contrary effects of inflation in eroding the real value of its financial wealth while increasing the nominal value of its physical wealth. In this fundamental measure, the fortunes of the college illustrated in Table 3 declined by some $11 million between 1989-90 and 1990-91, from real saving of $10.2 million to real dissaving of $.7 million.

The next four lines in Table 3 address two of the many questions that might be asked about the year's total real saving. The first two lines describe the distribution of total real savings between financial and physical wealth. Physical wealth fared better than did financial wealth in 1989-90 but had a slightly larger decline in 1990-91. The next two lines ask what would have happened to saving without the gifts that were targeted to increase wealth. Some of the increase in wealth on line 1 was the result of the explicit intentions of donors who gave the college money for the purpose of increasing its wealth, so that component might well be separated out from any change in wealth, or saving, that was due, instead to the college's decisions and external circumstances during the year. Without the gifts to wealth (to endowment and plant) of $8 and $9 million in the two years, the college would have saved in other ways some $2.1 million in the good year and lost a bit more than $10 million in the bad one. Again, governing boards would differ in their evaluation of these facts. Had the school's performance led to neither saving nor dissaving in those years, that might be considered good work by the board interested in real wealth maintenance, while it would be considered poor performance by a board that wanted, say, to catch up to Amherst or Swarthmore in wealth per student. So again, the global accounts are agnostic on policy aims.

College income is reported next in Table 3 in current dollars while its growth is reported in real terms, adjusted for inflation. Together they monitor the flow of total resources into the school over the year.

Direct monitoring of costs and spending levels and their real growth, as presented in the third section of Table 3, is a response to the criticisms of higher education in the 1980s and a conviction that real spending growth should be watched closely, both in detailed categories and broadly. Operating costs include both current expenditures and real depreciation as reported in Table 1. The year's deferred maintenance is reported as a separate line because of its usual neglect and its potential for causing serious long-term mischief. A board might adopt the policy that deferred maintenance should always be zero (giving top priority to protection of the physical plant, whatever the costs in other objectives). Or it might feel that deferred maintenance is simply one important aspect of performance that needs to be monitored attentively; that is, a board might conclude that deferring maintenance, like any other reduction in saving, can provide money to do other, more important, things. Again, global accounts inform policy by defining required maintenance spending and showing the cost of not doing it. Investment in new plant describes only spending for new physical capital.

The last section in Table 3 addresses an evaluation problem for well-endowed schools that report their financial assets at market values and thereby incur potentially large variations in reported income through capital gains and losses causes by market fluctuations. (Year-to-year comparisons of global performance will be hard to interpret if major changes in asset market value have dominated the numbers.) So in this last section of the table, the effect of the year's activities on the college's wealth are re-examined using a five-year moving average of asset income instead of actual asset income for each year. That smoothes out

the volatile element while still reflecting its underlying changes in a subdued form.

These data for 1989-90 and 1990-91 illustrate the effect nicely. Between the two years, the college's capital gains income fell by almost $12 million, so much of the striking difference in the effects of performance on real wealth between the two years was due to that sharp (and uncontrollable) decline in income and not, as it might first appear, to the way the college was run in the latter year. Indeed, the effect of operations on real wealth was, with smoothed income, better in the second year. Without that abrupt decline in asset income, reductions in deferred maintenance and the growth of current spending would have increased saving by $1.3 million in 1990-91.

Global accounts are agnostic on policy aims.

Now lets look at global accounting's ability to assist with economic planning.

Global accounts provide the framework for an economic planning model that has the scope and ability to integrate detailed management sub-plans while showing the global economic implications of the school's intended behavior and anticipated circumstances. Tables 4 to 6 illustrate such a model. Table 4 is a basic global economic plan; Table 5 is a sub-account giving more detail on planned current spending, "the operating budget;" and Table 6 gives the sort of evaluative summary data just described, here extended to include anticipated future performance over the period of the plan. All values are in current dollars with an assumed 5 percent inflation rate, and past accumulation of deferred maintenance is arbitrarily set at zero at the beginning of 1989-90. All planned and projected values are rounded.

Two years of historical performance data—1989-90 and 1990-91—are the starting point for projections of both anticipated circumstances (inflation, asset market con-

TABLE 4

Global Economic Plan
(CURRENT DOLLARS - INFLATION RATE 5%)

	1989-90 $	1990-91 $	PLAN PARAMETERS $	PLANNED 1991-92 $	PLANNED 1992-93 $	PLANNED 1993-94 $	...	PROJECTED 2001-02 $
1. COLLEGE INCOME								
Tuition and Fees	29,262,691	32,543,540	6.0%	34,500,000	36,600,000	38,800,000	...	61,800,000
Gifts and Grants:								
To Endowment	7,066,669	8,744,806	$9 m	9,000,000	9,000,000	9,000,000	...	9,000,000
To Plant	1,016,397	713,124	$1 m	1,000,000	1,000,000	1,000,000	...	1,000,000
All Other	12,664,824	13,951,045	$14 m	14,000,000	14,000,000	14,000,000	...	14,000,000
Asset Income:								
Interest & Dividends	17,039,521	15,859,257	6.0%	16,800,000	17,800,000	18,900,000	...	30,100,000
Appreciation	18,582,670	6,873,486	6.0%	7,300,000	7,700,000	8,200,000	...	13,000,000
Sales, Services and Other	1,950,970	2,724,059	6.0%	2,900,000	3,100,000	3,200,000	...	5,200,000
Auxiliary Income	11,599,559	11,862,813	6.0%	12,600,000	13,300,000	14,100,000	...	22,500,000
Total College Income	99,183,301	93,272,130		98,100,000	102,500,000	107,200,000	...	156,600,000
2. CURRENT EXPENDITURES								
Operating Budget Expenditures	62,425,303	66,924,329	On Table 5	70,900,000	75,200,000	79,700,000	...	127,000,000
Other Current Expenditures	6,304,914	5,634,728	On Table 5	6,000,000	6,300,000	6,700,000	...	10,700,000
less Current Acct Maintenance	703,276	642,167	$650,000	650,000	650,000	650,000	...	650,000
Total Current Expenditures	68,026,941	71,916,890		76,300,000	80,900,000	85,800,000	...	137,100,000
3. ADDITIONS TO CAPITAL STOCK								
Investment in New Plant	9,334,326	2,310,285	$2.0 m. constant	2,100,000	2,100,000	2,200,000	...	2,600,000
less Deffered Maintenance								
Real Depreciation	7,500,000	8,097,195	2.5% K-stock	8,500,000	9,000,000	9,500,000	...	14,600,000
less Maintenance Spending								
In Current Account	703,276	642,167	$650,000	650,000	650,000	650,000	...	650,000
In Plant Fund	3,477,560	4,639,692	6.0%	4,900,000	5,200,000	5,500,000	...	8,800,000
Total Deferred Maintenance	3,319,164	2,815,336		3,000,000	3,200,000	3,300,000	...	5,200,000
Total Additions to Capital	6,015,162	(505,051)		(900,000)	(1,000,000)	(1,200,000)	...	(2,600,000)
4. OPERATING COSTS								
Current Expenditures	68,026,941	71,916,890	As Above	76,300,000	80,900,000	85,800,000	...	137,100,000
Real Depreciation	7,500,000	8,097,195	As Above	8,500,000	9,000,000	9,500,000	...	14,600,000
Total Operating Costs	75,526,941	80,014,085		84,800,000	89,900,000	95,300,000	...	151,700,000
5. WEALTH (EOY)								
Financial Wealth								
Assets	346,203,972	358,726,081		373,500,000	387,100,000	400,200,000	...	481,100,000
less Liabilities	50,596,648	49,355,661	$50 m.	50,000,000	50,000,000	50,000,000	...	50,000,000
Net Financial Wealth	295,607,324	309,370,420		323,500,000	337,100,000	350,200,000	...	431,100,000
[Endowment Value]	[333,553,551]	[341,572,081]	$350 m.	[350,000,000]	[350,000,000]	[350,000,000]	...	[350,000,000]
Physical Capital Wealth								
Replacement Value	323,887,799	341,438,861		360,600,000	380,800,000	402,000,000	...	617,000,000
less Accumulated								
Deferred Maintenance	3,319,164	6,290,686		9,600,000	13,200,000	17,200,000	...	66,200,000
Net Physical Wealth	320,568,635	335,148,175		351,000,000	367,600,000	384,800,000	...	550,800,000
Net Worth	616,175,959	644,518,595		674,500,000	704,700,000	735,000,000	...	981,900,000

ditions, etc.) and planned college behavior (staffing, salaries, tuition, resource allocation, etc.). The heart of a planning process is, of course, the thoughtful specification of these "planning parameters"—projections of future intentions, plans and expectations. But in terms of the plan structure that is at issue here, after the college has decided on those planning parameters—how it wants and expects the components of the accounts to change in the future—a global economic plan will show the effects of that behavior on the college's real wealth over the period of the plan.

It is, then, a "consistency-and-implications" model. The pieces have to fit together over any year and they have to fit together from one period to the next, satisfying the truism that wealth at the beginning of the period plus income less spending has to equal wealth at the end of the period. Each period's performance is anchored in the past year's, and the projections are anchored in the most recent history.

The result is neither an optimization model nor an equilibrium model. It can be made into a "long-run financial equilibrium model" if a constant rate of growth of wealth is imposed; but that remains an option and not a characteristic. It is hoped that its more modest logical structure may well be of greater practical value than the more abstract alternatives in actual planning, administration, and governance. The global plan takes the concrete form of a Lotus spreadsheet that is easy to use to ask, repeatedly, the question, " What will be the economic implications of the following behavior, now and in the future?"

The data in Tables 4 through 6 are based on Tables 1 through 3. But it is important that they carry no implication about future plans or projections for any actual school. They are illustrative only of the *structure* of the economic plan. To make that very clear, planning parameter values in these tables have been entered as caricatures—most either as the constant rate of growth of 6 percent (nominal) or as a constant nominal quantity[18]—with the hope that a high level of artificiality will make it starkly clear that these tables deal only with a model structure and that no privileged information is conveyed.

A cost of artificiality, though, is that the numbers in these tables are less revealing of an actual planning exercise than they would be with more realistic parameter values. Nonetheless, they show that if a college, starting with the historical performance described in the first two columns, were to plan its spending and anticipate income as described by these rates and levels, it would

wind up as described in the last four columns. It would see increasing yearly dissaving, loss of more real financial wealth than physical wealth, real income growth hovering around zero with real operating costs that are increasing modestly, declining real new investment and declining but still positive real deferred maintenance.

It is hard to manage a place if you don't know what's going on.

If that pattern of behavior (and circumstances) continued until the academic year 2001-2, the college would find itself dissaving at an annual rate of $16 million, despite $10 million a year in gifts intended to increase wealth. Most of the dissaving would take the form of drawing down financial assets, but there would still be an accumulated deferred maintenance of some $66 million or a bit less than 10 percent of its total capital stock (all in 2002 dollars). A governing board, looking at these results, would have to conclude that the projected behavior under the projected circumstances isn't sustainable. Elimination of asset income volatility makes a significant difference in the evaluation of short-run performance. But predictably, it has a de-

TABLE 5

Global Economic Plan: Current Expenditure Component

	1989-90 $	1990-91 $	PLAN PARAMETERS $	1991-92 $	1992-93 $	1993-94 $	...	2001-02
OPERATING BUDGET								
Salary Pools:								
Faculty	10,194,014	11,415,331	6.0%	12,100,000	12,800,000	13,600,000	...	21,700,000
Administrative/Prof	6,029,465	6,315,789	6.0%	6,700,000	7,100,000	7,500,000	...	12,000,000
Weekly	11,568,273	12,101,430	6.0%	12,800,000	13,600,000	14,400,000	...	23,000,000
Total Salary Pools	27,791,752	29,832,550		31,600,000	33,500,000	35,500,000	...	56,600,000
Fringe Benefits	7,258,226	7,816,225	6.0%	8,300,000	8,800,000	9,300,000	...	14,800,000
Financial Aid	6,517,892	7,719,186	6.0%	8,200,000	8,700,000	9,200,000	...	14,700,000
Other Restricted Spending	2,720,321	3,505,429	6.0%	3,700,000	3,900,000	4,200,000	...	6,700,000
Manager's Budgets	18,137,112	18,050,939	6.0%	19,100,000	20,300,000	21,500,000	...	34,300,000
Total Operating Budget Expenses	62,425,303	66,924,329		70,900,000	75,200,000	79,700,000	...	127,000,000
Other Current Expenditures	6,304,914	5,634,728	6.0%	6,000,000	6,300,000	6,700,000	...	10,700,000
less Maintenance Spending in Current Account	703,276	642,167	$650,000	650,000	650,000	650,000	...	650,000
Total Current Expenditures	68,026,941	71,916,890		76,300,000	80,900,000	85,800,000	...	137,100,000

TABLE 6

Global Economic Plan: Summary
(CURRENT DOLLARS – INFLATION RATE 5%)

	1989-90 $	1990-91 $	PLAN PARAMETERS	1991-92 $	1992-93 $	1993-94 $	...	2001-02
1. SAVING – GAIN (LOSS) OF TOTAL REAL WEALTH:	10,171,785	(651,974)		(2,200,000)	(3,600,000)	(4,900,000)	...	(16,300,000)
Gain (Loss) Of Real *Financial* Wealth	4,156,623	(146,923)		(1,300,000)	(2,600,000)	(3,800,000)	...	(13,700,000)
Gain (Loss) Of Real *Physical* Wealth	6,015,162	(505,051)		(900,000)	(1,000,000)	(1,200,000)	...	(2,600,000)
Gifts to Increase Real Wealth	8,083,066	9,457,930	*Details*	10,000,000	10,000,000	10,000,000	...	10,000,000
Savings to Increase Real Wealth	2,088,719	(10,109,904)		(12,200,000)	(13,600,000)	(14,900,000)	...	(26,300,000)
2. INCOME	99,183,301	93,272,130	*on*	98,100,000	102,500,000	107,200,000	...	156,600,000
Real Growth Rate	-3.26%	-10.19%		0.12%	-0.45%	-0.39%	...	0.03%
3. SPENDING:			*Tables*					
Operating Costs	75,526,941	80,014,085		84,800,000	89,900,000	95,300,000	...	151,700,000
Deferred Maintenance	3,319,164	2,815,336		3,000,000	3,200,000	3,300,000	...	5,200,000
Investment in New Plant	9,334,326	2,310,285	4	2,100,000	2,100,000	2,200,000	...	2,600,000
Real Growth Rates:								
Operating Costs	4.51%	1.18%	*and*	0.93%	0.96%	0.95%	...	0.93%
Deferred Maintenance	36.27%	-18.99%		0.40%	1.13%	1.02%	...	0.26%
Investment in New Plant	4.35%	-76.36%		-14.18%	-2.25%	-2.32%	...	-3.10%
4. SAVINGS: GAIN (LOSS) OF TOTAL REAL WEALTH Using Smoothed Asset Income	7,276,151	8,600,747	5	2,600,000	4,000,000	(2,000,000)	...	(17,100,000)
5. ACCUMULATED DEFERRED MAINTENANCE	3,319,164	6,290,686		9,600,000	13,200,000	17,200,000	...	66,200,000

clining effect on the evaluation of smoothly projected future performance. So the plan reveals that something more fundamental than asset income volatility is producing unsustainable results.

Given the artificiality of these numbers, the results of these plan projections

---

Strategic information can be generated by global accounting.

---

probably don't deserve much more discussion. They should serve, however, to give a sense of the kind of strategic information that is generated by the global plan. It is, most generally, a description of the future resource implications of the behavior and circumstances envisioned by the college.

Premise and promises

The premise of the global accounts has been that a college's administration or governing board wants to have meaningful and accessible economic information about the college's performance. But that may be naive. The fact that the operating budget can be a political document is often acknowledged and usually described as regrettable, but it is also of considerable value in avoiding questions and discussions that might be time-consuming, tedious, and challenging to administrative decisions.

That fund accounts can selectively hide or reveal transactions is often convenient. So is the emphasis on endowment wealth, as though there were no other kinds of financial assets and no offsetting debt. And so on. But the difficulty with the manipulation of economic information, or selective optimism in its reporting, is the old one that plagues any departure from scrupulous efforts to report the economic facts: the first victim of distorted economic information is often the author of those distortions.

It is hard to manage a place if you don't know what's going on. This is a lesson learned and relearned in the contexts ranging from the Soviet planned economy to the current gyrations of state and city budgets in New York and California. Unfortunately, as the government parallel suggests, governors and mayors change and so do college administrations, increasing the temptation those transients face to keep their economic numbers looking good and to let the sober facts show up later, "but not on my watch."

More positively, and more importantly, global accounts appear to represent a marked improvement over fund accounting both in informing the long-run policy issues that confront colleges and universities, and in monitoring their economic performance. The information these global accounts present has proven to be the sort that induces and encourages the discussion of strategic fundamentals, of issues that are basic to the governance of the institution, issues that take the form "If we keep on doing what we're doing, or what we're planning to do next year, what will happen to our economic wealth?" Such elemental questions are not readily induced or addressed by the kind of economic information now available with fund accounts to colleges and universities.

Global accounts describe the effect of a year's activities, actual or planned, on all of the college's real wealth, on the distribution of that wealth between financial and physical assets, on deferred maintenance, on levels and real growth of income from its various sources, and of spending on it various objectives. This it does, in an environment of inflation with its opposing effects on the values of financial and physical wealth. Global accounts describe the whole of an institution. Their data are designed to avoid omissions and partial truths, to be clear and accessible, and to direct attention to the most basic economic implications of a college's behavior. ∎

APPENDIX A

TABLE 1-A

Global Financial Accounts

	1989-1990 $	1990-1991 $
1. COLLEGE INCOME:		
Tuition and Fees	29,262,691	32,543,540
Gifts and Grants:		
To Endowment	7,066,669	8,744,806
To Plant	1,016,397	713,124
All Other	12,664,824	13,951,045
Asset Income:		
Interest & Dividends	17,039,521	15,859,257
Appreciation	18,582,670	6,873,486
Sales, Services and Other	1,950,970	2,724,059
Auxiliary Income	11,599,559	11,862,813
Total College Income	99,183,301	93,272,130
2. CURRENT EXPENDITURES:		
Operating Budget Expenditures	62,425,303	66,924,329
Other Current Expenditures	6,304,914	5,634,728
less Current Acct Maintenance	703,276	642,167
Total Current Expenditures	68,026,941	71,916,890
3. CAPITAL EXPENDITURES:		
Investment in New Plant	9,334,326	2,310,285
Maintenance in Current Account	703,276	642,167
Maintenance in Plant Fund	3,477,560	4,639,692
Total Additions to Capital	13,515,162	7,592,144
4. FINANCIAL WEALTH (EOY):		
Assets	346,203,972	358,726,081
[Endowment Value]	[333,553,551]	[341,572,081]
less Liabilities	50,596,648	49,355,661
Net Financial Wealth	295,607,324	309,370,420
5. FINANCIAL SAVING:		
Total Financial Saving	17,641,198	13,763,096
Breakeven Saving (Inflation Offset)	13,484,575	13,910,019
Real Financial Saving	4,156,623	(146,923)
Real Net of Gifts to Endowment	(2,910,046)	(8,891,729)

ENDNOTES

1. Actually, 20 years ago Cornell professors Harold Bierman, Jr. and Thomas Hofstedt showed how misleading conventional budget deficits can be, using an analysis similar in some ways to this article (1973). Their effort got them an Andy Rooney segment on CBS, a front-page *Wall Street Journal* article; and strenuous objections from campus controllers and presidents, but no changes.

2. The structure of global accounts was developed in 1986-88, given a shot of practicality during my stint as Williams' provost in 1988-90, and refined in 1991. I enjoyed support from the Andrew W. Mellon Foundation through its assistance for the Williams Project on the Economics of Higher Education. William Bowen, Shawn Buckler, Keith Finan, George Goethals, David Healy, Robinson Hollister, George Keller, Duncan Mann, Charles Mott, Saeed Mughal, Will Reed, Joseph Rice, Morton Schapiro, David Schulte, and Winthrop Wassener gave me valuable insights and helped improve the analysis. I am especially indebted to Harold Bierman, Roger Bolton, David Booth, Anne MacEachern, and Michael McPherson.

3. These are similar to historical data from Williams' published sources, so no legal issues are raised by their use here. In the description of an economic plan below, I present transparently unrealistic and uninformative planning parameters to illustrate only the structure of the plan and nothing of Williams' expectations or intentions.

4. Tuition and fee income in these accounts is gross. An alternative would leave institutional student aid out of both income and expenditures and report as income only net tuition and fees.

5. "Adaption" refers to action to offset depreciation due to obsolescence, in the trilogy described long ago by Terborg. The other sources are depreciation due to use and depreciation due to the elements; these would be addressed by "renovation" spending as used here.

6. Under present practice some of the renovation and adaption is embedded in current spending but the largest part of renovation and adaption spending typically appears as capital spending (labeled "investment in plant"). So usually only a relatively small adjustment to reported current spending is needed to purge total current expenditures of what is more accurately capital spending. At Williams, the maintenance part of current expenditures was only $703,000 in 1989-1990 and $642,000 in 1990-91.

7. "Deferred maintenance" is often used to describe the accumulated result of past failures to spend enough on maintenance to offset real depreciation. It reduces the value of a stock variable. Here we used the phrase, too, to describe a flow—the extent to which this year's maintenance spending failed to offset this year's depreciation. As usual, this year's flow is an increment to the previously accumulated stock. Note that there is nothing necessarily pejorative about "deferred maintenance." Often it will be advisable to let physical capital depreciate.

8. The 2.5% is a conservative estimate. Economists (Schultz 1960; O'Neill 1971) have put it at 2% of the replacement value of plant and equipment per year. But estimates more carefully done by university capital planners get 1.5-2.5% for renovation and another .5-1.5% for adaption (Dunn 1989). So the 2.5% used in the text and tables appears to be a conservative estimate of the total depreciation and therefore of the spending needed to eliminate all deferred maintenance.

9. An important departure from the facilities planning literature lies in the fact that the global accounts identify the year's deferred maintenance without implying that it must therefore be prevented. Recognition of the cost of real depreciation is not the same thing as funding it. (See Dunn 1989, or Probasco 1991)

10. An issue lurks underneath the surface here. It is the classic neglect of the opportunity cost of capital as a real cost of production in colleges and universities (and nonprofits in general). So it is inaccurate to call "total current costs" total when they leave out, in the case of Williams, roughly $30 million a year of real costs of production, half again as much as is typically reported (Winston 1991). Two facts might recommend that we continue to leave them out, however: (a) the global accounts are concerned with the total flows of income and spending by the institution from and to outside agents, so it may be permissible to neglect a real cost of production that is paid, by virtue of the college's ownership of its capital stock, back to itself as imputed income, even though the resulting accounts seriously distort the costs of production; and (b) strategically, it may be unwise to try to persuade people of the good sense

of both the global accounts and an accounting of capital costs at the same time, though a courageous effort would take on both at once.

11. Though they may differ from endowment assets in other ways, the defining characteristic of these financial assets is that they are "owned" within the college, by a fund other than the endowment fund.

12. There is one awkwardness caused by the use of current market or replacement values for physical capital wealth in an inflationary environment. It lies in the need for an inflation adjustment to the value of the physical capital stock from year to year that doesn't appear here (as would be strictly appropriate) as nominal income. Strict adherence to the tautology would have to report the gain in physical asset value due to inflation as income (a physical capital gain) and then assign all of that income to saving, thereby justifying the increase in the nominal value of the capital stock. But since that portion of "income" is always "saved" and serves only to keep the replacement value of the capital stock in current dollars, the better choice seems to be to introduce an apparent violation of the stock-flow tautology rather than insert a large piece of funny money income explicitly into the body of the accounts. So the replacement value of physical capital reflects inflation within each year as well as showing the effect of net investment. As presented in Table 1, then, the tautology applies directly to financial saving and wealth but not to physical capital or total saving and wealth, unless inflation-induced "physical capital gains income" is included. (For the reader who'd like to confirm this relationship: the replacement value of the capital stock was $300,000,000 in 1989 while the inflation rate was (rounded) 4.85% over 1989-90 and 4.71% over 1990-91, so the inflation adjustments in replacement value are $14,553,473 and $15,240,777 in 1989-90 and 1990-91, respectively. With these, net physical wealth and net worth at the beginning of each period, plus saving and inflation adjustment will equal net physical wealth and net worth at the end of the period.)

13. In addition to Bierman and Hofstedt's brief fame for showing that budgets are often highly misleading—when MIT reported a $5 million deficit, they actually saved $100 million; Princeton's reported $1.5 million deficit went with $151 million in saving; and Harvard's $1.4 million deficit coincided with $314 in saving, *inter alia*—a number of others have tried to sound the same warning. William Nordhaus, economist and provost at Yale from 1986 to 1988, for instance, recently cautioned against relying on operating budget deficits and surpluses because "actions are generally taken to produce a balanced budget" (Nordhaus 1989, p.10).

14. Operating revenues are structurally a lot like a child's allowance, the part of the family income the parents assign for her to spend. Whether or not she can get by on, or even save from, her allowance is not an uninteresting question or one always viewed with dispassion. But it would be a mistake of some significance if the parents (or their creditors) were to represent the child's deficit or surplus on her allowance as

a measure of the family's economic fortunes for the week. So in the context of higher education, a number of Princeton faculty members were unimpressed with the university's recent and much publicized operating budget deficits, convinced that there had to be more going on there than met the eye (Lyall 1989). Global accounts make it clear that there was.

15. Initially for the 30 years since Williams was a small, all-male college.

16. The four alternative objectives that Dunn described for endowment wealth are relevant in this broader context of total wealth: (1) protect its nominal value; (2) protect its purchasing power, its real value; (3) have wealth grow as fast as operating expenses; or (4) increase wealth per student as fast as that of competing or peer institutions (Dunn 1991, pp. 34-5)

17. The details of getting from Table 1 to Table 3 are included in an appendix table.

18. In practice, three kinds of parameter values might be used to describe plans and projections: (a) rates of growth (constant or changing from one year to the next), (b) levels (constant in real or nominal terms or changing over time), and (c) functionally dependent parameters reflecting things like the way institutional need-based financial aid expenses depend on tuition decisions.

REFERENCES

Bierman, Jr., H. and T. Hofstedt. 1973. University Accounting (Alternative Measures of Ivy League Deficits). *Non-Profit Report* (May): 14-23.

Chabotar, 1989. Financial Ratio Analysis Comes to Nonprofits. *Journal of Higher Education* 60 (no. 2): 188-208.

Dunn, Jr., J. 1989. *Financial Planning Guidelines for Facilities Renewal and Adaption.* The Society for College and University Planning.

Dunn, Jr., J. 1991. How Colleges Should Handle Their Endowment. *Planning For Higher Education* 19 (no. 3): 32-37.

Garner, C. 1991. The Role of Funds. In *Accounting and Budgeting in Public and Nonprofit Organizations.* Jossey-Bass.

Harried A., L. Imdieke and R. Smith. 1985. *Advanced Accounting.* 3rd ed. John Wiley and Sons.

Harvard University. 1992. *Financial Report to the Board of Overseers of Harvard College.* Harvard University.

Lyall, S. 1989. Strife Over Style and Substance Tests Princeton's Leaders. *New York Times,* 4 December (B1).

Nordhaus, W. 1989. *Evaluating the Risk for Specific Institutions.* Yale University.

O'Neill, J. 1971. *Resource Use in Higher Education: Trends in Outputs and Inputs, 1930 to 1967.* The Carnegie Commission on Higher Education.

Probasco, J. 1991. Crumbling Campuses: What Are the Real Costs? *Business Officer,* 25 (no. 5): 48-51.

Schultz, T. 1960. Capital Formation by Education. *Journal of Political Economy* 68:6.

Swarthmore College. 1987. The Treasurer's Report. In *The President's Report, 1986-87.* Swarthmore College.

Williams College. 1991. *The Treasurer's Report, 1990-91.* Williams College.

Winston, G. and D. Mann. *Global Accounts: Reorganizing Economic Information for Colleges and Universities.* Forthcoming.

Winston, G. 1988. *Total College Income: An Economic Overview of Williams College, 1956-57 to 1986-87.* Williams College.

Winston, G. 1991. Why Are Capital Costs Ignored By Colleges and Universities and What Are The Prospects For Change? *Williams Project on the Economics of Higher Education, Discussion Paper No. 14.* Williams College.

APPENDIX B

Performance Calculations

		1989-90 $	1990-91 $
Saving – Gain (Loss) of Real Wealth:		10,171,785	(651,974)
Total Real Saving:	Y-X-[hK*(t-1)-(mc+mk)]+iK*(t-1)	38,209,833	28,498,822
Breakeven Saving:	iNFW(t-1)+iK*(t-1)	28,038,048	29,150,796
Gain (Loss) of Real Financial Wealth: Real Saving		4,156,623	(146,923)
Total Financial Saving:	Y-X-K	17,641,198	13,763,096
Breakeven Saving (Inflation Offset):	i(NFW)(t-1)	13,484,575	13,910,019
Gain (Loss) of Physical Wealth: Real Saving		6,015,162	(505,051)
Total Physical Capital Saving:	K-[hK*(t-1)-(mc+mk)]+iK*(t-1)	20,568,635	14,735,726
Breakeven Saving (Inflation Offset):	iK*(t-1)	14,553,473	15,240,777
Composition of Saving:			
Financial Saving		41%	23%
Physical Saving		59%	77%
With Smoothed Asset Income			
Saving – Gain (Loss) of Total Real Wealth: Smoothed		7,276,151	8,600,747
Total Saving		35,314,199	37,751,543
Gain (Loss) of Real Financial Wealth		1,260,989	9,105,798
Total Financial Saving: Smoothed		14,745,564	23,015,817
Spending:			
Deferred Maintenance:	hK*(t-1)-(mc+mk)	3,319,164	2,815,336
Real Yearly Growth		36.27%	-18.99%
Current Expenditures:	X-(mc+mk)	68,026,941	71,916,890
Real Yearly Growth		4.72%	0.97%
Operating Costs:	X-(mc+mk)+hK*(t-1)	75,526,941	80,014,085
Real Yearly Growth		4.51%	1.18%
Investment in New Plant		9,334,326	2,310,285
Real Yearly Growth		4.35%	-76.36%

K = new investment; K* = replacement value of capital stock; h = depreciation rate;
mc and mk = maintenance spending in Current and Capital-Budget, respectively (both included in X);
i = inflation rate; Y = income; X = (current expenditures + mc + mk).
(t-1) = end of previous period.

Colleges and universities are suddenly being taxed like business firms. What steps should institutions take?

Rendering Unto Caesar: The Movement to Tax Colleges

Cynthia Burns

The old saying is that the only guarantees in life are death and taxes. College and university administrators and faculty, however, have long felt that their institutions are immune from both. The medieval universities of Bologna, Oxford, Paris, and Salamanca have not died and are still teaching classes, as are Harvard (1636) and William & Mary (1694). And higher education has traditionally been exempt from taxes, like churches and other charitable institutions. As early as 1341 Philip VI of France proclaimed a royal exemption from taxes:

> To the aforesaid masters and scholars [at the University of Paris] now in attendance at the university, and to those who are hereafter to come to the same university...we grant...that no layman, of whatever condition or prominence...shall disturb, molest, or pressure other-

wise to extort anything from the aforesaid masters and scholars in person, family or property, under pretext of...tax custom, or any such personal taxes, or other personal exaction of any kind (Lucas 1994, p. 58).

Early American colonists continued this tradition by exempting Harvard College, as well as its president, fellows, and students, from taxation. From the origin of the Republic, U.S. federal and state governments have exempted colleges and universities from several forms of taxation such as income taxes, sales taxes, and property taxes.

But recently small towns and financially strapped cities have begun sending tax bills to private colleges and universities within their boundaries and asking public higher education institutions for annual "contributions." Newspaper readers now see headlines like "Nonprofits Eyed as Source of Additional City Revenue" (Siegel 1996) and "In Era of Fiscal Damage Control, Cities Fight Idea of 'Tax Exempt'" (Glaberson 1996), and find reports that the *ad valorem* property tax exemption is being questioned by political leaders in dozens of U.S. communities that are seeking new sources of revenue to sustain their public services (Healy 1995a).

Among the tax exempts, colleges and universities are of particular interest to poli-

Cynthia Burns is a doctoral candidate in higher education at the College of William & Mary. She holds a B.A. from Oral Roberts University and an M.A. in nonprofit management from Regent University in Virginia, and has taught religion at St. Leo College, served as an institutional research administrator, and directed a site program in Europe for an American university.

ticians for several reasons. Colleges own large tracts of property that can provide a town or city with a significant new source of revenue. Economic impact studies have estimated that towns lose hundreds of thousands and large cities millions of dollars annually as a result of the property tax exemptions given to higher education. (Of course, colleges also add many jobs and attract significant revenue to their localities.)

In addition, local political leaders perceive that institutions of higher education have large budgets and sizable endowments, and therefore can afford to pay for some services—fire, police, and road maintenance—that the town or city provides to all property owners, exempt and nonexempt alike. As one county lawmaker in upstate New York said, "There's only one billionaire in Tompkins County, and that's Cornell University" (Blumenstyk 1988, p. A19). Moreover, numerous universities have been turning over pieces of their operation, from dining halls and bookstores to grounds maintenance, to profit-making companies; and some universities are now earning considerable revenues from their sports programs and other quasi-business ventures. To a growing number of outsiders, colleges and universities no longer seem much like "charitable" enterprises with underpaid, struggling scholars and mostly poor students. They seem more like attractive businesses.

Getting the tax bill

Often city leaders seek to overturn the tax exemption on a college's or university's property by simply sending the campus administrator a tax invoice. Campus officials can either accept the new denial of exemption and pay the tax or attempt to defend the institution's centuries-old right to be tax-exempt and refuse to pay. When campus administrators choose to defend their right, a judicial battle usually results. Then the state's court system will have to determine the institution's exempt status by interpreting the state's tax laws (Oleck and Stewart 1994).

State laws usually limit the ability of town and city officials to challenge academic tax exemptions. First, under the doctrine of sovereign immunity, *public* colleges and universities, as property owned by state governments, cannot be taxed. "The general principle [is] that the sovereign cannot sensibly be thought to intend to tax its own property" (Ginsberg 1980, p. 299). The only exception is state-owned property that is leased to a for-profit corporation. Consequently, local officials can challenge only

Universities no longer seem much like charitable enterprises.

the tax-exempt real estate owned by *private* schools, colleges, and universities.

Second, state tax laws limit challenges to the property tax exemption for private institutions as well. (The laws governing property tax exemptions are determined by state legislatures, not by federal legislators or local laws.) State laws customarily grant a real estate tax exemption to nonprofit institutions that are organized for "charitable purposes," with none of their income benefiting private constituencies. In some states the property tax exemption is found in the state constitution (Wellford and Gallagher 1988; Bookman 1992). In such states—Kentucky, for example—local leaders cannot tax colleges without an amendment to the state constitution. However, in other states, where the provisions granting an exemption are statutorial, a university's tax-exempt status can be more easily disputed (Keeling 1990).

Third, in states where the property tax exemptions can be disputed, state law continues to prohibit local officials from challenging the exempt status of land so long as colleges use the property for educational purposes (Hill and Kirschten 1994). As a result, localities have had to resort to other means to get annual monies from higher education.

Four for the money

My review of recent legislative actions and of case law arising from property tax exemption challenges throughout the United States reveals that local leaders are employing four distinct strategies to exact tax payments from colleges and universities.

1. *Challenges to property used for non-educational purposes.* In this strategy, local leaders search for sections of a college's or university's property that are being used for auxiliary, quasi-commercial, or non-educational purposes, and then tax those sections. Thus, the tax-exempt status of residence halls, sports stadiums, income-producing parking lots, daycare centers, cafeterias, faculty housing, and vacant land being held for future college expansion are increasingly being disputed, and then resolved through the judicial process (Keeling 1990).

The outcomes of such incursions vary from state to state because the states vary in the way they define "traditional educational use." To illustrate, three similar cases litigated in different states yielded three distinct rulings. With *In re Swarthmore College* (1994) a Pennsylvania appellate court upheld the property tax exemption on a private college president's house and land because it was partly used to entertain college members and potential donors, activity deemed to be related to the college's educational function. In Tennessee, however, the court granted only a partial exemption for those portions of a residence used for entertainment since it claimed that only property "used purely and exclusively for carrying out one or more purposes for which the institution was created or exists" can be tax exempt (*Tusculum* 1980). A Texas appeals court went further. It denied the tax exemption for a college-owned domicile because it did not consider entertaining an educational activity (*Bexar Appraisal District* 1992).

Local challenges to colleges and universities for campus property that is used for non-instructional purposes have been going on for years. In 1899 the town of New Haven challenged some of Yale's property (*Yale University*) and the town of Cambridge sought taxes from Harvard in 1900 (*Harvard College*). As universities engage in a wider array of research, athletic, hous-ing, and unusual activities that may appear to be "non-instructional," administrators should expect the challenges to those activities to continue.

2. *Challenges to leased property.* Another tactic of town and city officials that goes back several decades is that of denying exemptions for portions of university real estate that are leased to for-profit corporations, such as a bookstore or dining hall. Municipalities are able to tax even public universities in this way because "immunity from local taxation does not extend to federal or state property leased to a private organization and used for the leasee's commercial purposes" (Ginsberg 1980, p. 300).

In the past, state courts have upheld the tax-exempt status of campus property leased to a for-profit firm if the firm's work is related to the school's, college's, or university's mission. At new Jersey's Blair

---

A fair proportion of colleges have agreed to make voluntary payments.

Academy, for instance, the court held, "The use of a catering system to feed the students and faculty of this boarding school cannot be regarded as a commercial activity or business venture of the school" (*Blair Academy* 1967). The tax exemption is usually denied, however, if the real estate is used for noneducational activities not closely related to the institution's exempt purpose (*Johnson* 1982; Segroves 1982).

In a recent court decision (*Stevens* 1988), the magistrate repealed the tax-exempt status of a community college's property leased to a restaurant franchise that provided food service to students, staff, and faculty. The court concluded that, because college officials gave the franchise operators complete control over the campus space it occupied, and because they did not supervise the operation of the franchise, the restaurant franchise was not exempt from taxation. Since more and more colleges and universities are seeking to reduce expenditures and augment revenues by privatizing, or outsourcing, some of their auxiliary services (Hackett 1992; Doctrow et al. 1996), this development is a cause for concern.

3. *Challenges to an institution's purpose.* A novel strategy for local officials is to repeal a college's tax-exempt status on the grounds that it is no longer organized for a tax-exempt purpose. While the tax statutes of many states specifically grant a property tax exemption to institutions organized for an

---

The plan should be clear about what the institution will do if challenged.

---

educational purpose, laws in some states limit the exemption to organizations that serve a "charitable" function. In these states, universities must meet the state's definition of being a "charitable" enterprise to remain tax-exempt (Hill and Kirschten 1994).

Definitions of what is a charitable purpose vary. In Pennsylvania, for example, to be considered charitable, the court ruled in 1985 that an organization must (a) advance a charitable purpose; (b) donate or gratuitously render a substantial portion of its services; (c) benefit a substantial and indefinite class of persons who are legitimate subjects of charity; (d) relieve the government of some of the burden; and (e) operate entirely free from a private profit motive (*Hospital Utilization Project* 1985).

In a bold move the town council in the town of Washington, Pennsylvania, south of Pittsburgh, decided to remove the tax-exempt status of 1300-student Washington and Jefferson College, the 11th oldest college in America (1793). The college is the biggest employer in town, like Dartmouth in Hanover, New Hampshire or Grinnell College in Grinnell, Iowa. The college objected; but in August 1994 the Court of Common Pleas of Washington County ruled that W&J met only one of the five criteria of a charitable organization: that it operated free of the profit

motive. It declared that the college had "grown into an enterprise of big business and...must pay its fair share of taxes" (*In re Appeal of City of Washington*).

On appeal from the college's lawyer, the appeals court reversed this decision and concluded that the college did meet the charitable organization criteria and is entitled to the property tax exemption. But the city of Washington's political leaders have appealed to the state supreme court (Healy 1995b), so the case has become one of possible historic significance. Meanwhile, several Pennsylvania legislators have submitted legislation to amend the state's property tax statutes to ensure that college and university properties remain tax exempt (Bell 1995).

So far, the assessors in other states have not yet turned to common law charitable purpose tests to challenge the tax exemption of entire colleges and universities. But this maneuver bears watching. It could have serious financial repercussions for academe.

4. *Payments in lieu of taxes.* A fourth tactic employed by city officials is not to challenge the tax-exempt status of colleges but instead demand annual payments *in lieu of taxes.* This is a rapidly spreading tactic. In this approach local political figures ask their colleges and universities—public as well as private—to give a voluntary gift of money or service to the town or city to help offset the cost of municipal services (Healy 1995; Glaberson 1996).

A fair proportion of colleges, both in states that restrict and those that allow property tax exemption challenges, have agreed to make voluntary payments. In 1990, for example, Yale administrators agreed to pay $4.2 million to the city of New Haven, Connecticut, and also agreed to place the university's golf course on the tax rolls (Hill and Kirschten 1994). A sample of other institutions that contribute annually to their city treasuries: Dartmouth $1 million; Harvard $970,000; MIT $900,000; UC Berkeley $200,000; Princeton $35,000 (Blumentyk 1988; Bookman 1992; Stepneski 1993).

A small but growing number of mayors are giving university officials the choice of either making voluntary annual contributions or having their tax-exempt status challenged through litigation. In 1994 Mayor Ed Rendell of Philadelphia issued Executive Order No. 1994-1 entitled "Payment in lieu of taxes," requesting all tax-exempt organizations (except churches and synagogues), including the 25 public and private colleges and universities in the city, to make payments equal to 40 percent of their property tax liability, or expose themselves to expensive litigation. All the Philadelphia colleges and universities have entered into agreements to provide monetary and service payments rather than risk a legal challenge (Bell 1995; Healy 1995a).

When institutions refuse to make the voluntary payments, some local officials have coerced institutions by strictly enforcing zoning and code regulations on each university expansion project, or by imposing either annual or per-use fees (Rudnick 1993). A more recent tactic is for state legislatures (New Hampshire, Rhode Island, and Nebraska) to initiate legislation authorizing city and town officials to levy payments similar to the real estate tax on colleges and universities to help pay for municipal services (Mercer 1994; Glaberson 1996).

As the financially pressed towns and cities search for new revenues, they are almost certain to continue to ask, coerce, or require colleges and universities, also financially strapped, to negotiate payments in lieu of taxes. Consequently, some attorneys are recommending that universities "cut the best deal as early as possible because the erratic nature of court decisions might lead to much higher payments" (Leland 1994, p. 6).

Planning for the tax people

Clearly, numerous colleges and underendowed universities could be forced to increase tuition, cut staff, and reduce salaries and services if they lose much of their tax exempt status or are compelled to make large annual payments to local governments. A few precariously financed colleges might have no choice but to shut down. What should institutions do?

From my study of this subject, it appears that several steps might be taken.

These steps would, in effect, constitute a strategic plan to prevent the loss of universities' exemption from property taxes, which they have enjoyed for centuries. The plan, I think, should have two goals: it should help prevent a challenge to tax-ex-

Universities need to be honest and disarming rather than huffy and presuming.

empt status, and it should enable the institution to make a knowledgeable, rational, intentional set of decisions if a challenge or request for payment occurs.

Colleges and universities should have a plan for becoming better citizens in their town or city. Maintaining good relations personally with local leaders, lending campus expertise to help solve town problems, encouraging students to volunteer with community groups, rewarding those faculty who serve on local community boards, helping local schools, participating in important initiatives, and contributing to the needy in town—these and other steps can help prevent town-gown tensions from rising (Leland 1994). Local business, religious, cultural, and political leaders can be invited to speak to classes and at major campus events. An economic impact study can document the many contributions and jobs that the college or university provides for the town or city.

The plan should also be clear about what the institution will do if challenged. Begin with a thorough analysis of the property tax exemption laws in your own state and those of other states. One observer notes that, "All too often an organization loses all, or part, of its property tax exemption due to a lack of knowledge as to the permissible scope of utilization of property under the law" (Bookman 1992, p. 189). The plan should collect evidence of how the institution carries out its tax-exempt purpose; and it should know the history and rationale for universities being exempt. If the college is richly knowledgeable about the issue, it will be better equipped to deal with any political pushes for taxes or payments.

Also, all outsourcing should be arranged in a way that the institution does not appear to be introducing commercial enterprises in its midst. Bookstores, sports programs, and other auxiliary services should evidently have an educational purpose. College housing, including fraternity and sorority houses, should either be college-owned and monitored or be owned by private or national entities and therefore taxable.

The plan should include the strategy that the college or university's leaders and lawyers will use if a challenge occurs. Since the institution can pay the tax bill, or fight fiercely to retain the exemption, or negotiate voluntary contributions, or seek to have the state laws altered, the plan should outline what actions will be taken in what order, who will make the decisions, and what resources will be used to implement the strategy.

Colleges and universities should recognize two other things. Many universities, hospitals, and other nonprofit organizations are unquestionably becoming more businesslike, as many business and political leaders are urging them to do; so the defense against property taxes cannot be on the same grounds that a defense might have been made in the 19th century or in the 1930s. Universities need to be honest and discerning rather than huffy and presuming.

The fiscal distress which has prompted municipal officials to assault the tax-exempt status of college and university property in search of additional revenues is not likely to diminish. So higher education should plan and prepare itself for further probable challenges to the centuries-old privilege it has enjoyed. ∎

REFERENCES

Bell, G. 1995. Where Have All the Charities Gone, or Have They? *Pennsylvania Bar Association Quarterly* 66(4): 168-176.

Blumenstyk, G. 1988. Town-Gown Battles Escalate as Beleaguered Cities Assail College Tax-Exemptions. *Chronicle of Higher Education* (June 29): A1, A19-A20.

Bookman, M. 1992. *Protecting Your Organization's Tax-Exempt Status: A Guide for Nonprofit Managers.* Jossey-Bass.

Doctrow, J., C. Sturz, and S. Lawrence. 1996. Privatizing University Properties. *Planning for Higher Education* 24(4): 18-22.

Ginsberg, W. 1980. The Real Property Tax Exemption of Nonprofit Organizations: A Perspective. *Temple Law Quarterly* 53: 291-342.

Glaberson, W. 1996. In Era of Fiscal Damage Control, Cities Fight Idea of 'Tax Exempt.' *New York Times* (February 16): A1, C17.

Grobman, G. 1994. *The Issue of Tax-exempt Status for Pennsylvania Charities.* The Pennsylvania Jewish Coalition.

Hackett, J. 1992. Productivity Through Privatization. In R. Anderson and J. Meyerson (eds.), *Productivity and Higher Education: Improving the Effectiveness of Faculty, Facilities, and Financial Resources.* Peterson's Guides.

Healy, P. 1995a. College vs. Communities: Battles Intensify Over City Efforts to Win Payments from Tax-Exempt Institutions. *Chronicle of Higher Education* (May 5): A27, A32.

Healy, P. 1995b. Pennsylvania Court Voids Ban on Private College's Tax Exemptions. *Chronicle of Higher Education* (September 29): A53.

Hill, F. and B. Kirschten. 1994. *Federal and State Taxation of Exempt Organizations.* Warren, Gorham, & Lamont.

Kaplin, W. and B. Lee. 1995. *The Law of Higher Education* (3d edition). Jossey-Bass.

Keeling, B. 1990. Property Taxation of Colleges and Universities: The Dilemma Posed by the Use of Facilities for Purposes Unrelated to Education. *Journal of College and University Law.* 16(4): 623-648.

Leland, P. 1994. *Responding to a Property Tax Challenge: Lessons Learned in Pennsylvania.* Marywood College.

Lucas, C. 1994. *American Higher Education: A History.* St. Martin's Press.

Mercer, J. 1994. States Weigh Bills to End Colleges' Tax-Exempt Status. *Chronicle of Higher Education* (February 23): A25-A26.

Oleck, H. and M. Stewart. 1994. *Nonprofit Corporations, Organizations, and Associations* (6th ed.) Prentice-Hall.

Rudnick, R. 1993. State and Local Taxation on Nonprofit Organizations. *Capital University Law Review* 22: 321-351.

Siegel, E. 1996. Nonprofits Eyed as Source of Additional City Revenue. *The Baltimore Sun* (February 12): A1, A5.

Stepneski, R. 1993. Rising Tax Pressure Hits Nonprofits. *Nonprofit Times* (April): 1, 36-39.

Wellford, W. and J. Gallagher. 1988. *Unfair Competition? The Challenge to Charitable Tax Exemption.* The National Assembly of National Voluntary Health and Social Welfare Organizations.

Credit cards are transforming campus financial exchanges.

Coming Soon: The Cashless Campus

Carole Ann Peskin and Marie McDemmond

An extraordinary thing is happening to colleges and universities. Cash is disappearing from an increasing number of American campuses. For financial planners the development raises some of the most important policy questions and planning needs in decades.

What began in the mid-1970s as a way to speed payments at campus dining facilities has become what we estimate to be a $2 billion to $3 billion a year operation in U.S. higher education. Today, credit cards are used for such payments as campus bookstore purchases, annual giving contributions, tuition for continuing education, athletic events, food purchases, vending machines, telephones, and special seminars and institutes. Several dozen institutions, from the University of Iowa to Michigan's Grand Valley State University,

which won an award from NACUBO for its touch-tone telephone registration and tuition payment scheme using voice response technologies, now accept credit cards for tuition. Kent State University accepts credit cards to pay for flying lessons, greens fees at the campus golf course, and for contributions to the campus radio station.

We conducted an informal survey of 69 institutions in 15 states—public, private, and community colleges—and found that 68 percent of the colleges and universities were accepting the 2" x 3 1/4" plastic cards for several kinds of purchases. Most of the fiscal officers thought the expanding use of credit cards was beneficial to the students; and most thought the credit cards were helpful to their institutions as well. This view is from campuses as varied as NYU, Golden Gate Baptist Seminary, Spelman College, and Joliet (Illinois) Junior College.

Carole Ann Peskin, a CPA, is Executive Director of Finance at Nova Southeastern University, Ft. Lauderdale. She attended Vassar, graduated from Ohio State, has an M.B.A. from Rider College, and Ed.D. from Nova Southeastern University. She previously worked as a financial officer at Trenton State College, at the Lawrenceville School, and at Westminster Choir College (all in New Jersey), and is author of several articles on college finances.

Marie McDemmond is President of Norfolk State University in Virginia. She was previously Vice President for Finance at Florida Atlantic University. A graduate of Xavier University in Louisiana, she earned an M.S. from the University of New Orleans and a doctorate in higher education finance from the University of Massachusetts at Amherst. She previously worked as a financial officer at Atlanta University, the University of Massachusetts, and Emory University, and serves on the board of directors of The National Coalition of 100 Black Women, Inc.

We found the credit card situation varies enormously from campus to campus, and most institutions are studying, experimenting, and inventing uses. The situation is in turbulent flux.

Four kinds of cards

There appear to be four different kinds of credit cards in use in U.S. higher education at the present time. Probably the oldest kind is the individual campus identification-and-charge card that permits students to charge books, art materials, and meals with their ID card. The charges are then billed to their student accounts. In effect the college is granting limited credit to its students rather than accepting commercial credit cards. This practice exists largely at smaller, private, well-endowed institutions such as Connecticut's Wesleyan University.

A second kind is the commercial credit cards such as Visa, American Express,

---

The situation is in turbulent flux.

MasterCard, and Discover. This is the most widely used system of accepting cashless payments. Some institutions, however, have a minimum transaction, such as Baldwin-Wallace College's $50 floor; others forbid the use of commercial cards for such things as parking tickets, lost library books, and dormitory damages.

The third kind is the so-called debit card. In this system the college or university issues its own card as with Duke's DukeCard, the University of Miami's 'CaneCard, and Clemson's TigerCard. Students are encouraged to deposit a sum of money with the university and then can use their university card to charge for nearly everything—cafeteria food, laundry washers and dryers, vending machines, bookstore purchases, video games, concerts, athletic events, library fines, parking fees—until the account is dry. Sometimes the students suggest new ways to use the card, as

when Seton Hall University (New Jersey) students urged that photocopiers be programmed to receive their debit cards. At Penn State nearly 19,000 non-regular students and visiting faculty use the Penn State Card during the summer months for conferences, athletic camps, food, and summer courses, depositing about $4 million in debit accounts and drawing down about $30,000 a day (*Collegiate Trends* 1993).

One observer (Nicklin 1993) estimates that at least 50 universities have their own debit card. At the edge of a few campuses, small business owners will accept the university's card as payment. For example, Mazzio's, an independent pizza parlor in Nashville, Tennessee, reports that its business has increased since it started accepting Vanderbilt University's Commodore Card in 1987. (For this, it pays Vanderbilt 15 cents on every sales dollar.) Some universities combine an experimental use of the debit card with that of commercial cards. Thus, the University of Pennsylvania issues faculty members a card after receiving a deposit, for use at the faculty club, but accepts only commercial cards at the bookstore.

The fourth kind, which a growing number of campus financial officers believe may be the card of the future, is Florida State University's Seminole Card. This hybrid, combined institutional/commercial card has *two* magnetic stripes on it: one is for the university's debit card, the other can be read by Visa and MasterCard machines. The Seminole Card can be used by students with 300 Tallahassee area merchants, who are electronically connected through Total System Services (TSYS), the country's second largest credit card processor. FSU gets a percentage of each purchase with its card from these off-campus locations, and earns about $250,000 a year from them.

John Carnaghi, Florida State's vice president for finance and administration, reports that he has had such interest in FSU's hybrid card that he has begun holding seminars for other campus financial planners from around the country about Florida State's innovative credit card arrangements—at $800 a session.

The credit card advantage

The cards offer higher education numerous advantages, including improved cash flow, reduced receivables and bad debts, streamlined service, increased sales at campus stores and services, and enhanced fund-raising potential.

Cash flow is improved because students who cannot pay their full tuition in cash or check immediately can settle their balances by credit card. Early payment by mail can also be encouraged. New York's Adelphi University facilitates credit card use by including a charge form in its registration packet to students. And more institutions allow students to authorize tuition payments via their credit card over the telephone.

Florida's Nova University has developed a way that students can use credit cards for deferred payment plans. Students merely arrange for post-dated charge authorizations at the beginning of a semester. With credit cards, colleges and universities which have traditionally had problems with bad debts and difficulties collecting money from students, have been able to reduce time-consuming and unpleasant collection activities. For instance, Virginia's Blue

Credit cards reduce unpleasant collection activities.

Ridge Community College reports that it has had a noticeable reduction in its bad checks since it introduced credit cards.

Most institutions do not as yet permit tuition payments via credit card by full-time regular students. But many have begun to accept credit card payments from part-time and non-traditional enrollees, whose access to financial aid is very limited. For instance, the University of Vermont allows charges by its continuing education students attending part-time but not by its full-time undergraduates.

Credit cards are increasingly being introduced into annual fund-raising efforts.

Edward Manson, Nova University's director of alumni affairs, contends that more first-time donors respond to phonathon appeals and mail solicitations when alumni are able to charge their contribution to a credit card. Kathleen Byington of Colorado State Uni-

Students tend to spend more on campus.

versity's development office says that with credit cards there are no "fulfillment problems," no waiting for checks in the mail, no need for reminders and follow-up phone calls, and no paperwork tracking pledges. The practice is spreading to Canada too. Canada's University of Saskatchewan accepts credit cards for fund-raising purposes. Credit cards are helpful also for donors living in foreign countries because neither the donor nor the university needs to bear extra fees for the currency exchange charges which banks impose on foreign checks.

Credit cards are also useful for sales and activities sponsored by the college or university: bookstore merchandise for alumni, alumni reunions, class directories, continuing education workshops, alumni travel tours.

Especially with debit cards, students tend to spend more at campus stores and eateries. After the University of Miami put dormitory washers and dryers on the 'CaneCard, they found a six percent increase in use by students in the first six months. Of financial importance, with debit cards the college or university earns interest on the money sitting in the student accounts. Duke University, for instance, says it earns about $200,000 a year in interest on the student's' deposits.

Some problems with cards

Credit cards have substantial costs for institutions, however, compared to cash payments. For one, there is the surcharge, or merchant fee, that banks and American Express charge. For every $100 charged on a card, the merchants charge the universities from $2 to $4 to handle the transaction. For example, card use at Nova University has climbed to about $17 million annually, and the university pays merchant and transaction fees of more than $300,000.

There are considerable new equipment costs if a college switches from cash to credit cards: dedicated phone lines, stripe readers, Zon terminals and other data-capture devices, personal computers, and customized software. Credit cards require systems integration, or a linkage of different equipment so they can "talk" to each other and use common data through such means as "value added retailer" software, or VAR. This can be quite expensive. The University of Miami spent $500,000 to install its debit card system over the past four years, and still spends $100,000 a year leasing additional equipment. And with this new equipment comes long hours of retraining university personnel.

Another issue is privacy. Credit card systems allow college officers to trace the electronic behavior of a student, what he or she did, where he went, what she purchased, and how she spends her time and money. This means universities have to take careful steps to control the access to and distribution of this data.

Once credit cards are accepted on campus for any purpose, there is usually continuous pressure to expand their use. So the cost effectiveness of these expansions needs to be calculated carefully in advance, especially since the reversal of credit card acceptance is very difficult. At California State University in Sacramento the officers discontinued the use of credit cards for 1991-92 because of the dollar losses from merchants' fees. The student outcry was so loud, however, university leaders had to reinstate credit card use in 1992-93.

Planning for a cashless campus

No chief financial officer, in our view, should be permitted to introduce credit cards, especially debit cards, without full consultation with other college and university leaders. To replace cash with credit cards is a major transformation in the way a college does its business. It requires thorough planning.

Among the vital questions that should be addressed are these. Why are credit cards being accepted, and for what reasons? Which cards will be accepted? Or will the institution introduce its own credit (debit) card? Is the university prepared to absorb the cost of credit cards? How will it balance those costs with new revenues? How will the charges be processed? What technology, staff training, and in-house banking procedures will be necessary?

Institutions contemplating a wider use of credit cards must negotiate the merchant rates offered by the various companies. With fairly high credit card volume fractional rate differences can translate into thousands of dollars a year for a college. A

Merchant fees are the major cost.

formal bidding process for rates and processing costs can help bring lower rates. Two other moves can help reduce merchant rates. One is to gather all of a university's banking operations into one master banking agreement, and then demand a very low credit card rate from that bank in return. Florida's Brevard Community College reports that it employed this approach quite successfully.

We believe that to achieve the lowest rates, only one or two cards should be accepted. A company is more likely to offer a favorably low rate if it can obtain most or all of a college's credit card business. In our survey, the lowest rate was 1.7 percent, quoted by two Ohio institutions, Cuyahoga Community College and Kent State University. Merchant fees are the major cost associated with credit card acceptance, so battling for the lowest possible rate is crucial.

Another possibility is the use of ISO's (independent sales organizations). These are companies that transmit their clients' credit card payments for electronic settlement to designated checking accounts.

ISO's can often perform these functions more cheaply than banks because their great volume gives them great bargaining

Credit cards are coming— fast.

power with the credit card companies. The University of California uses an ISO because the leaders say costs are lower than having their banks handle these transactions.

Credit card costs can also be reduced by the sophisticated selection of technology, adequate staff training, and continuous evaluations.

Whatever, credit cards are coming—fast—to American higher education. Credit cards can be especially important at institutions that are heavily tuition-driven, and those that have a large proportion of part-time and non-traditional students. The cards reduce receivables and collection expenses and clerical labor costs, and minimize bad debts. At the same time they accommodate the contemporary students' spending patterns and increase convenience for them. The new hybrid institutional/commercial card may even earn some money for hard-strapped colleges and universities in the years ahead. ■

REFERENCES

Collegiate Trends. 1993. Campus Card Systems Represent New Student Marketing Opportunities. 5(1): 1, 7-12.

Nicklin, J. 1993. Colleges Seeking New Sources of Revenue Herald Creation of the Cashless Campus. *Chronicle of Higher Education.* (3 February) A 29-30.

Universities may be on the brink of radically new exchanges of teachers and knowledge.

Good-bye to Ivory Towers

Philip Turner

I n the 20th century, a succession of technologies have emerged and been used in higher education: radio, film, broadcast television, satellite-based television, microwave transmission, and videotapes. These technologies have eased their way into U.S. colleges and universities without disturbing the basic patterns of life in academe. They have frequently made traditional classroom teaching a bit more vivid and stimulating, and have enabled some institutions to broadcast their courses to new populations or to schools outside the campus, often from a campus media center.

Philip Turner is the new dean of the School of Library and Information Science at the University of North Texas and associate vice president of academic affairs for distance education. Until August 1996 he was dean of the School of Library and Information Studies at the University of Alabama and assistant vice chancellor for academic affairs for the University of Alabama System. A graduate of Boston State College in mathematics, he earned a master's degree in library science and a doctorate in instructional technology at East Texas State University. He has taught courses in instructional design and written numerous articles and books, including *Helping Teachers Teach* (1993). In 1994 he received the Achievement in Managing Information Technology Award from Carnegie-Mellon University and the American Management Association, one of the few academics to receive this honor.

These technologies resemble an irrigation system. They carry information and ideas from a central source, flowing one way, to students, and watchers, and listeners.

Now yet another technology has arrived: two-way compressed video. Unlike the other technologies, this one promises to alter the patterns of teaching and learning in a fundamental way—by enabling two-way communication among colleges and universities all over the nation and much of the world. The splendid, sometimes monastic isolation of institutions may crumble; the ivory tower may be replaced by a network of colleges exchanging information and knowledge. Instead of a one-way irrigation system, higher education will be a network of two-way exchanges.

In addition to being dean of a school of library and information studies, I serve as administrator of the Intercampus Interactive Telecommunications System (IITS), a 25-site compressed video network in Alabama. This technology, which is a marriage of television, computers, telecommunications, and networks, presents planners with extraordinary opportunities. As a small example, several years ago I visited the president of a major university in our state to request that he connect his university to the IITS when he began using two-way compressed video. The president asked why I would want his noted university to be connected to the other colleges and universities in the state. I said there was a faculty member at his university that had an expertise that no one at my university possessed, and I wanted that person to teach a course at our university. His university did join IITS, and for the past two years that faculty member has taught via the network—not only to the University of Alabama (at Tuscaloosa) but also to University of Alabama students in Birmingham.

We are hardly alone. The schools of library science and information at Michigan, Berkeley, the University of South Florida,

Higher education will be a network of two-way exchanges.

and Texas Women's University have shared teaching resources. So have the engineering colleges at Auburn University and California Polytechnic Institute. Appalachian State University has taught classes to primary and secondary school students, and the students have also participated in other collaborative learning experiences (Walsh and Reese 1995). At our library school at the University of Alabama we regularly dial into other networks to bring in colloquium speakers such as the library directors at Georgia Tech and Southern Illinois University, the CEO of a major information agency, and an information specialist at the Bell South Corporation.

Two-way compressed video promises to revolutionize teaching, faculty hiring, and intellectual exchanges. Professors from many other campuses, business, religious, and political leaders, and experts from many fields outside academe will be teaching and joining seminars on each campus with network capacity. And institutions will be able to hold classes with many persons off-campus or in other parts of their state, or the nation.

This standards-based two-way compressed video represents a radical departure from previous tools in higher education. It has the potential for almost unlimited con-

nectivity; experts predict that connecting capability in the future could be 10,000 times as high as today's networks (Lewis 1996). A college or university's connectivity with the world's best teachers, experts, and innovators could very well replace the physical campus, the full-time faculty, and the variety of academic programs as the most significant factor in an institution's admissions or reputation in a few decades.

Soon no institution of higher education will be able to operate as a closed system. A constant two-way flow of an institution's knowledge product will be vital to its intellectual and financial health. Yes, for higher-level learning the presence of a scholar-teacher to provide motivation, guidance, methodology, and interpretation is an important component of the learning process. But the use of two-way video and audio actually provides many of the characteristics of an on-site faculty member. As Deborah Allen Carey pointed out in the previous issue of this journal (1996), video conferencing engenders a feeling of virtual presence for all participants.

While virtual presence is the major reason to employ two-way video and audio, another reason is cost. The infrastructure required to carry a compressed video signal between two sites can be 100 times less than that of a non-compressed signal, and transmission costs are correspondingly less. The quality of the compressed video signal does suffer in comparison with a non-compressed signal. But the pedagogical impact seems slight, and developments in compression algorithms in the past few years have improved picture quality, and should continue to improve video sharpness. Also, a digital-based system allows computer-based teaching and learning tools to be easily accessed while using two-way compressed video.

Getting started

Planning for the optimum use of two-way compressed video presents education planners with challenges of new complexity. Technology can bewilder even those who devote full time to keeping up with the technologies of distance education. But, driven by a desire to have human beings at both ends of the instructional process and by the need to control the costs of burgeoning technology on campus, colleges and universities are likely to make two-way compressed video the medium or choice. What decisions need to be made to optimize the initial investment, which can be considerable?

Connectivity could replace the physical campus, faculty, and variety of programs as the most significant factor.

I think decision makers planning for the use of two-way compressed video as an integral part of their instruction might benefit from the experience of others who have already introduced this technology. What is interesting is that most institutions have passed through a series of generations, mostly through trial and error. Let me describe what I think are the three generations.

In the first generation, a university's leaders usually decide to purchase the equipment necessary to digitize and compress the video and audio signals in order to deliver instruction to one or more distant sites much as they have been doing with other technologies. The main campus is still the "delivery" site and the outlying meeting rooms are called the "receiving" sites. The room designs usually reflect this one-way philosophy, with the receiving rooms having less sophisticated cameras and auxiliary equipment.

The sites are usually connected through leading a high-capacity digital telephone line. Most often this is a T-1 line with a capacity of 24 telephone channels (like a 24-lane highway). The sites communicate at a fixed bandwidth, which is achieved by selecting a certain number of telephone channels, from two to 24. The size of that bandwidth determines the quality of the video. A fixed bandwidth is selected because it is the least expensive way to connect, and also because it is the simplest way to connect and the simpler options are most appealing to newcomers.

Sometimes the college or university will want to deliver to more than one site simultaneously. In this case, a multi-point control unit, or MCU, will be utilized, allowing three or more classes to be held at the same time. In general, first generation users of two-way compressed video tend to mimic the use of earlier technologies, connectivity is limited to a few off-campus sites, and communication is via a fixed bandwidth. There is a great concern for logistics and for training the faculty to teach via the video.

The second generation of use usually begins when several things occur. Campus officials realize that digital-based technology is fundamentally different from its analog predecessors. As the monthly bills for the use of T-1 telephone lines continue to arrive, an examination of the network design often takes place. If a portion of the leased lines is not being used, some admin-

---

FIGURE 1

Sites D and E share a T–1 line to connect to the network. If site E is not involved in a conference, site D may use the full bandwidth to conference with sites A and B.

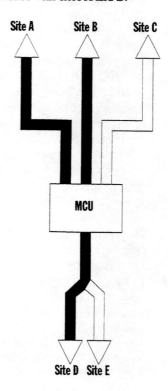

Site A   Site B   Site C

MCU

Site D   Site E

---

istrator is sure to question the wisdom of not using this expensive bandwidth. If the network operates at one fourth of a T-1 line (six of the 24 lanes of the information highway) some will complain that the quality of the video is not adequate. Networks using a fixed one half or more of the T-1 line will have critics that point out that most teaching and learning can be conducted at lower, less expensive bandwidths.

Also, other sites on campus will want to join the network and achieve connectivity to off-campus sites. The most cost-effective way to do this is by having several sites on campus share the "highway." So, in the second generation, devices are installed behind the CODEC, or coder-decoder, so that the user can select how many of the 24 channels are to be used every time there is a conference. This allows for the maximum use of the leased T-1 lines because the lanes in the

FIGURE 2

The video conference among sites A, D, and E is at one-half T–1, since sites D and E share a T–1 line. Site C is using one-quarter of a T–1 to connect the public switched network.

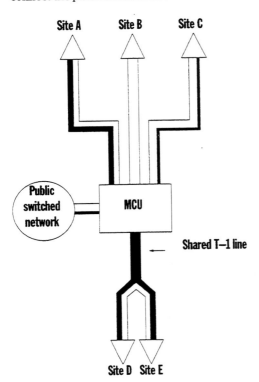

highway are no longer fixed. (See figures 1 and 2.) With *flexible* bandwidth capability, any site can select a very low bandwidth such as only two channels, lowering the cost of dialing out of the network.

Eventually, the real power of digital-based telecommunications technology, *connectivity*, occurs to most of the users in the first generation network. With a standards-based architecture, persons at another university—or industry or office—1,000 or 2,000 miles away are now available for colloquia, dissertation committees, or entire courses of study.

Enter the third generation?

Some persons are striving to use the Internet for desktop-to-desktop two-way compressed video connections since the Internet also uses digital telephone lines and is increasingly a household tool. But the quality of these connections is very low and definitely not acceptable for large-screen projections. Also, traffic on the Internet during peak usage is so heavy that video transmission is difficult, and this problem is likely to get worse. Because of these difficulties with the Internet, *separate* connecting lines to transmit video and audio will almost certainly be the choice for the future.

As ISDN (Integrated Services Digital Network) and ATM (Asynchronous Transfer Mode) services become available, and as cable television companies create technically feasible networks, the number of colleges and universities that develop their own interactive compressed video networks will decrease. Some institutions with a high volume of digital traffic may want to continue the use of leased-line private networks; but the vast majority will enter the third generation through the public-switched network and through networks carried by cable television. The explosive growth of desktop usage combined with the breakthroughs in compression capability and the decrease in line costs will drive this migration.

In this coming third generation, interactive video connections may be nearly as frequent and undemanding as telephone connections are today. Universities will no longer be limited to their on-campus teaching resources; they will be able to connect audibly and visually—with two-way exchanges—with scholars and experts from many places on the globe. Some campuses will become famous among students for their outstanding connectivity with leading teachers at other institutions and authorities in many parts of the country and the world.

What should planners do?

The third generation may be a decade or more away. In the meantime, higher education planners must help create strategies to guide their institutions through the first and second generations of connectivity. From my experience, I offer planners the following suggestions.

Maximize connectivity. While the high costs of high-compression video equipment have decreased in the past few years, the costs are still a significant barrier to many decision makers. The best way to justify the expenditures is as an investment in *potential connectivity*. As can be seen in Figure 3, the costs per connection fall dramatically as the number of sites in a network grows from two to ten. With two sites, assuming an outlay of $70,000 per room, the cost of one connection between the two is approximately $140,000. For ten sites, the cost for each of the 1,013 possible connections is only $691. Most institutions of higher education will build a network slowly, starting with two or three sties. But planners should stress the potential of greater connectivity in the future.

Connect to other standards-based networks. Try to connect your network with other networks. This can reduce potential connectivity costs dramatically. For example, in a four-site network there are 11 possible combinations of conferences, and 57 in a five-site network. If these two networks are connected, the potential connections jump to 1,013. The installation of a T-1 line between the Oklahoma and Alabama state networks enabled a wide combination of sites in each state network to communicate. The library schools of the universities of Oklahoma and Alabama conducted a series of colloquia for students at the two institutions and throughout the two states. An expert in pop-up books

for children at the University of Oklahoma held a discussion with students at her own campus as well as students in Tulsa, Oklahoma, and in Birmingham, Tuscaloosa, and Huntsville. The next week, an expert on Mexican copyright law from the University of Alabama held similar discussions with students in both states.

Connect to non-standards-based networks. In the last decade, numerous colleges and universities installed microwave-based analog networks. These can be linked to a digital network by installing a CODEC on the analog network and connecting this device to the MCU of the digital network. The analog network then becomes a "site" on the digital network, and the analog network

---

Interactive video connections may be as frequent as telephone connections are today.

---

gains the digital network's access to the public-switched network.

Satellite uplinks can also be connected to a two-way compressed network. So can digital networks that use little or no compression, simply by installing a CODEC on the non-standard network to enable it to function as a site on the two-way compressed video network.

Buy wisely. The challenge in purchasing equipment for a two-way compressed video site centers on selecting the CODEC, the IMUX (a device that allows for flexible bandwidth and for dialing out of a network), and the telephone company. Faced with the constraints of bidding regulations, some decision makers may choose one band of CODEC for the entire state's educational institutions. This has the benefit of maximum compatibility among sites; but swift technological advances can make good communication impossible between the same brand of CODEC produced four years apart. Also, the long-term existence of any one brand is not a certainty. The most important issue in selecting a CODEC brand is the track record of the company, including its after-sales servicing. A close second is the ease with which the CODEC

A well-designed system can adapt to a professor's teaching style.

---

can be upgraded. Third, make sure that the CODEC can use the bandwidth you want.

In selecting the IMUX device to connect you to the network, insist on the capability to dial out of your network. If you want to use various bandwidths and to share T-1 lines easily, be certain that the device can do this via software and does not require someone to set switches manually.

The choice of a telephone company is sometimes mandated. But the Telecommunications Act of 1996 is changing this. Nonetheless, it is extremely important to develop a good relationship with both the sales and the technical staff. Downtime on a network

translates into lost instruction and canceled conferences. Knowing exactly who to call to minimize the downtime is imperative.

Remember the people factor. In a study of those responsible for setting up the first sites in what has become the nation's largest two-way compressed video network—the Georgia Statewide Academic and Medical System—the respondents identified as the critical factor the person who makes the technology successful at that location (Stratford 1995). Thorough training for the technical staff, and for the faculty, was judged to be very important.

While training the faculty users is crucial to success, a well-designed system can adapt considerably to a professor's teaching style. With two-way compressed video, faculty teaching is closer to the informality of the telephone than to the formality of a television studio.

Preparing for tomorrow

In conclusion, I offer two other pieces of advice. One certainty with digital technology is that rapid change will occur. So net-

FIGURE 3

Cost of Connectivity

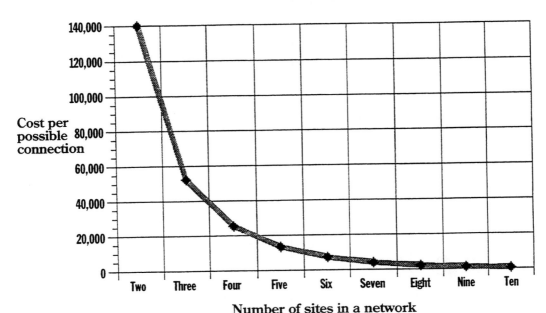

Number of sites in a network

work planners and developers need to provide for easy upgrading. Skipping over the first generation to the second can help employ the resources expended on the network more efficiently.

The barriers to sharing among colleges are many.

Second, this technology requires more than technical solutions. It requires risk-taking by campus leaders and a radical change in instructional philosophy. The barriers to sharing among colleges and universities are many, and the resolution of credit-hour allocation, scheduling, and tuition-sharing problems can be very difficult. Faculty fears about the "outsourcing" of some teaching are considerable, and must be dealt with through patient explanations.

But the move toward greater connectivity among institutions of higher learning seems inexorable both for financial and academic reasons. Planners should help create a campus environment that permits the greatest possible exchange of intellectual resources to become the norm in the next decade. ∎

REFERENCES

Carey, D. 1996. Distancing Your College Courses. *Planning for Higher Education* 24(3): 5-13.

Lewis, T. 1996. The Next 10,000 Years: Part II. *Computer* 29(5): 78-86.

Stratford, S. 1995. Critical Factors in the Start-up and Operation of a Two-Way Interactive Video and Audio Distance Learning Project. (Ph.D. diss., University of Alabama.)

Walsh, J. and Reese, B. 1995. Distance Learning's Growing Reach. *T.H.E. Journal* 22(11): 58-62.

Should states revise the way they finance state universities and colleges?

States and College Reform: New Jersey's Experiment

T. Edward Hollander

At the so-called education summit at the University of Virginia in 1990, President George Bush and the task force on education of the National Governors' Association agreed on some broad, ambitious goals. To help achieve these goals the National Governors' Association asked colleges and universities to increase their minority presence on campus, strengthen undergraduate education, increase retention, improve teaching, help strengthen the public schools, and help provide a more adequately trained work force. Surprisingly, the governors recommended

T. Edward Hollander, now professor at the Graduate School of Management, Rutgers University, was chancellor of the N.J. Department of Higher Education for 13 years until 1990. Dr. Hollander, who is also a certified public accountant, taught at Dusquesne University, and Baruch College before becoming vice-chancellor for finance and planning at CUNY and then deputy commissioner in the N.Y. State Department of Higher Education. He has also been chairman of the board of NCHEMS.

that competitive funding be considered to stimulate improvements in these areas. (National Governors' Association, 1990, pp. 22–27).

In New Jersey we were one of the forefront states to try competitive funding. We abandoned the formula funding that is still used widely and replaced it with a new system of incentive funding combined with base budgeting. In our scheme state institutions of higher education received a base of operating funds but had to compete for extra monies by planning initiatives for the problems on which New Jersey's leaders wanted more action (technological education, minority enrollments, strategic planning, etc.)

This article is a description of what we did, how, and why so that other states planning to introduce competitive funding might benefit.

The birth of funding formulas

How should America's 50 states give their state tax dollars to the state universities, colleges, and two-year colleges in their midst?

Prior to the 1950s, institutional budgets

We abandoned formula funding and replaced it with incentive funding.

were largely negotiated with the state's political and financial leaders. Institutions and their alumni put pressure on legislators and budget officials as each state college and university lobbied for a larger share of the funds for higher education (Millet, 1974).

To reduce the politicking and to arrive at more rational disbursements, Texas introduced formula funding after World War II, awarding monies to each institution according to a formula. The idea spread quickly across the states. By 1980, formula funding was employed in whole or part in 34 states (McKeown, 1986, p. 73).

The funding formulas were clear and objective. Legislators liked them because they increased harmony and equity and reduced infighting. Since the formulas were based largely on average costs per student, they provided generous financial support to state colleges and universities during expansion since the marginal cost of each new student was less than the average cost. So the public institutions liked them. State coordinating boards liked them because the formulas made their budgeting for state higher education easier. And college and university executives liked formula funding because it put a block of money in their hands to spend for their own priorities.

But funding formulas had some weaknesses. Since the system was based on enrollments, it encouraged public colleges and universities to grow, sometimes to the neglect of quality, and to compete fiercely for students. Except in states such as California, where each of the three tiers of higher education uses different formulas, differences in institutional mission are hard to take into account. With the power to allocate funds internally, many public institutions sought to emulate the research universities, often neglecting investments in undergraduate edu-

cation, teaching, and curriculum design, especially in states where the state coordinating agency failed to delineate institutional missions. Universities were rewarded for numbers, not for quality (Carnegie Council, 1980; Bowen, 1980).

Also, formula funding reduces budgeting to a technical process dependent on two variables: levels of enrollments and funding per student at each level. The formula-driven budget becomes the asking budget. Instead of public policy considerations, technical considerations determine the relative share each institution receives.

Worse, legislatures which were pressed to stimulate colleges to respond to new social problems, increase quality, and reform themselves but stymied by budget formulas felt forced to pass new laws for higher education. And state coordinating boards in the 1980s tried to stimulate change inside the state institutions through new regulations and enrollment allocations. These laws and regulations were often hurried, overly political, and poorly informed. Sometimes they intruded clumsily on college practices, or punished the high-quality campuses.

Legislative mandates and administrative regulations have turned out to be poor vehicles for higher education reform. The state budgeting process seemed a more effective instrument to encourage change and new directions.

Enter financial incentives

In the late 1980s, Tennessee, New Jersey, and a handful of other states came to recognize the potential of using the state budget as a facilitator of change. The idea was to put additional monies into the hands of those university leaders and faculties who support reform and who are willing to take risks to achieve it. Elected officials were encouraged to "put their money where their policy goals were."

But to pull away from formula funding, an alternative funding system was required. This was made easier in the 1980s because in a time of enrollment declines, presidents and faculties were looking for ways to move

The idea was to put additional money into the hands of those who support reform.

away from funding that was tied to the numbers of FTE (full-time equivalent) students.

New Jersey sends a larger proportion of its students to out-of-state colleges and universities than any other state, so its state colleges experienced sharp enrollment declines sooner than most other states. To obtain formula funds, they lowered admission standards to keep enrollments up, which in turn caused more young persons to leave the state because of the perception of declining quality in the state's public colleges and state university. It was a downward spiral.

So in 1978, New Jersey's board of higher education proposed a change in the way state institutions were supported by tax dollars, away from using enrollments as the entire foundation for funding. The proposal was that state funding should instead provide a base of money for each institution supplemented by new monies to be won by campus proposals for new programs and initiatives on priorities of the state. In 1981 the governor and legislators agreed to a change in financial policy and by 1985 incentive-based budgeting replaced enrollment-driven formula funding.

Under this new method, public college budgets are adjusted for salary increases but non-salary cost increases were covered by tuition increases. Additional funds are added to the colleges' base in the form of categorical aid (called priority packages). The state still set maximum enrollment levels, but enrollments no longer controlled the amount of

state dollars the university received. The purpose: to shift the focus of the campus leadership away from enrollment expansion toward program improvement.

What happened was that budget hearings quickly changed in nature to intense discussions of what were the state's priorities and why, and what kind of educational programs would best help achieve them. Since new funding was largely tied to campus plans to attack the state's priorities, the budget became the focal point for major policy decisions.

"Base budgeting plus," as the new financial scheme came to be called, was gradually accepted in the late 1980s, although some campus leaders argued that the new budgeting systems meant that the state was intruding on state college and university "autonomy" in setting educational priorities and that the state was "dictating" how New Jersey's public institutions ought to change.

The new budgeting system, it has to be admitted, was aided by two historic facts. One was the vigorous growth of New Jersey's economy in the 1980s. The other was the dedication of Governor Thomas Kean to improved lower and higher education for all New Jersey's citizens. As a result, public institutions increased their state support despite a slight enrollment decline.

What was the "plus" in "base budgeting plus?" We used three forms: performance budgeting, challenge grants, and competitive program grants. (I'm excluding categorical aid and funds for specified programs distributed on a matching or entitlement basis.) New Jersey benefitted from studying similar budgeting reform efforts in several other states (Holland and Berdahl, 1990).

Performance budgeting

Performance budgeting was pioneered by the state of Tennessee. Beginning in 1979,

New Jersey Appropriations per Student, 1967–1990

	1967	1979	1990
Institutional appropriations	$66.6 mill.	$320.4 mill.	$828.6 mill.
Enrollments	58,900	210,200	209,400
Appropriations per student	$1,131	$1,524	$3,957
% Increase (in real dollars)		–3.3%	2.9%

Tennessee allowed each of the state's four-year and two-year colleges to earn up to 5.45 percent of its budget by performing well in state-chosen areas that were measurable such as placement of graduates, students outcomes, and improvement of identified weak programs. Tennessee's is still the most ambitious program in the country, distributing more than $17 million a year for performance gains in selected areas.

Performance funding is without ambiguity. Institutions that achieve the performance goals the state leaders establish receive additional funding. Once allocated, the extra money for performance can be used however the institution chooses. The idea is simply to stimulate better performance and higher quality through financial incentives.

New Jersey has used performance budgeting to improve minority recruitment and retention. Public institutions that recruit more minority students, teach them more effectively, and retain them in larger numbers receive slightly higher funding for special programs than institutions that do not do so. There have been objections. "The poorest programs, not the most successful, should get the money." "It causes inequities because some parts of the state have fewer minority students." And, "Why punish a whole college for poor administration in one area?" But the state's institutions now are improving their programs for minorities to win the extra money for better performance.

Challenge grants

With challenge grants, the state challenges its public institutions to respond to the accomplishment of public policy objectives deemed important to the state's future. All institutions are sent a request for a proposal, or RFP, which would detail exactly how the college or university intends to reach the objective and what it will take. The proposals are examined in a competition, and the best ones are awarded extra money to accomplish the task.

New Jersey was particularly keen on this form of incentive financing, and developed what some believe is the most innova-

The one-time state teachers colleges were asked to propose bold programs to become among the best state colleges.

tive and successful program to encourage institutional change in the nation. Similar programs exist in other states—to establish chairs for outstanding professors, create research and teaching centers, or expand outreach programs (Holland and Berdahl, 1990). But the New Jersey challenge grants program appears unique so far both in its scope (all public and private colleges and universities) and in its pervasiveness of institutional challenge. Among the state objectives that colleges were challenged to accomplish: improved undergraduate teaching, assistance with secondary school improvements, more global issues in the curriculum, better and broader instruction in science and technology, and even "a change in mission."

The challenges were usually competitive, but could be negotiated. For example, Rutgers University—once private but now the state university—was challenged to become recognized as one of the ten best public universities in the country. The university accepted the challenge, and has received more than $150 million in additional capital and operating funds to finance its rise to national excellence. The university's progress toward agreed-upon objectives is monitored as part of its budget process. Similarly negotiated, non-competitive challenges were made and accepted by the New Jersey Institute of Technology, which has become one of America's more successful colleges for turning out black technicians and engineers, and the University of Medicine and Dentistry of New Jersey.

Even more interesting was the governor's challenge to New Jersey's nine state colleges. They were challenged to "become among the very best . . . in the nation" (*Annual Message*, 1985). The state appropriated $10 million extra to the board of higher education budget and invited the nine colleges to compete for the funds.

The one-time state teachers colleges were each asked to propose bold programs to transform themselves. Each proposal required a three-year strategic plan that included:

- a frank institutional assessment
- a vision for the future
- a projection of its future size
- a description of the students it intended to serve
- a plan for increasing the quality of its students and services for them
- a plan to refine and enhance the quality of its academic offerings.

A panel of three out-of-state college presidents was chosen to select the competition winners.

In the first round of competition, only five of the nine state colleges entered, and the selection committee chose two for funding. Two additional rounds of competition were held, and over the three years eight of the nine colleges received more than $33 million in funds. What is remarkable is that subsequent evaluations by the New Jersey department of higher education found that each of the eight colleges have met their grant objectives. So all of the challenge grant additions have remained in the state college budgets.

The success of the challenge grants program for the state colleges led to creating a similar one for New Jersey's 19 two-year community colleges. The state's objectives were: better minority representation on campus, closer cooperation with secondary schools, and improved programs in technology. As of 1990, 15 of the 19 community colleges had won competitive grants.

And in 1988, New Jersey's private colleges also asked to be included in the challenge grants program. The state generously obliged (*Annual Message*, 1988). Four priority areas were designated by the board of higher education: improvement of under-

graduate education, strengthening of the faculty, increasing minority enrollment, and contributions to New Jersey's economy. Sixteen of the independent colleges received small grants to begin planning for changes and their proposals. And in 1988 and 1989 the board of higher education awarded $16.3 million to eight of the sixteen private colleges that were successful with their proposals in the competition.

The challenge grants have had notable results. They bent some of the work of many colleges toward policies that the state thought important. They stimulated lots of strategic thinking and some inventive initiatives. They helped bring about change and innovations.

One of the principal outcomes was the empowerment of college presidents. Under formula funding the presidents had little discretionary money and little opportunity to move their state colleges in new directions. Challenge grants gave presidents a chance to mobilize their forces, to lead, to strategize, to design the new kinds of things college presidents dream of creating.

But challenge grants also brought risks for the president. The program was competitive and required management skills; the president could fail. The faculty and governing board might want to know why the institution lost in the competition. And the state's evaluation process meant that the college would be scrutinized annually to see how well the leaders and the faculty were implementing their successful proposal.

Competitive program grants

The third form of incentive budgeting was program grants. While challenge grants were for colleges and universities, program grants went to individual faculty and staff, or teams of faculty. The idea came from those of us at the board of higher education in 1983.

Faculty were solicited to respond to a "funding prospectus" that defined the objectives of the program (which emphasized improved undergraduate learning), the criteria for funding, and the rules for funding. The winning proposals in the competition were chosen by out-of-state faculty peers who ranked the quality and constructive nature of the proposals. The program was open to faculty of all public and private colleges and universities in New Jersey. Between 1984 and 1991, the state funded 1,433 proposals for $62.9 million, or an average award of $44,000.

The awards were in 12 categories. The most frequent proposals were in the use of computers in the curriculum, including subjects such as art and music; in the improvement of science, engineering, and technical education; and in the humanities, which included foreign language instruction.

The faculty union bitterly opposed the program.

The competitive program grants identified numerous ingenious professors, increased attention to undergraduates and classroom teaching, and stimulated individual faculty enterpreneurship. But the program grants were very controversial. Some faculty thought the enticements were improper. The union representing the state college faculty bitterly opposed the program because it gave extra money to some of its members and allocated resources directly from the board of higher education. Certain college presidents also opposed the program—some because it diverted money from the colleges, others because it made their faculty members responsive to statewide priorities rather than to institutional or research priorities.

When budget reductions were required in New Jersey in 1990–1991, the competitive grant program was one of the quickest to be cut out. Aside from support from the media, the state board of higher education, and members of the academic community who were able to introduce beneficial changes, the program had little political support.

So what?

Has the adoption of new forms of state budgeting for higher education made a difference in New Jersey? As chancellor of the state's department of higher education during the 13 years prior to 1990, I am not an entirely objective observer.

But the number of changes and increases in quality in the state's public colleges and universities has been noticeable to in-state persons and outsiders both. A near-orgy of strategic planning has intensified interest in each college's future, in minorities and better technological education, and in undergraduate teaching. Presidents at New Jersey's institutions have been able to lead a bit more actively. The media have praised New Jersey's efforts to raise quality (*Money*, May 1986; *The [London] Times Education Supplement*, October 14, 1987; *U.S. News and World Report*, October 26, 1987).

Legislative support for higher education grew, as did support for institutional autonomy. Two successful bond proposals for education were passed, one for $90 million in 1984 and the second for $350 million in 1989. Fund-raising for nearly all state colleges and universities increased dramatically, as did corporate support. Rutgers alone raised more than $150 million in a capital campaign, larger than any amount in the university's history.

What is astounding is how little the incentives to encourage change and higher quality cost. Of the $6.6 billion New Jersey spent on higher education between 1984 and 1991, only $120 million, or two percent, was spent on incentive financing:

New Jersey Appropriations for Higher Education, 1984–1991

	Amount (in millions)	% of Total
Institutions	$5,205	79%
Student Aid	647	10
Capital and Debt Finance	473	7
Other Aid	160	2
Challenge and Competitive Grants	120	2
	$6,605	100%

Yet, when a new governor came in in the fall of 1990 and the state faced a shortfall in state revenues, both the challenge grants and competitive grants programs were eliminated. (The state officials sharply cut the institutional base budgets also). Only categorical aid and financial incentive programs linked to student aid and minority recruitment survived in the 1990–91 fiscal year budget.

What is astounding is how little the incentives to encourage change cost.

New incentive fundings programs have succumbed to budget reductions in other states as well (Holland and Berdahl, 1990). It seems that the use of some small portion of a state's appropriation for the encouragement of better strategic planning, higher quality, and service to the state's greatest needs is not yet accepted as a desirable part of fiscal policy for education.

Thus, while the states' governors took a strong position at the 1990 education summit in Virginia in favor of allocating some part of their higher education expenditures to competitive financing, they have yet to convince most colleges and faculty leaders and many state legislators that incentive funding is a legitimate tool of state public policy.

In my view the reticence to use the state budget as a vehicle of reforms, strategic change, and higher quality could weaken America's efforts to respond creatively to rapidly changing national and world conditions. It leaves suggestions for resurgence and educational change largely in the rhetorical realm. Just as with all of us in our private lives, higher education institutions need to be encouraged and rewarded financially for daring to try something new and important.

■

REFERENCES

Agenda of the Board of Higher Education. Trenton: Department of Higher Education, State of New Jersey. September 1985; November, 1986; July 1987; July, 1988; October 1988; October 1989.

Annual Message. Trenton: Office of the Governor. 1985.

Annual Message. Trenton: Office of the Governor. January 12, 1988.

Bowen, Howard R. *The State of the Nation and the Agenda for Higher Education*. San Francisco: Jossey-Bass, 1980.

Carnegie Foundation for the Advancement of Teaching. *The States and Higher Education*. San Francisco: Jossey-Bass, 1976.

Department of Higher Education. *Out-Migration of College-Bound Freshman: New Jersey's Special Dilemma*. Trenton: Department of Higher Education, State of New Jersey, 1983.

Department of Higher Education. *Annual Report on Higher Education in New Jersey, 1986–87*. Trenton: Department of Higher Education, State of New Jersey, 1988.

Education Commission of the States. *The Education Agenda*. Denver: Education Commission of the States, 1990.

Holland, Barbara A. and Berdahl, Robert O., "Green Carrots: A Survey of State Use of Fiscal Incentives for Academic Quality," Unpublished Manuscript presented at the 1990 Annual Meeting of the Association for the Study of Higher Education, Portland, Oregon, November 1, 1990. College Park, Maryland: National Center for Postsecondary Study and Finance, 1990.

McKeown, Mary P. "Funding Formulas," In *Values in Conflict: Funding Priorities for Higher Education*. Edited by Mary P. McKeown and Kern Alexander. Cambridge, Mass.: Ballinger Publishing Company, 1986.

Miller, James L., Jr. *State Budgeting for Higher Education: The Use of Formulas and Cost Analysis*. Ann Arbor: University of Michigan, 1964.

Millet, John E. *The Budget Formula as the Basis for State Appropriations in Support of Higher Education*. New York: Academy for Educational Development, 1974.

National Governors' Association. *Educating America: State Strategies for Achieving the National Education Goals*. Washington, D.C.: National Governors' Association, 1990.

Hard times may require a different approach to decision making.

Statewide Planning During Declining State Support

Gertrude Eaton, Javier Miyares, and Ruth Robertson

In 1988 Governor William Donald Schaefer ordered that the state universities and four-year colleges (with two special exceptions)—13 institutions—be combined into one University of Maryland System (UMS), with a new central administration to provide a more efficient and more rational, collaborative network to serve the people of the state. The creation of UMS was accompanied by an increase in state financial support for the public institutions between 1988 and 1991 of more than 40 percent.

Then in 1991 the State of Maryland experienced the beginning of a three-year fiscal crisis, caused in large part by an economic recession, growing expenditures for public safety, and a sharp increase in Medicaid costs. (See Figure 1.) By fiscal year 1993, public higher education in Maryland endured nine successive budget cuts, reducing funding for the University of Maryland System by $124 million, or roughly 20 percent from the 1990 high. As UMS Chancellor Donald Langenberg, a respected physicist and former deputy director of the National Science Foundation and chancellor of the University of Illinois at Chicago, who was named UMS chancellor in July 1990, has observed, "Across the country higher educa-

Gertrude Eaton is associate vice chancellor for academic affairs in the University of Maryland System office. She received a B.A., M.A., and Ph.D. in English literature from the University of Pennsylvania, and has taught there, at American University, where she also worked as director of program and research development, and the University of Maryland.

Javier Miyares is assistant vice chancellor for academic affairs in the University of Maryland System administration. Though a graduate of the Universidad Católica Andres Bello in Venezuela, he also earned a B.A. and M.A. in sociology at the University of Maryland, where he is completing a doctorate in educational measurement and statistics.

Ruth Robertson is associate vice chancellor for academic affairs in the University of Maryland System office. She received her B.S. and Ph.D. in physics and materials science from Penn State. She has administered the physics department at Northwestern and the chemistry department at Princeton, and served as an academic planner for the University of Wisconsin system.

tion support is being squeezed out by health, welfare, and prisons."

The twin planning questions were: How does a state system office distribute such heavy and sudden reductions; and How might the reductions be used as an opportunity to improve individual campus strategic planning, mission clarification, and cost containment while at the same time establishing new collaborations and complementarity among the institutions? Further, how could the decline in state support be employed in a way that would help prepare each state college and university in Maryland for a new era of fiscal austerity and of stable or eroding state tax support?

One problem the relatively new University of Maryland System office faced was that the 1988 legislation strengthened the role of the state's coordinating board (Maryland Higher Education Commission) and its Secretary for Higher Education, and also promised the presidents of the 13 state

institutions considerable continuing autonomy. So the leadership role of Chancellor Langenberg and the Board of Regents was not entirely clear—an issue that complicates statewide higher education planning in many states (McGuiness 1990;

Across the country higher education support is being squeezed out.

Schick *et al.* 1991). Inevitably, disputes developed over who was responsible for what.

But the 1988 legislation did give the UMS Chancellor and staff three specific areas of accountability: assessment of student learning outcomes, program review, and cost containment and financial planning. The last two were to become the core of the UMS management of the reductions. Chan-

FIGURE 1

Higher Education's Changing Share of
the Maryland State Budget, 1985–1992

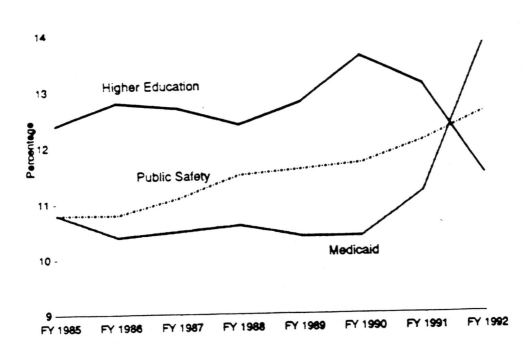

cellor Langenberg in his inaugural address spoke of the need for state colleges and universities to be more accountable for their educational programs and costs, and in 1991 he proposed that the state's 13 institutions become "a family of distinctive and complementary institutions." Distinctiveness implied a clearer mission for each campus, one that served a particular group of students rather than all students; and complementarity meant that each institution would be less isolated and independent and more mutual and interdependent.

In essence, the 13 state colleges and universities would act as a real *system*, as the governor and legislators intended in the 1988 law.

A UMS Accountability Group was created to address the legislative mandates. It included faculty and administrators from each state institution as well as central office staff, and gradually shaped a process and criteria for program reviews throughout the University of Maryland System.

The storm begins

When the first round of financial cuts came to the UMS campuses in 1991, the University of Maryland System officers distributed the reductions across the board to the 13 institutions and within the UMS staff, and each college or university made its own layoffs and cutbacks. But Chancellor Langenberg, sensing that the decline in the state appropriations would continue, issued a paper called, "Achieving the Vision in Hard Times," asking for a new way of doing higher education's business with better program reviews and cost controls, increased use of technology, and new fund-raising. It also asked each public institution to clarify its academic purpose and sharpen its strategy for achieving it.

Governor Schaefer was not happy with the across-the-board cuts, and several legislators and newspapers pressured the Chancellor and the 15-person Board of Regents of the University of Maryland System to set priorities and redeploy the limited resources. Also, the Secretary for Higher Education was beginning to propose priorities of her own for the University of Maryland Sys-

tem institutions. The University of Maryland at College Park, the "flagship" and largest state university, was completing its own restructuring, where it eliminated a whole school (Human Ecology, formerly Home Economics), 11 graduate programs, and 18 undergraduate degree programs, and seven academic departments, a move that had limited savings, however, since it was declared that no tenured faculty would be released.

The pressures on the System officials were well expressed by Pat Callan, executive director of the California Higher Education

Governor Schaefer was not happy.

Center: "The multicampus governing boards and central offices have neither taken nor stimulated major initiatives to set program priorities, to eliminate duplication, to streamline campus missions, or to encourage cooperation among campuses" (McCurdy and Trombley 1993). And Gordon Winston, a leading economist of higher education at Williams College, noted, "The fundamental challenge to college administrations...will be to induce a highly resistant community to understand that there's an economic reality within which they'll have to live, one that may include 'downsizing' and 'restructuring' and the biting of all sorts of personally painful bullets" (Winston 1993, p. 20).

Hence, in the summer of 1992, under mounting outside criticism for their seemingly *laissez-faire* response to reduced state funding, the UMS Regents—all appointees by the governor—made a commitment to Governor Schaefer that they would exert greater control over how budget cuts were made, and why. In early September 1992 they asked the chancellor for a redeployment plan by December 31, 1992. Chancellor Langenberg and his staff had only four months to devise a plan for further state reductions and reallocations within the 13-campus system and to make decisions.

The chancellor and his staff considered several options, including the merger of a few institutions, but concluded that radical structural changes would be politically unacceptable and would not yield short-term savings. (See Weinstein 1993.) So in the fall of 1992 Chancellor Langenberg wrote "Achieving the Vision in Hard Times: II." The plan was subtitled, "A Plan for Reinvesting the System's Resources," and it proposed redeployment in several areas throughout the state colleges and universities, including the reduction of several high-cost and low-productivity academic programs at the 10 regular degree-granting institutions. (Previous cuts had focused largely on administrators and staff and spared faculty.)

Push comes to shove

The question was, which programs would yield the most resources? Two groups were selected.

One was a list of academic programs that the governor's secretary for higher education had earlier drawn up as being of "low productivity," as defined by small and declining enrollments and few degrees awarded. Interestingly, this list had been sent by her office to the institutions for comment, and each institution responded that every program she targeted was indispensable. The other was a group of academic programs identified by the chancellor's staff as possibly duplicative, unusually high cost, and of questionable centrality to the mission of the institution. These included such programs as accounting, art, communications, computer science, law enforcement, nursing, social work, and theater.

Building upon a data collection process and the criteria already developed by the Accountability Group, the University of Maryland System office scrambled to conduct a swift review of all programs by cost, productivity, and centrality. The Regents themselves formed an Ad Hoc Committee of the Regents to work closely with the chancellor, and the Committee studied the analysis of the institutions' academic programs, then recommended closures to the full Board of Regents. On December 16, 1992 the Regents adopted a plan they called

Vision II, and urged that the program reductions be implemented by fall of 1993. The entire 13-institution network, and the system administration itself, was stunned by the rapidity with which the Regents acted. Several Regents confided that they had to act themselves because the individual campus presidents, administrators, and faculty were offering nothing to respond to the growing fiscal crisis.

In the first three months of 1993, each of Maryland's 10 degree-granting state colleges and universities in the system was given a two-hour public hearing, during which the Regents heard about the likely impact of their decisions from the presidents, faculty members, administrators, and students of the institutions. In a few cases, the Regents modified their decisions; but for the rest they required each president to offer alternative programs to be closed or downsized for the same amount of money if they didn't accept the Regent's choices.

For instance, at one institution the Regents had recommended eliminating the majors in physics and chemistry because of low enrollments, but reversed the decision when they learned the two majors were necessary for the training of science teachers. In another case, the Regents recommended the closure of a theater program because it seemed peripheral to the institution's main mission. But when it was demonstrated that the program had received some national recognition for excellence, they stipulated that it be downsized instead.

In May of 1993, the Board of Regents approved a total of 166 program actions: 60 bachelor programs and 35 master's degree and doctoral programs discontinued, reduced in size, or now offered cooperatively; 22 academic departments consolidated into 10 departments; two schools eliminated; and numerous program concentrations and certificate programs eliminated. In addition, reductions were made in several administrative areas. Of the cost savings, 75 percent went to the individual institutions and 25 percent went to the University of Maryland System's central office for reallocation within the system.

What made it possible

What enabled the cost reduction process to take place in only four months were several things.

One was that the UMS office had in place a program review process and criteria already agreed upon by the Accountability Group, and the Chancellor's staff had identified the outlier programs whose costs were high compared with similar programs at the same institution or at other institutions. The academic programs were the unit of analysis, and the UMS staff defined cost as direct cost only. (Figure 2 depicts the form used to collect the cost and pro-

FIGURE 2

Program Cost and Productivity

Institution's Name	XXX
Institution's FICE #	YYYYY
Department	Theatre
Program Name	Theatre
Degrees Offered	B
HEGIS Number	100700

I. PROGRAM FACULTY

FTE-FACULTY in Program: 12.8

# of Tenured Faculty: 4   # of Ten-Track Fac: 3

II. PROGRAM EXPENDITURES

Object of Expenditures	Gen. Instruct. State Supported Expenditures	Non State Supp. Expenditures	Total Instructional Expenditures	Research Exp Restricted	Research Exp Un-Restricted	Total Expenditures
Salaries – Ten/Track Fac	303,407	0	303,407	0	0	303,407
Salaries – Other Faculty	149,997	0	149,997	0	0	149,997
Salaries – All Other	111,685	0	111,685	0	0	111,685
Other Exp.	53,911	0	53,911	0	0	53,911
Total Prog. Expenditures	619,000	0	619,000	0	0	619,000

III. STUDENT CREDIT HOURS BY LEVEL – FY 92

Total Credit Hours Generated	5,302
Undergraduate LD	4,844
Undergraduate UD	658
Graduate I	0
Graduate II	0
Graduate III	0

IV. ENROLLMENT

Undergraduates Fall 1987	87
Undergraduates Fall 1991	86
Masters Fall 1987	0
Masters Fall 1991	0
Doctorates Fall 1987	0
Doctorates Fall 1991	0

V. DEGREES AWARDED

Bachelor's FY 88	11
Bachelor's FY 92	16
Masters FY 88	0
Masters FY 92	0
Doctorates FY 88	0
Doctorates FY 92	0

ductivity for a program, and shows the data for a theater program at one institution.) Program productivity was measured by the number of degrees awarded and the number of credit hours (SCH) generated, both

---

The entire network was stunned by the rapidity with which the Regents acted.

---

by level, and combined into full-time equivalent students (FTES).

Figure 3 shows the data for four dramatic arts programs. A key indicator is the cost per FTES, which was used to compare the relative cost of delivering similar programs at different institutions. Largely based on these data, the bachelor program in theater offered by institution A was discontinued because of low productivity, and the program at institution D was reduced by $100,000 because of its relatively high cost: $5,388 versus only $2,912 for institution C. Good data for the program reviews were a critical factor.

A second vital factor was leadership. Governor Schaefer and his insistence on cost containment and rationalization of the State's

FIGURE 3

Theater Programs at Four Maryland Institutions: Cost and Productivity Matrix

Dramatic Arts

	Institution			
	A	B	C	D
UG Enrollment: #	4	86	125	73
UG Enrollment: Chg in #	+4	−1	+6	+9
Grad. Enrollment: #	0	0	27	0
Grad. Enrollment: Chg in #	0	0	22	0
Bachelors Awarded: #	3	16	18	14
Bachelors Awarded: Chg in #	+3	+5	+6	+4
Masters Awarded: #	0	0	2	0
Masters Awarded: Chg in #	0	0	+2	0
Doctorates Awarded: #	0	0	1	0
Total SCH	399	5,300	7,533	3,027
% Lower Division of Total SCH	66%	87%	67%	63%
% Upper Division of Total SCH	33%	12%	29%	36%
% Graduate of Total SCH	0%	0%	3%	0%
FTES	13	176	253	100
FTEF	1.5	12.6	15	11.1
FTES/FTEF	8.6	13.9	16.8	9.0
# Core Faculty	1	7	9	9
# Tenured Faculty	0	4	4	6
St. Sup. Expenditures ($)	$33,173	$619,000	$736,794	$538,875
St. Sup. Expend/FTES	$2,593	$3,517	$2,912	$5,388
St. Sup. Exp.: Faculty Salaries	$32,361	$565,089	$684,121	$474,121
St. Sup. Exp. + Fringes	$43,421	$788,526	$942,030	$681,111
Research Expenditures ($)	$0	$0	$0	$0
Research Expend/St. Sup. Expend	$0	$0	$0	$0
Research Expend/Core Fac	$0	$0	$0	$0

All data are for FY 92 or Fall 91.
Chg in #: Change in # from FY 87 (for degrees) and from Fall 87 (for enrollments)

higher education system through clearer campus missions and complementarity rather than independence and duplication acted as a catalyst. The Regents, all major, full-time executives or professionals with other duties, were remarkably active. They were, of course, deluged with letters from special interest groups trying to protect their programs at particular institutions, assaulted verbally by angry faculty and students, and pestered by legislators hoping to exempt their own constituencies from the changes they advocated. At one point, in early 1993, a group of legislators moved vindictively to cut the budget of the University of Maryland System office an additional 26 percent. As a body the Regents argued against the deep cuts in the chancellor's office, but eventually had to accept a smaller cut.

Chancellor Donald Langenberg too showed leadership by trying to educate each of the Maryland public institutions about the new economic realities and how they could examine their own operations more effectively for costs, productivity, and centrality of campus mission. He met with the presidents repeatedly, but stuck to his demands that there be reasonable and strategic pruning as well as some deployment within the system to strengthen undergraduate education. And he had quiet, able assistance from vice chancellor for academic affairs, George Marx, whose judgment was trusted by many.

And then the backlash

Financial reductions and reallocations are never easy. The tactics to preserve the *status quo* were relentless and sometimes fierce. The presidents claimed that the System's actions challenged their autonomy, and invaded their authority to decide priorities and allocations on their own campus. They found the emphasis on distinctive mission limiting. Numerous campus leaders tried end runs around the Regents to their local legislators.

The presidents and their faculties complained that there had been insufficient consultation by the Chancellor and his staff and by the Regents as they studied which programs should be discontinued, downsized,

or consolidated. To some extent, they were right. Vision II was mostly a top-down effort. But repeated serious reductions required prompt decisions, and most institutional leaders had no action plans of their own.

Arguments about "access" were frequent, with institutions claiming ownership over "their" students. Colleges often allege that only a wide sprawl of academic programs will prevent denying access to some. They resist the idea of service to particular students instead of all. For example, in a disagreement over which institution should offer training in social work for Baltimore, the Regents supported a smaller institution with an urban mission rather than a larger institution strong in science, technology, and liberal arts, and ordered the large institution to reduce its program in social work.

Good data were a critical factor.

The Regents held firm to a belief that the greatest benefits accrue to students—and the state's taxpayers—when there is a strong correlation between institutional mission and academic programs. But most state institutions resisted the idea.

Many faculty claimed that the program reviews emphasized costs and productivity and largely neglected considerations of quality. And they argued that the Regents were usurping the rights of professors to determine the curriculum. But the Regents contended that the new era of stable or declining state support and of college costs rising annually 50 percent faster than the Consumer Price Index requires new emphases and modes of decision making. Also, being part of a state *system* calls for different ways of thinking about what each institution will distinctively offer to the state's young people and how each state college or university will complement each other's services. Quality of service to the state's people is also a form of quality that each institution has to consider; and value for each million dollars of taxpayers' money is not a consideration to be ignored.

One fascinating outcome of the System-directed reductions, which also sharpened campus missions and forced better financial analysis of academic operations at the campus level, is that it has impressed Maryland's law makers. Response to the reductions of $124 million and $10 million of internal cuts and reallocations meant *change* to legislators and the governor. Until specific programs were closed and reduced, many duplications decreased, and institutions were pressed into cooperative ventures, state government leaders saw no reason to restore funds. Now they believe the 13 institutions of the University of Maryland System are capable of meaningful change, especially if there are regular program reviews, financial oversight, and outcome assessments.

Numerous campus leaders tried end runs.

We think that in the coming decade, when the costs of running public colleges and universities will exceed each state's ability to provide increased support, the central offices, coordinating boards, or boards of regents will need to design ways to help the state colleges and universities make hard choices about academic priorities and less necessary offerings. In this difficult business two things will be especially valuable: good data and criteria to assist in the hard choices, and courageous leadership that can stand the attacks of special interests and those opposed to making changes for the new economic and social environment. ■

REFERENCES

McCurdy, J. and W. Trombley. 1991 *On The Brink: The Impact of Budget Cuts on California's Public Universities.* California Higher Education Policy Center.

McGuiness, A. 1990. *Perspectives on the Current Status of, and Emerging Policy Issues for, Public Multicampus Education Systems.* AGB White Paper No. 1, Association of Governing Boards of Universities and Colleges.

Schick, E., R. Novack, J. Norton and H. Elam. 1992. *Shared Visions of Public Higher Education Governance.* American Association of State Colleges and Universities.

Weinstein, L. 1993. *Moving a Battleship With Your Bare Hands: Governing a University System.* Magna Publications (Madison, Wisconsin).

Winston, G. 1993. New Dangers in Old Traditions: The Reporting of Economic Performance in Colleges and Universities. *Change* 25: January/February.

Planners in Delaware have developed some promising first measures for this much-discussed topic.

Closing in on Faculty Productivity Measures

Michael Middaugh

Three developments have fused to make faculty productivity a newly central concern in American higher education. Planners, provosts, and institutional researchers, as well as deans and faculty department heads, must now find some acceptable measures for this vexing issue.

One is the "collision course" described by education economist David Breneman (1994). The escalating costs of higher education, which are outpacing the rises in the Consumer Price Index, are colliding with the inability of states, the federal government, and the public to increase their funding of colleges and universities. Many states have tightened their appropriations; in 1994 10 of the 50 states actually cut their

Michael Middaugh is Assistant Vice President for institutional research and planning at the University of Delaware. He is a graduate of Fordham University and received a doctorate in education administration from SUNY at Albany. Prior to coming to Delaware, he held similar posts at two campuses in the State University of New York system. His work on the National Study of Instructional Costs and Productivity is supported by TIAA-CREF and FIPSE grants. At Delaware he teaches a course on educational planning and budgeting.

appropriations to public higher education in mid-year. A growing number of critics claim that costs in higher education are rising so fast primarily because many faculty are teaching less and being less "productive." Campuses therefore need better measures of faculty activities to allocate scarce resources.

A second development, connected with the rising costs issue, is the burgeoning "accountability" movement, with state officials, the media, and even trustees asking college leaders to explain in greater detail what they do and why. There are accusations of outmoded programs, too many courses (some with only a few students), abundant exemptions by tenured faculty from teaching, wasteful expenditures, administrative bloat, and general inefficiency. The 1994 *Chronicle of Higher Education Almanac* reported that 24 states were scrutinizing faculty workloads at their public institutions.

Third is the growing number of calls for colleges and universities to restructure or "reengineer" their operations for the new high-tech era (Markwood and Johnston 1994; Dolence and Norris 1995) and for the new economic, demographic, and international realities. Faculty members' reticence to change and their unwillingness to become

24 states are scrutinizing faculty workloads.

"more productive" in newly designed ways are often mentioned as obstacles to the modernization of higher education and possible new efficiencies.

Many professors, however, claim that faculty productivity can't be measured except in frivolous ways like the number of courses taught or research articles published, or by student evaluations. Also, there appears to be a clashing difference of opinion between what most tenured faculty call productivity and what some administrators and many students, state legislators, and parents believe is productivity. As two researchers who interviewed hundreds of professors at several kinds of institutions found:

> Our research indicates a good deal of commonality across institutional type. Many faculty define productivity in terms of research output: more specifically the number of publications and grants. Why? Because faculty believe that's where the rewards are.
>
> Quality teaching may be viewed as the highest priority by those who provide most of higher education's core funding; but almost three times as many episodes in our database deal with the centrality of research as with the importance of teaching. We observed a fundamental difference between the philosophy of faculty and the stated goals of public higher education. (Massy and Wilger 1995, p. 15).

Most parents, students, state officials, and general citizens contend that productivity consists of high-quality teaching and helpful advising during the nine-months of the academic year. But many faculty define productivity differently. As the two researchers write, "Academic productivity improvement may have become a meaningful goal, but new approaches must be invented."

We at the University of Delaware have been trying to create some useful new measures of faculty productivity, starting with *instructional* productivity, an effort that has begun to take on surprising national interest and funding. I think the effort may become an important new tool for educational planning and budgeting. I suspect the measures may also address the three challenges of cost reductions and reallocations, accountability, and possible reengineering.

It all began in 1989. Like many other higher education institutions across the nation, the University of Delaware, an institution with 21,000 students and a workforce of 3500 employees including more than 900 full-time faculty, had to weather severe financial constrictions in the early 1990s. When the budget reductions became inevitable, the university's leaders decided to protect, to the greatest extent possible, the academic core. A second principle was that reductions would not be across-the-board but targeted at specific programs. Thus, while the University of Delaware has cut

What are the reasonable bases for faculty trimming?

$34 million in recurring items from its roughly $360 million operating budget, 80 percent of the reductions have come from administrative and institutional support areas. Very little was taken from the university's 10 colleges.

By 1991 the administrative and support staff, reduced by nearly 200 personnel, was quite lean. Significant increases in state appropriations seemed unlikely, so further reductions had to, by necessity, embrace the academic units. How does a university make cuts within in the academic core? What are the factual underpinnings, the reasonable bases of faculty trimming and departmental or inter-college reallocations?

Digging for reliable comparisons

Delaware's senior vice president David Hollowell (the 1994-95 SCUP president) and the university's planner/institutional researcher (me) decided that the crucial first step for academic resource reallocations was to develop some reliable information about the faculty's "productivity," at least in one or two areas. Good data seemed essential. The data, however, had to be acceptable to the academics. They had to feel that the information being used for academic resource decisions described accurately how departments and programs compared with each other within the university, and possibly with similar departments and programs nationally.

Faculty allocations of attention are anchored to the trinity of teaching, research, and service; so productivity studies had to be done in that context. We met with department chairs, faculty committees, and the provost, with the planner/institutional research serving as notetaker and analytical center. It was agreed that of the trinity, the most appropriate first step in developing productivity measures should be teaching. But how does one measure *instructional* productivity?

Initially we examined the output measure of the number of degrees produced. But counting the number of degrees produced would have undervalued important service departments such as philosophy, which averages only 29-30 baccalaureates a year but teaches more than 20,000 student credit hours a year. We considered placement rates in curriculum-related careers or in graduate schools, but abandoned these as vulnerable to too many intervening personal and economic variables. So output measures were discarded. We focused instead on the teaching process.

We finally agreed that student credit hours are the best currency by which to measure instructional activity. There was also discussion about using teaching contact hours—the number of hours in class (teaching one course in economics, say, three times a week for one hour each yields three teaching contact hours)—but it quickly became apparent that the relation between contact hours and credit value varied across departments. My discussions with other institutions reinforced this observation.

The matrix gave us a sense of who was teaching how many at each level.

However, student credit hours, which are a product of multiplying the credit value times headcount enrollment—a four-credit course with 25 students yields 100 student credit hours—seemed the best, though not perfect measure, especially if the level of instruction was added in. But how should a university count those courses or laboratory sections taught by adjunct or supplemental faculty and by graduate teaching assistants?

We answered this query by developing a matrix to array student credit hours by both level of activity and type of instructor teaching those credit hours. (See Figure 1.) We

FIGURE 1

Student Credit Hours/Organized Class Sections

Taught by...	Remedial Level	Lower Division	Upper Division	Graduate Level
Regular Faculty FTE _____				
Supplemental Faculty FTE _____				
Graduate Teaching Assistants FTE _____				

divided the instructional faculty into three groups: regular, or those with recurring contracts for teaching, research, and service; supplementary, or those with limited-term appointments or those whose primary responsibility is other than the trinity of obligations; and graduate teaching assistants.

The matrix gave us for every department or program a sense of who was teaching how many at each level. We found it important, incidentally, to include all the student credit hours taught by faculty budgeted to a given department or program, regardless of whether the course is taught within that department or another unit, because otherwise interdisciplinary teaching and interdepartmental cooperation would seem less attractive.

Typically we considered lectures, seminars, labs, and discussion/recitation sessions all as organized class sections. Adding organized class sections to that for student credit hours in the matrix allowed us to capture zero-credit lab or recitation sections associated with credit-bearing lectures but which are not reflected in the purely student credit hour listings. This is the type of teaching most often done by graduate student assistants and which frequently escapes institutional scrutiny.

With our matrix the university was able to calculate the faculty's instructional productivity. Student credit hours taught per FTE faculty were arrayed by faculty type for each department. The matrix also allowed university leaders to answer internal or external questions about who exactly is teaching the undergraduate courses, a not inconsiderable piece of information given the allegations about faculty neglect of undergraduate teaching.

Looking at costs also

To consider possible reductions in academic resources the university also needed to know the costs of instruction in each department or program. But how can the costs of instruction best be measured? After discussions with deans and department chairs, we agreed that direct instruction costs—departmental salaries plus direct

support—was the best starting point since these costs are more uniformly defined across departments than are indirect costs.

For colleges and universities using generally accepted accounting procedures, every institutional accounting transaction number has a series of numerical codes attached to it, enabling the institution to track the transaction to a specific organizational

Other cost and productivity measures can also be derived from the data.

unit. Also embedded in the transaction number is an "object code" and a "function code" that specify the purpose of the expenditure (data processing, fringe benefits, etc.) and the function of the expenditure (instruction, research, etc.) By aggregating these transaction codes to departments or programs, it is possible to determine the costs of instruction, say, or public service, and to find out how much is being expended on salaries, supplies, or travel.

At the University of Delaware the decision to assign object and function codes to various expenditures is made jointly by the department chair and persons in the accounting office. This provides widespread confidence in the data that are used in cost measures.

The total department or program expenditures, by function, can then be used as numerators to establish cost ratios. When total student credit hours are used as the divisor, the quotient becomes "direct instructional costs per student credit hour." Similarly, when full-time-equivalent, or FTE, students (calculated from the student credit hours taught) is the divisor, the quotient is a fair measure of the per-student cost of instruction in the curriculum. A university with these measures can then examine the instructional productivity and cost ratios among the disciplines on campus—teaching loads and relative costs between, say, political science and history or between chemistry and physics.

Other cost and productivity measures can also be derived from these data. Suppose the chemistry department exhibits higher teaching loads and lower costs than the physics department. The university can turn to their ratios for direct research expenditures or direct public service expenditures per FTE faculty. If the direct research expenditures per FTE faculty in the physics department are substantially higher than those in the chemistry department, one can infer that the physicists are busier with research. The measures are thus useful in describing overall faculty activity (Middaugh and Hollowell 1992).

At Delaware, the deans and department chairs are now working with the Office of Institutional Research and Planning to develop cross-departmental, comparative measures of *non-instructional* activity that are appropriate for those academic disciplines which do not have access to substantial external research support (arts, classics, literature). We are also trying to devise measures for faculty functions that consume time outside the classroom, such as advising students, supervising dissertations, and serving on university committees.

Three caveats

We have found that three things are important to success in the anxiety-producing measures of faculty productivity.

One, all parties should have access to the data underpinning the decision-making process and should understand how the data are being used and interpreted. At Delaware, we conduct discussions with the University Budget Council, each of the deans of the 10 colleges, key committees of the Faculty Senate, and the department chairs. The opportunity for a frank exchange of information and ideas is crucial.

Two, instructional productivity and cost measures must constantly be described as "barometers" or rough indices. They are not empirical absolutes and should not be treated as such.

Three, productivity and cost measures are quantitative measures and do not address *qualitative* comparisons. A college

may be willing to accept lower instructional productivity and higher costs in a low-demand department or program with a national reputation for excellence. Quantitative measures are useful in resource allocation decisions but institutional leaders should avoid the pitfall of decisions based on numbers alone.

Going national for comparisons

In 1990 the University of Delaware chose a new president. He, the senior vice president, and the provost shortly after felt that the university needed to know how the instructional productivity and cost measures across the campus compared with those at peer institutions across the country as well. To that end, we initiated a National Study of Instructional Costs and Productivity, by Academic Discipline, in 1992.

We developed a survey for collecting comparable instructional productivity data, as well as data on direct expenditures for instruction, separately budgeted research, and separately budgeted service activity, all

Productivity and cost measures do not address qualitative comparisons.

consistent with the definitions used in the IPEDS Annual Survey of Institutional Finances. A total of 114 public institutions, from Carnegie Research I to Comprehensive II participated in the 1992-93 data collection efforts. We received data on 1700 departments and programs. We then issued a report of the findings so that each institution which participated was able to see how their ratios compared with those of other institutions, whose identities were masked. Appendix A displays a typical data array from the 1992 National Study for physics.

In calculating the mean for each category we excluded data which fell more than two standard deviations above or below the initial mean—the outliers—to provide a more "refined" mean. Participating colleges and universities therefore had an "average" workload and "average" cost of instruction against which to compare their own data. The data are intended to be used as a framework within which institutional policy questions can be raised.

The data from the National Study suggested that, among the 114 institutions participating, doctorate universities (such as George Mason, Miami of Ohio, and Northern Colorado) taught heavier loads at lower

> *It is vital that America's planners develop a defensible strategy for how they deploy their resources.*

costs in most disciplines than either comprehensive (such as Western Washington, Prairie View A&M, and College of Charleston) or research (such as University of California, Irvine, Mississippi State, and Virginia Tech) institutions. Appendix B displays the workload and cost ratio data, aggregated by discipline. The study raised an interesting question: Does the doctoral university approach to institutional resource deployment provide a model of greater productivity? The study also stimulated a great deal of interest in the process of data sharing about faculty productivity, but many suggested a second, expanded study to ensure that the 1992 findings were not sample dependent.

With financial assistance from the TIAA/CREF Cooperative Research Fund, a second round of data collection, with refined methodology, was undertaken in 1994-95. Private institutions have been included, and the number of research and doctoral institutions was tripled. And in August 1995, Delaware was awarded a large grant from the U.S. Department of Education's Fund for the Improvement of Post Secondary Education (FIPSE) to continue refining the data collection and comparisons. Soon U.S. higher education may have some quantitative measures of instructional productivity and costs to assist in campus planning, budgeting, and allocation of faculty resources.

I think it is vital that America's planners, institutional researchers, and policymakers act to develop a more defensible strategy for explaining how their colleges and universities deploy their resources in fulfillment of their mission. Though faculty productivity is controversial and difficult to measure to everyone's satisfaction, educators cannot afford to walk away from the issue. Forces outside academe may be forced to develop their own measurements. Also, professors who work skillfully to assign rough measures to everything from the incidence of homelessness in America to the productivity of the American economy might be viewed as hypocrites if they deny that measures, albeit rough ones, of their own productivity are impossible. ■

REFERENCES

Breneman, D. 1994. *Higher Education: On a Collision Course with New Realities.* Association of Governing Boards, Occasional Paper No. 22.

Dolence, M. and Norris, D. 1995. *Transforming Higher Education: A Vision of Learning in the 21st Century.* SCUP.

Markwood, R. and Johnston, S. 1994. *New Pathways to a Degree: Technology Opens a College.* WICHE.

Massy, W. and Wilger, A. 1995. Improving Productivity: What Faculty Think About It. *Change* 27(4) July/August: 10-20.

Middaugh, M. and Hollowell, D. 1992. Examining Academic and Administrative Productivity Measures. In C. Hollins (ed.) *Containing Costs and Improving Productivity in Higher Education.* Jossey-Bass.

APPENDIX A

University of Delaware Study of Instructional Costs and Productivity by Academic Discipline

		WORKLOAD RATIOS		COST RATIOS		EXTERNAL ACTIVITY RATIO
	Carnegie Classicification	Student Credit Hours Per FTE Faculty	FTE Students Taught Per FTE Faculty	Direct Instructional Cost Per Student Credit Hour	Direct Instructional Per FTE Students Taught	Sponsored Research/Service Per FTE Faculty on Appointment
Physics	Comprehensive I	603	20	106	3,177	0
Physics	Comprehensive I	409	14	139	4,182	0
Physics	Comprehensive I	571	19	126	3,788	0
Physics	Comprehensive I	142	5	174	5,218	0
Physics	Comprehensive I	813	18	69	3,100	0
Physics	Comprehensive I	385	13	92	2,730	0
Physics	Comprehensive I	326	11	218	6,491	0
Physics	Comprehensive I	1,104*	25	70	3,136	0
Physics	Comprehensive I	356	13	134	3,739	359,111
Physics	Comprehensive I	593	20	94	2,824	3,038
Physics	Comprehensive I	293	10	166	4,988	0
Physics	Comprehensive I	659	22	65	1,936	30,981
Physics	Comprehensive I	221	7	197	5,914	0
Physics	Comprehensive I	273	9	185	5,547	0
Physics	Comprehensive I	305	10	160	4,786	0
Physics	Comprehensive I	1,073*	24	73	3,284	802
Physics	Comprehensive I	520	17	109	3,256	0
Physics	Comprehensive I	536	18	87	2,610	0
Physics	Comprehensive I	507	17	138	4,153	6,280
Physics	Comprehensive I	608	20	107	3,188	172
Physics	Comprehensive I	602	20	75	2,225	0
Physics	Comprehensive I	511	17	146	4,383	3,266
Physics	Comprehensive I	759	17	87	3,909	27
Physics	Comprehensive I	650	22	110	3,268	0
Physics	Comprehensive I	646	22	85	2,508	0
Physics	Comprehensive I	387	13	176	5,239	5,490
Physics	Comprehensive I	570	19	85	2,552	0
Physics	Comprehensive I	377	13	135	3,955	12,995

APPENDIX A (continued)

	WORKLOAD RATIOS		COST RATIOS		EXTERNAL ACTIVITY RATIO
Carnegie Classification	Student Credit Hours Per FTE Faculty	FTE Students Taught Per FTE Faculty	Direct Instructional Cost Per Student Credit Hour	Direct Instructional Per FTE Students Taught	Sponsored Research/Service Per FTE Faculty on Appointment
Physics Comprehensive I	372	12	190	5,705	0
Physics Comprehensive I	649	22	131	3,936	0
Physics Comprehensive I	738	25	65	1,960	28,472
Physics Comprehensive I	932	21	55	2,468	2,363
Physics Comprehensive I	814	27	89	2,657	0
Physics Comprehensive I	614	21	145	4,304	0
Physics Comprehensive I	522	17	111	3,328	3,895
Physics Comprehensive I	1,196*	40*	49	1,447	1,275
Physics Comprehensive I	365	12	159	4,762	0
Physics Comprehensive I	357	12	195	5,838	0
Physics Comprehensive I	320	11	194	5,779	0
Physics Comprehensive I	561	19	95	2,817	0
Physics Comprehensive II	444	15	59	1,779	0
Physics Comprehensive II	180	6	222*	6,671*	0
Initial Mean	544	17	123	3,799	10,909
Standard Deviation	242	6	48	1,357	55,439
Tolerable Range	60 to 1028	5 to 29	27 to 219	1085 to 6513	
# of Outliers	3	1	1	1	
Refined Mean	500	16	121	3,729	
Physics Doctoral I	644	22	181	5,325	6,190
Physics Doctoral I	482	16	142	4,227	60,330
Physics Doctoral I	408	14	166	4,914	32,171
Physics Doctoral I	566	19	151	4,460	0
Physics Doctoral I	623	21	61	1,806*	38,797
Physics Doctoral I	1,114*	26	70	3,035	31,735
Physics Doctoral I	382	13	131	3,854	73,135
Physics Doctoral I	346	12	133	3,946	82,873
Physics Doctoral I	699	23	79	2,365	7,282
Physics Doctoral I	573	19	137	4,080	11,979
Physics Doctoral II	428	14	128	3,800	800

APPENDIX A (continued)

	WORKLOAD RATIOS		COST RATIOS		EXTERNAL ACTIVITY RATIO
Carnegie Classification	Student Credit Hours Per FTE Faculty	FTE Students Taught Per FTE Faculty	Direct Instructional Cost Per Student Credit Hour	Direct Instructional Per FTE Students Taught	Sponsored Research/Service Per FTE Faculty on Appointment
Physics Doctoral II	358	12	158	4,738	16,046
Physics Doctoral II	888	20	86	3,783	32,804
Physics Doctoral II	642	22	124	3,687	34,932
Physics Doctoral II	431	15	128	3,704	0
Initial Mean	572	18	125	3,848	28,605
Standard Deviation	212	4	36	917	26,618
Tolerable Range	148 to 996	10 to 26	53 to 197	2014 to 5682	
# of Outliers	1	0	0	1	
Refined Mean	534	18	125	3,994	
Physics Research I	361	12	210	6,075	88,261
Physics Research I	392	9	180	7,573	32,989
Physics Research I	161*	5	269	7,944	10,398
Physics Research I	461	16	195	5,752	0
Physics Research I	331	11	161	4,772	10,033
Physics Research I	432	15	244	7,264	22,455
Physics Research II	358	12	152	4,511	38,820
Physics Research II	466	11	231	9,547	133,818
Physics Research II	459	16	121	3,576	75,146
Physics Research II	343	12	208	6,058	48,590
Physics Research II	273	9	289	8,504	6,802
Physics Research II	565	19	85	2,518	4,691
Physics Research II	384	13	101	3,018	12,637
Physics Research II	503	17	181	5,297	57,717
Initial Mean	392	13	188	5,866	38,740
Standard Deviation	102	4	60	2,107	38,791
Tolerable Range	188 to 596	5 to 21	68 to 308	1672 to 10100	
# of Outliers	1	0	0	0	
Refined Mean	410	13	188	5,886	

APPENDIX B

Refined Mean Instructional Productivity and Cost Ratios, by Academic Discipline, by Carnegie Category

	# Institutions Reporting	Student Credit Hours Per FTE Faculty	FTE Students Taught Per FTE Faculty	Direct Instructional Cost Per Student Credit Hour	Direct Instructional Cost Per FTE Student Taught
1. HUMANITIES					
COMMUNICATION					
- Comprehensive Institutions	40	541	18	87	2,660
- Doctoral Institutions	13	617	20	80	2,484
- Research Institutions	13	610	17	88	2,849
FOREIGN LANGUAGES AND LITERATURE					
- Comprehensive Institutions	46	443	14	101	3,233
- Doctoral Institutions	14	496	17	87	2,585
- Research Institutions	12	449	13	91	2,832
ENGLISH					
- Comprehensive Institutions	53	540	17	77	2,403
- Doctoral Institutions	16	552	17	76	2,332
- Research Institutions	15	450	14	85	2,730
PHILOSOPHY					
- Comprehensive Institutions	38	761	23	71	2,223
- Doctoral Institutions	14	760	23	67	2,096
- Research Institutions	15	729	23	73	2,363
2. FINE ARTS					
THEATER/PERFORMING ARTS					
- Comprehensive Institutions	34	506	16	100	3,140
- Doctoral Institutions	11	383	13	154	4,560
- Research Institutions	14	400	12	161	5,144
ART					
- Comprehensive Institutions	49	458	15	106	3,282
- Doctoral Institutions	15	452	15	105	3,249
- Research Institutions	14	393	13	126	3,885
MUSIC					
- Comprehensive Institutions	47	347	11	146	4,511
- Doctoral Institutions	16	291	9	168	5,196
- Research Institutions	14	275	9	195	6,071
3. NATURAL AND PHYSICAL SCIENCES					
BIOLOGY					
- Comprehensive Institutions	56	579	19	99	3,043
- Doctoral Institutions	16	657	22	91	2,805
- Research Institutions	15	508	16	133	4,398

APPENDIX B (continued)

	# Institutions Reporting	Student Credit Hours Per FTE Faculty	FTE Students Taught Per FTE Faculty	Direct Instructional Cost Per Student Credit Hour	Direct Instructional Cost Per FTE Student Taught
CHEMISTRY					
- Comprehensive Institutions	49	498	17	124	3,815
- Doctoral Institutions	16	596	20	119	3,734
- Research Institutions	15	551	17	150	4,563
GEOLOGY					
- Comprehensive Institutions	19	580	19	105	3,391
- Doctoral Institutions	14	616	21	98	3,033
- Research Institutions	15	450	14	183	6,284
PHYSICS					
- Comprehensive Institutions	42	500	16	121	3,729
- Doctoral Institutions	15	534	18	125	3,994
- Research Institutions	14	410	13	188	5,886
4. MATHEMATICS AND COMPUTER SCIENCE					
MATHEMATICS					
- Comprehensive Institutions	54	638	20	70	2,183
- Doctoral Institutions	16	716	23	67	2,083
- Research Institutions	15	587	18	98	3,135
COMPUTER AND INFORMATION SCIENCE					
- Comprehensive Institutions	40	527	17	103	3,204
- Doctoral Institutions	13	655	21	106	3,191
- Research Institutions	14	475	15	154	4,662
5. BEHAVIORAL AND SOCIAL SCIENCES					
PSYCHOLOGY					
- Comprehensive Institutions	53	802	27	66	2,011
- Doctoral Institutions	16	728	24	75	2,274
- Research Institutions	15	750	24	85	2,912
ANTHROPOLOGY					
- Comprehensive Institutions	16	789	25	93	2,796
- Doctoral Institutions	10	641	21	77	2,459
- Research Institutions	11	551	17	98	3,131
ECONOMICS					
- Comprehensive Institutions	29	757	22	78	2,469
- Doctoral Institutions	14	707	23	75	2,428
- Research Institutions	11	586	20	100	3,207

APPENDIX B (continued)

	# Institutions Reporting	Student Credit Hours Per FTE Faculty	FTE Students Taught Per FTE Faculty	Direct Instructional Cost Per Student Credit Hour	Direct Instructional Cost Per FTE Student Taught
GEOGRAPHY					
- Comprehensive Institutions	27	804	26	67	2,126
- Doctoral Institutions	12	790	26	79	2,405
- Research Institutions	12	638	20	104	3,142
HISTORY					
- Comprehensive Institutions	51	728	24	71	2,192
- Doctoral Institutions	16	747	25	65	2,996
- Research Institutions	15	674	21	82	2,635
POLITICAL SCIENCE					
- Comprehensive Institutions	45	764	24	74	2,284
- Doctoral Institutions	16	762	26	72	2,218
- Research Institutions	15	659	20	87	2,772
SOCIOLOGY					
- Comprehensive Institutions	49	802	27	63	1,933
- Doctoral Institutions	16	879	28	60	1,866
- Research Institutions	15	729	22	70	2,276
6. PROFESSIONAL CURRICULA					
EDUCATION					
- Comprehensive Institutions	50	547	18	101	3,019
- Doctoral Institutions	13	505	18	102	2,873
- Research Institutions	12	384	13	188	5,459
ENGINEERING					
- Comprehensive Institutions	12	367	11	242	8,486
- Doctoral Institutions	8	280	12	185	5,573
- Research Institutions	11	305	10	297	8,861
NURSING					
- Comprehensive Institutions	30	248	8	204	6,250
- Doctoral Institutions	12	242	9	191	5,735
- Research Institutions	9	222	7	323	9,437
ACCOUNTING					
- Comprehensive Institutions	35	689	21	87	2,725
- Doctoral Institutions	15	765	25	93	2,845
- Research Institutions	12	687	22	102	3,156
FINANCE					
- Comprehensive Institutions	23	657	22	94	2,844
- Doctoral Institutions	13	733	24	95	2,880
- Research Institutions	11	593	17	134	4,165
BUSINESS ADMINISTRATION					
- Comprehensive Institutions	47	647	21	87	2,676
- Doctoral Institutions	12	690	22	90	2,720
- Research Institutions	11	608	19	131	3,678

How universities can reduce their legal costs while improving their legal services.

A New Approach to Campus Legal Services

Michael Roster and Linda Woodward

Colleges and universities are often accused of being unwilling to change. While the charge may have some validity about the academic core, it is largely untrue about many of the service areas in academe. For instance, many institutions have switched to outsourcing such activities as food services, facilities, maintenance, waste disposal, and mailroom services. A Connecticut firm, Collegiate Health Care, now manages the student health programs at colleges such as Cedar Crest, Rollins, and Trinity and at universities such as Alfred, Boise State, and Pepperdine. Outsourcing, or the turning over of services to an outside management source, is one of the major changes in campus operations during the past 15 years.

Michael Roster is the general counsel for Stanford University, where he received both his A.B. and J.D. degrees. Before he came back to Stanford in 1993 he was head of the bank regulatory practice at Morrison & Foerster, and managing partner of the firm's Los Angeles office.

Linda Woodward is the non-lawyer director of legal services at Stanford. She previously served as an administrator with two law firms, in Los Angeles and Palo Alto. She attended Cleveland State University and San Jose State University, and is an associate member of the ABA Law Practice Management Section.

In a *Wall Street Journal* essay last year, Peter Drucker predicted, "In 10 or 15 years organizations may be outsourcing all work that is 'support' rather than revenue producing, and all activities that do not offer career opportunities into senior management."

What is interesting about Drucker's prediction is that outsourcing is not driven exclusively by the need to reduce costs. Rather, outsourcing implies that (a) colleges should focus their resources on their core functions and consider buying at least some of their other services from organizations that perform those services as their core functions; and (b) institutions should be careful that any departments they retain do not become career dead-ends for persons in these departments.

One area of rapidly rising costs at many colleges and universities, and an area that is obviously not a core function at universities, is that of legal services. As the number of state and federal regulations has increased dramatically and as the nation has become more litigious, in-house legal departments typically have doubled or tripled in size during the past 15 years. At Stanford, for instance, the 13 attorneys on campus in 1980 had grown to an office with 21 attorneys and five paralegals by 1993, one of the largest in the country. In 1993 the benefits alone of the legal and support staff came to more than $1 million, and there were other costs such as law library books and continuing education courses for the university's lawyers. At the same time, the depth of expertise required to keep up with ever-changing and increasingly complex regulations is making it difficult, if not impossible, for lawyers to be generalists any longer.

In 1993, Stanford's law department, like other departments, was facing the challenge of doing more with less. The university's president and provost asked us to trim at least $500,000 from the department's budget, plus end the $300,000 deficit the department had accrued. The prospect of cutting expenses by reducing the staff by one or two attorneys meant that important, substantive areas would be underserved, and such an approach would not provide the budget reductions that were needed. It thus seemed time to consider a radical restructuring of the legal work at Stanford. Outsourcing struck us as one way to achieve a number of goals simultaneously.

Redesigning legal services

In analyzing the university's legal needs, several internal considerations were especially important, and one economic factor was noteworthy.

Internally, we needed the ability to draw on high levels of specialization from one or more major firms. We needed greater elasticity to be able to shift resources from one substantive area to another and to adjust workloads overall. We also had senior university officers who, though satisfied with the work of the legal office, thought it important to put educational and business decisions back in the hands of the faculty and administrators and no longer rely on lawyers to fill the management's decision gaps. And we had to reduce our costs.

At the same time, we felt compelled to redefine how outside counsel might function. Law firms traditionally bill for their services by the hour, prompting attorneys, consciously or unconsciously, to work very deliberately and run up the bill. We sought a new system that would force firms to work smarter, working as the university's in-house counsel has had to do with finite resources.

Stanford's solution was to seek firms to work on a largely fixed-price basis, with some of their attorneys in our office either full-time or on a regularly scheduled basis.

We solicited bids from 14 firms nationally and received other unsolicited materials. We then invited the 14 law firms to the campus to make two-hour presentations of their capabilities. All had considerable experience with higher education or were strong in areas important to Stanford such as environ-

In-house legal departments typically have doubled or tripled in the past 15 years.

mental law. We also invited the firms to an all-day meeting where we provided them with more information about our in-house operations, workload, and finances before soliciting specific bids from them. We even developed spreadsheets to assist the firms in predicting the levels of service that would likely be required in each substantive area.

We invited each firm to bid on one or more of three levels of service.

- *Turnkey operation.* This would eliminate the university's entire legal office, with a single outside firm providing all the legal services, including support functions such as a legal library, secretaries, and messengers.

- *Component operation.* This allowed bids individually on one or more of the 11 main areas of university need: academic affairs, benefits, business, environmental, government contracts, intellectual property, labor, litigation, medical affairs, real estate, and taxes and gifts.

- *Backup advice.* This permitted firms to offer special back-up expertise and counseling in any area where we might retain internal staff, but without the firm's meter running.

We decided to retain a small core of in-house attorneys on the general counsel's staff but link them with component bidders of three outside law firms. The in-house core would no longer litigate, and it would focus on the university's central activities: academic and medical affairs and related policy matters. The outside firms would assign people to be on-site to function as partners with the in-house lawyers.

Ropes and Gray of Boston was selected for benefits, nonprofit taxes, intellectual property, medical affairs, and backup advice on academic affairs. The San Francisco firm of McCutchen, Doyle, Brown & Enersen was selected to provide counsel on environmental, real estate, land use, and labor issues, and the related litigation. Another San Francisco firm, Pillsbury, Madison & Sutro, was chosen to handle government contracts, estates, business matters, and related litigation. A fourth firm offered to provide a fixed number of hours on international matters on a pro bono basis, and we have used them on a fee basis too for special international items.

Once we decided on the areas to be outsourced, we put together an implementation plan to assist the attorneys and paralegals who would be laid off. We brought in an organizational consultant to assist, and

Stanford has reorganized its legal department into a legal HMO.

confidential counseling was made available to the attorneys and paralegals to help them explore career options. Major changes, of course, create upheaval and much anxiety; but a sensitive, comprehensive program for the layoff candidates can be very helpful.

The new hard core

Stanford's legal team now consists of only six full-time equivalent lawyers. They are responsible for approximately one-fourth of the university's legal work. These inside lawyers are not supervisors of the outside lawyers, but practice with them as partners. Some of the outside firms' lawyers work on campus, but all attorneys handling Stanford matters have university telephone extensions and e-mail addresses, and are part of our weekly staff meetings. The only distinguishing factor among all the lawyers who provide Stanford's legal services is whose payroll they are on.

In effect, Stanford has reorganized its legal department into a legal HMO. Like an

HMO, the new incentive in the office is to *prevent* law suits and other legal wrangles. To earn a profit on its fixed-fee contracts, the outside law firms are stimulated to be proactive in

The blended outsourcing we are trying may be a surprisingly viable new approach.

educating clients to reduce legal risks. For example, attorneys now train laboratory managers to understand environmental compliance rather than just defending the university when a law suit arises. The attorneys have held more than 40 seminars and roundtables since the office's reorganization in September 1994.

The financial incentives now are for all attorneys to be focused on the efficient use of their time and skills and not to amass a large number of billable hours on each task. No longer does the legal staff sit through two-hour university committee meetings; lawyers attend only that portion of the meeting where legal advice is needed, or provide legal advice before the meeting to the appropriate committee members.

The dollars for legal services are now budgeted differently. All attorneys—in-house and from outside—record their time, and at the end of each month the total time is plugged into a composite matrix designed to show how much time was spent in each substantive area and for each of the university's elements. The matrices allow us to track all professional legal output and budgets, provide early warnings for major variances, and help develop next year's budget.

An important element of the reorganization is a newly aggressive effort to get information out to university people in the form of roundtables, newsletters, and legal bulletins. Quarterly reports are sent to most internal clients showing them the total amount of legal services budgeted for their area versus the actual services provided. We have also introduced occasional assessment meetings with clients, where attorneys ask them if they are satisfied with the legal services they are receiving and what legal problems they see coming down the pike.

How has it gone in the first 18 or so months? We believe quite well. The outside firms are learning to manage university needs within a fixed budget, and the university expects to see another saving of $500,000 to $800,000 this year from what had been an $8 million budget. And

Stanford has higher legal expertise than ever in numerous areas. Our client survey shows high satisfaction so far in all areas.

Reengineering is a trendy word. But redesigning the management and costs of legal work at colleges and universities is something more institutions might explore. For educational support services, the blended outsourcing we are trying may be a surprisingly viable new approach. ∎

Financial planning must include better management of each institution's endowment.

Growing the Endowment in a High-Risk Environment

Charles Tharp

I n his poem, *Dover Beach*, Matthew Arnold, himself an educational reformer, wrote of a "darkling plain...where ignorant armies clash by night." He might well have been describing the annual debate on many U.S. campuses in the 1990s over their budgets. Financial discipline has emerged in the 1990s as a pre-eminent concern.

The financial strains have caused numerous colleges and universities—especially private institutions—to look more closely at the way their endowments are performing. Some universities have already made major changes in the management of their endowments; but others are only be-

Charles Tharp is a principal of Charles Tharp Associates in Washington, D.C., consultants on investment policy and structures for endowments and pension funds. A graduate of Yale, he earned an M.A. in international law at England's Oxford University, and has worked as an investment adviser to corporations, as head of the U.S. government's Pension Benefit Guaranty Corporation, and from 1989 to 1995 as treasurer and chief investment officer at Oberlin College, where he reduced expenses while enlarging the endowment measurably. His recent clients include The World Bank, the Kingdom of Jordan, and several foundations.

ginning to understand that wise management of their endowed assets is a strategic way to increase operating income over the long term. Unfortunately, trying to squeeze greater growth from an endowment in the late 1990s requires special thoughtfulness because of the rapidly changing and increasingly high-risk environment.

Endowments are a distinctive feature of American higher education. At least 20 U.S. universities have endowments larger than $1 billion, with Harvard's at $9 billion. Another 200 colleges and universities have endowments of more than $100 million, and perhaps 500 more of the nation's 2,200 four-year institutions hold assets of more than $25 million (*Chronicle* 1997). Managing such large amounts has become a serious business.

Harvard University now has a staff of 150 to do so; and one of its portfolio managers, Jonathan Jacobson, has drawn faculty criticism because he earned $6.1 million last year ($200,000 salary plus performance bonuses), 25 times as much as Harvard's president. Jack Meyer, head of Harvard Management, defends the huge compensation by saying, "John has provided over $300 million in value added to the endowment in the past five years." Jacobson's portfolio of stocks has generated a 30 per-cent annualized return, double that of the Standard and Poor's 500 Index, so Meyer claims, "Jon is the biggest benefactor Harvard has ever had" (Bary 1996).

At 1500-student Berea College in Kentucky, vice president for business and finance Leigh Jones was able to contribute more than $16 million to the college's 1996-97 budget from earnings on the college's $485 million endowment. To help him with the endowment he uses the chair of the trustee's investment committee, who is a venture capitalist with Primus Venture Partners in Cleveland, and retains Cambridge Associates, a Boston-based investment consulting firm (Cropper 1996). Berea's endowment includes investments in real estate, venture capital projects, and foreign stocks (19%).

Berea College is far from alone in its purchase of foreign stocks. A survey of college investments revealed that in fiscal 1995-96, an average of 9.5 % was invested in foreign securities, up from 2.4 % in 1990-91 (Nicklin 1997). And the University of Vermont, in an effort to increase the return on its $101 million endowment, has put $4 million into a risk-arbitrage fund, which invests in companies involved in mergers, spinoffs, and acquisitions.

The big three

To grow an endowment a college or university must manage three factors:
- the endowment spending rate
- investment policy for the endowment
- fund raising, to add to the endowment

The three factors are separate but not independent. A high annual spending rate (6% or more) gradually reduces the size of the endowment by lowering the reinvestment rate. Shrewd investments result in endowment growth and better returns for use in meeting operating expenses, as do new monies from fund raising. There are less obvious correlations too. For instance, a few studies have indicated that when alumni and other donors perceive that the college has conservative financial policies and/or successful investment returns on its

endowment they are likely to donate more money to the college.

I will not discuss fund raising, even though it is very important for endowment growth. But I want to suggest some ways that institutions should approach the endowment spending rate and the handling of their investments.

The endowment spending rate is the most difficult factor to control because it is critical for the institution's annual financial needs and is also central to the long-term stability and growth of endowment assets. (The endowment's payout is the amount of funds transferred each year from the endowment for use in the school's annual

How should a college balance the need for income for annual expenses with the desire to increase the endowment?

budget.) How should a college balance the need for income for annual expenses with the desire to increase the endowment for the future? How should it balance the claims of present faculty and students with those of the cohorts of the future? I think institutions should do some financial modeling as a starting point for understanding the choices.

At Oberlin College we extensively modeled the probable results of different investment scenarios and spending levels, and of different spending formulas. The president and Board of Trustees had determined to avoid the mistakes of their predecessors in withdrawing too much from the endowment each year, and had agreed that a new endowment spending formula was needed. The old rule had been to withdraw up to 5.5% of the endowment's current value for use in the annual budget; but budgetary pressures often caused the endowment spending rate to rise even higher. This practice still goes on at many colleges, with some institutions drawing 7% or more. After study, we developed a new formula to balance the college's operating income needs with protection of its capital and provision for long-term endowment growth.

Our approach was based on that developed at Stanford University (Massy 1990). The idea underlying the Stanford formula is this: the endowment spending rate each year should be based on the previous year's level of endowment payout, plus an annual inflation adjustment. This protects the institution's budget by starting with the actual sum provided the previous year, plus an inflation estimate. But there is also an embedded target payout rate—say 4% or 5%—taken as a percentage of a moving average of the endowment's market value over the past two or three years. This "smoothing" formula moves the payout back toward general levels even if the market results have been volatile. Thus, if the market lifted the value of the college's endowment up 3% three years ago, up 8% two years ago, and down 14% in the current year, the college would have its 4% or 5% payout rate based on the average of the past *three* years, not on the current 14% downturn.

The two key questions for Oberlin College were: (1) what target rate to establish, and (2) what balance to strike between the needs of the annual budget and the needs for endowment growth in making annual adjustments.

We knew from experience what damage a 5% or 6% payout rate could do over time. And we observed with keen interest the results of a more conservative 3.5% or 4% payout rate at a competitor such as Swarthmore College, which grew its endowment from half that of Oberlin's 30 years ago to twice that of Oberlin's today. Oberlin's president and board chose an endowment spending target of 4%.

On the second question, they decided to weight the college's budget needs at 60% and the endowment growth needs at 40%, and to smooth market volatility by valuing the endowment over a 36-month moving average of market prices. This combination gave greater security to the annual budget expectations while reserving a healthy weight for long-term savings. Here is the formula we adopted:

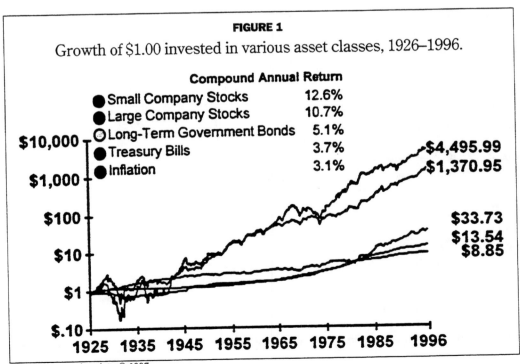

FIGURE 1

Growth of $1.00 invested in various asset classes, 1926–1996.

Compound Annual Return

- Small Company Stocks — 12.6%
- Large Company Stocks — 10.7%
- Long-Term Government Bonds — 5.1%
- Treasury Bills — 3.7%
- Inflation — 3.1%

$4,495.99
$1,370.95
$33.73
$13.54
$8.85

Source: Ibbotson Associates © 1997

$$.6 \, (xg) + .4 \, (yz) = P$$

where x = previous year's payout in dollars

g = expected growth from other sources of revenue, expressed as 1.0 plus the percentage rate of change

y = market spending rate, expressed as a percentage

z = market value of the endowment, defined as the average of the prior 36 months' market values.

P = payout in dollars

Thus, to arrive at a good endowment spending rate two ingredients are essential. One is the smoothing formula to protect the college's or university's annual income from the endowment from the zig-zag swings of the market. (Swarthmore has even placed their venture capital investments in a special fund outside the regular endowment to further insulate the college from a sudden drop in asset values.) The other is a low—and strictly adhered to—spending target of, say, 3.5% or 4% to immunize the endowment from erosion by inflation and to permit endowment growth through reinvestment compounding.

The second ingredient requires a very strict financial discipline to prevent incursions into the endowment corpus. (I recall one college treasurer telling me, when I asked why his spending rate was routinely 9% or 10%, "We have only $30 million, so we might as well spend it.") It is essential to have a conservative spending formula in place before embarking on an aggressive investment program. To do otherwise is to expose the institution to dangerous levels of risk.

How to invest for the future

As colleges and universities seek to manage their endowments more strategically in the late 1990s, the one thing that must be kept in mind is risk. This is the greatest challenge of asset management today. If the decade of the 1960s was the golden age of stockpicking and go-go portfolios, and the 1980s was the heyday of asset allocation, the 1990s is the decade of risk management. Today a

college's investment committee does not manage stocks, it manages risk.

In the 1960s numerous colleges and universities improved their endowments considerably by investing in growth stocks and new high-tech companies. But when the stock market collapsed in 1973-74, with a 52% fall in U.S. equity markets in 24 months, followed by double-digit inflation in the late 1970s, the damage to higher education was considerable. The 1980s became the boom time for S&P Index funds and other large, diversified "passive" funds that

The 1990s is the decade of risk management.

could offer returns equal to that of the market and reduce a board's exposure to criticism. In the decade between 1980 and 1990, the Salomon Broad Bond Index rose 127%, more than doubling its value, but the S&P Index rose 212.6%, more then tripling. From 1994 to 1997 common stocks have had another surge, again led by "brand-name" stocks and new high-tech firms. (See Figure 1.) But a number of older investment hands, including Federal Reserve chairman Alan Greenspan, have grown wary. Risk management is now primary.

How does a college manage risk? I suggest that two sets of actions are necessary. The first set of actions is to get the management of your portfolio in order. The second set pertains to managing your managers.

It is dismaying, but a majority of colleges and universities, including some famous ones, need to improve their strategic management. Oberlin, a remarkable academic institution, was an example. Oberlin in 1950 and 1960 was one of the wealthiest institutions in the nation, measured by endowment per student. By the 1980s this had changed. At one point its endowment returns ranked last among the 33 colleges it considered its peers. The college's holdings of common stocks was 20% below the NACUBO mean. About 30% of its endowment was in cash or cash equivalents. The college's financial condition had slipped to the point where a new president had to recruit new talent for the trustee investment committee and develop a fresh strategic vision.

To move toward superior portfolio management, the first step is an *assessment* of the exact state of the endowment and the college's essential needs. It is imperative to know the true economic value of the endowment's assets and liabilities. There is no need to survey every asset or need of the institution; simply conduct a survey of present resources and commitments. For the inventory of assets, a college needs a conservative accounting approach to valuation, done by a qualified staff or by an outside auditor, or both. This is especially important for assets such as land, real estate, venture capital, and foreign securities.

And *financial reporting* needs to be frequent and accurate. At Oberlin, the trustees believed they had less than 10% of the endowment sidelined in cash. So their quarterly reports asserted. But investigations revealed that the equity managers also held cash instead of common stocks, so actually more than one-third of Oberlin's total endowment was not in the market.

Peer comparisons are helpful too. How well are similar institutions with similar size endowments performing? Is your institu-tion behind, roughly even with them, or ahead? What is their distribution of investments compared to yours? Be sure to include the most outstanding performers among your set of peers so that you have a realistic sense of what can be accomplished. These benchmarks are extremely helpful in evaluating the performance of the managers of parts of your endowment.

With accounting, better reporting systems, and performance measurements an institution is ready to make fundamental changes in the endowment's structure and handling. At Oberlin we closed down loss-making operations, reinvested the cash, let go underperforming managers, and re-structured the portfolio. (See Figure 2.)

Which assets are best?

Now you are ready to construct an integrated investment model for the institution. The endowment model will have a subpart which includes the flow of funds from new gifts, including the maturation of deferred giving programs, and the payments from the endowment for current use by the college. Most important, you will have to decide on asset allocation (Williamson 1993).

Studies have shown that up to 90% of long-term investment returns depend heavily on asset allocation, or what propor-

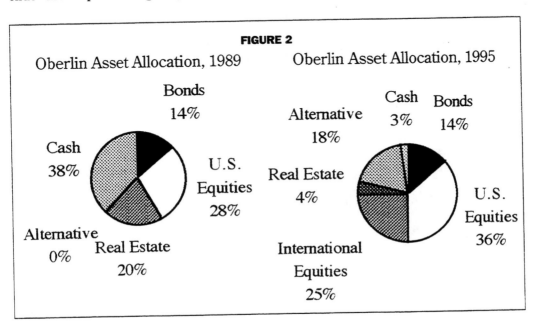

FIGURE 2

Oberlin Asset Allocation, 1989

- Bonds 14%
- Cash 38%
- U.S. Equities 28%
- Alternative 0%
- Real Estate 20%

Oberlin Asset Allocation, 1995

- Alternative 18%
- Cash 3%
- Bonds 14%
- Real Estate 4%
- U.S. Equities 36%
- International Equities 25%

tion of funds you put to work in each investment class over time (Ibbotson and Brinson 1993). How you allocate assets is more important than what stocks or bonds you choose, when you buy or sell your investments, or which professional firms you choose to manage your funds. The major

---

How you allocate assets is more important than what stocks and bonds you choose.

---

classes of investment alternatives, in order of risk, from least to greatest, are:

- cash equivalents
- U.S. investment-grade bonds
- non-U.S. fixed-income securities
- U.S. common stocks
- non-U.S. common stocks
- real estate
- venture capital, or private securities
- special situations

This list is not exhaustive. Some universities invest in commodities, junk bonds, oil wells, or prime farmland like Washington's Whitman College, where 7% of the $167 million endowment is in farms (Mercer 1996).

Constructing the asset allocation model can be done in-house if sufficient skills among the staff, trustees, and professors of finance are available. But most colleges will need to bring in an outside expert to help.

The college or university will need to set some long-term performance goals for (1) the endowment fund as a whole and (2) each asset class in the endowment. These choices will depend on the risk and reward levels of each asset class, how large the endowment is, and how much risk the institution leaders are able to handle.

At Oberlin we inserted benchmarks of achievement in our contracts with the managers of each of our classes, discussing these goals up front and reaching a clear agreement. Sometimes managers would propose weaker bogeys, for obvious reasons. It's important to have benchmarks that are fair and realistic, but sufficiently ambitious. It's also important to monitor the transactions of the investment managers that the university selects through such means as monthly reconciliations, telephone calls, and bringing in the lead managers to report to the trustees regularly on their progress.

The choice of investment firms to manage the asset classes—bonds, foreign stocks, real estate, venture capital investments, emerging growth stocks, etc.—is the second most important endowment decision after asset allocation. (Colleges with very small endowments may choose to turn over their endowment funds to a single, multi-capability firm.) Be careful, however, of hiring too many outside managers: too many to oversee properly, too many slivers of funds on too many plates.

In selecting investment firms to manage the college's assets, your institution should keep a few things in mind.

1. Be sure to establish a benchmark of expected returns for each asset class, with an explicit understanding of the risk parameters, against which the firm is to manage the allocation.

2. Decide early who will have the authority to hire and fire the asset manager, and who will conduct the search for the best firms to manage each asset. (A search consultant may be needed, and the annual *NACUBO Endowment Study* lists the firms used by other colleges (NACUBO 1996). Typically, the institution's financial staff will investigate the firms and recommend the hiring decision to the trustees' investment committee, who will make the final choice.

3. Your issue of a request for proposals from prospective managers should describe the expectations and risk parameters, and should ask for detailed information about such things as the size of the firm in capital and in personnel, assets under management, performance data, some client names to contact for references, the background of the account manager

who would handle the college's account, and the firm's investment philosophy and procedures. I suggest that international firms not be overlooked in the searches, especially for investments in foreign securities.

4. In discussing the finalists, hold round-table discussions among the administrators and trustees (and the consultant, if one is used).

5. In negotiating the contract, be certain that the benchmark against which the firm will be judged, termination provisions, fiduciary insurance, and other key items are crystal clear. Every precaution should be taken so that there is no misunderstanding whatsoever. The written agreement should contain all these items to minimize later disagreements (Spitz 1992).

The new, risky climate

What is risk? One definition puts it, "Risk is how likely it is that one morning I may not have enough to pay my bills." For a college, that would translate to not having sufficient endowment returns for next year's operating budget. What if the stock market falls by one third, and the 4% expected from your $90 million endowment, or $3.6 million, was suddenly only 4% of $60 million, or $2.4 million?

Many academics, and most of Wall Street, define risk mainly in terms of price volatility—the likely rises and falls in stock and bond prices. Others define risk as the relative chances of making high returns or none at all. For instance, venture capital deals or investments in possible new oil fields can bring extraordinary returns. But venture capital start-ups can collapse, and oil wells can come up dry. Generally, high-risk investments can yield high returns or big losses, while low-risk investments yield lower returns but little chance of sizable losses.

With the U.S. stock market recently trading at record high levels, with instability in such places as China, the former Soviet Union, and the Middle East, and with foreign currencies shifting frequently, the investing environment has become more risky. At the

same time, higher education's voracious needs for more income have become ever more intense. What should university financial planners do? Risk management has become paramount in the late 1990s.

Again going back to Oberlin, we used our endowment model to perform simulations of hundreds of possible scenarios, varying both market conditions and asset allocations. One purpose of the simulations was to test probabilities and risk tolerances. Would the college officers be willing to take a 5% chance of a 20% increase in endowment if it meant a 10% chance of a 20% loss? The simulations were valuable.

We were able to quantify the tradeoffs, and we learned some things we did not know. For example, the risk-reward frontier was not a continuum. Diversification using some additional asset classes could reduce volatility without reducing expected returns.

Investment in foreign stocks is one example. Recent studies show that returns on U.S. stocks tend to be equal to, or only a half percentage point lower than, returns on foreign stocks if the currency risk is hedged. But if the currencies are not hedged, the low correlations between U.S. and foreign stock returns mean the volatility of a portfolio holding both kinds of assets can be significantly reduced. So Oberlin College decided to in-

It's important to monitor the transactions of the investment managers the university selects.

crease its international exposure substantially. Oberlin was not alone. In Indiana both Earlham College and the University of Notre Dame now have more than 20% of their endowment dollars invested in overseas stocks and bonds (Nicklin 1997), as do dozens of other colleges and universities. Remember, you are managing risk, not stocks.

Asset diversification—the wise and prudent allocation of assets—has become a key feature for good endowment management in higher education. However, some forms of diversification may carry too high a risk. "Alternative" investments in limited partnerships with limited disclosure is an example. Likewise for the use of derivatives, which can be a valid tool for hedging risk but can be the opposite when hedge fund operators use them to leverage up risk and a client's exposure. A good rule for col-

---

What if the stock market falls by one third?

---

leges is: "Don't invest in what you don't understand, and don't approve what your asset manager can't explain."

At Oberlin, our endowment performance went from 33rd among 33 peer institutions in January 1989 to returns that were above the median by June 1995. With an endowment of $203 million in 1989 and $288 million in 1995, we generated $147 million in investment returns, including the money taken by the college for its annual budgets. Strategic endowment management can make a substantial difference for an institution's financial (and academic) health.

Harvard's endowment, for instance, has risen from $1.8 billion in 1977 to $9.1 billion in 1997, helping that university maintain its eminence. Atlanta's Emory University, with an extraordinary 22.5% annualized return over the past five years, has zoomed to a $3 billion endowment, greater than that of M.I.T., Cornell, or Columbia. Yale, with only 22% of its endowment now in U.S. common stocks and increased diversification into venture capital, leveraged buyout funds, real estate, hedge funds, and foreign stocks, had a 25.7% return on its endowment in 1996 and has grown its endowment

to $4.9 billion (Bary 1996). Georgetown, Loyola University in Illinois, Grinnell College, Occidental College, and Wake Forest are among those who have increased their endowments *10-fold* over the past 30 years (Wingert 1993).

With colleges and universities facing a more constricted financial future in the coming decade, they will need to devote more expert attention to the management of their endowments. Keep the endowment payout rate as low as possible (3.5% to 4.5%). Allocate your assets wisely. And manage for risk as well as for high returns. ∎

REFERENCES

Bary, A. 1996. Harvard's Men. *Barron's*, December 2.

Chronicle of Higher Education. 1997. February 14: A35-36.

Cropper, C. 1996. Where the Education is Built on Principal. *New York Times*, July 7.

Ibbotson, R. and Brinson, G. 1993. *Global Investing: The Professional's Guide to the World Capital Markets*. McGraw-Hill.

Massy, W. 1990. *Endowment Perspectives, Policies, and Management*. Association of Governing Boards.

Mercer, J. 1996. Stocks, Bonds, and Farmland. *Chronicle of Higher Education*. July 28: A27-28.

NACUBO. 1996. *The 1995 NACUBO Endowment Study*. National Association of College and University Business Officers (NACUBO).

Nicklin, J. 1997. More Colleges Look Overseas to Diversify Their Endowments. *Chronicle of Higher Education*, March 21: A41-42.

Spitz, W. 1992. *Selecting and Evaluating an Investment Manager*. National Association of College and University Business Officers (NACUBO).

Williamson, J.P. 1993. *Funds for the Future: College Endowment Management for the 1990s*. The Common Fund Press.

Wingert, D. 1993. *The Growth of College Endowments, 1960-1990*. The Common Fund Press.

More colleges and universities are using debt to pay for strategic changes and capital needs. Is it wise?

The Strategic Use of Debt Financing

David Hornfischer

I t is now widely known that the finances of most colleges and universities are under pressure. Moreover, institutions are trying to make strategic changes, modernize their facilities and equipment, and reengineer their operations to harness the new digital technology. Naturally, they have raised tuition fees and intensified their fund-raising from alumni, foundations, friends, and corporations.

What is less known is the extent to which numerous colleges and universities are now borrowing money from the capital markets. Nearly one-third of America's 3,600 institutions of higher education have issued debt, Standard & Poor's claims. According to a Morgan Stanley report, in the first half of the 1990s alone U.S. colleges and universities may have borrowed $45 billion. Debt has been increasing in much of public and private higher education. In 1996 $9.1 billion in tax-exempt debt was issued to public and private institutions, up from $6.8 billion in 1995.

David Hornfischer is vice president for administration and finance at the Berklee College of Music in Boston. A graduate of Trinity College in Connecticut and an M.B.A. recipient from the University of Massachusetts at Amherst, he also graduated from General Electric's three-year Financial Management Program. He previously worked at Amherst College as assistant treasurer and coordinator of computer systems.

Some colleges abhor debt. Rice University in Texas even has a charter that prohibits borrowing money. Others have a philosophical bias against debt similar to that expressed by Henrik Ibsen in his play *The Doll House*: "There can be no freedom or beauty about a home life that depends on borrowing or debt." Trustees especially can be very reticent about borrowing, particularly since universities are non-profit organizations with little chance of enhancing their revenues to pay off the debt. Some institutions have an unwritten rule that no new construction on campus should ever begin until all the money for the project has been pledged or collected. Where a campus has not used debt before, the administrative leaders may need to work with the governing board to develop the urgency of capital needs and a comfort with the idea of going into debt.

But many U.S. colleges and universities have come to regard debt not as a blemish on their financial reputation but as a strategic and natural way to sustain the quality of their operations. The effective use of debt can enable a campus to take on capital initiatives that will produce long-term benefits.

Two for the money

The case for debt in higher education is really a two-fold one. The *strategic* case argues that long-term benefits should be paid for from the funds of several generations. The *economic* case contends that the use of debt allows institutions to keep their own funds invested.

Strategically, colleges and universities have three major capital needs: new construction, introducing new scientific and technological equipment, and renovating their old structures and reducing the deferred maintenance that has accumulated through poor stewardship over the years.

A large building project is often a strategic necessity to permit the institution to ratchet up its quality or move into an emerging field such as biotechnology or

Nearly one-third of America's 3,600 institutions have issued debt.

international commerce. Dartmouth College, for example, recently issued $30 million in 30-year bonds to construct and equip a new psychology building and some related facilities. Likewise, at Berklee College of Music we plan to borrow $10 million to renovate a recently purchased building for our urban campus. For numerous colleges, new residence halls for students are funded by long-term debt since the housing revenues can be pledged to meet the debt service payments.

A second strategic planning initiative— to retrofit the campus for the new technological age we've entered, thus attracting more students and possibly reducing some costs—is an ideal project for debt financing. Hundreds of campuses have borrowed to keep up with the rapid advances in technology or for the latest scientific equipment for engineering, medicine, the arts, or the sciences. At Berklee we are in the midst of a multi-million dollar effort to upgrade our music library with a digital technology that will allow a classroom teacher to select a piece of music from the library, download it to a classroom computer, play it and display it to the class, and demonstrate various

changes to the piece through a synthesizer keyboard. A project such as this requires new wiring infrastructure, new hardware and software, training programs, and extra staff to convert data from older formats to digital.

Financing for new technology, however, is more complex than for a building project. Given the rapid changes in technology, today's technology could be obsolete before the debt is paid off. The same is true for specialized medical equipment, dining room services, and energy control systems. So these projects require a different type of financing from the traditional 30-year fixed-rate issue. One option might be to include a tax-exempt lease whose duration is matched to the useful life of the project. Another might mix some longer-life assets, such as a building renovation, into a combined financing whose term might be only, say, 15 years. A third approach might be the use of a tax-exempt statewide pooled fund where one state agency pools projects from a number of tax-exempt institutions. (At Berklee, we have found the pooled approach to be the most flexible, least costly, and most administratively simple approach to short-term financing.)

A third class of strategic projects that may merit debt financing is renovating facilities that have been neglected. The 1995 update of the Association of Physical Plant Administrators (APPA) 1988 report, *The Decaying American Campus: A Ticking Time Bomb*, notes that an estimated $26 billion of deferred maintenance and aging equipment is still outstanding at America's 3,600 colleges and universities, with $5.7 billion classified as "urgent." The APPA survey also reports that 56 percent of U.S. institutions have renovation or construction projects in process to correct their deferred maintenance problems, and that 19 percent of both public and private campuses are using tax-exempt debt to fund those projects.

The actual percentage of colleges and universities that are using debt to finance their facilities repairs and renovations is higher if we include *taxable* debt. For instance, Yale and Dartmouth are no longer able to use tax-exempt debt because they have already issued more than the Internal Revenue Service's limit of $150 million debt per institution. Yale faced up to its long-term needs through a creative issuance of 100-year bonds to fund (in large part) the huge deferred maintenance (said to be $2 billion) to its historic New Haven campus.

The economics of debt

The economic case for debt in higher education is usually linked to an endowment management strategy which calculates that the expected return on well-invested endowment assets is greater than the cost of debt. This case has certainly been easier to make in years like 1995 and 1996, when the average college endowment had returns of 15-17 per-

---

Hundreds of campuses have borrowed to keep up with the rapid advances in technology.

---

cent because of a rising stock market. There is a risk though because the endowment may underperform in some years of recession.

The economic case for debt was enhanced by tax changes in the early 1970s which made *private* colleges and universities also eligible to issue tax-exempt debt. Because investors do not have to pay taxes on the interest from tax-exempt bonds they purchase, interest rates are lower. Today long-term tax-exempt rates average about 5.5 percent compared to rates of more than 7.5 percent for taxable debt. The U.S. Congress, however, has since placed several limits on tax-exempt debt such as the institutional cap of $150 million and investment arbitrage limits on monies received from the bond issue but not yet spent.

Several noted private universities have decided that tax-exempt or current low-interest debt is strategically a smart way to finance capital improvements. Harvard University, whose endowment reached $9 billion in December 1996, has almost $1.5 billion of debt outstanding. If Harvard's en-

dowment is structured to produce a long-term total return of 9 percent but its debt costs are roughly 6 percent, the 3 percent difference provides Harvard with almost $5 million of marginal return a year. Harvard is not alone. In a 1994 report, Moody's Investors Service reported that while the median endowment for all eight Ivy League universities was $1.7 billion, it was leveraged by an average debt level of almost $450 million. The Ivy League average debt is about 26 percent of their endowments. For all U.S. private colleges and universities, Moody's reports that the debt-to-endowment ratio is closer to 35 percent.

Assuming the same 3 percent spread between endowment returns and debt costs, the median U.S. college gains additional $720,000 of funds a year—roughly the equivalent of returns on an additional $8 million in endowment.

State colleges and public universities have also become active players in the debt market. Their issues tend to be general obligations of the state higher education system, and legislative approval is usually necessary to authorize the issue. Their issues also are rated by external rating agencies who will evaluate the credit quality of the state itself and the extent to which state appropriations are used to fund the state colleges and universities. Moody's notes that this is more important in a state such as New York which provides 40 percent of SUNY's budget than in Michigan or Virginia, where the state contributes only about 14 percent of the public universities' budgets.

Who lends?

How does a college or university arrange to borrow money? The process is complex and subject to an array of government tax regulations and legal limits. Small colleges and first-time borrowers should work with an independent financial adviser or underwriting representative early in the process. Larger universities also should use an expert financial adviser, although some institutions have added such a person in-house because of the frequency of their debt issuances. Institutional lawyers will probably be

needed too to work with state agencies and the financial community to insure compliance with tax and other regulations. Legal counselors are also helpful in advising college administrators of the most appropriate

An estimated $26 billion of deferred maintenance and aging equipment is outstanding at America's colleges and universities.

wording for board of trustee votes to comply with complex tax rules.

Most states have special authorities to issue debt, and numerous banks and underwriting firms have been willing to arrange loans. In 1995 the leading underwriters for tax-exempt debt were Lehman Brothers, Goldman Sachs, Merrill Lynch, and Smith Barney. But recently several larger firms such as Salomon Brothers and First Boston have left the higher education financing market because of narrowed profit levels and the reduced market capacity caused by the national government's $150 million limit on large institutional borrowers. But some smaller firms and regional banks have entered the college debt market, sometimes providing personalized advising.

College and university executives need to do their homework before approaching state agencies, banks, or other capital markets. The institution's financial administrators and planners should team up with a financial consultant to summarize the institution's financial position for both internal and external evaluations of the potential transaction. An internal ratio analysis should help the trustees determine the level of debt at which it can feel comfortable.

The key measures of a college's financial strength are the size of its endowment (often measured by endowment dollar per student), a strong tradition of budget control, and a balance sheet that is not already burdened by heavy debt. Enrollment strength is also a key factor. This is mea-

sured by the geographic spread of the enrollment base, the stability of applications and the selectivity ratio, the reasonableness of tuition charges compared to peers, and a financial aid approach that is not merely buying enrollment through widespread pricing discounts or (in state universities) numerous tuition waivers.

The financial adviser can be especially helpful in assisting colleges and universities without large endowments or abundant applicants to enhance the credit quality of their bonds. These steps include the use of a quality bank's (rated AA, or AAA) letter of credit, purchase of bond insurance from an insurer such as MBIA or Connie Lee, or the pledge of various college assets such as mortgages, future tuition revenues, or residence hall rents as collateral. Such steps may bring new restrictions on the college budget, but they will allow the bonds to be sold at lower interest rates, saving the campus considerable money over the long run. The financial adviser can also make introductions to and get bids from lending sources.

The underwriters may also suggest some financial engineering strategies such as the use of swaps to limit interest rate risk or one or two creative repayment schedules that better fit debt servicing within the

Borrowing money is not a free lunch. Debt has to be repaid from future operating budgets.

institution's financial plan. The adviser may also locate a private placement source who is willing to take on the additional credit risk of an underendowed college in exchange for a higher interest rate that meets the income objectives of its loan portfolio.

Many of these same issues will be analyzed in a more formal way by rating agencies such as Moody's Financial Services or Standard & Poor's, who will evaluate for the potential bondholders the likelihood of the college's debt being repaid. Their analysts have recently been challenged by changes in the format of financial statements of private colleges and universities mandated by the new standards 116 and 117. Accounting changes for *public* institutions also are promised by the Accounting Standards Board. The new standards make institutions appear a bit richer because they include gains on endowment assets and on buildings and equipment values in their new category of "net assets."

No free lunch

It is imperative that budget and planning committees, faculty leaders, and all campus administrators understand that borrowing money to finance capital needs, major changes, or growth is not a free lunch. Debt has to be repaid from future operating budgets. Debt service adds a new, fixed expense item to the annual budget. And if payments for debt principal and interest exceed 7 percent of the annual budget, an explanation will be necessary to the outside lenders. Also, if revenues from enrollment, or donor support, or government appropriations decline, a fixed debt service cost can become burdensome; and a management failure or a faculty's refusal to fix the finances could put an institution in bankruptcy.

One rule of thumb for institutions already in debt: limit any new debt issuance to the amount that the college is already paying annually on its existing debt principal. Also, always include the institution's chief financial officer in the strategic planning or restructuring process so that the full financial ramifications of any strategic initiatives and transformation are fully understood.

One other thing: the rating agencies place a great deal of importance on the strength and soundness of a college's or university's leadership. So make sure that the presidential, academic, financial, and trustee leadership is determined, astute, and responsible before soliciting a major loan. Also, lenders will often want to know

exactly how the college's use of a loan's proceeds relates to the institution's strategic plan to make the institution more attractive, higher quality, and stronger overall, and how the college or university will be able to handle the debt repayment.

> *Lenders will often want to know how a loan's proceeds relate to the institution's strategic plan.*

In these years of rapid changes and rising costs for higher education, effective use of creative financing arrangements are absolutely necessary. Delaying a strategically beneficial project until gift funds are available may have adverse consequences. Debt can help universities respond quickly to new needs. The institution that understands how to use debt wisely and strategically, and is willing to instill the added discipline to pay off the debt, has an additional tool to finance its strategic plans—and in doing so, help its faculty teach and its students learn better. ∎

REFERENCES

Augustine, J. 1996. College and University Financial Statements Under SFAS Nos. 116 and 117. *Journal of Financial Statement Analysis* 1(4): 1-15.

Hornfischer, D. 1996. A Dynamic Capital Spending Model. *NACUBO Business Officer* 29(9): 46-48.

Kaiser, H. 1996. *A Foundation to Uphold: Preliminary Report*. Association of Physical Plant Administrators. July 22.

Moody's Investors Services. 1996. *Moody's Higher Education and Other Not-for-Profit Ratings: Trends and Analysis*. July.

Smith Barney Higher Education Finance Group. 1996. *Financing Higher Education*.

Standard & Poor's. 1996. *Viewpoint on Higher Education*. Summer.

Better planning and reforms are necessary to reverse growing public skepticism.

Rethinking Capital Campaigns

Peter Buchanan

The time has come to change the way American colleges and universities plan and conduct capital campaigns. The recent billion-dollar campaigns and the numerous other efforts in the hundreds of millions, some of which now go on for a whole decade, face a rising crescendo of criticism from within and without the academy. The public is beginning to suspect campuses are more interested in obtaining more money than in providing better education—greed rather than need. And people inside the university wonder where all the collected money goes. A reassessment and major changes are in order.

It is not that most campuses do not

Peter Buchanan is president of the Council for the Advancement and Support of Education (CASE) in Washington D.C. A graduate of Cornell University, he earned an MBA from Columbia's Graduate School of Business and an Ed.D. from Columbia's Teachers College. He has served in the Marine Corps, worked in business, and has been vice president for planning and resources at Wellesley College and vice president for development at Columbia University, where he directed a $600 million capital campaign.

need a larger endowment and additional money for renovations and a new building or three. Before I left Columbia University in 1990 I proposed a new $1.15 billion campaign (following a $600 million campaign we had just completed), and a majority of the deans were disappointed at the sum because their needs were so acute. And indeed, for 1993 Columbia University is estimating a deficit of $30 to $40 million. Even Princeton, Grinnell, Pomona, Swarthmore, and Wellesley, the nation's richest institutions in endowment per student, could use additional funds. Yale has $1 billion of deferred maintenance; and hundreds of other colleges need newly equipped laboratories, better libraries, more scholarships for low-income students, and refurbished residence halls. There are abundant and compelling reasons for the profusion of capital campaigns.

But the way that higher education carries out its crusades for new buildings and larger endowments has not changed since the 1950s and 1960s, when the United States economy was growing fast, enrollments were increasing, and faculty salaries were disgracefully low. Conditions have changed, and the media and the public are now suspicious rather than supportive.

Major fund-raising drives need to change.

Having spent 13 years planning, preparing for, and directing large fund-raising campaigns on campus, and the past two years as president of CASE, the national association for campus fundraisers, alumni directors, public relations executives, and publications editors and designers, I have developed some ideas about how the planning and performance of capital campaigns might be reformed. In this article, I offer six of these to higher education leaders for consideration and possible adoption.

Planning to begin

1. Get your house in order before you begin. Numerous institutions are prompted to begin a major fund-raising effort because they foresee, or are already operating with, a considerable financial deficit. More money, they believe, will allow them to continue what they are now doing. But it is unseemly to ask others for support before you have done all you can to reduce expenses, elimi-

Planning for a campaign should begin years ahead.

nate duplication and wasteful practices, and make your college as efficient and productive as possible. Planning for a campaign should begin years ahead with internal improvements and judicious pruning in the operating budget.

It is no secret that many colleges and universities offer too many courses and programs, allow professors to teach too little, employ administrators and aides who are not entirely necessary, spend excessively for athletics, and tolerate some low-quality operations. The public and alumni have become more aware of these slipshod practices. So the first consideration in planning a capital campaign is to make sure your institution is as efficiently administered as it can be. Individuals, foundations, and corporations are more disposed to give

if they are convinced a university has squeezed out careless, spendthrift, antiquated, and low-quality practices, and has balanced its budget.

It is of utmost importance to announce your top priorities and stick to them.

You should also try to increase the percentage and amount of alumni giving, improve your operations in the cafeteria, bookstore, residence halls, and other semicommercial campus ventures, and be certain that your endowment is skillfully invested. After demonstrating that you have done everything you can to reduce costs, you should also increase available revenues before you ask others for financial help. People are more likely to help those who have first helped themselves, especially in today's climate of austerity.

2. Develop a strategy and choose the most urgent needs. Before you begin to solicit capital funds, be certain you have a strategic plan for where your institution wants to go in the next 10 years. The strategy should be specific with clear priorities, and not be vague or rhetorical. This will help you decide what the most urgent priorities are for investment.

It is of utmost importance that colleges clearly announce their top priorities, explain why they are crucial for the future, and stick to them during the campaign. With a strategic action plan in hand, institutions can cost out their capital needs with some precision and develop a detailed financial plan, which then serves as a foundation for the fund campaign. Many donors will want to know where your institution wants to go, what the priorities are, and why, before they consider a major gift.

Strategizing in preparation for a fund-raising effort provides a chance to confer widely and build a broad commitment to improving the financial situation at your campus. A campaign can lift campus spirit as well as open pocketbooks. Failure to see a campaign as much more than an effort to attract dollars is a common form of lost opportunity.

A proper strategic action plan also moves beyond a college's own ambitions and indicates how the college will address the intellectual and economic needs of the region, state, and the country in the next quarter century. Keep in mind that a capital campaign is usually the most visible aspect of the university to the public (except for its sports program), so the explanation of your priorities must make sense to the media, business, and political leaders, and to the general citizenry, as well as to faculty, staff, and students.

How big? How long?

3. *Decide on the size and duration of the campaign.* No fund raiser in a competitive environment has failed to witness the desire of several trustees, some leading alumni, and a few deans and vice presidents to have a campaign larger than the college's chosen peers or chief competitors. It is disturbing to discover how recklessly or arbitrarily many colleges and universities choose the size of their campaign. Even feasibility studies to determine from chief prospects what sum might be realistic are sometimes ignored.

Timid presidents and vice presidents for development will tend to choose a goal they can attain easily and appear successful. Ambitious trustees and presidents will sometimes select a goal based on institutional envy or extravagant hopes rather than reality. How should an institution choose the proper size of its campaign ?

I believe the best strategy may be to determine the dollars needed for the absolutely urgent needs of the institution, and then expand that sum by the smallest sum the alumni, public, and friends can understand. Or, if the college is small, poor, or relatively new to major fund campaigns, stick to the indispensable capital needs only. Thus, if an institution has a compel-

ling need for $15 million of new buildings and renovations and $25 million of new endowment, especially for student scholarships, it might designate its goal as, say, $45 million or $50 million.

It has recently become fashionable to have five-year, even 10-year campaigns. I believe this is a mistaken trend. Campaigns should be as brief as possible, and very pointed, not lengthy and vague. I think few campaigns should last longer than three years, perhaps with an extra year to solicit the large, advance gifts.

Campaigns should be as brief as possible.

4. *Choose a capital campaign or a general campaign.* Nothing has caused so much cynicism about capital campaigns in the past decade as the way colleges and university leaders count receipts toward the campaign goal. Failing campaigns have thrown in government research grants and orally promised money from future wills, as well as all annual giving toward the campaign goal, to make it appear "successful." It is definitely time to reform the way we count contributions to the special campaign. People have begun to chuckle about higher education campaign accounting; and faculty wonder how a $25 million capital campaign that is proclaimed to have "gone over the top" could have produced only $16 million in new capital for buildings and endowment.

I think every college or university should decide whether it will run a *capital* campaign or a *general* campaign. Capital campaigns should be strictly for new monies for designated capital needs (buildings and endowment). General campaigns can count annual alumni giving, gifts of paintings or used scientific or computer equipment, and every gift (but not government grants) that comes in during a specified time. The kind of campaign a college chooses should be made transparent in advance, and alumni and others should be clear as to what will be counted and what will not—in advance. If you run a general campaign, you should never call it a capital campaign.

If you run a general campaign never call it a capital campaign.

As I said, a capital campaign should be only for buildings, vital equipment, and endowment. I would even recommend that it be limited to buildings, equipment, and endowment that are designated by the strategic plan as top priorities. An offered gift, for instance, of $7 million for a new contemporary art museum that is not a campus priority should either be redirected to a vital need, accepted with a maintenance endowment but not counted, or refused because it is not a building the campus needs or wants in the future.

A new and indispensable document for every fund raiser is now being prepared by a blue-ribbon panel called The Campaign Reporting Advisory Group, representing CASE, NACUBO, the Association of Governing Boards, and the American Association of Fund Raising Counsel, with publication expected in 1993. Among other standards, the report says, "Deferred gifts should be reported only when assets are transferred;" "Oral pledges should not be reported;" and wills may be reported only if accompanied by "an irrevocable instrument" and then should be reported as a campaign gift minus inflation during life expectancy. For example, a $100,000 pledge by a 65-year-old male in his will would be reported as a gift of roughly $49,500, its real value by the time the person dies at the expected age of 83 years old.

Organization and training

5. *Decide how your institution will organize the campaign.* Will it be centrally directed and administered or decentralized and merely coordinated? Will it be run professionally by outside fund-raising experts and the vice president for development or led by the vice president and president and run entrepreneurially by deans, directors, department chairs, even individual faculty, with the help of a large cadre of trained alumni volunteers? How much will the institution budget for the campaign staff, communications, and travel?

Those universities that have experience in major fund-raising and have a large group of devoted alumni and alumnae will probably opt for a less centralized campaign. I think the growing variety of funding sources and the need to make hundreds and hundreds of calls will increasingly require a many-pronged, decentralized effort, with every dean active alongside numerous alumni volunteers.

A reminder: volunteers need to be trained and guided so that they are effective. Too many campuses turn volunteers loose with little sense of proper protocol and productive approaches. A clumsy approach to a potentially receptive donor can have painfully negative consequences. Also, colleges and universities have different traditions and styles of loyalty that must be taken into account. (Duronio and Loessin 1991).

Volunteers need to be trained and guided.

6. *Educate and explain thoroughly.* In the past several years I have become convinced that one of the major reforms needed for campaigns is a much larger expenditure of time, money, and publications to educate faculty, students, alumni, and the public about the details and uses of the campaign. I have been guilty of neglect in this area myself.

We forget that to outsiders, including most faculty and staff, capital campaigns are mysterious. Terms such as "nucleus fund," "deferred gift," "feasibility study," "case statement," and "restricted endowment" are an enigma to most people. Even the meaning of the word "capital" is not evident to most non-economists. Few persons understand that the actual campaign usually begins a year or so before the campaign is announced publicly, as the president, vice president for development, alumni leaders, trustees, and deans quietly visit the 50 to 150 persons and foundations likely to give "lead gifts" of $1 million to $20 million (or more) so that a "nucleus fund" of roughly one-third to one-half of the campaign total can be pledged before the campaign is officially begun. Many persons don't realize that 90 percent of the campaign dollars usually comes from less than 5 percent of the donors.

Proper presentation can prevent misunderstandings. People need to understand that when their campus sets a large endowment goal, the university will be able to spend only five percent of that total; an endowment addition of $50 million brings only $2.5 million a year more to the operating budget. On the other hand, if the $50 million is prudently invested it will produce another $50 million every 15-20 years in constant dollars *forever* since capital sums can be doubled in value five or so times over a century with astute investments.

Higher education must do a much better job of explaining what campaigns are, exactly why they are imperative, and how they work. Educators must explain especially the direct connection between the dollars raised and the human and academic benefits. This may require more open discussions of what is now taboo—why and how colleges prepare two or three years in advance to launch a campaign.

It also means, despite its dangers, that institutions must inform the media earlier and better so that the uninformed sniping is reduced. Even America's better newspapers have been known to write astonishingly ignorant editorials because they do not understand how universities are financed. Colleges, on the other hand, have

We forget that capital campaigns are mysterious.

often failed to explain how donations to their capital campaign will benefit young people, the public, and the nation. When campus leaders complain that television, radio, or newspaper stories are inaccurate, they seldom reflect on how much effort they made to get the story straight in the first place through professional meetings.

We need to bear in mind what one of the wisest of all fundraisers in higher education's history, Harold "Si" Seymour, wrote in his classic book (Seymour 1966, p. ix): "The vineyards of philanthropy are pleasant places and...if these vineyards are to thrive and bear their best fruit, they must always have first-class attention." ∎

REFERENCES

Duronio, M. and B. Loessin. 1991. *Effective Fund Raising in Higher Education.* Jossey-Bass.

Management Reporting Standards for Educational Institutions: Fund Raising Campaigns. 1992. CASE/NACUBO.

Seymour, H. 1966. *Designs for Fund Raising: Principles, Patterns, Techniques.* McGraw-Hill.

V. Strategies, Leadership, and Administration

A university president suggests how institutions can begin redesigning themselves.

How to Start Restructuring Our Colleges

Clara Lovett

Many college and university leaders have acknowledged in the past couple of years that, given the public scrutiny of our institutions and shrinking state and federal budgets, some fundamental changes are needed in our higher education system. But no consensus has emerged about what changes would be most desirable.

As Theodore Marchese, executive editor of *Change* magazine, put it in an editorial a few months ago: "We have much clearer ideas about the need for change and the dysfunctions of the present system than we do about what a new system might be like."

Clara Lovett is president of Northern Arizona University. She did her undergraduate work at the University of Trieste in her native Italy and at Cambridge University in England, and earned a doctorate in history at the University of Texas, Austin. She taught at Baruch College of the City University of New York and studied as a Guggenheim Fellow. She has also served as chief of the European Division of the Library of Congress, dean of Arts & Sciences at George Washington University, and vice president of academic affairs at George Mason University in Virginia. An earlier version of this article appeared in *The Chronicle of Higher Education*.

While no one change would transform the system, he noted, "the right five or seven might."

It seems to me that it is not difficult to identify pieces of our current system in which we could make changes that —while not earthshaking in themselves—would produce considerable benefits.

The academic calendar is a good place to begin. Everyone recognizes it for what it is: a relic of an agrarian society in which able-bodied men and women were needed in the fields at certain times of the year. What are we getting for our reluctance to let go of cherished old customs? On most campuses, we get some faculty members who work 11 or 12 months a year—because they engage in research or other professional activities during the summer—but who get paid for only 9 or 10 months. We get others who teach during the summer for a fraction of their regular salaries. We get students whose progress toward graduation and opportunities for on-campus summer employment are curtailed. We get underused facilities during some months of the year and overcrowding during others.

A 12-month academic year divided into three equal segments, or into shorter modules for some programs, would benefit everybody by promoting a more even use of facilities throughout the year. Students would gain a less crowded campus and would face less competition for part-time jobs during the school year. They still could work full time to earn more money for tuition during any terms they choose to take off. Those who decide not to take any time off at all would be able to graduate sooner, opening up spaces for new students.

Faculty members would be able to teach for two segments and then use the next segment to conduct experiments, work on important manuscripts, travel to other institutions, or do other academic work. And because of the additional revenue produced by higher enrollment in the "summer" segment, professors could be paid on a 12-month basis.

Sounds simple and sensible, doesn't it? Yet this kind of change requires that many constituencies think differently about the system they share. Faculty leaders and administrators surely can restructure academic programs and work assignments around a 12-month academic year. But trustees and legislators need to help, at a minimum, by providing funds to shift faculty members to 12-month contracts before the added tuition revenues from higher summer enrollment kick in. They also need to abandon traditional fiscal practices, such as providing support only for the traditional academic year and ignoring the summer term.

Leaving industrial practices behind

If the academic calendar is a relic of the agrarian age, several other pieces of the system are artifacts of the early industrial age—when teachers colleges, land-grant universities, and many of our research universities were developed. Our degree requirements reflect a faith in the efficiency of the industrial assembly line, a concern for product standardization, and a preoccupation with time management that Frederick Taylor, the legendary American efficiency expert, would have loved.

Research findings, to say nothing of the common-sense observations of thousands of faculty members, tell us that this industrial-

age system is not working well. In contrast to the middle- or upper-class white male students of an earlier era, today's students start college with many different learning styles, levels of preparation, and personal goals. They do not fit the academic assembly line, and it makes little educational sense to try to force them onto it.

Most educators agree that communication, critical thinking, and quantitative reasoning are the principal elements of an undergraduate education. Movement away from the current emphasis on seat time and

Pieces of the system are artifacts of the early industrial age.

credit hours to an emphasis on academic competence, which students would demonstrate on broad-based exams, would have several advantages.

Academically talented and motivated students would have a chance to earn a degree in less time than the traditional four years (now often stretched to five anyway). And since grades for individual courses would matter less than proven competence in broader areas of expertise, students would be less likely to seek out easy courses, and professors would be less tempted to try to obtain good ratings from students by watering down course content or grading standards. Less emphasis on the accumulation of credit hours and time in the classroom probably would also reduce the need to expand physical facilities, and thus the need to raise money to do so.

Institutions wishing to move toward competence-based exams could draw on the experience of the assessment movement, now more than 10 years old. From the work done to develop better ways to assess students' learning, faculty members can learn to articulate appropriate educational goals and develop new ways to measure students' achievement of them.

Where in higher education can we expect resistance to systemic change, such as credit and degrees based on demonstrated academic competence? Perhaps from faculty members, long accustomed to the allocation of academic resources based on the production of student credit hours. Perhaps from academic administrators, who might find it harder to predict student enrollment or to estimate a semester or two in advance how many classes will be needed or how much tuition will be generated.

Institutions moving in this direction would need strong support from their trustees and, where appropriate, from elected officials. Trustees and public officials would have to work closely with campus leaders to protect institutions against any large fluctuations in enrollment and revenue that might occur during the transition. In public colleges and universities, for instance, the traditional financing formula, based on the number of "full-time equivalent" students, might have to be modified or replaced for a time by block grants, as is commonly done when a new campus or school is created.

Students and work

Student employment provides yet another point for beneficial change in our academic system. Over the past decade, education researchers—including Alexander Astin, Arthur Levine, and Arthur Chickering—have provided information about why students work and how they use their earnings. Students work to put themselves through college if their families cannot afford to pay or are unwilling to do so. Other students work because they want more spending money, because they want the experience, or simply because they enjoy working.

One hears many complaints about this fact of college life. Faculty members, in particular, note that academic rigor diminishes when students work more hours than they study. Trustees, legislators, and parents fret about the length of time it takes students to graduate when they have to work as well as study.

Given that most students are employed during college, why not make employment *on campus* an integral part of their experience, perhaps even a requirement for gradu-

ation? To a large extent, we already do this with graduate students, who assist their professors with teaching and research. Why not

What if students transferred evidence of academic competence instead of credit hours?

apply the same model to undergraduates? Smaller institutions, which might find it difficult to provide part-time jobs for all students, would at least employ all seniors. Larger institutions might be able to find jobs for all juniors as well.

While some undergraduates could be employed by academic departments, as, indeed, many already are, others could work in maintenance, security, administrative services, alumni affairs, and fund raising. Money to pay the students would come from existing jobs—for example, one full-time support position could be converted into two or three part-time ones.

The jobs would not necessarily be related to the student's major. In fact, paid employment in unrelated areas might teach students new skills, such as tolerance, conflict negotiation and resolution, and an appreciation of cultural diversity in the workplace.

Would students object to the change? Yes, if it turned out that on-campus jobs paid less than comparable jobs off campus. This change would require administrators to stop using students merely as a contingent work force in less-than-critical jobs. And students would have to stop thinking of on-campus jobs as sinecures, to be abandoned without a moment's hesitation at exam time or when a friend proposes a trip to the beach. Administrators would have to hold students to their work obligations, because students would be filling—and sharing—responsible, reasonably well-paid jobs previously held by full-time staff members.

Students already are working, so why are we not moving more boldly in this direction? On many campuses, administrators and staff members resist the systemic changes that would be required to employ large numbers of students in responsible jobs, because they fear losing their own positions if fewer full-time employees are needed. Some administrators are reluctant to change job descriptions and hiring practices, citing students' propensity to disappear at holiday or exam time. This would change, I believe, if campus managers started thinking of, and treating, students as part of their core work force, not as "contingent" workers. And more on-campus employment for students might reduce the demand for more and more financial aid.

Stumbling toward graduation

Let's also look at the tortuous paths many students take to graduation. We know that most students do not earn a baccalaureate degree in four years, or an associate degree in two years. Many take longer because, among other reasons, they attend more than one institution, change majors, or take time off to travel or earn money for tuition. Many institutions make life difficult for such students. Our rhetoric extols the freshman who stays at the same institution, sticks with one major, does not fail any courses, is not employed, and gets out in eight semesters. Yet the biographies of ac-

Will supporters and critics assist the innovators who are trying to imagine new forms?

complished men and women tell us that success in life has very little to do with this kind of linear, lockstep progress through the curriculum.

What if students transferred evidence of academic competence instead of credit hours? What if the most general and critical skills—writing, oral argumentation, and mathematics, for example—were required in all majors? Transfers or changes of major would not automatically impede a student's

progress to graduation, provided he or she had built up a portfolio of basic academic skills that could be tested by the faculty of the new institution or degree program.

The benefits? Faculty members would be assured of a more consistent level of student preparation, which surely would make teaching easier. Trustees and legislators would, in time, see more students graduating in four or two years and find the pressure on campus facilities reduced. And students

Trustees do not yet understand that they are in the driver's seat of educational Model T's.

would not lose credits when they transferred or changed majors, as they often do now.

Despite the salutary effects of the changes I've suggested, they are sure to draw naysayers. Some students will object to the challenge of mastering an array of skills and taking broadbased exams instead of just passing one course at a time. It is true that they would be required to make intellectual connections that they seldom make under the current credit-hour system. And numerous faculty members— even some of those who say they want students with better, more consistent preparation—will be reluctant to give up their favorite courses or modify departmental requirements.

And what of higher education's supporters and critics? Proposals for basic changes will test their values and resolve. Will they assist the innovators who are trying to imagine new forms of higher education and develop new means of delivering it? Or will they continue to believe that our agrarian-age and early industrial-age practices can meet the needs of information-age students?

At both private and public institutions, trustees and legislators are trying to increase accountability, implement new management strategies, and monitor graduation rates, job placements of graduates, and other indicators of institutional effectiveness. They have become frustrated, as anyone can attest who has attended meetings of the Association of Governing Boards of Universities and Colleges in recent years.

With few exceptions, trustees and legislators do not yet understand that they are in the driver's seat of educational Model T's. Tinkering with the engine to reduce fuel consumption and rearranging the seats to accommodate more passengers do not address public concerns about the quality of education or the productivity of our colleges and universities. Redesign of their institutions might.

From the experience of other sectors of society, including business, we know that successful design (or redesign) starts with simple ideas. Why not start with very simple changes, such as the 12-month academic calendar, required on-campus employment for upperclassmen, and competence-based degrees? ■

Are traditional forms of presidential leadership and faculty governance outmoded?

Wanted: New Leadership for Higher Education

Barry Munitz

I had a dream the other night, and a nightmare…. The nightmare was that I dreamed I was the CEO of Monsanto—and had to run the corporation like a university.

Richard J. Mahoney
Chair/CEO, Monsanto Company

Radical changes are occurring that will alter fundamentally the nature of the university as we have known it for nearly a century. They will also transform the shared governance model we have followed since the 1950s (AAUP 1966; Mortimer and McConnell 1978). These changes will force adjustments in how faculty teach and how stu-

Barry Munitz is Chancellor of the California State University, a 23 campus system of the state universities, and Immediate Past Chair of the Board of the American Council on Education in Washington, D.C. For the past four years he has chaired the State's Education Round Table and he is chair-elect of the California Business-Higher Education Forum. He received a B.A. in Classics from Brooklyn College and a M.A. and Ph.D. from Princeton in Comparative Literature. After teaching at Berkeley and serving as Clark Kerr's assistant on the Carnegie Commission on the Future of Higher Education, he worked as Academic Vice President of the University of Illinois system, as Chancellor of the University of Houston, and as president of a Fortune 200 corporation. He has written widely on organizational theory, higher education, and planning and governance.

dents learn, how colleges and universities are financed, and how institutions are administered. They will require that colleges and universities restructure their management processes and modify their traditional notions about academic leadership.

Universities do not change easily, and major shifts in U.S. higher education have been rare. There was a dramatic shift from the many small, all-male, often religious and classically-oriented colleges of the early 19th century to the establishment in 1865 to 1900 of new land-grant colleges that were coeducational, polytechnic, oriented to work, and open to the working classes. From roughly 1890 to 1920 the German model of education and research introduced academic specialization and departments, deans, graduate schools and research, and large private and state universities (Veysey 1965). After World War II the GI Bill opened a new era of higher education with new community colleges, teachers colleges turned into comprehensive universities, adult and evening education, and the rise of federal-grant multiuniversities.

We face a different metamorphosis

The coming transformation may be especially difficult because, in contrast to the other three, this change will take place in

261

an environment of socio-economic triage. (Triage is the process of allocating scarce commodities or services among the many needing them only to those most likely to benefit from them or those most likely to contribute importantly to the community. In its best known medical metaphor, it focuses on those most likely to survive.) The other major changes in higher education occurred with the expectations and delivery of more money and broad public support. Never before has American higher education had to make radical adjustments with inadequate resources and with a dangerously weakened base of public support.

Between 1990 and 1993 public spending on higher education in the United States declined by $7.76 billion (including budget cuts and inflationary losses) (*Report of the States* 1994). In California, the portion of the state budget going to higher education in the past five years has gone from 13 percent to less than 9 percent. And the

When we are questioned, we act defensively.

costs of higher education are going up faster than the Consumer Price Index (Baumol and Blackman 1995). There is little prospect of major new public infusions of money. It is not available, and more state and federal allocators feel it is not deserved.

There is, however, still an impression among many faculty and some administrators that as soon as the economy gets better, the money will roll in again. Tied to this naive optimism are those who believe that with a bit of trimming here and there and with better fundraising and public relations, a college or university can get by until the recovery begins and then business can continue as usual.

Contrast this assessment with that of the noted higher education watcher Clark Kerr:

> In the early 1990s, we are again in a sad decade for higher education in the United States. Financial resources, particularly for public insti-

tutions, are in jeopardy. Productivity increases in our economy are at a low point for the past century. Other competitors for public support—such as for the renovation of our infrastructure, and assistance for children and youth—are more demanding (and often rightly so). Public confidence in higher education has been reduced by the flight from teaching, by political dissension on campus, by scandals of many sorts. Once again there is a fear of a new "ice age" (1994, p. 217).

There also remains considerable feeling in academe that the public will soon return to an appreciation of how valuable professors and their institutions really are. This feeling continues in the face of more and more people asking with growing bluntness, "What exactly are we paying for?" They worry about decreased attention to undergraduate teaching for their children in order to subsidize graduate seminars and research, about anarchic curriculums, misguided faculty reward systems and measures of productivity, and the increasing politicization of some activities.

Business leaders are not the only ones who view higher education as one of the few professions where the producers define the product with minor regard for the customers and where the quality of that product and its producers is rarely assessed and systematically improved. Indeed, words such as "product," customer," and "management" tend to be regarded like profanity in a Victorian parlor. Surveys show that voters in many states now view public colleges and universities much as they do other public agencies: self-regarding bureaucracies wasting too many taxpayer dollars. And polls reveal that a majority of those interviewed feel that the most prestigious colleges and universities are increasingly elitist, out of touch with most citizens, overpriced, pampered, loosely managed, and relatively unconcerned about society's most urgent problems and undergraduate learning needs. From the Business-Higher Education Forum to the Education Commission of the States, our patrons and stakeholders bemoan the widening gap between the priorities for which they *send* resources and the objectives for which higher education institutions *spend* it.

Thomas Kean, the former governor of New Jersey and now president of Drew University and co-chair of a new panel to study the national investment in higher education, says:

> Here is the reality plain and simple…People are questioning our mission and questioning who we are. They claim we cost too much, spend carelessly, teach poorly, plan myopically, and when we are questioned, we act defensively (*Stress on Research* 1994).

If so, what then?

The challenge, therefore, is not just a matter of telling "our story" more effectively. New patterns in the economy, demographics, government spending policies, technology, public attitudes, international exchanges, and the expectations of students and their families demand that colleges and universities change fundamentally, as U.S. business firms and local and national governments have begun to do. And the restructuring will have to be done in a new climate of tightening finances, as is happening in health care. Donald Kennedy, the former president of Stanford, recently wrote (1994):

> We know (because Nobel laureate Herbert Simon and others have been telling us) that organizations seldom achieve major economic or directional shifts—even when these would plainly yield important gains—unless the external pressures are intense… We now face that kind of pressure…. It can be used by university leaders to direct major institutional reconfiguration.

But who is to direct the reconfiguration?

The standard reference on the desirable approach to campus policymaking is the "Statement on Government of Colleges and Universities," issued jointly by the American Association of University Professors, the American Council on Education, and the Association of Governing Boards in 1966, when faculty power had reached unprecedented heights during education's explosive growth period. The "Statement" was embellished by the AAUP in separate position papers in 1969 and 1970 (AAUP 1969, 1970).

According to these documents, "The faculty has primary responsibility for cur-

riculum, subject matter and methods of instruction, research, faculty status, and those aspects of student life which relate to the educational process." In all these matters the president and trustees should "con-

Who is to do the reconfiguration?

cur with the faculty judgment," which "can be overruled only in rare instances and for compelling reasons stated in detail."

However, the same documents say that the president and his or her staff have "a special obligation to innovate and initiate." The Statement and AAUP papers did not envision that colleges and universities might face serious financial difficulties or that dramatic developments in society would press academic institutions to redesign the way they operated. Thus, in the late 1990s we still have the hallowed tradition of "shared governance" with faculty members controlling most core academic issues and with the president and trustees "obtaining needed capital and operating funds" and somehow trying to "innovate and initiate."

The reality in recent years though is that too many professors have been resistant to urgings that hard decisions need to be made, and too many institutions have experienced reactions ranging from suspicion to hostility about suggestions for restructuring their institutions and prerogatives. There is a widespread reluctance to select priorities for action, and to help design the coming transformation of higher education. To quote Donald Kennedy again (1994):

> University faculties have unwritten understandings, and one of them is that they usually criticize one another's discipline only in private. In a recent round of harsh budget cuts at Stanford, we involved a group of distinguished faculty from all fields…. They frequently worried that we were cutting too much 'across the board,' and not singling out whole programs for elimination. Yet they could not develop a consensus on which programs should go. There was private advice to us, of course, on what victim 'the administra-

tion' might select—and in nearly every case the recommended deletion was a discipline far from the domain of the recommenders.

To question the behavior of some faculty in times of severe economic pressure and societal change is not to deny the strength, character, and composure of most of America's professors. The creativity and skill that most faculty demonstrate while carrying heavy teaching schedules and lightened paychecks is beyond dispute. Our best faculty consult around the world, improving lives from the inner city to outer space. On some campuses faculty have begun program evaluations and reallocations. And many, especially in the colleges, teach in an inspiring and illuminating way.

But many faculty members tend to view their own institution as different from all others in society, and largely exempt from the need for renovation. So the traditional checks and balances, the multi-level reviews, and the shared governance model which served us well in times of growing enrollments, resources, and public confidence need to be reconsidered. The underlying values of the shared governance model must be preserved, but processes that more easily permit action, change, and reforms should be explored.

The education economist David Breneman, a former college president Harvard professor, and new dean at the University of Virginia's School of Education, suggests frankly (1995):

> The collegial nature of most colleges and universities, emphasizing consultation and shared decision making, seems poorly suited to the sorts of wrenching changes that lie ahead.

On the other hand, many presidents seem equally reluctant to "innovate and initiate," even though many campus executives recognize that inertia or hunkering down could put their institutions at risk. When the better faculty step forward to help redesign their own professional world, are they really invited by their presidents to participate in the institution's leadership? Do provosts and presidents honor and reward those scholars who bring their imaginations, knowledge, and experience to bear directly on their own institution's problems?

One of the most dangerous tendencies among presidents today is an inclination to tell those outside higher education that they really have little influence over their institutions. When presidents or chancellors say to an audience of political persons, business men and women, or general citizens that, "You must recognize that we college presidents don't really control our institutions," it makes us sound inept, cowardly, or dishonest. The public does not believe it, or accept it. Leaders in other sectors believe that presidents actually have enormous influence over their institutions, particularly when resources are very tight. If presidents do not use their influence and authority both within their own institutions and in national settings, the public's faith in higher education and its capacity to make adaptive changes will collapse.

In a recent column in *The New York Times*, William Honan wistfully recalled the

There is a widespread reluctance to select priorities for action.

college and university presidents of yesteryear as "striking figures" who did not shrink from pressing their institutions in new directions or speaking out on the important issues of their time. Where are such leaders today? Honan asked. Few of today's presidents, provosts, or deans have spoken out on human rights, attacks on the National Endowment for the Humanities or National Public Radio, welfare reform, school reform, health care, international trade, crime and drug use, or family responsibilities toward the young. Honan argued that the current leaders of higher education are "a new breed" characterized by "timorousness." Certainly today's presidents view their position quite differently from the likes of James Conant, Arthur Flemming, William Friday, the Rev. Theodore Hesburgh, Robert Maynard Hutchins, John Kemeny, Clark Kerr, and Herman Wells.

The argument against taking a personal stance on broad social issues is traditional and clear. Presidents assert that they have enough responsibility undertaking the enormous range of assignments tied directly to educational and intellectual pursuits. They are concerned about diluting this mandate if they attempt to engage issues beyond those responsibilities. Indeed, they worry whether their institutions's relative independence would be threatened, and even whether they would be inviting retaliation if they become participants in what they perceive to be a political process beyond their legitimate boundaries. Many state quite clearly that they lack the expertise and/or the mandate.

My concern is that academic executives understand the distinction between taking a personal/political stand and helping the state and the country address more than just specific higher education issues by hosting and framing the debate. From an institutional perspective the president's responsibilities might reasonably be focused upon raising the issues, gathering a variety of perspectives, creating a context for analysis and focusing upon potential resolutions—everything short of political pressure—but far beyond the recent tendency to avoid any public policy involvement. If administrators ask the faculty to exercise the same authority and courage at their own institution that they demonstrate around the world, then presidents must acknowledge their own power internally, and to engage public policy convictions externally.

Out of the quandary

If the times require a transformation at many colleges and universities, and if the current patterns of shared governance and reluctant leadership greatly inhibit substantial changes, what then?

The administration of colleges and universities in the next decade, when we have to rethink and redesign the delivery of higher education in a triage atmosphere of diminishing financial resources and weakened public confidence, needs to be radically reconceived. A new kind of leadership is required to manage in higher education's very different environment. Pop philoso-

pher and comic George Carlin refers to this situation as "vuja de"—one we've never seen before and hope never to see again.

Managing an institution's financial cutbacks require different skills and different procedures. Kenneth Boulding noted during the recession of the 1970s that, "The

Shared decision making seems poorly suited to the sorts of wrenching changes that lie ahead.

manager of a declining institution is required to think of more things that haven't been thought of. In a growing institution the stakes are easily corrected; in a declining institution they are not" (1975).

Supervising structural changes at a college or university also requires a different style of executive leadership. Leaders of major academic change must be willing to take risks and be accountable, must have a strong sense of daring and possess great courage and tenacity, must know how to sell the new departures to many constituencies, and must develop workable leverage and constraint mechanisms to alter internal patterns and behaviors. They must be organizational architects and passionate builders and reshapers, willing to surrender being liked for being respected.

To do this, however, presidents must be recruited, supported, and rewarded by their faculty and trustees for trying new approaches and candidly confronting current challenges. If presidents are asked to lead toward basic changes but are rewarded for calm mediation, then institutions create the same treacherous tension as when they ask young faculty to focus on undergraduate teaching and then honor major research.

In a perceptive paper, Judith Eaton, former president of two community colleges and of the Council for Aid to Education and now chancellor of the new Minnesota State College and University system, observed (1995):

Today's leadership style is rooted in the 1970s and 1980s…. What worked in the 1970s and 1980s, though, is not working so well in the 1990s…

Higher education leaders need a new set of tools. Rather than placating constituencies, they are being called on to use conflict constructively…. Rather than fiscal moderation, they must be prepared to practice fiscal boldness…. Rather than avoiding controversy, they need to be able to engage the tough issues….

The 'high risk' leader taking up these new tools will need to enjoy taking chances, thrive on challenge and change, and find public censure bearable. He or she will have to value respect over affection, vision over short-term gain, and genuine disagreement over polite accord.

In sum, the current stalemate needs to be broken by the willingness of colleges and universities to accept a different kind of presidential leadership and a renovated governance partnership.

Is the idea of a new kind of stronger presidential, decanal, and faculty leadership in academe utopian? Will a majority of American faculty and their official representatives come to see that shared governance in its present form is an outmoded concept now that, as retiring dean of arts and sciences at Harvard Henry Rosovsky noted in his final dean's report (Rosovsky 1991), faculty teaching loads have grown lighter, outside sources of funding for faculty more varied and influential, and commitments and loyalties to activities and groups outside their institution more substantial? And will a majority of campus executives demonstrate the same courage and commitment they are seeking from their faculties?

I believe a new style of presidential and faculty leadership, one that is more appropriate to transformational change during a time of declining financial support, is not only desirable; it is also possible. But several other changes will need to pave the way.

To usher in the new era

The first change needed is in the selection process and criteria for presidents. At present three of the most important attributes that a successful presidential candidate must have at the great majority of institutions is a strong record as a teacher and scholar, some experience with administration that went smoothly and without controversy, and a proper disdain for academic management. Each of these three attributes seem open to serious question.

To be a transformational leader in higher education requires a major talent for managing organizational change, skill with people, and a dedication to intellectual life, as well as an ability to speak and write well, to disseminate and sell ideas and new ventures. Having been a distinguished physicist, literature professor, or economist may help, but may not be essential. Indeed those skills and habits often conflict with executive patterns. What is essential is that one know how to find and care for great teachers and

Administration needs to be radically reconceived.

scholars. Ex-governors, corporate leaders, campus vice presidents of finance, development, or student affairs, and others, can be, and occasionally have been, excellent university leaders. The narrow qualifications for a college presidency should be broadened. While claiming to seek visionary, adept leadership skills for large complex organizations, faculty at too many institutions screen out those candidates who are most interesting to the best trustees, then the board selects from those left the person who is least comfortable to the faculty.

The requisite that the candidate should never have been controversial or in trouble with his or her faculty is also subject to challenge. It results in "safe," shrewdly evasive, survivor presidents who would rather compromise than fight. It almost guarantees a relatively passive and non-entrepreneurial person because people who have battled for greater excellence, less economic waste, and new ways of doing things are almost certain to have made some enemies. The key question should be: have his or her enemies been the right ones? Have the difficulties been understandable and the results positive? Search committees should seek out movers and shakers and insist on studying the causes of professional or personal controversies, rather than shunning all persons who have been embroiled.

Currently the national academic grapevine prefers peace to pressure. This climate creates an irony: the more we know about a candidate for president, dean, or department chair the less likely we are to hire her or him.

The third change necessary is a new attitude toward the leadership and management of academe. Colleges and universities often distrust persons who set out to learn the difficult craft of university administration and who discuss their leadership aspirations openly. In business, the potential leaders are usually identified fairly early and are deliberately assigned positions in marketing, finance, foreign sales, and manufacturing or engineering so that they will develop the all-around expertise necessary for top management. Their professional ambitions are understood and monitored. At most colleges and universities, however, a comparable grooming of possible future leaders would be frowned upon if not strongly criticized as inappropriate to the historical values of campus administration. Intriguingly, the view that promising young women and men who show leadership potential should be trained and encouraged is evident in every organizational environment—religious, economic, athletic, political, military, interest group—except that of higher education.

But the only way we will have education leaders who are imaginative, strategically daring, and professionally trained is to depart from higher education's traditional view of campus leadership as the last bastion of proudly amateur management. After all, a dozen or so U.S. universities have annual budgets of a billion dollars a year, and hundreds of colleges and universities have operating budgets of a quarter billion dollars or more. U.S. higher education is bizarrely antiquarian in trying to run contemporary institutions as it did a half century ago. Today's universities resemble corporate holding companies, as Steven Muller, the ex-president of Johns Hopkins University, points out (1994):

[There has been] a transformation of the corporate structure of the university, from a centralized single entity into a holding company. True, faculties of law, medicine, and more recently, engineering had been earlier components of the university.... Generally some sense of community also continued to prevail. [But] as...the number and individual size of professional schools increased, each division began more and more to assume a corporate character of its own. This involved the structuring not only of each division's budget but of its own management as well....

A mega-sized university holding company no longer musters much sense of community.... [Moreover] the arts and sciences, or liberal arts, no longer constitute the acknowledged and determining core of the university. This erosion...is one of the significant and disturbing features of the current state of the research university in the United States.... In effect, therefore, the president no longer has a constituency in which the presidency can take root.

Higher education is trying to manage itself as if today's colleges and universities were still snug, little, collegial communities of 2,000 or so souls as they were in the 1920s. Colleges and universities have become huge, fragmented, complex, and very expensive enterprises. But our attitude toward their management is stuck in old notions of amateur and unobtrusive administrators, working collegially with a cooperative faculty who all share the same values. It seems grotesquely and perhaps suicidally inappropriate.

Maybe a new government

To urge that major colleges and universities should be led by a different kind of person and should be more adventurously managed, with a keener financial sense, inevitably suggests that the traditional notions of a single faculty senate, shared governance, and faculty control over major areas of university life may need to be revisited. Today, there are graduate student unions and other worker trade unions on campus; a third or half of the actual teaching force is not represented in the senate; there are perhaps a dozen senates (at the larger universities); colleges have competent and devoted staff members who have little voice; extremely accomplished alumni in leadership positions are learning to serve on visiting committees, evaluation teams, or school advisory bodies; there are new campus experts on digital technology; and more. The players in today's governance game may be stuck in a round of musical chairs where there are too many seats and the music is loud and dissonant.

Higher education's view of leadership is the last bastion of amateur management.

A forward-looking response is neither unimaginable nor unreachable. If the strongest, most caring faculty join with the most competent and courageous presidents, deans, and vice presidents to examine how new management patterns can serve both their interests, we will survive the triage crisis and be better for it. To question the faculty's governance role and reward system is not to undo their essential functions, any more than to question how we recruit and train campus leaders undermines the skills and importance of university presidents.

Our colleges and universities once lived on the colorful periphery of American life. Now the powerful intellectual base demanded by modern information-rich society puts higher education under everyone else's microscope. We can, we must foster a new generation of higher education leaders—faculty and administration—with academic integrity and fiscal management skills, to guide colleges and universities in the 21st century.

While reading a biography of James Bryant Conant, I came across a letter he wrote to his sister soon after he was appointed president of Harvard in 1933:

> It is the most thankless job in the U.S.A.... If the president does the right thing he can count on almost unanimous howls of disapproval.... I have few illusions about the posi-

tion. It will be very interesting and, I hope, satisfying; but on the whole, unpleasant and trying—a very, very lonely job.... Pray for me. I shall need it. ∎

REFERENCES

American Association of University Professors (AAUP). 1966. Statement on Government of Colleges and Universities. *AAUP Bulletin* 52 (4): 375-379.

AAUP. 1969. Policy on Representation of Economic and Professional Interests. *AAUP Bulletin* 55 (4): 489-491.

AAUP. 1970. Student Participation in College and University Government. *AAUP Bulletin* 56 (1): 33-35.

Baumol, W. and S. Blackman. 1995. How to Think About Rising College Costs. *Planning for Higher Education* 23 (4): 1-7.

Boulding, D. 1975. The Management of Decline. *AGB Reports* (September–October).

Breneman, D. 1995. *Higher Education: On a Collision Course with New Realities.* AGB Occasional Paper No. 22.

Eaton, J. 1995. Where Have All the Higher Education Leaders Gone? *Council Comments* 2 (6): 1-2.

Kennedy, D. 1994. Making Choices in the Research University. In J. Cole, E. Barber, and S. Graubard (eds.), *The Research University in a Time of Discontent.* Johns Hopkins University Press.

Kerr, C. 1994. *Higher Education Cannot Escape History: Issues for the 21st Century.* State University of New York Press.

Mortimer, K. and T. R. McConnell. 1978. *Sharing Authority Effectively.* Jossey-Bass.

Muller, S. 1994. Presidential Leadership. In *The Research University in a Time of Discontent.*

Report of the States. 1994. American Association of the State Colleges and Universities.

Rosovsky, H. 1991. Annual Report on the Faculty of Arts and Sciences, Harvard University. Reprinted in the *Harvard Gazette* (11 October).

Stresses on Research and Education at Colleges and Universities: Institutional and Sponsoring Agency Responses. 1994. Report of Collaborative Inquiry Conducted Jointly by the National Science Board and the Government-University-Industry Research Roundtable (July).

Veysey, L. 1965. *The Emergence of the American University.* University of Chicago Press.

How vital—really—is vision to planners and education leaders?

The Vision Thing in Higher Education

George Keller

L ately there has been expanding talk about how the planners and leaders in higher education need to "reinvent" America's colleges and universities for the changed conditions in the nation. If any educational group intends to reinvent its university or college it will need to have some idea of what the newly invented institution might look like. It is not sufficient to move away from existing problems, inefficiencies, and outmoded structures and programs. Toward what new directions should the group move? They will require a vision of what the renovated university or college could or should become.

The need for vision seems so obvious. Individually we have visions of becoming firemen, great violinists, major league pitchers, fashion models, famous authors, competent doctors or nurses, or owners of our own store or business. We labor to make ourselves more physically fit or financially

George Keller is editor of *Planning for Higher Education* and an award-winning consultant and education scholar and writer in Baltimore. He did his undergraduate and graduate work at Columbia; and has taught and administered at Columbia, SUNY, the University of Maryland, and the University of Pennsylvania. He is the author of many articles and reviews, and the book *Academic Strategy* (1983). This article is based on an invited address to the annual meeting of the American Council of Learned Societies in April 1994.

shrewd. We struggle to have a happy family life or a merry circle of friends. Collectively we often work to make the town we live in one of the loveliest and best run, to have our college be the friendliest and best teaching institution in the region, or to see that the United States is a land of opportunity and freedom for all citizens, as Martin Luther King, Jr. did so magnificently. Nearly all humans carry a dream in their pockets, a vision of what could be one day in the future.

Somehow through evolution, mysteriously, human beings have been provided with two kinds of vision. One is the animal recognition of material objects and movements with our eyes. The other is the ability to see with our minds, to imagine a new political condition, an ideal vegetable garden, a novel law school program. We can look back in time as we do with reflection, regret, or reevaluation; and we can look forward to conceive of a larger or smaller institution, a different organizational structure, a more strategic mode of operating in the decade ahead, or a new kind of international society linked by electronics and clever software. We are intelligent animals, intricately equipped for both sight and imagination. As one essayist recently wrote:

Our bodies demonstrate, albeit silently, that we are more than just a complex version of our animal ancestors to which a little dab of rationality has been added; and conversely that we are also more than an enlarged brain, a consciousness somehow grafted onto or trapped within a blind mechanism that knows only survival. The human form as a whole impresses on us its inner powers of thought (or awareness and action). Mind and hand, gait and gaze, breath and tongue, foot and mouth—all are isomorphically part of a single package, suffused with the presence of intelligence.[1]

The history of U.S. higher education is replete with stories of persons who imagined, who saw ahead in their minds a new kind of college or university: Charles William Eliot and Nicholas Murray Butler who transformed urban colleges for gentlemen into great universities at Harvard and Columbia; Emma Hart Willard, who envisioned young women studying as undergraduates as young men did; the Holy Cross fathers who imagined a Roman Catholic university in the wilds of northern Indiana at South Bend; president Wallace Sterling and provost Fred Terman who envisioned a post-World War II, Harvard-like university at Stanford for people on the West Coast; U.S. Congressman Justin Morrill of Vermont who imagined and fought for a new kind of public college in every state "to promote the liberal and practical education of the industrial classes"—the land-grant college; and Frank Aydelotte who envisioned an Oxford-like college in Swarthmore, Pennsylvania.

As I said, the need for vision seems obvious, and natural. Human beings are imaginative, envisioning creatures. Civilizations, and colleges and universities, are built and maintained and improved by people who possess a vision about a kind of life or institution different from the one that exists.

Phooey on vision

Yet in the 1990s there is a growing cynicism about vision. When IBM's new chairman, Louis Gerstner, was questioned at a press conference about how he intended to halt the decline of the corporation, he responded:

> There have been a lot of questions as to whether I'm going to deliver a vision for IBM. I would like to say that the last thing IBM needs right now is a vision. What it needs is very tough-minded...strategies for each of its businesses.

And Robert Eaton, the new chairman of the Chrysler Corporation, told the *Wall Street Journal*, "Internally we don't use the word vision. I believe in quantifiable short-term results—things we can all relate to, as

Human beings have been provided with two kinds of vision.

opposed to some esoteric thing no one can quantify." Billionaire William Gates, chairman of Microsoft Corporation, has sneered, "Being a visionary is trivial."

In higher education, a similar, growing disdain for vision can be heard. The new mood was perhaps best expressed in Richard Chait's opinion article in the September 22, 1993 *Chronicle of Higher Education*. In his view, "The 'vision thing' has been elevated nearly to the level of religion in higher education." But Chait contends, "The virtues of vision have been exaggerated. The concept should be enshrined in the pantheon of panaceas that already includes management by objectives, zero-based budgeting, quality-control circles, and TQM." Chait believes "these are not the times for heady visions," and he argues for an Adam Smith-like *laissez-faire* approach by campus administrators:

> For all the emphasis placed upon vision, observers of higher education would be hard pressed to cite more than a dozen or two colleges...that have been successfully "reinvented..." More often institutional priorities and opportunities emerge from individual and departmental initiatives...
>
> Freed of the obligation to craft a compelling and comprehensive vision college presidents can concentrate on crucial, if mundane, tasks like controlling costs, increasing productivity, diversifying their work forces, assessing quality and streamlining operations...
>
> Few professors are disposed to be guided, let alone summoned, by the North Star of a presidential vision...Presidents may do better to nip at the heels of the laggards, to contain the strays to the extent possible, and wait importantly, to nudge the entire herd along.[2]

Richard Chait is a member of the higher education faculty at the University of Maryland's School of Education, along with scholars Robert Birnbaum and Frank Schmitlein. Chait and his colleagues at Maryland have been leaders in the higher education studies field in deriding attempts to improve leadership, strategic planning, quality of service enhancement, and vision in academe. Adhering to the incrementalism of political scientist Charles Lindblom, who wrote that, "Patching up an old system is the most rational way to change it, for the patch constitutes about as big a change as one can comprehend at a time,"[3] the Maryland school of skeptics believes in the beneficent "hidden hand" of multifold and scattered initiatives, chiefly by the faculty.

In this the Maryland scholars reflect the views of dozens of college and university presidents I have met who feel they are able to be little more than highly paid janitors and dignified spokespersons, and who

The caretaker view of college leadership has become a perilous one.

are convinced that passive, unobtrusive administration of the semi-anarchic status quo is the only "realistic" course. They also concur with the view of Clark Kerr and others who argue that the new power of federal grant agencies, state commissioners of higher education, ambitious scholar-entrepreneurs in their midst, the courts, special-interest racial, gender, and ethnic groups, and the accrediting bodies prevent academic executives from having a vision of their own for their institution. In the words of Clark Kerr during his 1963 Godkin lectures at Harvard:

There is a "kind of lawlessness," in any large university…and the task is to keep this lawlessness within reasonable bounds…The president becomes the central mediator… among groups and institutions moving at different rates of speed and sometimes different directions…He has no new and bold "vision of

the end." He is driven more by necessity than by voices in the air.[4]

This Ronald Reagan-like perspective on modern academic leadership is, I think, a salutary caution, particularly against the sometimes hyperbolic claims for "reinventing" the university and those academic management texts which assume that campus deans and presidents have the charisma and power of England's Henry IV. To "reinvent" is to make over completely, or to reestablish in a very different form an already established institution. This is not very likely to happen. Universities are among the oldest, most conservative, and slowly adaptive organizations in Western civilization.[5]

The new demands

But the caretaker view of college leadership—administration without vision, patching up and nipping at the heels of the professorial laggards—has become a perilous one to advocate at the end of the 20th century. It is also flawed in its analysis and suppositions.

For one thing not having a vision is a kind of vision. To imagine that a college will remain pretty much the same over the next 15-20 years in the face of radical changes in demography, technology, and finances is an apparition—and a decision about the future—as much as a vision to double in size or to become more multicultural.

For another thing, if an institution has no vision, other persons or outside agencies may force a new mission, usually a more restricted or specialized one, on the institution. For a third item, a concentration on the basics—"good, solid blocking and tackling," as IBM's Louis Gerstner puts it—is quite appropriate for an organization that is badly run and in trouble because of ineptitude and neglect, and its lack of vision. The first priority for poorly run colleges, after all, is to get their house in order. TQM, well done, has been a considerable help to some colleges in this situation. But if a university is functioning fairly well, the priority becomes: what should it do in the future to maintain its position and excellence? Or to move to a slightly higher level of quality?

There are larger reasons for vision in higher education, however. It is not an historical accident that the calls for greater attention to the future began in the late 1960s and reached an almost nagging emphasis in the 1970s and 1980s. Herman Kahn and Daniel Bell (who invented the term "post-industrial society") in 1967, Michael Young in

How can a university decentralize and still have a coordinated effort?

1968, and Peter Drucker in 1969 were prominent among those who pointed out that North America and Western Europe were at the edge of major social, technological, demographic, and economic changes.[6]

After the 1965 amendments to the Immigration and Nationality Act, the United States began admitting more immigrants (including 150,000 to 300,000 illegal entries) each year than all the rest of the developed world combined, ushering in a new period of multiculturalism. The personal computer was introduced. The traditional two-parent family began disintegrating. Since the family has long been the co-educator of children, the change has meant new problems for the schools and cities. Out-of-wedlock births have increased rapidly to the point where 30 percent of all babies are now born in that way. Adult education has become a giant, growing addition to the customary youth education for many colleges and universities. And America faces new financial pressures from Japan and other countries abroad and from escalating expenses for crime prevention and prisons, pollution, pensions for the elderly, and health care from inside the nation. In short, the environment has become very turbulent, and educators are increasingly being asked to respond to the radical changes and "reinvent" their structures and services for the new environment.

A second source of pressure for greater vision is from those who think that the increasing decentralization and fragmentation of universities and many colleges demands something to hold the institution together—what two business professors have called "superordinate goals." These are "significant meanings or guiding concepts that an organization imbues in its members."[7] In effect, a vision of where the institution is going seems necessary to bind together the loose coupling of many campus parts.

As colleges grew larger, and as numerous universities (and some community colleges) expanded to 25,000 to 40,000 students in the 1970s, educational leaders pushed decisions out of the president's and academic vice president's office to the schools, departments, and divisions. This frequently resulted in quasi-independent medical, business, or law schools, or departments of physics or economics, or maintenance or student affairs divisions. The question thus becomes: How can a university decentralize and at the same time have a coordinated effort? As two scholars put it:

> How can people in the far reaches of these flatter organizations know where it is heading? The development of a shared organizational vision represents a response to this problem.[8]

There are other pressures to create a vision. Colleges and universities have long lead times. Change at most campuses is remarkably slow, with long debates over the processes, details, and educational policies. New facilities often have to be planned for five to eight years in advance. And students are preparing for work in society 10 to 20 years from the present. Therefore, a vision that imagines the institution 10 years hence is an enormous help. Also, arriving at a desirable vision for the institution's future circumvents some of the fierce discussion about the details of the present situation and immediate reallocations. A vision enables academics to think seriously about the purposes, priorities, and distinctiveness of their college or university without threats to current positions and arrangements.

Then too, Henry Mintzberg of Canada's McGill University has argued that strategic planning is largely instrumental. It provides reasonable priorities and detailed steps after the leaders have formulated a vision. For him, "Planning does not promote significant change in the organization so much as deal with it when it is introduced by other means." To him "A plan as vision—expressed in imagery, or metaphorically—may prove a greater incentive to action than a plan that is formally detailed, simply because it is more attractive and less constraining."[9] A vision with some emotional content is often more likely to spur action toward a rearranged college than a well-conceived strategy; and it gives faculty members a greater freedom to invent.

Vision's key ingredients

Vision is not the same as a mission statement, which is almost always a bland stew of platitudes, beliefs, and vague goals. Vision is a combination of gut values and a tangible goal.

The gut values need to be ones that are part of the college's tradition and that at least a large minority of people on campus already subscribe to. If the values articulated in a vision are too idealistic or vague, the vision will be treated cynically. The values must be genuine and specific. For example, a rigorous, historic liberal arts college might say, "Our college will continue to educate a small number of very able undergraduates for the highest positions in society through intense and scholarly study with exceptional scholar-teachers." Or, a major, large state university might advocate something like benefactor Ezra Cornell did when he established Cornell University: "I would found an institution where any person can find instruction in any study," thus giving equal value to poultry science, forestry, and labor relations and to history, literature, and science.

But if a college proclaims it will be a place giving primary importance to the cultivation of every individual's personal and intellectual growth—as half of America's colleges seem to do in their catalogs—when faculty union members, the director of athletics, or the dean of students actually have other priorities, the values will be only a fanciful bro-

mide rather than an authentic expression of gut values. L. L. Bean, the Maine clothing and camping merchant, said in 1947: "Sell good merchandise at a reasonable price, and treat your customers as you would your

The vision must have a tangible outcome.

friends, and the business will take care of itself." These were Bean's gut values.

But it is not enough to express one's deepest values in the vision statement. The vision must also have a tangible outcome. It should be an inspiring picture of a different future, something that seems slightly out of reach but achievable if enough people work on it, as when President John Kennedy proclaimed in 1961 as a vision, "before this decade is out, of landing a man on the moon and returning him safely to earth."

The tangible outcome is tricky. It should not be too definite and detailed, yet vivid enough to allow persons to imagine a new and better set of conditions and services and to strive toward their fulfillment. For instance, in 1909 Henry Ford said his vision was, "to democratize the automobile." The statement did not suggest the Model T but made it clear that the Ford Motor Company would concentrate on low-cost cars, not Cadillac-like vehicles. The vision implied a target audience and the kind of automobile with which the company would seek preeminence.

There are two kinds of tangible outcomes. One is that of setting a clear, unambiguous target. Here are some fictional examples of targeting:

"Within the next 20 years our university will become the near-equal of Harvard for Southern youths and adults."

"We will become widely known as the best managed and financially open private college in our region."

"The college will in the next 10 years be the finest teaching institution among state colleges in our state."

"Our state university will be smaller, more focused, and regarded as one of the top 10 or 12 public universities in the nation."

The other kind of tangible outcome is that of institutional transformation, of picturing a slightly "reinvented" institution to meet the emerging realities of the next decades. Again, some fictional examples:

> "The university will have more Blacks, Latinos, and Asians among its students and faculty, and reorient its curriculum and scholarship to be more international and multicultural."

> "Our university will employ the most advanced technology for teaching, financial planning and controls, and new linkages with other academic, cultural, and scientific entities."

> "Recognizing the increase in state and community colleges, this historic state university will enlarge its graduate education, research, and leadership in professional education, admitting fewer undergraduates and chiefly those of demonstrated scholarly interests."

Misconceptions and fallacies

One of the most common errors that critics of vision make is their assertion that vision requires a charismatic or exceptionally clairvoyant president. This is patently untrue. Some department chairpersons have created extraordinary collections of scholars in their department. I have often been told that a "visionary" financial officer has kept some institution's eyes on long-term financial strength rather than short-term expenditures. Three times in my travels I have encountered directors of buildings and grounds who take unusual pride in their work and staff and have a vision of what the campus grounds and horticulture will look like in the next decade.

Another error is that visionaries are dreamers, ambitious utopians who can't and won't pay attention to costs, details, and current problems. They lack realism, with realism usually defined as accommodation to the status quo and small, incremental changes at the edges. The fact is that good visions usually emerge from attention to the myriad workings of the institution, not a neglect of such attention. And even small changes can't be carried out effectively unless one has a vision of the direction toward which the small changes should be made.

Some of the most acerbic critics of "vision" have an implicit vision of their own

about where the college or university should be going, although there is also a small but growing band of higher education scholars who seem resigned to drift, semi-anarchy, and lack of fiscal priorities or controls as the only satisfactory way of administering a varied, rambunctious, and quarrelsome collection of specialized scholars. To them, a vision seems confining rather than a bonding agent which provides purpose and distinctiveness to an institution competing with numerous other of the 3,500 colleges and universities in the United States.

However, there are several key ingredients that educators who would develop and promote a vision must possess. One is a sense of history, of what works and doesn't in social organizations, especially during times of change. Another is a willingness to understand the public's view as well as the parochial campus interests. Peter Drucker once expressed it this way:

> [The visionary leader] has to establish himself as a spokesman for the interest of society in producing, in performing, in achieving...He has to become the proponent, the educator, the advocate. The manager, in other words, will have to learn to create the "issues."[10]

The vision of an education leader should connect the private interests of the professors and staff to the public urgencies of society in the years ahead.

Educators and planners also need to sharpen their imaginative thinking. Faculty members are passionately devoted to "critical thinking" but they say very little about *creative thinking*, which is in our time has

Colleges lack sufficient powers of social invention.

become essential. Our colleges and universities, as well as America's other institutions, lack sufficient powers of social invention. No one ever used creative thinking about social life better than Alexis de Tocqueville, when he observed Americans, identified the central features of young

America, and constructed a pattern for future developments in this country.[11] In recent years more strategic planners and educators have become adept at analyzing the thrusts and novel features of society and have begun to help create visions and strategic plans to implement the visions.[12]

An emotional lever for change

In a remarkable new book Antonio Damasio, one of the world's leading neuroscientists, has provided scientific evidence of "Descartes' error," the notion that there is an area of the brain that is capable of pure, objective thought.[13] Damasio and others have demonstrated in the past decade that every part of the brain is tied to emotion and to physical movements. People are creatures of their genetic material, their environmental conditioning, and their emotions.

Visions have emotional power. They help us organize our knowledge and supply hope, passion, and direction. They help

Visions speak to our entire selves.

give meaning to our lives. Visions speak to our entire selves rather than just to dry-as-felt goals or quantifiable objectives.

If colleges and universities are to reform their structures, finances, and services they will have to possess some vision of how they will do so, and why. The vision for any institution should combine its tradition, culture, and core values with the emerging conditions in society and with the public's expectations about higher education's role and behavior in the new environment.

The vision may take root in one of a university's colleges which is led by a far-sighted dean. It can originate with department or division chairs, or with a courageous vice president. It can be forced by a strong, forward-looking Board of Trustees if the president and faculty drag their feet. Whatever its source, each college and university should design a vision for itself. David Riesman once wrote,

There has always been room for innovation and fresh starts in American higher education, even if this freedom, which rested partly on expanding enrollments and funds, is more circumscribed now. What is really lacking is strong and visionary academic leadership.[14] ∎

NOTES

1. Leon Kass, *The Hungry Soul: Eating and the Perfecting of Our Nature* (Free Press, 1994), 75-76. See also George Keller, "Neuroscience and the New Foundations of Transformational Planning." Paper presented at the 29th Annual Conference of the Society for College and University Planning, on July 26, 1994, in San Francisco.

2. Richard Chait, "Colleges Should Not Be Blinded by Vision," *Chronicle of Higher Education*, September 22, 1993, B1, B2.

3. Robert Dahl and Charles Lindblom, *Politics, Economics, and Welfare* (University of Chicago Press, 1976), 86.

4. Clark Kerr, *The Uses of the University* (Harvard University Press, 1963), 35, 37.

5. It is instructive to read medieval historian Charles Homer Haskins' *The Rise of Universities* (Cornell University Press, 1957).

6. Herman Kahn and Anthony Weiner, *The Year 2000: A Framework for Speculation* (Collier Macmillan, 1967); Daniel Bell, "Notes on the Post-Industrial Society," *Public Interest*, No. 6 (1967): 24-35, No. 7 (1967): 102-118; Michael Young (ed.). *Forecasting and the Social Sciences* (London: Heinemann, 1968); Peter Drucker, *The Age of Discontinuity* (Harper & Row, 1969).

7. Richard Tanner Pascale and Anthony Athos, *The Art of Japanese Management* (Warner Books, 1982), 125.

8. James Collins and Jerry Porras, "Organizational Vision and Visionary Organizations," *California Management Review* 34 (Fall 1991): 1.

9. Henry Mintzberg, *The Rise and Fall of Strategic Planning* (Free Press, 1994), 292-293.

10. Peter Drucker, *Managing in Turbulent Times* (Harper & Row, 1980), 218.

11. Alexis de Tocqueville, *Democracy in America* (Oxford University Press, 1947).

12. George Keller, *Academic Strategy* (Johns Hopkins University Press, 1983).

13. Antonio Damasio, *Descartes' Error: Emotion, Reason, and the Human Brain* (G. P. Putnam's Sons, 1994).

14. Quoted in Keller, 164.

Lots of effort, but do they say anything?

Are Mission Statements Worthwhile?

Walter Newsom and C. Ray Hayes

Most devotees of academic planning believe the planning process should begin with a mission statement or a clear statement of what a college or university does, for whom, how, and why. The mission statement should be a declaration of the special purposes of an institution and whom it intends to serve. It is a revelation of the college's reason for being.

From the mission statement should flow the goals and objectives of the college or university and therefore the activities which the institution's members will pursue. The mission statement should focus the attention of both those who plan and those who implement the plans — at least that is the theory. In the past we have subscribed to the theory

---

Walter Newsom is professor emeritus of management in the College of Business and Industry at Mississippi State University. Dr. Newsom received his undergraduate degree from the University of Michigan and two additional degrees from the University of Missouri.

C. Ray Hayes is the Executive Vice President for Finance & Administration at Texas A&M University-Corpus Christi. Previously, he held several administrative appointments at Mississippi State University. He received his M.B.A. from Mississippi State.

and to the importance of mission statements.

In recent years, however, both of us have been dismayed at several university mission statements we have seen because they did so little to focus activity. Rather, the statements seemed to represent a compromise designed to offend no one and at best to limit a few options. So we decided to conduct a small study to learn more exactly whether colleges were creating pointed mission statements from which specific objectives and lines of activity could derive.

We selected 142 institutions in eleven southeastern states, all listed in the *HEP'88 Higher Education Directory*. We then chose every fifth institution for a systematic sample and classified each as public, private, or sectarian as listed in the categories of the directory. Our questionnaire was sent to the president of each campus, and we asked each to send us a copy of the college's mission statement, if it had one. We sent a follow-up letter two months later to those who had not replied. Of the 142 institutions, 114 replied, or 80 percent. Not overwhelming, but a large enough percentage to hazard some generalizations. Of the 90 public institutions solicited, 69 percent returned written mission statements; of the 21 privates, 57 percent sent statements; of the 31 sectarian,

61 percent mailed mission statements. Altogether, we had 93 mission statements to read and analyze.

For our analysis of the 93 mission statements, we used a variation of the eight dimensions used by Pearce and David (1987) in their survey of Fortune 500 companies' corporate mission statements. We used seven dimensions—e.g., Target Clienteles, or Constituencies the College Wants to Serve—and examined each statement separately to determine which of the seven dimensions the statement contained. (See Table 1.) We also analyzed the responses for other elements.

What's the Mission?

All but two of the respondents indicated their college had a mission statement, suggesting that a large percentage of colleges and universities in the United States have a statement. We asked where the mission statements can be found on campus. Most respondents (91 percent) said the statement was located in their catalog of courses; also prominent were the faculty handbook and key documents to the board of trustees.

We were also interested in learning whether colleges and universities were active in reassessing or rewriting their mission statements. Eighty-four percent indicated they had "reevaluated" their mission statement in the past five years, and 70 percent said they had "rewritten" theirs. Colleges and universities appear diligent in keeping their statements up-to-date. Why? Accreditation purposes was the chief reason, with administrative reasons and strategic planning as the second and third reasons most frequently cited.

In response to the question "Was the mission statement used, and if so, how?" most did not list any use! A few said they used the statement during program evaluations or in the consideration of a proposed new program, but few claimed they used it for strategic-planning directions. Most striking of all, in analyzing each mission statement, we found that a relatively small percentage of statements were specific in most of the seven dimensions (Table 1). Public universities were likely to get specific about the geographic region they served, while private and sectarian institutions were specific most often in their philosophy and public image.

It does not cost a public institution much to identify the region it serves. And private and sectarian colleges need to describe the philosophy that separates them from other institutions. But most of the mission statements are amazingly vague, evasive, or rhetorical, lacking specificity or clear purposes.

Non-Statements of Mission

Where do these findings leave the traditional belief that planning should begin with a clear statement of mission? We suspect it may demolish the idea.

It appears to be the case that most U.S. colleges and universities have a mission statement. Many institutions even dust it off every few years for a visit by an accrediting team, or for a new round of program reviews, or when a new president arrives. Hundreds of manhours of expensive administrator and faculty labor are spent to reassess or rewrite the document. But while institutions think they must have a mission statement, they feel no obligation to say anything specific in it. Although the statement itself is

Few colleges find much use for their mission statements.

regarded as essential, its content seems utterly unimportant. We found that when we hid the institution's name, most of the colleges or universities could not be identified from their statements because they all read alike, full of honorable verbiage signifying nothing. Not surprisingly, few colleges find much use for their mission statements. They are usually not guidelines for serious planning.

Does this mean mission statements are

Table 1. Percent of Colleges Whose Mission Statements Contained Specific Purposes

Dimensions of Mission	Public	Private	Sectarian	Total
1. Target clienteles: What constituencies does the college want to have?	30%	50%	19%	30%
2. Products: What outputs beyond general teaching, research, and service does the college intend?	31%	42%	31%	33%
3. Geography: What specific location will the college serve?	74%	25%	0%	54%
4. Commitment: What will be emphasized for survival or growth?	43%	58%	25%	42%
5. Philosophy: What are the college's specific beliefs, values, and philosophical priorities?	31%	67%	75%	44%
6. Self definition: How does the institution view itself?	36%	50%	19%	35%
7. Public image: What reputation does the college wish to have among the public?	46%	75%	94%	58%

a waste of time? In their present form, we would answer, yes. But we found a few documents that were quite courageously specific, and these seemed to point the way for planners. If universities can find a way to substitute the vapid consensus of the present statements for a sharp, specific definition of their distinctive role in society, then mission statements can be the proper beginning for activities like a planning exercise, program reviews, curriculum design, and admissions. ∎

REFERENCE

Pearce, John, and David, Fred. "Corporate Mission Statements: The Bottom Line." *Academy of Management Executive*, I (May 1987), 109–115.

Colleges need to get the process right.

Sheep in Wolves' Clothing, or How Not to Do Strategic Planning

Rebecca Stafford

O ften, when I have taught in strategic planning seminars, participants bring their mission statements and the strategic academic plans of their institutions for discussion. Most of them are astonishingly similar. I suspect the campus administrators attending these seminars could not match the planning documents of the other institutions correctly even though the colleges and universities represented are of different kinds (Newsome and Hayes 1990-91).

Who cares? one might ask. I do, for one. And so should the faculty and leaders of these institutions. We live in turbulent times, and money, good students, and fresh ideas are scarce. Serious planning, clear

---

Rebecca Stafford is the new president of Monmouth University, New Jersey. Previously she was president of Chatham College in Pittsburgh and of Minnesota's Bedmidji State University. A graduate of Radcliffe College who earned her Ph.D. at Harvard, she has taught sociology, served as dean of arts and sciences at the University of Nevada, Reno, and worked as executive vice president of Colorado State University. The author of articles and books, she has given strategic planning workshops, and taught at Carnegie-Mellon University's summer College Management Program.

priorities, and hard choices are imperative.

A good strategic plan for a college or university is expected to scan the regional and local environment of the school, to have a deep knowledge of the college's clientele and its competitor institutions, to honestly assess the college's strengths and weaknesses, and then to derive a limited set of purposes (or mission) and select the strategic emphases and initiatives to implement those special purposes. It should clearly proclaim the college's niche in the 3400-institution higher education marketplace, or, to put it more academically, the unique contribution the college can make to U.S. higher education. Kenyon College should have a very different strategic plan from Ohio State. Stevens Institute of Technology should have a different strategy from California Institute of Technology. And Pittsburgh's Chatham College (for women) should have different priorities from Hollins College in rural Virginia. Real strategic plans cannot, by definition, look alike.[1]

What is going on here? I think a central problem is the confusion of consultation with creation. Consultation with the numerous constituencies in the college or university is vital. One of the great benefits of a planning process is the opportunity it allows for discussion among various groups

279

about the direction, priorities, and purpose of the institution. But the creation of strategy—like most acts of creation—ought to be accomplished by a small, special group, or even by one or two persons, and then submitted for criticism. It should not be written by several committees. The wider the involvement in the actual formulation, the more likely a college is to have a vague, politically unassailable plan that is hard to distinguish from other vague, pallid plans. In the attempt to incorporate the conflicting ideas of the numerous constituents and not to offend any group, all the priorities and the uniqueness are wrung out of the plan.

What is wrong with many collegiate strategic plans is that they are the outcome not of research, sound financial thinking, academic priorities, and courageous decisionmaking but of a poorly led, intensely political process wherein each constituency is allowed to add its particular pork projects to the barrel. The purposes of the college expand, the goals increase in number and scope, and the strategic initiatives multiply like rabbits (Schmidtlein and Milton 1988-89). This may be marginally acceptable behavior for the U.S. Congress, but it should not be the way a college or university behaves in charting its future.

Some modest proposals

I have found seven weaknesses that characterize many of the more platitudinous university plans and render them almost useless as decision-making directives for future operations and growth. These weaknesses—and their correctives—derive not just from planning seminars but from my numerous consultations with administrators and faculty at a variety of colleges and universities over the past decade.

1. *The vision, or mission statement, should define precisely the principal business of the college or university.* If the college thinks it should modify its mission in the coming decades because of changing conditions, that should be transparently clear in the statement. The mission should be specific enough to exclude other kinds of academic activity. Microsoft, for example, creates and sells

computer software. It does not manufacture computer hardware, computer chips, or devices for the hearing impaired.

Academic mission statements, however, rarely make such choices. Instead, they claim "to explore, understand, and improve ourselves, society, and our world," as one statement read. Or they are committed to "personal, social, and intellectual growth and to personal integrity coupled with a concern for others" and promise "to graduate citizens of the world who lead responsible, reflective, and creative lives." One state university plan said its purpose was: "Teaching at all levels from associate through doctoral level programs as well as continuing education and non-credit programs; [conducting] pure and applied research, scholarship, and creative activity; providing high-quality education at a reasonable cost; assessing and responding to

Few colleges identify what they are really good at.

the needs of the state, the nation, and the international community at large, not to mention enhancing the economic development of the state and providing public service." I would be hard-pressed to conceive of a single academic activity that could not be included in that statement. Admittedly, large state universities have a broader mission than smaller liberal arts colleges; but they too should designate some priorities for themselves among the several public institutions in the state and among the state universities in their region. The key questions are : Exactly what will your college concentrate on doing, and for whom? How will it accomplish this specific mission?

2. *An action strategy should be based on a thoughtful and credible assessment of the future environment for the school.* It is amazing how many colleges and universities conduct a scholarly assessment of the demographics, economy, technological changes, and political situation surrounding them—and then ignore or contradict the assessment. For ex-

ample, the plan of one university I recall pointed out that many of its students were first-generation attendees, interested largely in career preparation programs at the bachelor's degree level. The appraisal specifically noted a decline in enrollment in the university's graduate programs. Yet, the plans for this university urged a stronger concentration on liberal arts subjects and the establishment of new doctoral programs. A college I remember noted the shrinking pool of traditional college-aged students and the intense competition from the better-known colleges in the area, then proposed in its plan to grow enrollment by one-third and increase the college's selectivity.

Surely, environmental changes should not dictate a college's policy. But neither should universities and colleges plan utopian or foolishly ambitious efforts that swim against the torrent of new sociological, intellectual, and economic conditions. Higher education is not excluded from Darwinian adaptability.

3. *The strategic plan should build on the strengths of an institution and seek to eliminate weaknesses.* Relatively few colleges identify the activities at which they excel. They seem to fear giving offense to the weaker elements in their operations. And often, when they do list their strengths, they are so vague that the strengths cannot be used to create a competitive advantage or seize a market niche. For instance, one university listed as its two main strengths that it was the only one in the northeast corner of the state and it was committed to excellence. Another university, puffed with pride, lists as its distinguishing strategy its quality education, dedicated faculty, high-quality students, affirmative action program, attractive campus, ability to attract research grants, the internship program, and athletics.

Even fewer institutional plans are honest about weaknesses, though lack of money pops up often. It is probably a case of not wanting to hang one's frayed clothing in public. But if a college fails to identify its shortcomings, how can it develop strategies to eradicate them? I do remember one

university that mentioned problems with program isolation and inflexible scheduling, weaknesses that could be eliminated in an action plan.

4. *The strategic initiatives in a plan should be few and quite specific.* Colleges and universities should lay out the three to five directions on which the institution will focus attention and resources to build a comparative advantage and achieve its pointed mission. But the goals of many strategic plans I have examined are far too numerous to provide any guide for action. Often they are not compatible with the particular situation the college faces, and some are internally contradictory.

For example, one university plan listed 16 priority goals: providing a more positive environment, improving the quality of teaching and advising, increasing support for faculty scholarship, developing new delivery systems, providing for international experiences, improving institutional research and planning, stabilizing enrollment, increasing funding, utilizing space more efficiently, increasing the quality of administrative services, enhancing the university's image—well, you get the picture. Another university plan I recall had 12 objectives, from establishing an assessment system to "taking a leadership posi-

Without priorities a college has a mere shopping list.

tion in higher education." For one thing, many of these goals are *operational* improvements not new *strategic* initiatives. For another, they point to so many initiatives that faculty and administrators must feel overwhelmed and disheartened.

Also, many of the strategic plans I have examined read like the mantra of higher educational professionals. The initiatives are not only too numerous but they also lack specificity and usually refer obscurely to enhancements, improvements, commitments, and strengthenings. It is a curious language crafted to make people feel good rather than to act upon. It proclaims exalted aims rather than delineates specific moves.

5. *The plan should contain new courses of action in priority order.* Hardly any strategic plans I have seen prioritize their suggested initiatives. In fact, the authors of one plan, after concluding that the institution's current programs urgently had to be exam-

---

The time has come to shed woolly thinking.

---

ined to reduce expenses where feasible, quickly added that the planning committee did not try to identify any priorities for either increased or decreased funding. Another planning document I recall listed several broad goals, insisting they were in no priority order, then it recommended that the readers turn to an appendix, where there were four tightly packed pages of other equally important priorities.

The definition of a priority is something that "comes before in time, order, or importance." One simply cannot have 15 or 20 "priorities." Planners must decide what should be done first or which is more important. Without priorities a college has a mere shopping list not an understandable plan of action. Again, campus politics, cowardice, the desire to hurt no one's feelings, indecisiveness, and ignorance about how best to leverage organizational change all contribute to the unwillingness of many planning groups and campus leaders to give precedence to some initiatives over others.

6. *The strategic plan should suggest areas where the university can trim expenses and which programs should be reduced or discontinued.* Plan after plan I have read proposes that the college grow, increase, enhance, develop, improve, and expand. Almost none proposes to combine, substitute, shrink, or—heaven forbid—delete. This is true even for institutions where enrollments and finances are declining!

Occasionally, planners will suggest that the campus appraise all the academic programs, using good criteria such as quality,

student demand, centrality to the purpose of the institution, and costs. But either the program and department appraisals are not carried out or the final appraisals are reported in such a way that nearly every program seems to be of equal quality, popularity, importance, and cost. Therefore, no program can be eliminated or even reduced. The often-described proliferation of courses, faculty, and staff, recently labeled "lattice and ratchet" pressures (Pew-University of Pennsylvania Higher Education Research Program 1990) thus pushes on. And colleges and universities are increasingly accused of behaving like bloated government agencies rather than like wisely managed and financially responsible intellectual entities.

7. *The strategic plan should always include estimates of the costs of the strategic initiatives.* While I have seen two or three exceptions over the years, almost none of the plans estimate the amount of funding or point to the sources of revenue that will be necessary to implement the plan. At most, the plan will mention that "increased funding will be necessary to carry out the plan." Several of the briefer plans I have read include proposals for higher faculty salaries, more financial aid, increased numbers of faculty and staff, a new building or two, new academic programs, and more modern technological and scientific equipment. These proposals can add up to tens of millions of dollars! Yet the plans usually contain no cost data and only a vague suggestion about a capital campaign in the near future.

Colleges and universities can only frustrate their constituencies and look ridiculous to savvy outsiders if they do not consider as an integral part of each plan where the money will come from and roughly how much will be needed. Strategic plans that omit financial planning as an essential component only further the "Ivory Tower" stereotype.

Wolves and sheep

Colleges and universities that engage in strategic planning are supposed to be like wolves—streamlined carnivores constantly on the alert for the feeble or sick or those peripheral to the pack's health and welfare. Wolves police their own members to strengthen the pack's dominance of its particular territory. Wolf packs have survived harsh climates, lean years, and hunters, and still they flourish.

But the strategic plans of too many colleges and universities do not help them to function as cagey wolf packs but rather as herds of sheep obliviously overgrazing the landscape, mindlessly ignoring the herd's real long-term needs, and being too fearful to act collectively and boldly for their own longevity.

The plans usually contain no cost data.

Some fat-sheep colleges and universities will continue to graze heedlessly because of their reputations, large endowments, or partisan advocates in the state legislature. But for most, the time has come to shed woolly thinking and wish-list planning and resolutely sharpen their mission, determine their special character and their niche among the 3400 institutions of higher education, build on their strengths, and concentrate on change through the successful achievement of a few, well-chosen strategic actions. These actions should be persistently implemented, supported in part by reductions in some other areas, and be cost effective and fundable.

Colleges and universities need to become wolves in woolen suits, fierce and shrewd protectors of their own futures. They should stop being faint-hearted sheep with wolf-like howls and dense rhetoric, bleating when they should be acting and strategically and courageously. ∎

ENDNOTE

1. The literature abounds with guidance on strategic planning, but I like three sources: George Keller, *Academic Strategy* (Johns Hopkins University Press, 1983); Douglas Steeples (ed.) *Successful Strategic Planning: Case Studies* (Jossey-Bass, 1988); and Patrick Below, George Morrisey, and Betty Acomb, *The Executive Guide to Strategic Planning* (Jossey-Bass, 1990).

REFERENCES

Newsome, W. and C. R. Hayes. 1990-91. Are Mission Statements Worthwhile? *Planning for Higher Education,* 19 (2): 28-30.

Pew-University of Pennsylvania Higher Education Research Program. 1990. The Lattice and the Ratchet. *Policy Perspectives,* 2 (4): 1-8. *See also,* Massey, W. 1989. A Strategy for Productivity Improvement in College and University Academic Departments. Paper presented at the Forum for Postsecondary Governance, Santa Fe, New Mexico.

Schmidtlein, F. and T. Milton. 1988-89. College and University Planning: Perspectives from a Nationwide Study. *Planning for Higher Education,* 17 (3): 1-19.

Why planning sometimes stumbles, and how colleges can increase its success.

The Two Cultures of Academe: An Overlooked Planning Hurdle

Robert Newton

A t the 1991 SCUP annual conference in Seattle I encountered several academic administrators who observed that the conference had a dearth of sessions designed specifically for academic planning. The purpose of SCUP, one person said, seemed to be the adaptation of corporate and architectural planning models to higher education. Several of these administrators, and many faculty I know, are uneasy that the spread of such business planning techniques will erode traditional university values.

On the other hand, the strategic planning literature and articles about the behavior of professors and high school teachers

Robert Newton is associate academic vice president at Boston College. A graduate of the University of Scranton, he holds graduate degrees from Fordham, Yale, and Harvard. He served as headmaster at New York City's Regis High School, a selective Jesuit secondary school, and taught at the University of San Francisco before coming to Boston College in 1980. He is the author of numerous articles on curriculum and academic organization issues.

charge that most faculty and teachers have been reluctant to change despite radically new conditions, seem oblivious to crucial matters such as money, enrollments, and public opinion, and prefer "organized anarchy" (Cohen and March 1974) to a coherent institutional purpose, harmonious new initiatives, and thoughtful organizational adaptation.

I think both camps are right. Moreover, I believe the tension is indigenous to the *universitas magistrorum et scholarium*, the corporate body of masters and students. A university or college is necessarily both a corporation, or organized, business-like body or guild, and a very personal, sometimes contentious community of teachers and learners. Though numerous scholars have written about the "culture" of individual institutions in higher education (Clark 1980, 1987; Dill 1982; Kuh and Whitt 1988; Schein 1985; Tierney 1988, 1990), I think every good college and university has within it *two* cultures, not unlike the two mindsets that C.P. Snow described in *The Two Cultures* 33 years ago (1959).

These two cultures in academe make

college or university planning an especially difficult venture, a fact not always sufficiently acknowledged. And it means that higher education planning requires an unusual degree of mutual understanding and respect, of diplomacy, and of generosity of spirit. It suggests that higher education planning will always be different in its procedures and unusual in its style.

To get the two cultures to agree on one collaborative course of strategic action for the institution requires an exceptional understanding of the history and nature of the university and a special kind of leadership.

The corporate community

The one culture—the corporate community—tends to view universities mainly as business organizations, as pieces of the $140-billion, 3400-institution U.S. higher education industry, delivering education and training to clients at a price they can afford. Persons in this culture point out that universities have substantial capital assets and huge operating budgets. (Major U.S. universities today have annual budgets of a half billion to one billion dollars a year.) Many colleges and most universities contain residence halls, scientific laboratories, restaurants, parking garages, sports arenas, libraries, offices, theaters, student centers, classroom buildings, religious chapels, and power plants. The campus police force at some suburban and rural institutions can be as large as the law enforcement division of their surrounding towns.

People of this culture are mindful that modern colleges and universities have a highly differentiated workforce: experts in accounting and finance, personnel, psychological counseling, institutional research, admissions and financial aid, construction and maintenance, alumni relations, purchasing, fundraising, government lobbying, athletic coaching, public relations, computer programming, information and records management, mail distribution, and book acquisition, not to mention in-house legal counsel and job placement offices (Rehder 1979). Almost none of these

professionals has anything direct to do with teaching and learning. And among these staff persons unruly students and outspoken professors are often mentioned as a source of problems for the smooth functioning of the college.

The corporate community is involved with market research and publicity, government aid programs, classroom design and furniture, competitive strategies and comparative advantages, serving the customer, and cost-efficiency ratios. They are responsive to outside publics: the press, school guidance counselors, legislators and other politicians, alumni, minority leaders, the courts, potential employers, parents, church officials. They experiment with total quality management to improve their services; they accept measurable performance targets and administrative hierarchies; they use outside experts, from architects to auditors. Many in this culture believe that the university's scholarship and teaching would collapse in a few years without their diligence.

Every good college and university has within it two cultures.

In this culture, central planning, and continuous change and adaptation are necessary, supervision is normal, the financial condition of the institution is of vital interest, and the physical appearance and working condition of the facilities are important. The university usually is viewed as a business enterprise—of a significantly different kind. The corporate community may boast that "our university is one of the largest employers in our region," or that "ours is a well-run organization."

The community of scholars

The second culture—the community of scholars—views the college as a near-sacred institution with a special and indispensable mission, a mission that is more similar to that of medicine and religion than to that of industry and commercial services.

For many faculty, teaching is not just part of a job description but an integral component of a vocation that passes on the best of civilization's accomplishments. Students are not consumers or clients, but neophyte members of a select intellectual community devoted to exploring the perennial questions of humankind and the best new ideas and methods of inquiry of the scholarly disciplines. Knowledge is important not just to prepare for a career but for its own sake, and one of the duties of the masters is to inspire students to extend the heritage of knowledge, great ideas, and great art.

Members of this culture believe they are the central, driving force of the college's vitality, reputation, and success. The university changes and moves forward through the work of individual scholars; changes should emerge from the bottom up rather than from the top down. Under the benevolent and seldom intrusive guidance of a department head or dean, individual teachers and scholars set their own teaching and research agenda and decide what courses should be taught.

Members of the second culture believe they are the central, driving force.

The organization is held together by collegiality and persuasion and not by administrative direction and compliance. The academic organization chart should be simple and flat rather than complex and hierarchical, resembling a small cottage enterprise rather than a complex corporation. To those in this culture, faculty and students are only loosely joined to the institution, and are free to pursue the vague, general purpose of the university in their own idiosyncratic ways. Evaluations are based on flexible, professional, peer judgments rather than on precise and management-determined standards.

Finances, enrollments, and physical plant operations are the concerns of others. Planning, marketing, recruiting outstanding students, and campus architecture are the distasteful task of non-academic personnel, whose duty it is to provide for those in the scholarly culture, just as hospital administrators minister to physicians. Teaching, research, and learning are the central and real business of the campus; all other campus business is operational support for the academic mission.

Planning, assessment, and change

The complications caused by the coexistence of these two cultures —the corporate and the scholarly—are illustrated by looking at three activities: planning, assessment, and institutional change.

Planning in the corporate community is viewed as an activity that is necessary, rational, comprehensive, and fairly centralized. It should be strategic, a series of coordinated actions to strengthen or reposition the college in relation to its competitors and to opportunities or threats in the environment. The planning process places considerable reliance on data: applicant pools, space, revenue and expenditure analysis and projections, faculty workloads, construction costs. The process also monitors external forces—demographic shifts, changes in government funding and regulations, economic fluctuations—that affect the college.

Criteria should be established against which alternative courses of action can be weighed. Timetables and measurable results are useful, as are the assignment of tasks to specific persons or departments to implement the strategic plan.

In contrast, those in the university's scholarly community view planning as mostly intuitive, piecemeal, and decentralized. Individual professors and departments should set the scope and direction of their own and their discipline's activities.

Planning sessions should resemble a colorful town meeting rather than seminars with statistics and agendas. The values, needs, and preferences of the academics, not quantitative data, financial facts, or external changes, are central. There is a disdain for overly systematic planning approaches and their accompanying terminology. Personalities, research priorities, and internal politics more than comprehensive planning should determine the university's future. The scholarly culture sees consensus as uniting and democratic, hard decisions as divisive and disruptive. Academics view precise objectives, timetables, and measurable results as bureaucratic measures imposed by people who do not understand the subtleties of higher learning.

As for assessment, the university's corporate community tends to view it as a difficult but reasonable new demand by legislators, government agencies, taxpayers, parents, and employers who want to know how much students are really learning in college. It makes sense to focus on results rather than processes. They find the behaviorist premises—learning objectives, program design to reach the objectives, delivery system, and the assessment of outcomes to see if the design and delivery met the hoped-for objectives—logically sound. This culture sees little reason that intellectuals should not be able to measure what they are accomplishing. Isn't assessment of a student's progress a vital ingredient in education?

The members of the scholarly community, on the other hand, view the assessment movement as a simplism concocted by persons who are ignorant about the purposes and achievements of higher learning. They reject the behaviorist approach to teaching and learning. Rather, most scholars view themselves as intellectual midwives who help students become more accurate and precise, more philosophical, more tolerant of other's views, more open to beauty, elegance, and artful expressions, more committed to inquiry and questioning, more aware of the glories of their heritage and faith, more creative in their thoughts, and much more. They reject the production-oriented notion that a university should churn out graduates with measurable skills and knowledge for successful careers. To this culture, the assessment movement is an attempt by philistines to control the content and manner of instruction by prescribing outcomes.

Planning sessions should resemble a colorful town meeting.

The two cultures also differ on how change should take place at a college or university. To illustrate this, look at one change: the diffusion of computers and communications technology on campus.

To those on the corporate side of the university, the campus needs a comprehensive plan for changing to a more highly technological mode of operation, which is indicated by comparisons with other innovative organizations. After a study of where computers and scholarly communications and research are likely to go in the future, a multi-year strategy should be developed, with hardware and software standards, distribution schedules, funding sequences, and a promotion effort to inform everyone. Mandatory training programs should be developed to assist everyone in using the new equipment, and additional support persons should be hired. Faculty and support personnel should be provided with new equipment they are expected to use so that the university can stay at the cutting edge of modern technology and its possibilities.

To those on the scholarly side of the university, technology is a useful tool for the dissemination and discovery of knowledge, but its uses vary a great deal from department to department, office to office, and person to person. Engineering faculty, economists, physicists, sociologists, and English composition instructors may prefer certain kinds of technology while scholars in theater, law, and molecular genetics may prefer other kinds—made by other manufacturers.

> *The assessment movement is an attempt by philistines to control the content and manner of instruction.*

The diffusion of technology among faculty tends to be reactive rather than proactive, disorderly rather than neatly planned. Change should be stimulated by clever, enthusiastic persons in each department or school. University administrators should accommodate the requests of individual scholars rather than create some comprehensive purchasing plan, with the aid of outside consultants, for everyone on campus. Change is necessarily uneven, with some departments with professors who stimulate others through their own creative use of computers or teleconferencing rushing ahead, and other departments lagging behind.

E pluribus unum?

How can colleges and universities carry out a single, widely accepted strategy or an organizational change if each campus contains two distinctive cultures, both of which are indispensable to the successful functioning of the institution? Without a commitment to preserve the intellectual core and the values that support it, a university will lose its purpose and defining characteristic. But without the expertise to operate a contemporary, forward-looking educational corporation, a university will lose its viability.

Though the tension between the two campus cultures is ineradicable and perennial, I suggest there are three steps that institutions can take to bring the two cultures closer together.

One strategy is to help both cultures recognize that they are inextricably en-

twined and that neither can exist without the other. The corporate culture exists *for* the scholarly community culture; the scholarly culture exists only *with* the support of the corporate culture. Those who understand the complementary roles of the two cultures—planners, deans, the president and academic vice president, senior faculty, enlightened trustees—need to keep reminding both sides of the contributions of the other and correcting expressions of provincialism.

Historically, the community of scholars is the original culture, and academic purposes should guide major institutional decisions. And the chief academic officer, among peers on the organizational chart, should be regarded as the first among equals. At the same time, the scholarly culture must recognize that a modern college or university is a large, multifaceted organization, much of whose operation is beyond the expertise of faculty scholars and student leaders. Scholars have no grounds to be supercilious.

On primarily administrative issues, from budgeting to architectural planning, those in the corporate culture should consult the community of scholars. On primarily academic issues, from new programs to research proposals, those in the scholarly community should consult the appropriate members of the corporate community. By consulting each other, and sitting on committees together, persons in both cultures are most likely to avoid cultural isolation and to appreciate each other's talents.

If a considerable number of people in the two campus cultures appreciate each other, praise and respect each other, and if scholars can recognize the many tasks of running their institution as well as the demands of their own discipline while support staff persons recognize the requisites of creative teaching and scholarship, the chances of unified, collaborative planning are vastly increased.

The second step is to delineate clearly the decisionmaking spheres of the corporate and scholarly cultures. Conflict usually occurs when one culture interprets the other as straying inappropriately into its domain. As Ken Mortimer and T.R. McConnell famously noted (1978), there are three decisionmaking domains:

1. decisions that should be made by the scholarly community;
2. decisions that should be made by the corporate leaders; and
3. decisions that require the expertise and participation of both cultures.

In the domain of the teachers and scholars are decisions about the design of individual courses, requirements for degrees, structure of the curriculum, evaluation of student achievement, development of library collections, and assessment of the qualifications of candidates for appointment and promotion. Clearly in the administrative sphere are decisions of financial stability, maintenance of facilities, budgetary control, campus security, and compliance with government regulations and legal procedures.

It is more difficult to define the areas of overlap. But the construction of academic facilities, student admissions and activities, salaries and benefits, overall academic program design and new programs, and strategic planning are examples. The type and degree of involvement by each of the two cultures should vary with the issues. For example, in expenditures on academic computing, the faculty's role in setting the priorities should be authoritative but the administrators' role in deciding the funding and implementation should be paramount.

Issues on which the decisionmaking is shared present a special challenge. Not only do these decisions require unusual tolerance, understanding, and cooperation, they also require an accommodation to different styles of decisionmaking: the more rational, financial, and outcomes-centered approach of the corporate culture and the more intuitive, principled, and process-centered approach of the academic culture.

The third step is for each college or university to appraise its own competitive situation and the kind of academic services it offers, and then to mix the corporate and scholarly cultures in an appropriate balance

for its planning. Some colleges, for instance, are at ease with an educational corporation that efficiently provides students with services that the public wants. At such institutions the corporate culture should be allowed to have a stronger influence on the planning, setting of priorities, and pace of change. Other colleges or universities, however, subscribe to the view of the campus as a scholarly enclave focused less on

The corporate culture exists for the scholarly culture.

preparing individuals for the workplace than on exploring perennial questions and advancing knowledge. At these institutions the scholarly culture should play a stronger role in decisionmaking.

Or, if a college is in financial difficulty or undergoing radical changes the corporate culture may have to be stronger in the planning process. But if a college is determined to improve the quality of its faculty, teaching, and scholarship the academic culture may need to be primary in shaping the planning.

Obviously, university planning is most likely to be balanced if an institution has key individuals in both cultures who are at home both in the world of the educational corporation and in the community of scholars. Such men and women should be groomed, nourished, and honored. It is an abundance of persons who understand the necessity of both cultures that makes integrated institutional planning successful. ∎

REFERENCES

Clark, B. 1980. Academic Culture. *Yale Higher Education Research Group, Report No. 42.* Institute for Social and Policy Studies.

Clark, B. 1987. *The Academic Life: Small Worlds, Different Worlds.* Carnegie Foundation for the Advancement of Teaching.

Cohen, M. and J. March 1974. *Leadership and Ambiguity,* 2d ed. Harvard Business School Press.

Dill, D. 1982. The Management of Academic Culture: Notes on the Management of Meaning and Social Integration. *Higher Education* 11:303-320.

Kuh, G. and E. Whitt, 1988. *The Invisible Tapestry: Culture in American Colleges and Universities.* ASHE-ERIC Report No. 1. Association for the Study of Higher Education.

Mortimer, K. and T.R. McConnell. 1978. *Sharing Authority Effectively.* Jossey-Bass.

Rehder, R. 1989. The Bureaucratic Drift in the Governance of Higher Education: Insights from Organizational Theory. *Educational Technology* 19: 7-15.

Schein, E. 1985. *Organizational Culture and Leadership.* Jossey-Bass.

Snow, C.P. 1959. *The Two Cultures and the Scientific Revolution.* Cambridge University Press.

Tierney, W. ed. 1990. Assessing Academic Climates and Cultures. *New Directions for Institutional Research No. 68.* Jossey-Bass.

Tierney, W. 1988. Organizational Culture in Higher Education. *Journal of Higher Education* 59:2-21.

A new scientific theory may have some salutary ideas for educational strategists.

Can Chaos Theory Improve Planning?

Marc Cutright

Since the 1983 publication of George Keller's influential book, *Academic Strategy: The Management Revolution in American Higher Education*, many hundreds of America's 3500 colleges and universities have conducted strategic planning. Ten years later Keller acknowledged that a number of these efforts had failed to produce strategic changes (1993). Earlier Frank Schmidtlein (1988-89) and Larry Jones (1990) estimated that possibly half of all planning efforts may have been fruitless. A 1994 study by Jack Schuster and some colleagues who conducted a study of planning on eight campuses found mixed results and several outright failures (Schuster *et al.* 1994).

Why have such a large number of institutions that have tried to introduce changes in order to respond to radically changing external conditions met with so little success?

Marc Cutright is director of university relations at the University of Tennessee at Chattanooga. A graduate of Lindenwood College in Missouri, he is completing his doctorate in education at the University of Tennessee at Knoxville. He has worked in institutional advancement at Northwestern University and North Georgia College, and was a Fulbright Scholar to Canada for 1996-97, at the University of Calgary.

The offered reasons are many. But I find most persuasive the argument of Canada's Henry Mintzberg, admittedly a corporate and not an education planner, who contends that many of the failed planning processes have been overly rational, quantitative, and linear processes that neglected intuition, artfulness, and sudden social and human shifts (Mintzberg 1994; Keller 1994).

I suspect, based on some limited experience, that a portion of the strategic efforts were unsuccessful because the planners and campus leaders failed to recognize the role that luck, surprises, strange incidents, personnel quirks, and unpredictable turbulence play in an institution's life. Colleges too easily assume that society's evolution is reasonably orderly, predictable, and tidily sequential. Indeed, social scientists often base their views on the so-called rational choice theory. But there is probably a significant element of chaos and disorder in the evolution of human—and educational—history, and in people's choices.

In the past 30 years scientists and mathematicians have developed a new theory about the natural world called chaos theory, the origins of which were explained with magnificent clarity in James Gleick's best-selling book, *Chaos: Making a New Science* (1987). Though the science deals with physical events rather than social events, I believe some of its postulates may help college and university planners improve the success rate of their strategic decision making and restructuring.

The element of chaos

Chaos theory is generally acknowledged to have been initiated by MIT meteorologist Edward Lorenz, who, while working on computer models of the weather in the early 1960s, found that tiny changes in weather conditions could produce enormous, chaotic changes in weather patterns. Those chaotic functions are said to demonstrate *extreme sensitivity to initial conditions*, or to *influx*. This has become popularly known as "the butterfly effect," where it is said that the fluttering of a butterfly's wings in Asia might eventually help cause a tornado in Texas. Lorenz had unveiled a discontinuous, erratic, unpredictable side of nature.

Chaotic systems are dependent on *feedback*. As opposed to Newtonian concepts, which clearly differentiate between cause and effect, feedback is the notion that each effect becomes part of the cause in the subsequent iterations of the pattern. Small factors thus can—but not necessarily will—become vastly multiplied over time. Peter Senge explored this notion for organizational behavior in *The Fifth Discipline*.

But what allows chaotic systems to develop any sense of pattern, to stay within boundaries? Or, as James Gleick asked, "In a universe ruled by entropy, drawing inexorably toward greater and greater disorder, how does order arise?" (1987, p. 7) It is because of what scientists call *attractors*, elements of a system that have a drawing power or organizational strength. For example, a pendulum swinging back and forth is attracted by gravity toward its lowest point. A system can have multiple attractors, which establish organization. The presence of a great many attractors results in unstable, complex patterns called *strange attractors*. (Parker and Stacey 1994).

Chaotic systems often demonstrate a self-similarity. That is, they replicate themselves in different sizes, as blood vessels do from thick aorta to hair-like capillaries. This self-similar structuring is called *fractals*, meaning a geo-

metric pattern that is repeated at ever smaller scales to produce irregular shapes and surfaces that cannot be expressed by classical geometry. A snowflake is a fractal structure; on microscopic examination, the basic pattern is continuously repeated. One analyst, Margaret Wheatley, has attempted to adapt chaos theory to organizations, believing that "the best organizations have a fractal quality to them. An observer...can tell what the organization's values and ways of doing business are by watching anyone..." (1992, p. 132).

To summarize, a chaotic system is one in which apparently random or chaotic ac-

Colleges too easily assume that society's evolution is reasonably orderly, predictable.

tivity is in fact very complexly patterned. The patterns are created by attractors but modified or disrupted by the introduction or infusion of small and large bits of turbulence. Chaotic systems exhibit fractal structuring at various levels of the system. The infinitely varied interactions of turbulence and attractors make pattern predictability immensely difficult in the near term and impossible over the long term.

Does chaos theory, which describes systems and turbulence in the *natural* world, have any application to *social* life? A few scholars have tried, using enormous quantities of numbers, and have claimed to find similarities, especially in economics and electoral politics (Priesmeyer 1992; Brown 1995). Some financiers have also tried to use chaos theory to understand how financial markets operate, but they have so far mostly despaired (*Economist* 1996). However, a growing number of social practitioners have accepted the idea of non-linearity—that in the real world events change not according to some predetermined, predictable formula but under the influence of many different factors: tiny, surprising, and sometimes cataclysmic.

My own view is this. While chaos theory is a highly mathematical conformation of some patterns in nature, it suggests a few approaches that we in academic organizations might keep in mind, especially if we are planning new patterns for our college or university in the midst of increasing social turbulence in the environment. These approaches could possibly improve the success rate of strategic planning efforts.

Planning with chaos

Organization analyst James Begun recently wrote, "Chaos and complexity theory invite us to explore the 95 percent of the organizational world that we have avoided because it is too dark, murky, and intimidating" (1995, p. 334). The challenge, Begun wrote, is not to apply chaos theory directly to our institutions but to discover some similar dynamics within our human systems. I think such discovery might help education planners who are helping to renovate their institutions. Here are some ways that chaos theory might help strategic planning.

1. *Life is unpredictable, semi-chaotic; so plans should be short-term, and flexible.* As in nature, social life has "butterfly wings" whose fluttering causes unpredictability through iterative dynamics, far out of proportion to the seeming insignificance of their genesis. The American G.I.Bill was such a butterfly flapping. The bill's supporters at the closing weeks of World War II believed its most significant feature would be its unemployment benefits for returning veterans. Yet more than two million veterans instead jumped at its financial assistance to attend college. As a result, access to higher education and higher education's service to adults were both transformed (Kiester 1994).

One could identify other butterfly effects: Martin Luther King's actions and speeches, the discovery of questionable uses of indirect research cost monies at Stanford and other campuses, introduction of the Internet, and the proliferation of rock bands and their music. These and other seemingly small developments cause expanding disorder in traditional social and collegiate life.

So, planners should do two things. Recognizing the certainty of uncertainty, they should plan only for a fairly short time frame, three or four years at most. Elaborate long-term predictions are folly. As with the weather, short-term predictions can be quite accurate but long-term predictions are not. Planners should also keep plans pointed but relatively detail-free and flexible. Specific changes and new resource allocations ought to be clear, but flexibility to respond to sudden perturbations is a must. As Henry Mintzberg reports, "The more elaborate the planning procedures become...the greater seemed to be their failures" (p. 295).

2. *Recognize that life is nonlinear as well as linear; so planning should be multifaceted and interactive.* Linearity means relationships can be portrayed by a straight line on a graph, that things are determined by their initial conditions in a logical way. Campus plans are often overly directive, one-way, highly rational, linear. But as in nature, so-

> *Chaos theory invites us to explore the 95 percent of the organizational world we have avoided.*

cial life seems nonlinear as well. As James Gleick says, "Nonlinearity means that the act of playing the game has a way of changing the rules" (p. 24). Multiple attractors can destablize; the effects of feedback can be significant and can regulate as well as alter. Nonlinearity in planning recognizes the peculiar dynamics and causal relationships at the institution.

Some colleges believe that an institutional plan is the sum of individual plans by departments and schools. But collation can at best identify individual desires and preferences, and it is based on a linear, upwardly directed information path. It neglects feedback and the strong force of organizational attractors, and this process lacks the connectivity between the various elements of an institution. As Keller has written, "A university is more than the aggregate of its parts" (p. 141). Strategic formulations should be nonlinear, acknowledging the complex, causal interplay to which universities are subject, not naively linear or overly rational.

3. *Colleges and universities have strange attractors; so planning should identify and employ these factors.* Attractors are the forces that help organize the system despite the turbulence, and they prevent total chaos. They establish boundaries, and they give a general direction for the future. At colleges and universities, these are usually the institution's traditions, its "saga," its institutional culture, and its long-time purposes. To impose new purposes and new ways of operating without discovering and reconciling those attractors at the institution is likely to result in an unrealistic and unworkable strategy of action.

Failure to recognize the existence of a college's attractors also fails to recognize the fractal structures as well. A college may profess a deep dedication to high-quality teaching, but unless this commitment is a goal and motivator at all levels of the organization the dedication will not be reflected in the experience of the students.

4. *Feedback is essential; so seek the widest possible amount of information for planning.* Chaos theory suggests that feedback, the constant interplay of cause and effect, the return of information about the output of a system to reshape its input, is a central determinant of complex natural systems. Higher education too needs lots of feedback and a wide net of information, evaluation reports, data, and results.

Thus, good environmental scanning, financial data on costs, assessments of student learning, Internet data banks, reports from employers, and discussions among the different stakeholders and scholars of the institution are all imperative to understand how a university functions, how it is performing, and how it relates to its environment—and how it might perform less chaotically and better.

Frequently, rich feedback will result in conflict and new turbulence on campus. But turbulence not only increases chaos, it also produces additional creativity and new alliances. Conflict is inevitable. The trick is to use it constructively. There is no doubt that

quick, conflict-free planning is faster. But this is false economy. A plan that is rich in feedback and in frequent disagreements and conflicts is more likely to be accepted eventually and more efficiently implemented.

Former college president James Fisher notes that "in a misguided sense of democ-

Flexibility to respond to sudden perturbations is a must.

racy" faculty, students, staff, trustees, and alumni are often included in an "unending and totally unproductive morass of committee meetings, faculty meetings, formal and informal dialogues" (1994 p. 62) that lead to paralysis or lowest-common-denominator compromises instead of necessary new strategies. This seems to be the case often. A president or college dean should be strong, decisive, and visionary. In fact, a president should, through the promotion and implementation of a strategic planning process, become a system attractor, a basic element in the formation of the organization's pattern.

But she or he will achieve a finer planning outcome if maximum feedback is employed to design the plan—without surrendering to the feeble, do-nothing compromises that Fisher mentions because of the fear of conflict that haunts many campus leaders.

5. *The future can be created; so strategic planning is necessary.* Much of the unpredictability in social affairs derives from our inability to discern which factors in the environment—which butterfly wings—will be absorbed by the system and gain great power from iterative dynamics, far out of proportion to the insignificance of their genesis. But this does not mean that planning in higher education is futile.

Rather, the primary lesson is that the future is an invention. Factors in the external and internal environments are strong shapers of the future, but so are dreams, values, and ambitions. Campus plans can also be butterfly wings, influencing the course of an institution's life, longevity, quality, and service. From chaos theory we realize that seemingly small efforts, created in partnership and applied with consistency, gain power over time, and can affect more people's lives than we imagine.

Chaos theory also suggests that the linear suppositions of much of contemporary social "science" and of some kinds of long-range

Campus plans can also be butterfly wings.

planning have only limited applications, and can contribute to failures in education planning. Cognizance of the principles of chaos theory can enable colleges and universities to "roll with the punches" delivered by our unpredictable environment and the realities of campus cultures while creating wiser, more flexible strategies for the near-term future. ■

REFERENCES

Brown, C. 1995. *Chaos and Catastrophe Theories*. Sage.

Begun, J. 1994. Chaos and Complexity: Frontiers of Organizational Science. *Journal of Management Inquiry* 3(4): 329-335.

Economist. 1996. "Chaos Under a Cloud." January 13: 69-70.

Fisher, J. 1994. Reflections on Transformational Leadership. *Educational Record* 54 (Summer): 60-65.

Gleick, J. 1987. *Chaos: Making a New Science*. Penguin.

Jones, L. 1990. Strategic Planning: The Unrealized Potential of the 1980s and the Promise of the 1990s. *New Directions for Higher Education*. 70: 38-41.

Keller, G. 1994. Review of *The Rise and Fall of Strategic Planning*, by Henry Mintzberg. *Planning for Higher Education* 23(1): 38-41.

Keller, G. 1993. Strategic Planning and Management in a Competitive Environment. *New Directions for Institutional Research*. 77: 9-16.

Keller, G. 1983. *Academic Strategy: The Management Revolution in American Higher Education*. Johns Hopkins University Press.

Keister, E. 1994. The G.I. Bill May be the Best Deal Ever Made by Uncle Sam. *Smithsonian* 25(8): 129-139.

Mintzberg, H. 1994. *The Rise and Fall of Strategic Planning*. Free Press.

Parker, D. and Stacey, R. 1994. *Chaos, Management, and Economics: The Implications of Non-Linear Thinking*. (Hobart Paper 125). London: The Institute of Economic Affairs.

Priesmeyer, H. R. 1992. *Organizations and Chaos: Defining the Methods of Nonlinear Management*. Quorum Books.

Schmidtlein, F. and Milton, T. 1988-89. College and University Planning: Perspectives from a Nation-Wide Study. *Planning for Higher Education* 17(3): 1-19.

Schuster, J., Smith, G., Corak, K. and Yamada, M. 1994. *Strategic Governance: How to Make Big Decisions Better*. ACE/Oryx Press.

Wheatley, M. 1992. *Leadership and the New Science*. Berrett-Kohler Publishers.

*Pay attention to the characteristics
of those creating your strategy!*

Those Persons Who Do Your Planning

Karen Gonçalves

Campus leaders seem to have little difficulty setting up a strategic planning process. But they often have great difficulty in implementing the action plan after one is agreed upon (Schmidtlein and Milton, 1988–89; Keller and McCreery, 1990). Fortunately, several experiences I have had with colleges during their planning, and research I recently conducted, suggest that there may be a way to assist universities in coming to closure on strategic decisions and in implementing the strategic plan.

I was prompted to notice the new factor while I was working several years ago with two colleges that were engaged in strategic planning. What struck me was the difference

Karen Gonçalves is President of Delphi Market Research, Inc. in Arlington, MA. She received an M.B.A. and Ed.D. in higher education administration from Northeastern University, where she also taught for several years. She was on the faculty of Babson College briefly and at Bentley College for many years. Before starting her own firm she was assistant director at Institute for New Enterprise Development and a senior consultant for Arthur D. Little, Inc. She won SCUP's Annual Student Paper Competition in 1990.

in the makeup of the planning committees at the two institutions.

One client chose for the planning committee the head of each department or functional area as well as a few persons who opposed the idea of the plan. The committee thus included the obvious line officers plus a few dissidents, who, it was hoped, would shed their objections through participation in the process. I labeled this a "traditional" planning team.

The other client also selected persons from several departments but only sometimes the head. Usually the person most widely recognized as the hardest-working, most creative, and influential in each department or area was selected, as well as a few of the most forward-looking administrators. I saw this as a "radical" planning group.

Within the traditional team, "turf" warfare, interpersonal disputes, and hidden agendas were rife, and most of those opposed to planning remained unconvinced about developing a broad strategy. As a result the final plan was weak, cliche-ridden, and late in coming out. And attempts at implementation were half-hearted or sabotaged.

Within the radical group, the plan was completed on schedule and was rather blunt and innovative. The plan elicited considerable support and even some enthusiasm throughout the organization, and the follow-up implementation went smoothly. We updated the plan annually four times, each time with a few new persons who were also seen as "comers;" and it was remarkable how smoothly changes were made and implementation carried out.

Three years later the client with the "traditional" planning members formed another strategic planning team. This time it included younger academics and a few specially chosen persons who had no official position. Despite a turbulent environment for this college, the new planning team completed their work on schedule, gained considerable support for their plan, and helped implement about half of what they had proposed.

To me the contrast in performance seemed to be related to the kind of people chosen to devise the strategic action plan. So I decided to see if the people who are asked to carry out the planning are a crucial factor in the success of the planning process and its implementation.

Enter the early adopters

As a person trained in marketing, I knew there was a small body of research on the diffusion of innovations. How did innovative products, whether jogging sneakers, credit cards, or personal computers, come to be accepted? What kind of persons are most likely to first try new products or services? And how did acceptance spread? Diffusion research began several decades ago to understand the buying behavior of farmers who were offered improved, highly productive hybrid corn but continued to plant the older, less desirable corn.

Diffusion researchers have learned that three kinds of persons are especially influential in launching an innovation (Rogers, 1976, 1983; Danko and MacLachlan, 1985; Leonard-Barton, 1985). The most receptive persons are labeled "innovators." These people are risk-takers, quick to gather new knowledge and adopt new patterns of behav-

ior. Eager to do things before anyone else, innovators were the first people to buy VCR's; they are persons who travel to Bangkok, the Amazon jungle, or Budapest when

"Early adopters" are the most influential in getting an innovation accepted.

most Americans take trips to other parts of the United States. Innovators tend to be much younger, have a high level of self-confidence, education, and income, and are unusually avid to improve their social status or esteem.

The second most receptive group to accept new products or ideas is called "early adopters." This group, say researchers, is the most influential one in getting an innovation accepted. Early adopters share some traits with the innovators, but they differ on several dimensions (Robertson, 1967; Tolbert and Zucker, 1983; Mahajan, Muller, and Bass, 1990). Like the innovators, the early adopters tend to be above average in income, education, and social accomplishment. But while early adopters are interested in new ideas, products, or ways of doing things, they tend to explore and discuss new products or ideas fairly thoroughly. Early adopters accept new practices only after they weigh whether the new practices will hurt them socially, economically, and professionally and whether the new practices will hurt or benefit their organization. Early adopters are usually seen by others as effective persons and workers, as opinion leaders, and as worthy of emulation.

The third group is called the "early majority." They are more cautious and less self-confident, less well-educated. They tend not to weigh the pro's and con's of the innovation themselves but to emulate the early adopters. If the early adopters buy or adopt a new idea, the early majority will usually do so too; if the early adopters do not buy or commit, they too will refrain. The early majority is a large force in commercial, social, or institutional change, but one heavily influenced by the early adopters.

Kerry Bunker, head of leadership research at the Center for Creative Leadership in Greensboro, North Carolina, finds a similar breakdown. In research he conducted for AT&T, he found four groups:

1. *Risk-takers*. Those comfortable about jumping into new situations but not adept at it. They are frequently seen as trendy, opportunistic, or reckless.
2. *Adapters*. These are open to calculated risks that are based on enough information and on discussions with key people. They are perceived as enterprising but judicious.
3. *Copers*. These can cope with change if necessary but are uncomfortable doing so. They prefer to work in a stable environment. They are viewed as reluctant but moderately able adapters.
4. *Resisters*. These are neither comfortable with change nor able to learn new ways without resentment. They like to do what they know already. They are seen as obstructionists and preservers. (Fox, 1991)

To my knowledge, no one in higher education has ever used diffusion of innovations theory to help provide successful outcomes in strategic planning, although several persons have applied it to educational settings (Caffarella et al., 1982; Basch and Sliepcevich, 1983; Milne and Anderson, 1984; Broyles and Tillman, 1985; Schachter, 1986).

I wondered, was it possible that the reason some strategic planning exercises went better than others was that the college leaders at certain institutions carefully selected "early adopters" for their planning committees, while others appointed the usual department heads, deans, faculty and union spokespersons, and vice presidents? If so, how can planners identify the early adopters on their campus?

Looking into the question

I decided to conduct a small study among 110 private colleges and universities in New England to find out from their presidents what kind of persons—as viewed by most faculty and staff—were involved in planning at their institution. I also wanted to see if the characteristics of their planners matched those of the influential "early adopters" from diffusion of innovations research. I used a mail survey, preceeded by a telephone call to each institution, and an offer to see the results. I expected a yield of 60% to 65% and got a yield of 75%.

> *Presidents often seem to have a profile of early adopters in their head.*

I asked the presidents to rate their planning team members on twelve characteristics. Actually the diffusion researchers find nine characteristics to be associated with the early adopter group. They are:

1. *Moderate risk-takers*. They measure higher than average on risk-profile tests but are not high-risk persons.
2. *Fairly self-confident persons*. Poised, secure, undaunted.
3. *Younger than average* in the potential pool.
4. *Innovative*. Persons who are comfortable with new ideas, approaches and strategies, and who are emulated by many others in the group.
5. *Highly educated*. More and better education in their youth and continued enhancement of their intellectual capital as adults, compared to the potential pool.
6. *Effective people*. Highly competent, good at getting things done.
7. *Leaders*. Their opinion is respected. They are persuasive, influential.
8. *Well-established and integrated* in the social structure of the organization, or unit of organization—or among peers nationally.
9. *High-income earners*. They earn slightly more than the average person in their age group or professional group.

I decided to eliminate the ninth characteristic—income—because of the difficulty of collecting the data reliably. And I decided to add four additional distinguishing traits that I believed were important to academics to the list:

1. *Respect among others on campus.* How highly a person is regarded by her or his colleagues.
2. *Seniority* at the institution where he/she currently works.
3. *Stability.* Absence of inconstancy, volatility, contradictory allegiances.
4. *Wisdom.* Good sense, good judgement, discerning, and humane.

I also asked each of the 110 presidents to rank what they regard as the traits of an "ideal" strategic planning team for their institution. When the results came in, a jury of seven persons experienced in planning—faculty and administrators—reviewed the findings with me. What I found is described in Table 1.

The ideal team traits drawn by the presidents closely matched the profile of early adopters in non-academic settings. Presidents seem to have a profile of early adopters in their heads. To my surprise, most campus presidents rated their own planning teams as being reasonably close to the ideal team in most characteristics. This suggests that numerous institutions may already select planning groups that have a fair number of early adopter characteristics.

Note, however, that the actual institution planners tended to be less risk-taking,

Planners need to be innovative and be moderate risk-takers.

less innovative, and less respected by their peers, and a bit less stable and wise than presidents would like. The actual teams also used fewer younger persons and fewer people without seniority on campus.

I realize this study is only a fragment of evidence, that the 12 characteristics are not easy to identify in others, and that much more research needs to be done to validate the idea that colleges and universities should screen their planning committee members to pick as many early adopters as possible if they wish to have their strategy accepted and implementation go more smoothly. I was encouraged, however, that all seven jurors I used said they themselves could readily identify the women and men on their campus who fit the early adopter profile.

What kind of team?

In interviews with college leaders, I find that they are under enormous pressure to put

TABLE 1
How Presidents Characterize their Ideal and Current Planning Teams

MEAN SCORES[1]			SCALE[2] 1 2 3 4 5 6 7	
Ideal Team	Current Team			
2.84	3.84	high risk-takers		low risk-takers
6.26	5.38	weak		strong
3.98	4.12	young		old
1.73	2.89*	innovative		staid
6.52	6.40*	poorly educated		well educated
6.48	5.39	ineffective		effective
1.89	2.52*	influential		not influential
2.29	2.39*	well established		not established
1.48	2.36*	highly respected		not respected
3.36	2.76*	senior		junior
1.78	2.42*	stable		unstable
1.63	2.67*	wise		foolish

[1]* denotes a statistically significant difference between means at the 5% level
[2] "ideal" team = - - - - - - -, current team = _____

senior people and current deans, vice presidents, and elected faculty officers on their strategic planning groups. More recently, they have been lobbied to make sure the planners are a sufficiently diverse group by gender, ethnic background, religious preference, color, and even political leanings. Clearly, these considerations must be attended to.

But planning also needs to be effective (Chaffee, 1984). The planners need to be innovative and moderate risk-takers. As policy advisers and deciders about the future, they need to be stable, effective, influential persons who are self-confident enough to handle the inevitable criticism that any new strategy receives.

Most institutions will clearly need to pay attention both to the politics and psychology of team selection and to the quality of the strategy team and its effectiveness in breaking down the older ways of operating. But I believe the seriousness of the situation at many American colleges requires leaders to pay much greater attention to the use of early adopters. Presidents need to pick persons who can analyze, choose, innovate, decide, and influence others. They should give less attention to the representation of less germane factors.

The special qualities of those persons doing the planning are more important than their representativeness.

If university planning is to work, the special qualities of those doing the planning are more important than their representativeness. To the maximum extent possible, college leaders should avoid in-house politics in selecting the planning group, and concentrate instead on achieving beneficial institutional change through the inclusion of early adopters. ∎

REFERENCES

Basch, C. and E. Sliepcevich, "Innovators, Innovations, and Implementation: A Framework for Curricular Research in Health Education," *Health Education*, 14:2 (1983), 20–24.

Broyles, I. and M. Tillman, "Relationships of In-service Training Components and Changes in Teacher Concerns Regarding Innovations," *Journal of Education Research*, 76: 6 (1985), 364–71.

Caffarella, E., et al., "Predicting the Diffusability of Educational Innovations," *Educational Technology*, 22:12 (1984), 212–41.

Chaffee, E.E., "Successful Strategic Management in Small Private Colleges," *Journal of Higher Education*, 55:2(1984), 212–41.

Danko, W., and J. MacLachlan, "Research to Accelerate the Diffusion of a New Innovation: The Case of Personal Computers," *Journal of Advertising Research*, 23:3(1983), 39–43.

Fox, J., "How to Take Risks," *Amtrak Express* (May-June 1991), 17–19.

Keller, G. and A. McCreery, "Making Difficult Educational Decisions: Findings from Research and Experience." Paper presented at the SCUP Annual Conference, Atlanta, Georgia, July 31, 1990.

Leonard-Barton, D., "Experts as Negative Opinion Leaders in the Diffusion of a Technological Innovation," *Journal of Consumer Research*, 11:3 (1985), 914–26.

Mahajan, V., E. Mullen and F. Bass, "New Product Diffusion Models in Marketing: A Review and Directions for Research," *Journal of Marketing*, 54:1 (1990), 1–26.

Milne, J. and J.S.A. Anderson, "The Microelectronics Education Program: Dissemination and Diffusion of Microelectronics Technology in Education," *Programmed Learning and Educational Technology*, 21:2(1984), 82–87.

Robertson, T.S., "The Process of Innovation and the Diffusion of Innovation," *Journal of Marketing*, 31:1 (1967), 14–19.

Rogers, E., "New Product Adoption and Diffusion," *Journal of Consumer Research* 2(1976), 290–301.

Rogers, E., *Diffusion of Innovations*, 3d edition (Free Press, 1983).

Schacter, H. "State Coordinating Agencies and Academic Innovation" *Higher Education*, 14:3–4(1986), 333–42.

Schmidtlein, F. and T. Milton, "College and University Planning: Perspectives from a Nation-Wide Study," *Planning for Higher Education*, 17:3(1988–89), 1–19.

Tolbert, P. and L. Zucker, "Institutional Sources of Change in the Formal Structure of Organizations: Diffusion of Civil Service Reform, 1880–1935," *Administrative Science Quarterly*, 28:1 (1983), 22–39.

Comparing your own operation with the very best can be a new route to improvements.

Benchmarking: The New Tool

Steven Stralser

I n the 1880s the Singer Sewing Machine Company became known for its unusual new manufacturing process: mass production. People came to visit the upstate New York factory to inspect the novel way they produced their low-cost sewing machines; and a few visitors later introduced similar production techniques in their own companies.

Today, some colleges and universities have begun visits to other, more innovative campuses and to high-quality operations in the business world to learn from the most innovative and very best, much as visitors once trooped to Isaac Merritt Singer's factory. The visits are part of a new method of improving institutional performance and introducing major changes on campus called benchmarking (Blumenstyk 1993). (Benchmark, like the words standard, criterion, hallmark, touchstone, and yardstick, is a colloquial term meaning "a point of reference to which practices can be compared and evaluated.")

Steven Stralser teaches marketing and entrepreneurship at the University of Arizona and is completing a Ph.D. program at the Center for the Study of Higher and Continuing Education at the University of Michigan. He has also taught at the University of Michigan's Business School and is a consultant in strategic planning, technology transfer, and new venture formation.

For example, when the University of Mississippi's School of Education and its dean, James Payne, recently decided to improve the School's organizational processes and behaviors, teams were formed to study various corporations known for their excellence in certain areas. From IBM they learned how to make meetings and committees more productive; from a local utility they discovered how to enhance town-gown relationships through greater faculty and staff participation in community organizations; and from Federal Express they found out how valuable training and teamwork can be in producing better quality and faster service (Payne and Blackburn 1993).

Benchmarking, which one scholar describes as a "continuous, systematic process for evaluating the products, services, and work processes of organizations that are recognized as representing best practices for the purpose of organizational improvement" (Spendolini 1992), is suddenly being recognized as reasonable extension of TQM (Total Quality Management), where campus teams try to streamline college processes to reduce costs, improve cooperation, and raise the quality of service on campus (Rush 1994). Visiting another university to observe its remarkable financial aid office, or its outstanding freshman mathematics classes and tutoring, or its effective marketing and public relations methods, seems to motivate lagging groups as invocations, statistics, and threats usually do not. Also, some academic departments or campus units tend to believe they are already first-rate and in little need of change; so benchmarking comparisons can be eye-opening, humbling, and conducive to considerable changes for the better. Travel, as the saying goes, is broadening.

But benchmarking is not a simple matter of visiting the finest competitors or the paragons in some area, and transplanting their practices into your own institutions. As statistician and TQM guru, W. Edwards Deming once said, "It is a hazard to copy. It is necessary to understand the theory of what one wishes to do" (Watson 1992). Colleges should understand that what works at some corporation may not work in higher education organizations, and that extraordinary procedures at a Quaker college or big state university in a farm state may not work at a Baptist college or a private urban university like Tulane or the University of Southern California. Campus cultures differ from corporate cultures; and within higher education there are many different cultural styles among America's 3,500 colleges and universities. Still, though educational benchmarking is young it is proving to be a novel and sometimes expeditious new method of stimulating planned changes.

Anatomy of benchmarking

Robert Camp, a pioneer practitioner, provides a good definition of corporate benchmarking, as developed largely by David Kearns, the former CEO of the Xerox Corporation and former U.S. Undersecretary of Education under President George Bush (Camp 1989):

> Benchmarking is the continuous process of measuring products, services, and practices against the toughest competitors or those companies recognized as industry leaders.

Note that this definition describes it as "continuous" and as a "process" and not just a one-time measurement. Colleges may wish to make their benchmarking more selective and episodic rather than continuous. But, like corporations who visit Japanese

manufacturing plants or the most innovative companies in Germany, Illinois, or California, educational institutions can use benchmarking as a means of organizational learning (Senge 1990).

Benchmarking is not a simple matter of visiting the finest competitors.

There are really two parts to benchmarking: performance benchmarking and process benchmarking. Performance benchmarking, which precedes, compares one institution's performance in some important area with another's. The difference between the performance at one's own operation and that of the superior one is known as "the improvement gap." A university may compare such things as

- cost per credit hour in some academic discipline,
- percentage of annual giving by alumni,
- retention at each semester's end, and
- number of staff in the student affairs operation, and costs per student.

For instance, Oregon State University developed eight performance indicators to compare OSU's funding relative to its peers. With benchmark data the university was able to gain new support to fund needed changes (Johnson 1993).

Performance benchmarking is particularly useful to answer the question: "What areas on campus need to improve?" Once improvement gaps have been identified, the next step is to move into process benchmarking.

Process benchmarking is learning about the processes that enable the institutions or companies to display unusual performance excellence, then adapting those processes to your own institution. Often, improved processes at one university will come from several sources, some of them non-educational organizations. For example, researchers at Belmont University in Tennessee found the best practices applicable to their campus at several kinds of organizations (Belmont University 1994);

- Employee involvement and morale, from a financial services firm
- Innovations, from a travel agency
- Customer research, from a television station
- Integrated use of latest technology, from a large law firm.

As one observer wrote (Dunn 1992):

A college or university is a small city. It may consist of real estate, facilities, roadways, utility systems, housing, restaurants, retail stores, public safety services, transportation systems, computer technology, research initiatives, and power plants.

Most of these functions have operations similar to those in commercial organizations. So colleges and universities can learn a great deal from the best non-educational enterprises:

- A campus concerned about its transportation and cleanliness may wish to look at the Walt Disney Company's entertainment operations in these areas.
- A research university worried about faculty productivity might study the Rand Corporation's productivity assessment process.
- A college with complaints about its financial aid and bursar's offices could learn from examining the processes at an exceptionally user-friendly bank.

It is important that colleges identify certain specific areas of activity to study before they visit other institutions. Otherwise they will descend into "organizational tourism" (APQC 1993).

The vital parts

In some of the literature, benchmarking is advocated as a systematic, highly structured process (e.g. Spendolini 1991). But competition among colleges is more collegial than it is in the business arena, and campuses have fewer dollars and personnel to carry out continuous, systematic benchmarking.

Thus I think there are six fundamental steps for collegiate benchmarking:

- Determining what to benchmark
- Forming a team to do the benchmarking
- Discovering who to benchmark
- Collecting and analyzing data

- Using the data to redesign your own operation
- Assessing improvements in your operations.

Step One: Determining what to benchmark. One obvious place to start is with those operations on campus which draw the most complaints. These improvement gaps can be determined through focus group interviews, or staff, student, and faculty surveys. Another way to find some areas to benchmark is to tag those operations that are reported to be done with exceptional excellence at other colleges or uni-

There are really two parts to benchmarking.

versities. For instance, one might read about or hear repeatedly about another campus where the landscaping is unusually beautiful or where instruction in the sciences is innovative and amazingly effective.

Who decides? It depends. Deans of schools seem to be especially active in starting the benchmarking, perhaps because business, engineering, law, and other professional schools are frequently rated by outside evaluators. But presidents, vice presidents for administration, department chairs, or campus planners and architects might also initiate some benchmarking, and set aside some money to carry it out.

Step Two: Forming a team. Benchmarking is most effective if it is performed by a team. The team should be no smaller than three persons or larger than six persons. Members should include at least one person who will be able to implement the process changes, but should also include persons involved in the process being studied.

Step Three: Discovering who to benchmark. Solid research is important at this stage. Institutions should explore possibilities through:

- Education and business journals and newspapers
- Public domain databases
- Higher education associations and their leaders

- Market research on potential students and employers.

The office of institutional research may be a rich source of performance benchmarking data since these officers often collect comparative data, and frequently know which operations on campus are in need of improvement. The IR staff are usually especially capable in primary and secondary research techniques about university performance.

Step Four: Collecting and analyzing data. There are two kinds of data to be collected. One is the on-the-scene observations, interviews, and notetaking. Experienced benchmarkers report that personal site visits are the most rewarding method of collecting information. The other is quantitative data: financial data, performance statistics, and the like.

It is important that a college prepare and plan before any team visits. What are the specific research questions and comparative data on which the visit should concentrate? Vague, unfocused visits are seldom productive. As one author reminds us (Spendolini 1992):

Universities can learn a great deal from the best non-educational enterprises.

> Interacting and visiting with other organizations is what attracts many to the benchmarking process...Experienced benchmarkers, however, tell a different story. If the initial planning and preparation stages of the process have not been completed carefully, the process of collecting and analyzing benchmarking information can be unproductive or even counterproductive.

Step Five: Redesigning your own operation. This is the hardest part. As with strategic planning, hard decisions are very difficult to make; and specific renovations, actual changes, and reallocations are much harder to implement, even if the data clearly suggest the changes that should be made. Adaptation of the best practices for one's own campus is "where the rubber meets the road." At this stage, the commitment of the president, vice presidents, or deans—to higher quality performance and

It is most effective when performed by a team.

to definite changes to improve instruction and services on campus—is essential.

Step Six: Assessing improvements. After making changes in some campus operation, it is necessary to monitor the performance of the modified process to see if the consumers feel better served and if the results of the changes are significant.

How do colleges learn?

Benchmarking is likely to be viewed suspiciously by college and university professors and seen as a threat to staff in some departments and units. It might be regarded as just another management fad, like the TQM craze of the early 1990s or zero-based budgeting. Admittedly, it is another time-consuming procedure, and, according to a recent study, each benchmarking effort could cost from $10,000 to $20,000.

But most colleges and universities already have a platform for benchmarking in place with departmental rankings, program reviews, peer comparisons, and magazine rankings in such journals as *U.S. News & World Report* and *Money.* Benchmarking thus can be represented as the logical next step to already existing comparisons and rankings.

Also, higher education is a natural for benchmarking. While benchmarking is sometimes viewed as industrial espionage in business circles, colleges and universities are remarkably open and comfortable sharing information about their operations. Most institutions are even likely to be flattered if others ask to come study the secrets of their exceptional performance.

Benchmarking can be a help to planning too. Planners can learn how other institutions have adapted to their changed environments or how they are responding to the new high-tech world that educators live in. Benchmarking also can sharpen people's sense of the differences among U.S. colleges in their local cultures, traditions, administrative styles, and attitudes toward quality service and change.

So, while benchmarking may face considerable challenges, it is neither radical nor very complicated. In fact, it should seem natural for colleges to keep improving and

Higher education is a natural for benchmarking.

learning from those in higher education and business who are doing the most fascinating new things and are performing at extraordinarily high levels of excellence. Colleges and universities should not only foster learning in their students but also foster learning within their organization so they can grow in quality, stature, and value. Two higher education scholars put it nicely:

> What is education itself—our core mission—but continuous improvement through learning? Surely we want to endorse that idea as a description not only of our educational goal but also of our organizations as a whole (Sherr and Lozier 1991). ∎

REFERENCES

American Productivity & Quality Center. 1993 *Planning, Organizing, and Managing Benchmarking Activities: A User's Guide*. Houston, Texas.

Belmont University Long-Range Planning Commission. 1994. *Benchmarking Quality Team Manual*. Belmont University Center for Quality and Professional Development.

Blumenstyk, G. 1993. Colleges Look to "Benchmarking" to Measure How Efficient and Productive They Are. *Chronicle of Higher Education*. September 1: A41-42.

Camp, R. 1993. A Bible for Benchmarking. *Financial Executive* 9 (July-August): 23-27.

Dunn, J. 1992. Decision Processes. *College and University Business Administration*. NACUBO.

Johnson, J. 1993. *Total Quality Management in Education*. University of Oregon.

Ogilvie, T. 1993. Lost in Space: Typical Benchmarking Problems. *Management Review* 82 (September): 20-22.

Payne, J. and J. Blackburn. 1993. Learning Through Benchmarking. *Journal for Quality and Participation* 16 (September): 62-65.

Rush, S. 1994. Benchmarking—How Good is Good? In W. Massey and J. Meyerson (eds.) *Measuring Institutional Performance in Higher Education*. Peterson's.

Senge, P. 1990. *The Fifth Discipline: The Art and Practice of the Learning Organization*. Doubleday/Currency.

Sherr, L. and G. Lozier. 1991. Total Quality Management in Higher Education, in *New Directions for Institutional Research*, No. 71. Jossey-Bass.

Spendolini, M. 1992. *The Benchmarking Book*. AMACOM.

Watson, G. 1992. *The Benchmarking Workbook: Adaptive Best Practices for Performance Improvement*. Productivity Press (Cambridge, MA).

How to develop the research necessary for your enrollment management program.

Tracking and Understanding Your Students

Craig Clagett and Helen Schneider

n the past decade a growing number of American colleges and universities have replaced their comparatively simple and artful admissions office with a more sophisticated and quasi-scientific enrollment management operation. Enrollment management is a coordinated effort to influence the size and characteristics of a college's student body—through systematic recruitment, admissions processing, pricing, financial aid, advising, retention measures, and other policy initiatives. Conceptually it links research on how students choose their college, student-institution fit, and retention so that institutions can manage their enrollments more successfully from the time a student starts inquiring about colleges to the time he or she graduates. Some colleges include alumni tracking too.

A prerequisite for enrollment management is an understanding of the forces that influence individual decisions about college choice and persistence in college. Institutions therefore need to create a student flow model, from initial inquiry through application, enrollment, persistence, degree completion, and job or post-graduate study. Enrollment management should be founded on solid information. As two scholars have said:

> The single most critical element in all this effort is accurate, timely, usable information. Our ability to influence our enrollments to any degree is a direct function of the information ... available. (Claffey and Hossler 1986, p. 106.)

In this article we explain how you can set up the information infrastructure to support the new efforts at enrollment management. And we offer several examples of enrollment research to illustrate how it might be done. It is important to do the research right. As Michael Dolence reported in this journal four years ago, more than half the institutions that try to establish enrollment management programs fail (1989-90).

Craig Clagett is director of institutional research and analysis at Prince George's Community College in Maryland. He earned his Ph.D. in government and politics from the University of Maryland at College Park. He serves on the editorial boards of the *AIR Professional File* and the *Journal of Applied Research in the Community College.* Past president of AACC's National Council for Research and Planning, he is author of numerous articles and co-author of *The Institutional Research Practitioner* (1990).

Helen Schneider is director of research and analysis for the Maryland Independent College and University Association. A graduate in economics from the University of Virginia, she earned her M.B.A. from the University of Delaware.

In the beginning

Enrollment managers need information of six kinds, or answers to questions at six stages of a student's experience.

- How widely known is the college? How do prospective students view the college? What other institutions are the prospective students considering?
- How effective are the college's recruiting activities? What factors differentiate your college from its closest competitors and influence the choice of your admitted students? How can the college increase its yield?
- What influence does financial aid have on student decisions to enroll, and to remain in your college? What do students perceive to be the campus culture, and what influence does this culture have on retention or attrition?
- What proportion of a freshmen class persists to graduation? Which subgroups have a higher average attrition? Why do some students persist while others do not?
- How successful are your alumni in their postgraduate endeavors? What proportion remain involved with the institution, and why? What characteristics describe alumni donors?

As you can read, the results of admissions recruiting are now being measured increasingly not just in terms of the numbers, test scores, and characteristics of the new students but by the number who become well-adapted and successful students and who become productive alumni. Enrollment management represents a significant shift in attitude among university administrators toward students and what becomes of them.

How do you set up an information system to undergird enrollment management? We suggest five steps.

1. Review the literature, and visit colleges that have a successful system.
2. Develop a performance monitoring indicator system.
3. Construct longitudinal cohort tracking files.
4. Identify patterns in aggregate student behavior.
5. Conduct survey and focus group research to illuminate key student decision points.

In reviewing the literature, you should know it falls into two kinds. One kind is the books and articles written in the past 10 years to advocate the use of enrollment management. The other is the more diverse body of literature that includes recent research and describes successful information-gathering: on student college choice, student-institution fit, pricing and financial aid, student attrition, and other topics. A familiarity with national findings will help you decide how best to set up your own institution's research. Understanding student behavior is essential to influencing it—and to changing your college's academic culture to improve enrollment and retention.

The recruitment literature includes research on how students choose a college (Litten, Sullivan, and Brodigan 1983; Zemsky and Oedel 1983; Lay and Endo 1987), on student-institution fit (Williams 1986) and on impact of pricing and financial aid (Litten 1984; Leslie and Brinkman 1987; Huff 1989). The persistence literature includes several useful reviews (Pascarella 1982; Tinto 1987) as well as numerous case studies. There is also a literature on the in-

Enrollment management represents a significant shift in attitude.

stitutional research necessary for enrollment management (Davis-Van Atta 1986; Glover 1986). And this article presents an approach that has proven successful at both a small, fairly selective liberal arts college and a large, open-door community college.

Visiting colleges and universities that have installed an information system is also extremely helpful, especially in hearing and seeing first-hand the way the data is gathered, by whom, and with what success.

Monitoring performance

As a second step, your college will need to establish performance monitoring indicators, or PMIs. These are simple counts or ratios that report the status of enrollment at a point in time. PMIs should be developed with the consultation of the offices responsible for each stage of the enrollment process. With PMIs a college can evaluate the performance of each unit and oversee the whole enrollment picture.

Most colleges already track some PMIs for the recruitment phase: inquiry, application, and enrollment. At a minimum, the enrollment management team should

How data are organized requires a great deal of attention.

have clear expectations about the number of applications, offers of admission, and resulting enrollment anticipated for the planning term. Since the college and its faculty will want to know the characteristics as well as the magnitude of enrollment, the college should also monitor the SAT or ACT score distribution of the applicants, admits, and enrollees, the racial/ethnic composition at each stage, the school background, geographical origins, and other relevant items.

More and more colleges are now monitoring student persistence patterns, especially over the first two semesters, since this is usually the time of greatest attrition. Persistence rates for different populations—athletes, African Americans, students with the lowest scores at entry, or engineering students—can be reported separately. And some institutions have begun tracking their graduates: the number going to graduate or professional schools, the percent obtaining program-related employment, and those traveling or entering the military. The tracking system may need to be supplemented with surveys later—to find out about satisfaction with academics during college, say, or to learn about postgraduate activities.

A frequent problem of PMIs is how to organize the data for policy studies and college use. Standard transcript files and frozen term files are not ideal for student flow studies. How the data are organized requires a

great deal of attention so that the PMIs can be readily useful to planning changes.

The third step is to construct longitudinal cohort tracking files. You'll need data systems to parallel the student flow continuum from inquiry to post-graduation. (For overviews, see Ewell, Parker, and Jones 1988; Bers 1989; and Palmer 1990.) Free-standing tracking files for selected entering cohorts of students preserve data values and facilitate data analysis.

The data elements in such files fall into three categories. First are the student attributes such as demographic and academic background variables. Second are the student progress variables recorded each term, such as credit hours attempted and earned and the grade point average. Third are the outcome measures for graduates, and for those who leave without completing the program.

Tracking numerous cohorts simultaneously is complex, and there is usually little variation in successive years. So it is sufficient to track classes entering every third year. Students should be tracked for six to eight years to handle the growing number of undergraduates who study part-time, stop out for a year, or whose attendance is interrupted (Ewell 1987).

From data to analysis to policy

The PMIs will provide an overview of what is happening with campus enrollment, and the cohort tracking files will supplement the information gleaned from the PMI summary statistics. But the goal is to discern patterns in aggregate student behavior that will guide further research (Terenzini 1987). Hence, the fourth step.

A good approach for yielding the student behavioral data of most interest is to develop a standard analysis that provides both trend data for several cohorts and for subgroup analysis within a given cohort. To illustrate, suppose 50 percent of all students entering your college in the fall of 1991 had earned at least 60 credits after two years. You find that the percentage earning at least 60 credits after two years in the class entering three years earlier in 1988, was over 70 percent. This decline should alert the institution to study why student progress toward a degree is slowing.

You need to anticipate future research needs. Try to identify the subgroups of students that will be of research interest to your college. These may include identifiers for remedial students, non-native English speakers, scholarship recipients, athletes, students in honors programs, arts and music majors, and other groups of special concern. If this is done, it is relatively easy to examine attendance patterns and outcomes for subgroups by running the standard analysis against the appropriate variables.

The fifth step is to conduct survey research and focus group studies. Along the continuum from inquiry through the post-graduate relationship students face a series of decisions: whether to apply, whether to enroll, whether to stay at the college or transfer, whether to be a generous and loyal alumnus or not. Colleges need to know as much as possible about these student decision points, especially about what factors influence the decisions.

For this information, survey and focus group research—and in-depth interviews—are most useful. You should conduct these at key points in the college experience. Focus groups, where 8 to 12 students respond to a skilled questioner's queries, are especially good for a reality check about your college's image and position compared to the competition, for evaluating your promotional materials, and for learning the needs of particular student groups. They are also a source for discovering ways to improve service and for generating new ideas. You should maintain files for survey data that can be linked to the longitudinal data for further analysis.

Three vivid examples

To help give you a better sense of how tracking can be done, we offer three illustrations of the approach that characterizes a comprehensive enrollment management system. The illustrations are all drawn from the research at a large, open-admissions community college in suburban Washington, D.C. Reflecting the county's population, the college has a majority African American student body. Three-fourths of the students attend part-time; half say they intend to transfer to a four-year college or university. Clearly, the research needed at

Focus groups are especially good for a reality check.

a four-year college would differ in scope and emphasis. But nonetheless, these examples demonstrate how colleges can address specific questions.

One: a focus group study of delayed-entry students. Nearly two-thirds of the high school graduates of this county do not attend college the year following their graduation. The college wanted to learn why this is so. The institutional research office organized a series of focus groups with current students who had delayed their entry to college.

The focus group discussions revealed that most of the students had postponed college to continue working in jobs begun while in high school. Jobs and careers provided a sense of purpose to these students; many cited job skill development or a desire to change careers and leave dead-end jobs as their reasons for entering college. The time out of school, they felt, provided them with motivation, money, and confidence to start college.

The students saw themselves as a special group, more mature and motivated than the 18-year-olds, yet not really "adult" returning students. They often described a sense of pride they had from paying for their college education, unlike the 18-year-olds who relied on their parents and the government for financial support. Without exception they felt they were more committed to their studies than the younger students. They admitted, however, that they had feelings of doubt about their ability to keep up academically with the traditional students just out of high school, but most found these fears quickly dispelled in their first classes. (The lack of a standardized admissions test requirement was a factor for many in choosing the community college rather than a four-year institution.)

The focus group revelations enabled the admissions office to target its messages to this group more effectively, stressing the non-intimidating aspect of the two-year college, career advancement, and an appeal to the pride and maturity of these delayed-entry students. The information gathered also prompted the college's academic leaders to schedule additional evening and weekend classes so that these hard-working students could complete their degree without quitting their jobs.

Two: geo-demographic market analysis. This community college serves a county that has a population larger than that of five states in the nation, and is very diverse. So reliance on county-wide census data for planning and admissions purposes can be misleading, obscuring pockets of poverty, prosperity, and ethnic groups. This led the research office to employ "lifestyle cluster analysis," a geo-demographic tool used by business firms. The underlying premise is that people tend to cluster in neighborhoods that reflect their

> *By geo-coding the college was able to see its students in a new light.*

economic, social, or religious values ("birds of a feather flock together").

Geo-demographic enrollment analysis enables a campus to know more about who its current students are and where to find more students like them. Cluster analysis systems based on national data can be purchased, and these may be useful for universities or elite colleges that have national student bodies. But this community college decided to develop its own. An internally created system avoids licensing fees, uses local rather than national data, and emphasizes lifestyle factors particularly important to college planning, such as age and educa-

tional levels. Using cluster routines included in the office's statistical analysis software, and a set of local demographic data, the college's researchers identified 24 distinct neighborhood types within the county (Boughan 1990).

Residents of these 24 neighborhoods had different lifestyles, aspirations, and educational needs. By geo-coding student address lists—identifying the U.S. Census tract and thus which cluster each student resided in—the college was able to see its students in a new light. Contrary to expectations, the cluster analysis revealed that the community college's highest penetration was in the upscale clusters. The analysis also revealed that credit courses attracted different clusters from non-credit courses.

The college found that residents of mostly white, lower-middle-class and blue-collar neighborhoods had the highest A.A. degree completion rate, but a very low transfer rate to four-year colleges. Residents of mostly black, middle-class clusters had a comparatively low A.A. degree attainment rate but a fairly high rate of transfer to four-year institutions. The county's largest cluster—well-educated young singles and new families, mainly living in garden apartments and at the beginning of their careers—had a unique outcome pattern: low rates of graduation and transfer but an extraordinary rate of continuing enrollment. For this cluster a high percentage were already college graduates, so many were using their community college to upgrade their skills and learn new things. The geo-demographic market analysis has yielded a wealth of new insights about how the county's residents were using their community college.

Three: patterns of attendance analysis. External agencies are increasingly asking for college graduation rates. At this community college, the graduation rate was under 15 percent. The college needed to know why it was so low, so it could design programs to improve the completion rate.

Tracking students over an eight-year period, the college found that more than one-fourth of the first-time students attended only that one semester. Another third—the "stop-outs"—had interrupted patterns of attendance. Those most likely to graduate were those who attended semester after semester uninterruptedly. While only 12 percent of the cohort graduated within eight years, a majority of those who

Knowing the students better seems an indispensable knowledge frontier.

attended six or more consecutive semesters received a degree.

Many who had "dropped out," had actually transferred to a four-year college or university. And analysis of seven entering cohorts found increasing numbers of students transferring to senior institutions without earning their A.A. degree. This contributed to a decline in A.A. degree attainment rates.

Concurrently, the research office initiated a project to follow the fall 1990 entering class in depth. The median credits earned after two semesters was six. Less than two percent were at a pace to graduate in the allotted two years, and after two terms nearly one-fourth of the students had yet to earn a single credit.

The college discovered that the credit accumulation was so slow because many students were taking non-credit remedial courses. Three-fifths of the entrants who took placement tests needed remediation in at least one area of reading, composition, and mathematics. Moreover, the extent of remedial need was severe for numerous students. For example, after three semesters only eight percent—one in twelve— were ready to take the introductory college mathematics course for credit. These findings prompted a review of the remedial programs at the college.

As enrollment becomes more of an issue for many colleges and universities and the potential students become more diverse than ever, it will be incumbent for higher education institutions to know more about their students and student choices than ever before. And the quality movement, which preaches staying close to one's customers, will also require closer tracking and better understanding of your college's clientele. For any institution that plans to improve its academic services, knowing the students better seems an indispensable knowledge frontier. ∎

REFERENCES

Bers, T. 1989. Using Student Tracking Systems Effectively. *New Directions for Community Colleges,* (no. 66). Jossey-Bass.

Boughan, K. 1990. *The PG-TRAK Manual: Using PGCC's Custom Lifestyle Cluster System.* Office of Institutional Research and Analysis, Prince George's Community College.

Claffey, M. and D. Hossler. 1986. An Integrated Enrollment Management System. In *Managing College Enrollments,* D. Hossler (ed.). New Directions for Higher Education, (no. 53). Jossey-Bass.

Costello, D. 1989. The Development of a Performance Indicator System: A New Direction for Enrollment Management. In *Bringing Technology to the Issues.* North East Association for Institutional Research.

Davis-Van Atta, D. and S. Carrier. 1986. Using the Institutional Research Office. In *Managing College Enrollments,* D. Hossler (ed.). New Directions for Higher Education, (no. 53). Jossey-Bass.

Dolence, M. 1989-90. Evaluation Criteria for an Enrollment Management Program. *Planning for Higher Education,* 18 (1): 1-13.

Ewell, P. 1987. Principles in Longitudinal Enrollment Analysis: Conducting Retention and Student Flow Studies. In *A Primer on Institutional Research,* J. A. Muffo and G. W. McLaughlin (eds). Association for Institutional Research.

Ewell, P., R. Parker and D. Jones. 1988. *Establishing a Longitudinal Student Tracking System: An Implementation Handbook.* National Center for Higher Education Management Systems.

Glover, R. 1986. Designing a Decision-Support System for Enrollment Management. *Research in Higher Education,* 24 (1): 15-34.

Hossler, D. 1987. Enrollment Management: Institutional Applications. *College and University,* 62 (2): 106-116.

Hossler, D. 1991. Evaluating Student Recruitment and Retention Programs. *New Directions for Institutional Research,* (no. 70). Jossey-Bass.

Hossler, D. and F. Kemerer. 1986. Enrollment Management and Its Context. In *Managing College Enrollments,* D. Hossler (ed.). New Directions for Higher Education, (no. 53). Jossey-Bass.

Huff, R. 1989. Facilitating and Applying Research in Student Financial Aid to Institutional Objectives. In *Studying the Impact of Student Aid on Institutions*, R. Fenske (ed.). New Directions for Institutional Research, (no. 62). Jossey-Bass.

Lay, R. and J. Endo. 1987. Designing and Using Market Research. *New Directions for Institutional Research,* (no. 54). Jossey-Bass.

Leslie, L. and P. Brinkman. 1987. Student Price Response in Higher Education. *Journal of Higher Education,* 58 (2): 181-203.

Litten, L. 1984. Issues in Pricing Undergraduate Education. *New Directions for Institutional Research,* (no. 42). Jossey-Bass.

Litten, L., D. Sullivan, and D. Brodigan. 1983. *Applying Market Research in College Admissions.* College Entrance Examination Board.

Palmer, J. 1990. *Accountability Through Student Tracking: A Review of the Literature.* American Association of Community and Junior Colleges.

Pascarella, E. 1982. Studying Student Attrition. *New Directions for Institutional Research,* (no. 36). Jossey-Bass.

Terenzini, P. 1987. Studying Student Attrition and Retention. In *A Primer on Institutional Research*, J. A. Muffo and G. W. McLaughlin (eds). Association for Institutional Research.

Tinto, V. 1987. *Leaving College.* University of Chicago Press.

Williams, T. 1986. Optimizing Student-Institution Fit. *In Managing College Enrollments,* D. Hossler (ed). New Directions for Higher Education, (no. 53). Jossey-Bass.

Zemsky, R. and P. Oedel. 1983. *The Structure of College Choice.* College Entrance Examination Board.

How colleges can reduce the hassle that students have with administrative offices.

Redesigning Student Services

Julie Karns

I t's the first day of the semester. A student is prevented from registering for classes. The registrar's office sends her to the bursar's office, where she is told there is a problem with her previous semester's balance of payments. But the person at the window has trouble interpreting the account statement, so a long line of frustrated students listens while the student tries to solve her personal financial problem in public. The befuddled clerk at the bursar's window, aware of the growing line of students, commands the student to go to another building to straighten things out at the financial aid office, where she goes, angry, to the rear of another line.

The delivery of student administrative services in U.S. higher education is famous for its level of frustration and "hassle." Anecdotes about the ordeal of registration and financial accounts abound on most campuses, and cartoons about the process are sometimes included in the semester's first issue of the campus newspaper. Faculty

usually refer to the process with humor and annoyed resignation. Higher education's methods of handling student administrative details is often uncoordinated, ineffective, and a principal source of dissatisfaction among college students.

It is becoming increasingly evident that the way colleges and universities handle their student administrative services needs to change. There are several reasons for doing so. For one, unpleasant experiences with campus administrative offices contributes to student dropouts and transfers to other colleges. Although little research has been done on the institutional obstacles to retention, at least one analyst (Anderson 1985) has pointed out that administrative procedures often are an obstacle to student persistence. For another, an increasing number of minority students, youths from immigrant families, foreign students, and first-time college goers are entering universities today; and these students require better advising and more caring treatment.

Also, students have become more informed consumers, demanding a level of university administrative service comparable to that which they receive from other entities in society. This is particularly true for the increasing number of adult students (25 years and older) who are returning to campus. As one observer notes (Giczkowski

Julie Karns is Vice President for Finance and Treasurer of Rider University. An alumnus of Translyvania University in Lexington, Kentucky, Ms. Karns is a CPA. Prior to joining Rider, she served as Vice President for Finance and Administration of Pratt Institute in Brooklyn, New York. Her responsibilities at those institutions have included financial analysis and reporting, budgeting, cash management, and labor relations.

1990), these adults students "have been conditioned to believe that the customer is always right. Consciously or not, they see themselves as customers who are free to take their tuition money elsewhere if they are not satisfied." The Total Quality Management (TQM) movement is also pressing colleges to provide better services to their student "customers."

Then too, with the tuition and college costs rising one-third faster then the Consumer Price Index in the past decade, the need for improved financial counseling, aid, and assistance has grown enormously. This is especially so for students from poorer families who often lack family models for wise long-term financial management. Finally, there is the urgency for each campus to streamline its operations to reduce expenditures. Though many colleges have experienced declining enrollments, the administrative personnel performing academic support services grew by 61 percent between 1975 and 1985, or more than 100,000 persons (Grassmuck 1990), and continues to swell. At the institution at which I work, Pratt Institute, enrollments declined more than 20 percent between 1980 and 1990; yet over the same period faculty ranks declined by only seven percent and the ranks of managerial and clerical employees actually increased by 19 percent. Universities must reorganize how they provide administrative services in order to halt the swell in administrative staffing. The classic tripartite division of student administrative services model into offices of the bursar, registrar, and financial aid represents an antiquated model.

Where's the problem?

The first task for universities is to conduct an analysis of why the present scheme of student administrative services is ineffective. When an institution understands why and where the existing structure is dysfunctional, its administrative leaders can then rethink and reorganize. I believe most campuses will find three primary difficulties, as we did.

Lack of good advice and counseling. The biggest failure in the present arrangement is the lack of adequate advising and direction for students. There are published catalogs and student manuals, but little or no personal instruction or guidance. In the traditional model, staff who interact with students have responsibility for both counseling and transaction processing. At peak times such as the beginning of each semester, the processing of registrations and student payments takes precedence and there is little time for advising students. Without proper advice, many students get confused about how to proceed.

This is especially a problem in the area of financial counseling. Eighteen-year olds, including many from modest-income families, are expected to negotiate a $20,000 to $30,000 annual investment at private colleges and universities, or $10,000 to $15,000 costs at public and state institutions. Given the number of broken families and the economic squeeze on middle-income families, and given the variety of grants, loans, jobs, and work-study jobs, most undergraduates

> *The division into offices of bursar, registrar, and financial aid represents an antiquated model.*

live on the edge financially and are confused about financial aid possibilities. (About five percent of all students currently do not repay their loans, including about 10 percent of African American students.) In his book on retention, Vincent Tinto (1987) says that fluctuations in financial aid can affect persistence: "For some students, especially those whose financial situations are already tentative, such changes over the short term may well spell the difference between college and at least temporary withdrawal."

Inflexible staffing patterns. The persons who work in the bursar, registrar, and financial aid offices typically have narrowly defined areas of skill and expertise. They often lack the knowledge required to respond to a student's questions about policies and procedures unrelated to their own department and to make appropriate referrals to other offices. In the traditional structure there is little cross training and staff

---

Students frequently complain about a "run-around" in administrative student services.

---

sharing, which not only prevents adequate guidance to students but also results in overstaffing and reduced promotion opportunities for staff persons. Inflexible staffing is a common cause of frequent student complaints about a "run-around" in administrative student services.

Uncoordinated policy making. In most colleges and universities the three offices of bursar, registrar and student records, and financial aid report to different institutional divisions. The bursar often reports to the controller or treasurer; the registrar usually reports to the vice president of academic affairs or of administration; and the director of financial aid may report to the vice president for student affairs. This reporting structure lends itself to fragmented decisionmaking and policy inconsistencies. Academicians are often unaware of financial policies, and registrars or bursars may be unaware of the implications of their actions for the college's cash flow.

Also, the roles of the three offices are changing. Registrars are being pressed to provide information on such subjects as when students drop out and why, faculty workloads, and the comparative costs of academic programs. With the escalation of tuition, financial aid administrators are becoming more like deans of students, with an "ever-increasing role of integrating student services with the academic function while addressing business needs" (Fisher 1986). No one office appears to be coordinating policies about student services,

records, and charges or assuming responsibility for structural change to accommodate the changing functions of student service administrators.

Planning the new model

After such an analysis, I believe many institutions will conclude that planning for a new student administrative services model is imperative, one that both improves services to students and reduces costs for the institution. That is what we began to do over a four-month period in February, 1991 at Pratt Institute, with the campus president's blessing.

We organized a seven-person planning team consisting of the two top administrators in the three departments—bursar, registrar, and financial aid—and the assistant vice president for finance and administration, a newly created position to improve all student administrative services and enhance the Institute's financial analysis and reporting. A survey of student services provided evidence of the need for change and suggestions about the directions for change. We sought the advice of the department heads and the academic advising staff. To ensure top-level support, we also sought the advise of two groups that determine Pratt's administrative and academic policies: the Administrative Management Committee (the college's senior officers) and the Dean's Council.

Because Pratt's non-administrative employees are represented by unions, we consulted with Pratt's human resources professionals and then the union representatives. We made clear our desire to create a higher standard of student services while reducing expenditures in the student services area. The union leadership recognized the need for reform and helped alleviate anxiety among employees about the proposed changes.

We also employed an outside consultant and auditor to check for flaws in our rethinking and internal controls. In all these consultations we found help in the list of conditions conducive to change in higher education that is spelled out by Creamer and Creamer (1988), especially for identifying potential impediments to change.

The team then developed the customary mission and goals. Our three-part mission was:

- to improve student administrative services so that they contribute to satisfaction with Pratt and help retention;
- to increase efficiency in this area so that costs are controlled, and if possible reduced;
- to restructure the way student administrative services are delivered to accomplish both better and increased efficiency.

To carry out the mission, the team agreed on four strategic goals:

- to project a single, coordinated view of Pratt's student policies, services, and procedures to all students, faculty, parents, and staff;
- to separate to the greatest extent possible advising, counseling, and information services from operation functions;
- to automate standard transactions as much as possible to allow staff to focus on student service and problem solving;
- to give more control to students through student-initiated transactions (registration, records inquiries, finance-related matters) by more intensive use of technological hardware and software.

At the end of four months we arrived at a new model for administrative services. In place of the three traditional offices of bursar, registrar, and financial aid, Pratt would group its services according to three new functions (see Figure 1):

- information, advising, and counseling
- operations and processing
- analysis and reporting of data.

We thought this new division would better meet student needs, providing a central place to obtain information and receive counseling, a behind-the-scene group to process all data, and an office to provide transcripts to students, data to state and federal offices, and analyses to in-house management.

Steps of the reorganization

Once a university decides what it wants to do and what new structure is necessary to carry out the change, it must then implement its planned transformation. At Pratt Institute, we did the implementation in four phases: redesign of policies and procedures, reorganization, staff development, and systems enhancement.

Redesign policies and procedures. Students need a single center where they can get answers to questions they have and advice on problems that arise. And faculty need a central place to which they can refer students. So we created an Information Center where students make inquiries about academic, financial, or recordkeeping with a much reduced wait. If the problem is complex, or if detailed counseling about financial matters is desired, students are encouraged to make an appointment

---

FIGURE 1

Student Administrative Services Duties

Information and Counseling	Operations and Processing	Analysis, Reporting, and Services
Reception/Referrals	Billing	Management Reporting
Faculty/Staff Liaison (Service)	Payment Processing	External Reporting
Financial Counseling	Grade Processing	Faculty/Staff Liaison (Data)
Student Employment	Degree Audit	Space Management
Veterans Services	Transcript Prep/Distribution	Database Administration
Leave Counseling	Loan Administration	Programming Changes
Appeals	Program Changes	Student Account Collection

with one of the counselors or the director of the information and counseling division. The staff member who first talks to the student summarizes the student's problem in writing so the other staff person who will meet with the student can research the problem and formulate options before the

The union leadership recognized the need for reform.

student arrives for the appointment. The advising division also runs financial aid workshops, contacts students about financial assistance possibilities, handles registration appeals, arranges leaves of absence, and helps students find campus jobs.

The operations and processing group is not expected to deal with complex student difficulties or provide advice, but they are trained to answer basic questions about policy and procedures. Their role is to process academic and financial information promptly and accurately. The internal and external analysis and reporting group issues reports and studies of many kinds, but it also assists the operations group with instruction about data processing and use of technology.

Reorganization. To determine which division everyone in the old bursar, registrar, and financial aid offices might be best suited, we asked each staff person to complete a staff profile detailing the duties he or she performed. It also asked employees what they most enjoyed and disliked doing in their current positions. Next, we circulated a full set of the new position descriptions, both clerical and administrative, of the reformed student services structure (see Figure 2), and each staff person filled out a position preference form listing up to three positions for which they wanted to compete. Some positions were filled immediately, without interview, based on the person's qualifications and experience. Other positions elicited much interest and required interviews.

The support of the union was crucial at this point. The union was asked to comment on the revised clerical position descriptions, and the consultation paid off. For example, when one person formally complained that no upgrade had been given even though the new position required wider duties and new responsibilities, the union supported the Human Resources Office's contention that while the work was more varied the degree of difficulty and skills required did not justify an upgrade.

FIGURE 2

Student Administrative Services
Unit Staffing

Information and Counseling	Operations and Processing	Analysis, Reporting, and Services
Director	Director	Director
Assoc. Dir. – Financial Aid	Office Manager	Associate Director
Sr. Financial Aid Counselor	Asst. Dir. – Fin'l. Processing	Credit Manager
Financial Aid Counselor (3)	Senior Financial Assistant	Information Specialist
Student Employment Coord.	Financial Assistant (4)	
Information Center Asst. II	Asst. Dir. – Acad. Processing	
Information Center Asst. I (2)	Records Mgmt. Asst. II	
Academic Service Asst. II	Records Mgmt. Asst. I (3)	
Academic Service Asst. I		

Staff development. Key to the change in student administrative services was a major effort to train the staff. One scholar noted that, "The improvement of people in the work setting depends on their ability to give and receive information, to empathize and understand, and to listen and receive feedback" (Dalton 1989). So communications training became a central element in staff development. Pratt's Human Resources staff created an in-service training program, stressing the need to offer appropriated referrals to the students. We used role-play and group discussion to emphasize the importance of good listening skills, friendly telephone technique, and readiness to "go the extra mile" in courtesy and help. We also covered ways to defuse tensions and resolve conflicts.

Because Pratt has a substantial foreign student population, the Director of International Affairs conducted a workshop on the special needs for communicating with this population. The Vice President of Student Life addressed the staff on her office's services and how the administrative student services group could best collaborate with her department.

We spent much time too on technical skills training. The systems and reporting unit developed a "counseling module" within the administrative computing system to provide read-only access to student academic and financial records, and everyone was instructed how to provide students with advice on a single visit. We held evening workshops to offer hands-on experience in researching student problems; and we sent supervisors and staff to outside training sessions to show that we were investing n their personal skills development.

To improve the leadership skills of the supervisors, Pratt trained all of them in spreadsheet applications on the computer, developed a course in effective writing, and suggested that each attend an outside workshop on supervising staff decision making, managing conflict, and team building. Managers were urged to instruct in an improved student orientation program and during parents' weekend, and to initiate training programs for all their new student employees. Supervisors designed an employee recognition program with monthly awards for quality service. One innovation—that all staff wear name tags daily—not only allowed students to identify individuals for praise and criticism but also increased awareness of courtesy and personal assistance.

> *Key to the change in student administrative services was a major effort to train the staff.*

Systems enhancement. Our fourth phase was to improve productivity and service through better use of technology. We instituted tape download of external financial aid information and are installing optical scanning technology to process grades and student timesheets. At numerous universities students can now register by telephone or review their transcripts and financial accounts through ATM-like systems, and we intend to do this too.

Progress and pitfalls

We are evaluating the changes we made, and are still refining; but we are encouraged so far by the new structure of student administrative services. Our greatest achievement is the new Information Center. The staff in this area have quickly developed broad knowledge and have already earned a reputation from the students for listening, caring, and providing very helpful advice. We certainly have a more able and informed group of employees than we did two years ago. We created advancement opportunities for five minority staff members, two managerial and three clerical, where none had previously existed. And in reorganizing, we reduced the number of positions from 35 to 27, and cut the department budget by $210,000, a 19 percent drop.

But Pratt's changeover has been hampered by two things: lack of time for leadership and resource restraints. While the departmental managers have the experience and ability to lead, competing demands on their time make it difficult to do justice to their champion roles. Lack of money to put in place the new technology to relieve the staff from inputing that students can do themselves has caused some overload during peak periods, and frustrations which still surface occasionally in dealing with students.

I believe the new model for administrative student services that some colleges like Pratt Institute are experimenting with is a reform that more institutions will need to plan for, especially with the more competitive and financially constricted environ-

Our greatest achievement is the new Information Center.

ment that lies ahead. As George Keller has noted (1983), "Without new monies and additional students, a university's chief hope for increased productivity, higher levels of academic productivity, and better management is to improve performance of the people already at the college and make every new appointment count." Training all staff members and restructuring higher

education's services for students to make the services more user-friendly seems a must for the 1990s. ∎

REFERENCES

Anderson, E. 1985. Forces Influencing Student Persistence and Achievement. In *Increasing Student Retention: Effective Programs and Practices for Reducing the Dropout Rate*. L. Noel, R. Levitz, D. Saluri and Associates (eds.) Jossey-Bass, 44-61.

Creamer, D., and E. Creamer. 1988. Predicting Successful Organizational Change: A Case Study. *Journal of College Student Development* 29(1): 4-11.

Dalton, J. 1989. Enhancing Staff Knowledge and Skills. In *Student Services: a Handbook for the Profession*, 2nd ed. U. Delworth, G. Hanson, and Associates (eds.). Jossey-Bass, 533-551.

Fischer, M. 1986. The Need for Organizational Integration in Financial Aid Administration. *The Business Officer* 20(5): 34-38.

Giczkowski, W. 1990. Colleges Must Learn to Cope With Market-Oriented Adult Students. *The Chronicle of Higher Education* 36(29): B2.

Grassmuck, K. 1990. Big Increases in Academic-Support Staffs Prompts Growing Concerns on Campuses. *The Chronicle of Higher Education* 36(28): A1.

Keller, G. 1983. *Academy Strategy: The Management Revolution in American Higher Education*. Johns Hopkins University Press, 64.

Tinto, V. 1987. *Leaving College: Rethinking the Causes and Cures of Student Attrition*. University of Chicago Press, 82.

Anniversaries can be moments of intense planning as well as celebration.

Planning for a Centennial

Nancy Sureck

Most colleges and universities use their 50th, 100th, 150th, or 200th anniversary as the occasion for a series of celebrative events and historical looks backward. These events are usually emotional, sentimental, and memorable, and occasionally merry. But centennials are also a time of intense introspection and planning for the future. A little known fact, one that I have seen repeatedly, is that a centennial—or milestone anniversary—celebration is as much about the future as it is about the past.

Centennials induce plenty of nostalgia. They provide an opportunity to remember the college's most influential teachers, to honor the most distinguished graduates,

Nancy Sureck is president of Centennial Celebration Consultants in New York City. Her experience includes 10 years as a public affairs commentator for Voice of America broadcasts to Africa; public relations for ABC-TV and NBC-TV; publicity for clients such as Bob Hope, Danny Kaye, and the Texaco Corporation; centennial coordinator for the Metropolitan Opera; and director of special events for the 100th anniversary of the Statue of Liberty. A graduate of Sarah Lawrence College, where she served on the Board of Trustees for seven years, she founded her firm in 1987 and has done anniversary celebrations for clients such as The New York Stock Exchange, Broadway: 100 Years in Times Square, Volunteers of America, Carnegie Hall, the *Wall Street Journal*, and consulted for several educational institutions.

and to capture the memories of the oldest graduates. They allow a college to look back with pride. But the question naturally arises, What should we be doing for our next hundred years? And other questions ooze into consciousness. How have we most distinguished ourselves in the past century? What do we really stand for? Do we need to change? If so, how?

These questions lead naturally into some strategic planning for the next few decades. In three out of four cases in academe, the anniversary and planning that accompanies it also prompts a capital funds campaign for building renovations, scholarships, new construction, and more endowment dollars.

In addition, centennials and special anniversaries are a wonderful opportunity to make a university better known regionally or nationally, even globally. Colleges seem to worry a lot about their image. A centennial is a great time to correct an image if the public has an inaccurate view of your institution. It can also enhance your image, or partially change your image in preparation for some new directions you are racing toward. For instance, during the centennial of Carnegie Hall the directors felt that most people associated Manhattan's Carnegie Hall almost exclusively with classical music, and they were hoping to develop a more diverse audience. So Carnegie Hall's centennial leaders dug out photographs and posters and reminded everyone that Carnegie Hall had also housed performances by Booker T. Washington, Judy Garland, Benny Goodman, the Beatles, and many jazz stars.

Getting ready

If your college or university has a milestone anniversary coming up, you need to plan for it carefully. I have found that preparations need to begin three to four years in advance. Two years does not allow enough time for certain major events, and five years is too distant, causing trouble and lack of focus.

The institution should assemble a small internal group to spend a half day thinking about how the centennial should be handled. Should it be splashy or quiet? Should an outside expert be consulted? Who should be the campus centennial director? What are the college's priorities among the constituencies they want to reach? How should the celebration be paid for? What will be the exact date of the celebration? (This is often a contentious mat-

---

Centennials are an opportunity to make a university better known.

---

ter. Does a college celebrate the date when it got its charter? When it bought some land? When it opened its doors to students?) And when will the celebration be held—September to May of the anniversary year, or January 1 to December 31, or for five or six intensive months around the actual day of the founding?

If I am consulted at the beginning, I usually ask for a one or two-day planning session with the key people. At a university, that would probably be the chief officers and selected trustees, persons in public relations, alumnae affairs, development, the library or archives, admissions, student leadership, the media center, and planning, and a few of the professors who have been around longest. I call it "the think tank." We

begin with the largest question of all, Why are we having a celebration? Or, to put it another way, what does the institution want to accomplish with its birthday bash? The answer to this question will shape the entire centennial, and give it focus and purpose.

Does the college want to stress its venerability and national importance? Does it wish to use the publicity to clarify or reinforce its image? Does it want to use the celebration to increase applications, especially from outside its region and among males? Does it hope to launch new strategic priorities during the anniversary year? To lay the groundwork for a new three-year fund-raising campaign? To restore pride among graduates? To get an edge on one or two specific long-time competitors? What are the two, three, or four principal goals?

I press to get directly into specific, detailed wording, and reach agreement in writing on exactly what the institution hopes to accomplish. An outsider like me can help keep the goals overarching and pull them away from the excessively territorial interests of some insiders. Only after a college has very clear goals for its centennial can it plan its strategies about how to achieve those goals.

Closely allied is a second major question, Who does the institution especially want to reach? Are political and corporate leaders the principal audience? All the alumnae and the institution's friends? The college's townies? The general public on the West Coast or in the Southeast? Other cultural and educational institutions? High school college advisors? Intellectuals in certain foreign countries? Depending on the answers to this question, campus leaders can then begin to sense what exhibits, events, parties, publications, and publicity are proper, and where the placements will be most important.

How big a celebration?

Next is the issue of scope and budget. Should the celebrations take place mostly on campus? Should they be statewide? Or national? Even international? It is not unusual for universities—and other cultural institutions—to try to do too much, over too wide an area, with too little money. The scope of the project must fit the institution's financial capabilities. It is better to do several things really well than do many things in a slipshod manner, especially if one of your messages is that you are a high-quality enterprise.

Preparations should begin three to four years in advance.

Sometimes, as with the Statute of Liberty Centennial, the scope of the celebration can be expanded through aggressive fundraising for the centennial. A few corporate sponsors or several affluent and very dedicated older graduates may decide to contribute to a more comprehensive and dramatic celebration. But for colleges, such fundraising usually collides alongside the capital campaign that is being inaugurated with the centennial. A solid centennial for a small college might cost less than $200,000, for a larger institution from $200,000 to $500,000, and for a large major university roughly $400,000 to $1 million.

Once these essentials are settled, an institution is ready to structure the work of the centennial. Who will do what? My experience suggests that centennials should be run from the center. They cannot be done raggle-taggle, led by hundreds of well-intentioned volunteers, though volunteers can be very helpful on many occasions as aides, chaperones, and assistants. So a university needs a small, decisive centennial team and a campus-based director, and perhaps an expert consultant.

Consultants can be helpful at the conceptual stage, but they can be especially helpful at getting things done and taking care of details. They can direct a university to filmmakers, banner makers, poster artists, window display experts, medallion makers, calligraphers for awards, manufacturers of plates, T-shirts, and mugs, photographers, graphic designers, caterers, and arrangers of exhibits. They can rent a hot-air balloon or a comedian. They train staff, guide archivists, help assemble press kits, and help place stories in papers, magazines, and on television. They know celebrities, and can rent a sailing ship or a 1920 automobile for your 75th anniversary. They know that a scholarly book of history takes 36 months to produce, major exhibits take 18-20 months to prepare, and gala dinners take 6 months. Perhaps most important of all, a consultant takes the pressure off the regular college staff, who usually have little extra time to run all the events of a centennial.

A crucial appointment early on is the position of centennial archivist. This is vital. Someone must spearhead the treasure hunt for old photographs, memorabilia, and especially objects of historic worth. Many of these found objects can become publicity stories or fundraisers at an auction: the baseball shirt the current governor wore during his senior year on the college team, the bowler hat of some famous 19th-century dean, a photo during a student drama production of a now-illustrious Nobel Prize scientist. Then-and-now stories are great favorites for alumnae and the media.

The institution will need a "mark," or centennial design, to go on all stationary, flags, and special merchandise during the celebration year. There probably should be

What do you want to accomplish with a birthday bash?

a documentary film, a contest or two, some oral history projects, a special symposium, and maybe two books: one scholarly, the other a coffee-table picture book. All these projects will require a detailed calendar and timetable for production.

There should be a major event to kick off the centennial year, and a gala party, possibly black tie, to end the celebration. At the very end there should be a final, smaller, thank you party for all those who worked on the centennial, at which time a specialty medallion, paperweight, or pin is given to each person.

The importance of culture

Each institution has its own culture and style. The *Wall Street Journal* is not quite like the *Chicago Tribune*. Yale University is not quite like Indiana University. Berea College is not quite like Reed College. A centennial, or major anniversary celebration, should fit the school or enterprise. Some will be folksy, some highly intellectual and artistic. Some college celebrations will have religious overtones, some will stress how the college helped shape the work and industries in its area. Know your institution's special culture. Appropriateness is a must. Fit is essential.

But appropriateness for the future is important too. So use the centennial as a time to reassess, to look hard at what changes may be necessary for the next several decades. If you do engage in strategic planning, try to keep it separate from the centennial committee; but keep the centennial planners informed of any notable, new strategic priorities and facilities needs that

the futures group arrives at. For example, if your university hopes to emphasize the arts much more in the years ahead, the celebration group can do special displays on the theater or studio arts programs of the past. Or, if your university intends to become stronger in science, a focus on science over the years can be featured.

I have found that centennials are a time when many people ask, Where is the institution going from here? and, How will we be different in the future? Somehow, for

The centennial is a time to reassess.

many Americans the past is linked to the future, the past is prologue.

One last thing. Centennials are a time for fun. There are rediscovered camaraderies, renewed friendships, gatherings of unusual warmth with spirited, even jolly talk. Centennials are marvelous occasions to unite a college's community or a university's diverse constituencies in fresh bonds of loyalty and mutual assistance, and to foster new feelings of appreciation. Plan for them well. ∎

ABOUT THE EDITOR

George Keller is an education consultant and writer, one of America's leading scholars of higher education, a noted strategic planner, and an award-winning editor and education writer.

He took his undergraduate and graduate degrees from Columbia University, where he served as a faculty member in political science and a college dean. He later worked as assistant to the chancellor of the SUNY system and to the president of the University of Maryland system. Until recently, he chaired the program in Higher Education Studies at the University of Pennsylvania's Graduate School of Education.

Keller is author of more than 100 articles and reviews and has lectured at several universities. His 1983 book *Academic Strategy: The Management Revolution in American Higher Education,* is in its seventh printing and was named in two polls of college educators—by the *New York Times* and *Change* magazine—as the most influential book of the past decade. He also edits the journal *Planning for Higher Education.*

His awards include *Atlantic* magazine's Education-Writer-of-the-Year, the Sibley Award for education magazine editing, the U.S. Steel Foundation Medal for "distinguished service to higher education," and the Casey Award from the Society for College and University Planning for "distinguished achievements in the field of education planning."

He is completing a new book with the aid of a Pew Charitable Trust research grant.

Other Titles Available from The Society for College and University Planning

Special Planning for Special Spaces $29.95
    edited by Persis Rickes

Transforming Higher Education—   SCUP Members $50
A Vision for Learning in the 21st Century   Nonmembers $60
    by Michael Dolence and Donald Norris

Doing Academic Planning—   SCUP Members $50
Effective Tools for Decision Making   Nonmembers $60
    edited by Brian Nedwek

Campus Architecture—   SCUP Members $50
Building in the Groves of Academe   Nonmembers $60
    by Richard P. Dober

Campus Planning   SCUP Members $40
    by Richard P. Dober   Nonmembers $50

Ecodemia: SCUP Members $20
Campus Environmental Stewardship   Nonmembers $25
    published by the National Wildlife
    Federation, 1995
    by Julian Keniry

Society for College and University Planning
4251 Plymouth Road, Suite D
Ann Arbor, Michigan 48105 USA

Telephone: (313) 998-7832
Fax: (313) 998-6532
Email: scup@umich.edu
Website: www.scup.org